Maritime Strategy and Sea Control

This book focuses on the main methods of obtaining and maintaining sea control by a stronger side.

During times of war, sea control, or the ability of combatants to enjoy naval dominance, plays a crucial role in that side's ability to attain overall victory. This book explains and analyzes in some detail all aspects of sea control and describes and analyzes the main methods of obtaining and maintaining it. Various theoretical aspects of sea control also include the views of naval classical thinkers. This book also utilizes historical examples to illustrate the main methods of sea control. Each chapter focuses on a particular method, including destroying the enemy forces by a decisive action, destroying enemy forces over time, containing the enemy fleet, choke point control, and capturing important enemy positions/basing areas. The aim is to provide a comprehensive theory and practice of the struggle for sea control at the strategic and operational levels of war.

The book will be of much interest to students of naval strategy, defense studies, and security studies.

Milan Vego is Professor of Operations at the Naval War College, Rhode Island, United States, and the author of ten books, including *Naval Strategy and Operations in Narrow Seas* (Routledge, 2003) and *Operational Warfare at Sea* (Routledge, 2008).

Cass Series: Naval Policy and History
Series Editor: Geoffrey Till
ISSN 1366-9478

This series consists primarily of original manuscripts by research scholars in the general area of naval policy and history, without national or chronological limitations. It will from time to time also include collections of important articles, as well as reprints of classic works.

Maritime Strategy and Sea Control

Theory and practice

Milan Vego

Routledge
Taylor & Francis Group

LONDON AND NEW YORK

First published 2016
by Routledge
2 Park Square, Milton Park, Abingdon, Oxon OX14 4RN

and by Routledge
711 Third Avenue, New York, NY 10017

Routledge is an imprint of the Taylor & Francis Group, an informa business

© 2016 Milan Vego

British Library Cataloguing-in-Publication Data
A catalogue record for this book is available from the British Library

Library of Congress Cataloging-in-Publication Data
Vego, Milan N.
  Maritime strategy and sea control : theory and practice / Milan Vego.
    pages cm. — (Cass series—naval policy and history)
  Includes bibliographical references and index.
  1. Sea control.   2. Naval strategy.   I. Title.
  V163.V45 2015
  359'.03–dc23
  2015021353

ISBN: 978-1-138-90827-7 (hbk)
ISBN: 978-1-315-69452-8 (ebk)

Typeset in Baskerville
by Apex CoVantage, LLC

Contents

Preface

This work is a sequel to the book *Operational Warfare at Sea: Theory and Practice*, published by Routledge in 2009. It explains and analyzes in a much greater detail sea control in all its complexities. It also describes the main methods of obtaining and maintaining sea control. The subject of sea control is often discussed, but the true meaning of the term "sea control" or "control of the sea" is all too often either misunderstood or not understood at all. For example, many naval officers firmly believe that just by having a naval presence in a certain sea/ocean area one also possesses sea control. Many also confuse power projection and sea control or sea denial as one side of the same coin. The need for a work that explains and analyzes in some detail all aspects of sea control seems obvious. In a war between two strong opponents, the principal objective of each side would be to obtain and maintain sea control or control of the sea. Among other things, a side that fails to achieve that objective would have great difficulties in defending and protecting its military-economic potential at sea and in supporting friendly troops on land. In such a case, the weaker side has to shift to a strategic defensive and conduct sea denial. Perhaps it is needless to say that no country possesses sea control in peacetime. Struggle for sea control starts with the first encounter of the opposing forces in combat. It consists of the related and mutually dependent phases of obtaining and maintaining sea control.

This work consists of nine chapters. In each chapter, a certain theoretical aspect is illustrated by examples from naval history. Theory without examples from past naval wars is unconvincing, dry, and lifeless. Whenever possible, the views of naval classical thinkers are also presented and interpreted. The first chapter, "Strategic Framework," explains the linkages among national or grand strategy, military/theater strategy, and naval/maritime strategy; the distinctions between a political strategic objective and military/naval strategic objectives and between strategic offensive vs. defensive in a war at sea; and the strategic distribution of one's naval forces. The next chapter, "Sea Control," explains the true meaning of the term, misconceptions on sea control and its importance, as well as the degrees of sea control in terms of the factors of space, time, and force. Chapter 3, "Obtaining and

Maintaining Sea Control," discusses the prerequisites for a stronger side for obtaining control of the sea, along with the advantages and disadvantages of central and exterior strategic positions and of the concentration vs. dispersal of one's naval forces. It also explains the dynamics of obtaining sea control on the open ocean and in enclosed/semi-enclosed seas (popularly called "narrow seas"). Each of the remaining five chapters describes, at the operational and tactical levels, one of the main methods used for obtaining sea control. The first three of these chapters describe and analyze methods of destroying enemy naval forces in the struggle for sea control. Chapter 4, "Destroying the Enemy's Forces by a Decisive Action at Sea," discusses the concept of the "decisive naval battle" and "major fleet-vs.-fleet operation" in obtaining sea control, and Chapter 5 describes the destruction of enemy naval forces by a decisive action at their bases. Chapter 6, "Destruction of the Enemy's Forces over Time," explains attritional methods in destroying enemy surface ships, submarines, and aircraft as practiced by a stronger side at sea. Chapter 7, "Containing the Enemy's Forces," discusses the naval blockade, posing a threat to critical positions/areas, and strategic diversion as methods of neutralizing the weaker side at sea. "Choke Point Control," Chapter 8, describes in some detail methods of a stronger side to obtain and maintain control of the straits/narrows. The last chapter, "Capturing the Enemy's Important Positions and Basing Areas," describes and analyses this important but relatively neglected method of obtaining seas control. This work does not end with a "Conclusion" chapter because naval theory should not offer definitive views on certain subjects. It should be very general in its nature. Naval theory can only develop a way of thinking but cannot and should not offer prescriptions. Hence, one of the purposes of naval theory is to present various theoretical concepts coherently, logically, and in a clear and understandable language.

This work required the active participation and support of several individuals. I am greatly in debt to Mr. Andrew Humphrys (Senior Editor, Military, Strategic and Security Studies at Routledge) for his interest in the project and his great patience in dealing with my numerous delays in submitting the manuscript. My thanks are also due to Professor Geoffrey Till (Series Editor, Naval Policy and History) for giving his approval for my book proposal. He has also approved several of my past book projects. Many thanks also for the superb work of Fred Dahl, who copy edited my manuscript, and Tina Cottone, the project manager and the rest of the team at Apex CoVantage.

Maps

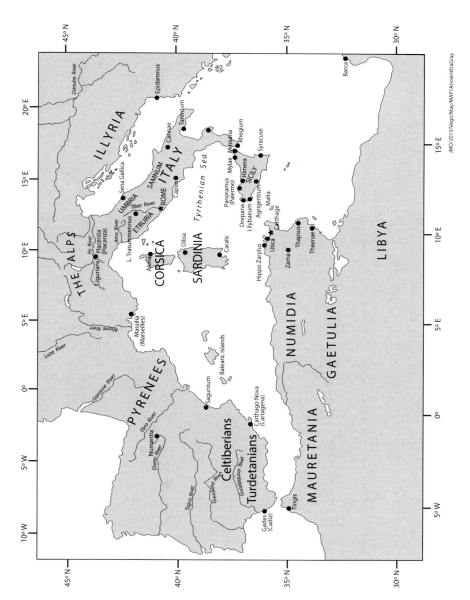

Map 1 The Mediterranean in the Ancient Era

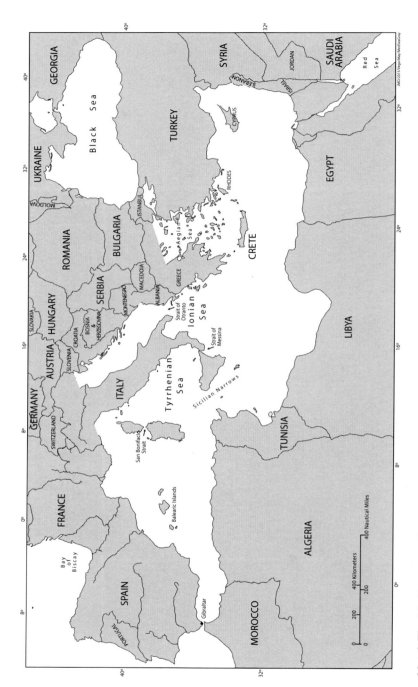

Map 2 The Mediterranean Sea

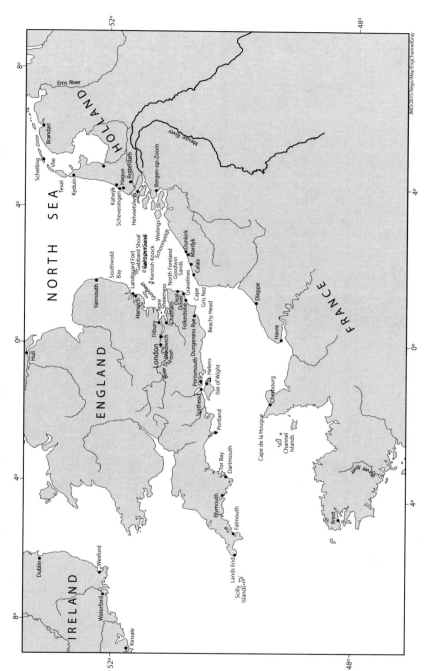

Map 3 The English Channel in the Seventeenth Century

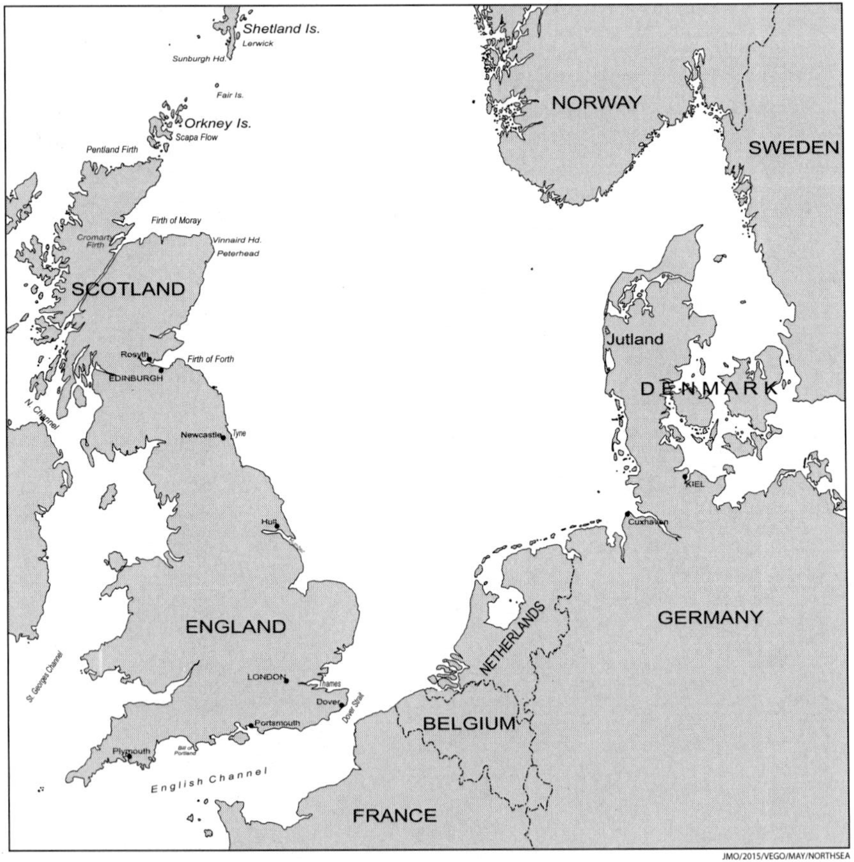

JMO/2015/VEGO/MAY/NORTHSEA

Map 4 The North Sea

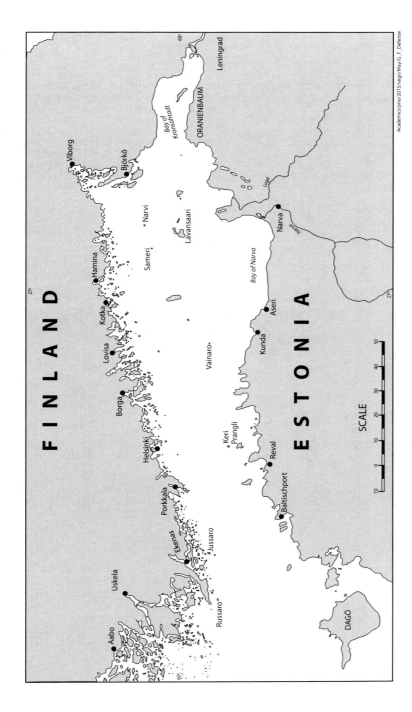

Map 5 Gulf of Finland, 1942

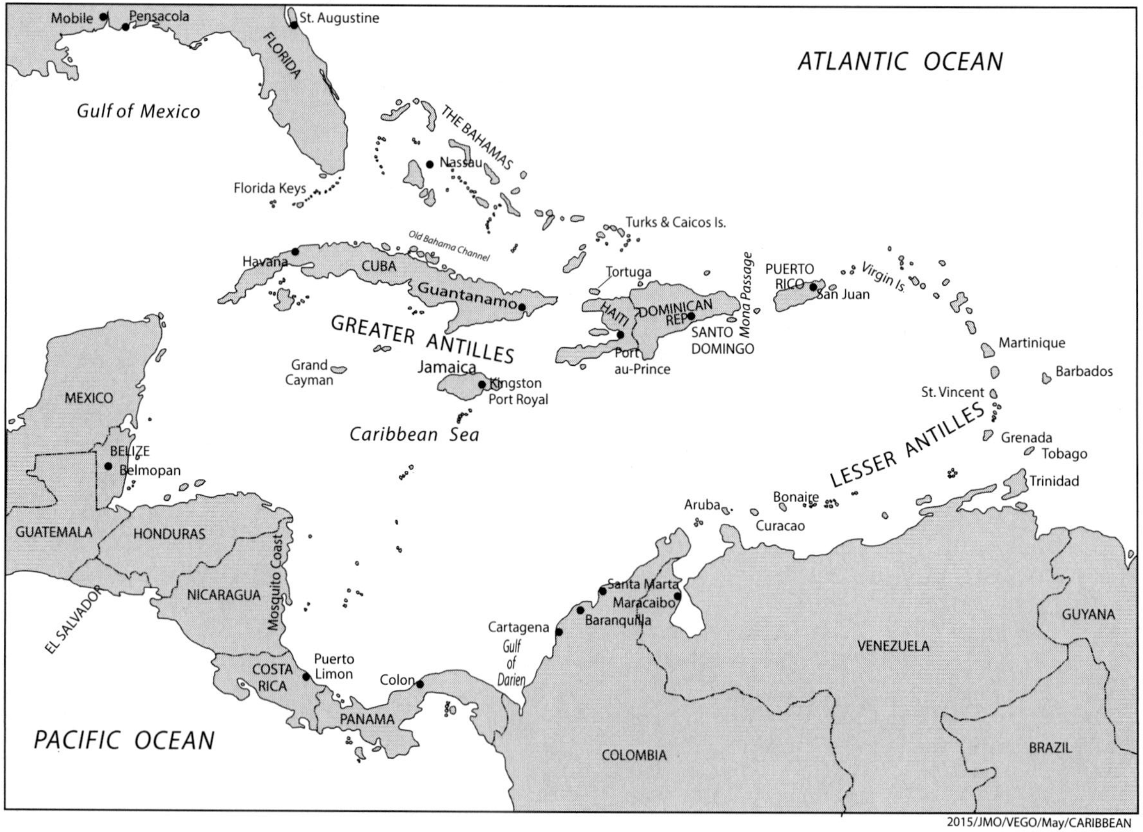

Map 6 The Caribbean Sea

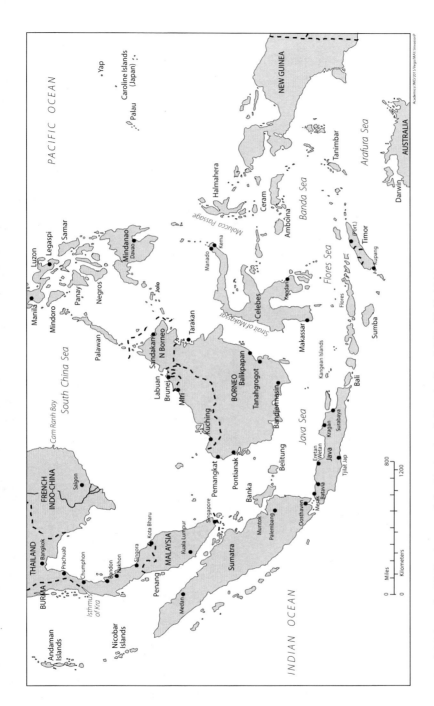

Map 7 Malaya, the Philippines, and the Netherlands East indies (NEI), 1941–1942

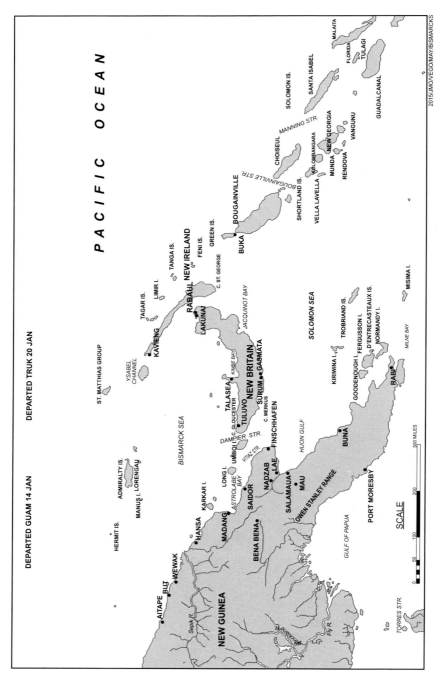

Map 8 The Bismarcks, Eastern New Guinea, and the Solomons, 1942

Abbreviations

ABDA	Australian-British-Dutch-American
AIP	air-independent propulsion
ANZAC	Australian and New Zealand Corps
ASCM	antiship cruise missile
A/S	antisubmarine
ASV	airborne surface vessel
ASW	antisubmarine warfare
AUV	autonomous underwater vehicle
B.E.F.	British Expeditionary Force
BC	Before Christ
C2	command and control
CENTPAC	Central Pacific
CINC	commander in chief
CO	commanding officer
CSG	carrier strike group
DC	depth charge
EM	electromagnetic
ESG	expeditionary strike group
F.A.A.	Fleet Air Arm
FAC	fast-attack craft
FEAF	Far East Air Force
FFL	light frigate
HWT	heavy-weight torpedo
IW	information warfare
km	kilometer
LACM	land attack cruise missile
LCG	littoral combat group
MCM	mine countermeasures
MEU	Marine expeditionary unit
MEZ	maritime exclusion zone
MPA	maritime patrol aircraft
MTB	motor torpedo boats
NATO	North Atlantic Treaty Organization

NEI	Netherlands East Indies
nm	nautical mile
OKM	Oberkommando der Marine (Supreme Command of the Navy)
OKW	Oberkommando der Wehrmacht (Supreme Command of the Wehrmacht)
PI	Philippine Islands
R.A.F.	Royal Air Force
SAG	surface action group
SC	submarine chaser
SDV	swimmer delivery vehicle
SSK	conventionally powered attack submarine
SSN	nuclear-powered attack submarine
SWPA	Southwest Pacific Area
TBM	tactical ballistic missile
TEZ	total exclusion zone
TF	task force
TG	task group
ULF	ultralow frequency
USSR	Union of Soviet Socialist Republics
VLF	very low frequency
WMD	weapons of mass destruction

1 Strategic framework

In the modern era, war at sea has not been conducted in isolation from the war on land and in the air. The navies and air forces have a significant but invariably supporting role because the outcome in a war is ultimately decided where humans live – on land. At the same time, the experience in the modern era shows that a war cannot be ultimately won without control of the sea and the air. No navy, regardless of its numerical strength and the quality of its personnel, can possess the optimum capabilities in all war-fare areas. The task of obtaining, maintaining, and exercising sea control – sometimes arbitrarily called the "struggle for sea control" – is conducted by the stronger side at sea in time of war. Although one's naval forces have the most important role, the services of the country's armed forces and often the navies and other services of allies/coalition partners also participate in such a struggle.

Policy and strategy provide the framework for the employment of the armed forces in a high-intensity conventional war and in operations short of war. Policy should always dominate strategy. At the same time, they should not be in conflict with each other.[1] Among other things, the domain of policy includes decisions to enter or not to enter a war and whether a war will be offensive or defensive. Policy also determines the political, diplomatic, legal, and other limitations on the employment of one's military forces.

In its simplest terms, strategy can be defined broadly as the process of interrelating and harmonizing the ends with the means. The articulation of national interests, objectives, and commitments with the use of the instruments of national power (political, diplomatic, military, economic, informational, scientific, technological, and so on) is called *national security strategy* (or *grand strategy*) – the art and science of using the instruments of national power to attain the political ends articulated by the national or alliance/coalition's political leadership. For each instrument of national or alliance/coalition power, there is also a corresponding *supporting strategy*. The importance of each supporting strategy depends, among other things, on whether a particular instrument is applied in a time of peace or war and on what policy determines the objectives to be. In a war, national strategy is principally concerned with determining national or coalition/alliance political objectives and providing strategic guidance to subordinate operational commanders, with determining the desired strategic end state, and with determining conditions for and the timing of war termination.

The boundaries between policy and strategy are often blurred or even indistinguishable. The upper part of strategy is closely linked to policy, a domain of statesmanship. It is there that the entire war effort is coordinated.[2] Carl von Clausewitz (1780–1831) made it clear that strategy depends on policy because war is the continuation of policy by other means. Normally, the military can act only within the framework determined by national or alliance/coalition strategy. Generally, the greater the limitations on the military leadership's freedom of action, the greater the military resources that are required to accomplish the given strategic ends. In practice, measures taken by the military leadership are often compromises between purely military needs and political realities. One of the major responsibilities of the highest military leadership is to point out to the political decision makers the critical need to determine and articulate clear and militarily achievable strategic objectives. Therefore, policy should never demand what is militarily impossible.[3] At the same time, the political leadership should not unnecessarily limit the military leadership's freedom of action.[4]

One of the most difficult problems in developing and executing strategy is balancing one's ends and means. This process is very difficult. It is more an art than a science. A lack of balance can result in a mismatch (inadequate means to achieve the stated ends) or a disconnect (sufficient means but an unwillingness to use them to achieve the stated ends). Clearly, a sound strategy should not have a serious mismatch or disconnect; otherwise, regardless of performance at the operational and tactical levels, the entire effort will end in failure and could even be fatal.

A mismatch between one's ends and means creates a certain degree of risk. The level of risk is largely a matter of one's judgment. Risks can occur due to many factors, such as overrating one's capabilities and/or underestimating the enemy's. They also can be the result of making willful or unintended faulty strategic assumptions. Calculated risks are incurred deliberately.[5] The degree of risk can be greatly reduced by scaling down one's ends or increasing one's means modifying, altering, or even abandoning one's ends. Another solution for resolving mismatch is to find a novel way of using one's sources of military and/or nonmilitary power.

Military strategy is the art and science of using or threatening to use military instruments of power to accomplish the political objectives of national or alliance/coalition strategy.[6] It is principally concerned with converting political strategic objectives into military strategic objectives, improving the country's or alliance/coalition's geostrategic position, providing a vision of the character and duration of the future war, and determining the theater of primary and secondary efforts and the distribution of forces among several theaters.

If a nation-state has vital interests to preserve or defend in several theaters, then strategy should be developed and applied in each theater.

Hence, a distinction is made between national military strategy and *theater strategy* – the art and science of developing integrated strategic concepts and courses of action, directed, within a theater, toward securing the objectives of national and alliance/coalition policy and strategy by the use of force, the threatened use of force, or operations not involving the use of force. National strategic objectives must dominate theater strategic objectives.

Military or theater strategy can be *offensive* or *defensive* in its main purpose. In an offensive strategy, the intent can be to seek to drastically change the balance of power, either regionally or globally. The attacker might also attempt to make some modest adjustment to the balance of power. In a defensive strategy, the objective is to preserve the status quo. The ultimate purpose of military (or theater) strategy could be the enemy's destruction or annihilation or the weakening of his power over time. The first, arbitrarily called *strategy of annihilation*, aims to overwhelm the enemy and make him unable to resist one's demands. It is viable only if one's power is overwhelming; otherwise, the hostilities will be protracted, requiring such a commitment of resources that one or both sides would be exhausted before either was defeated. A *strategy of attrition* (or *erosion*), in contrast, is designed to convince the enemy that settling the political dispute will be easier and to make the outcome more attractive than continued hostilities. It is intended to erode, or wear down, the enemy's strength and thereby weaken his will to fight, rather than destroy his ability to resist.[7]

Military (or theater) strategy can be symmetrical or asymmetrical. In a *symmetrical strategy*, the aim is to match one's superior strength against the enemy's similar strength but using innovative methods in the employment of military and nonmilitary sources of power. An *asymmetrical strategy* aims to offset one's numerical and qualitative weaknesses and vulnerabilities by applying nonconventional means.

Subordinate to military/theater strategy is naval or maritime strategy. *Naval strategy* can be defined as the science and art of using all naval sources of power in support of the national military strategy. In contrast, *maritime strategy* is the science and art of using both naval and non-naval sources of power at sea. Naval classical thinkers did not agree with one another on what constitutes naval or maritime strategy. For instance, the influential British blue-water navalist Sir Julian S. Corbett (1854–1922) defined maritime strategy as the principles that govern a war in which the sea is a substantial factor. For Corbett, the paramount concern of maritime strategy is to determine the mutual relations of the army and navy in a plan of war; once this is done, and not till then, naval strategy can begin to work out the manner in which the fleet can best discharge the function assigned to it.[8] Yet he confused strategy and operational art by arguing that naval strategy determines the movements of the fleet, while maritime strategy determines what part the fleet must play in relation to the action of the land forces.[9]

French vice admiral and notable theoretician Raoul Castex (1878–1968) differentiated between land and naval strategy on one hand and what he called general strategy (*strategie generale*), or military strategy, on the other. General strategy unifies the actions of the armies and fleets whenever they have to operate together. In his view, as infantry is the queen of battle, so the army is the queen of general strategy. Everything has to be subordinated to the army because its success means the success of the general strategy. The navy is often to the army what the artillery is to the infantry, an indispensable support that permits it to accomplish its objectives.[10]

In generic terms, maritime strategy is principally concerned with determining the naval aspects of the military (or theater) strategic objectives; using or threatening to use one's sea power; enhancing the country's or alliance/coalition's maritime strategic position; providing the vision of the character and duration of the future war at sea; determining (under the guidance of political-military leadership) whether war at sea will be primarily offensive or defensive, or a combination of these two; determining the primary and secondary theaters; and allocation of forces to each theater.

The objectives of naval/maritime strategy must be determined in consonance with the political and military strategic objectives. Policy determines what objectives should be pursued by strategy in case of war.[11] Clausewitz, in his *On War*, wrote that the most essential factor in trying to bend the enemy to one's will is the political object (or objective) of war. The latter, in turn, determines both the military objective to be accomplished and the amount of effort it requires.[12] Clausewitz also noted that sometimes political and military objectives can be identical. This is usually the case in a war of conquest. In general, when the military objective and the political objective are identical in scale, if the political objective is reduced, the military objective must be reduced proportionately.[13]

The political strategic objective should be expressed clearly and concisely. This would seem to be a relatively easy task for decision makers. Yet, all too often, political objectives are ambiguous, poorly defined and articulated. The reason is that politicians prefer not to be too specific for fear that if the objectives are not accomplished, domestic opponents and foreign leaders will consider the entire effort a failure. Hence, foreign policy objectives are often defined in terms of aims or goals rather than objectives. However, these terms should be used in expressing national or alliance/coalition interests. They are of little or no use to military commanders and their planners.

The intensity of a war is directly related to the importance of the political objective.[14] The lesser the importance of the political objective, the easier it is to abandon it.[15] A war in which the political strategic objectives for both sides are considered vital will be fought to the utmost exertion[16]

Political strategic objectives can be limited or unlimited in scope. *Limited political objectives* range from the threat of the use of force to capture some strategically important area/position to changing an enemy's behavior or policy on a certain issue. In war with a limited objective, it is often sufficient to occupy or capture the disputed area in order to accomplish the war's objectives.[17] For example, the Russo-Japanese War of 1904–1905 was conducted for a limited objective for both sides. Both Russia and Japan disputed control of an area that did not belong to either of them. Japan was unable to completely defeat Russia, but that was unnecessary. This was also the case for Russia. Neither Japan nor Russia wanted to fight to the very end. Thus, they were unwilling to commit utmost efforts and sacrifices, which might have led to a complete exhaustion.[18]

In a war with an *unlimited political objective*, as was the Allies' war against Japan in 1941–1945, the objective is a complete defeat of the enemy armed forces, the removal of the enemy's political leadership, and/or even the overthrow the enemy's social system. Unlimited objectives can also include the conquest of the entire country or groups of countries or even the extermination of the entire population of the hostile state.[19] Like any objective, a political objective could be positive or negative. A *positive objective* seeks to gain or obtain control of or to capture additional territory, whereas a *negative objective* is to prevent the stronger side from extending its control.[20] A positive war objective does not necessarily require an offensive posture, and a negative war objective need not be achieved only through defensive means.[21]

After the political objectives of a war are determined, the next step is to derive *military strategic objectives* as well. A military strategic objective defines which sources of military power should be used to achieve all the aspects of a political strategic objective. The well-known and influential British theoretician B. H. Liddell Hart (1895–1970) asserted that the military objective should be governed by the political objective, subject to the basic condition that policy must not demand what is militarily – that is, practically – impossible.[22] If the political objectives are unlimited, so are the military objectives. Yet a limited political objective does not necessarily mean a limited military objective. Both the political purpose of a war and the military strategic objectives must be in consonance with each other; otherwise, the overall war's objectives will be adversely affected.

A war should be conducted not with the sole aim of defeating the enemy's military forces but rather of accomplishing the overall political objective. There is a great danger in determining military strategic objectives that are inappropriate for the accomplishment of the political objectives. One's military strategic objective might have unintended consequences or effects on the enemy. For example, accomplishing a given military objective may alter that balance of power in such a way that the resulting political situation is actually less favorable to the victor. Another serious problem is that the selected military strategic objective may not result in the accomplishment of one's political purpose. Sometimes too much emphasis on the political aspects of the situation can lead to the selection of a political strategic objective that, while highly desirable, is unattainable with the military means at hand.

Normally, political and naval strategic objectives should be physically located in the same maritime theater. Yet sometimes this is not the case. For example, in the Seven Years' War (1756–1763), the British political objective was the conquest of French Canada. However, the British main naval effort was not in North America but in European waters. The reason was that freedom of action against French Canada could not be obtained unless the French fleet was defeated or neutralized in their home waters. Hence, the main maritime theater was the English Channel and eastern Atlantic washing France's coast.[23]

The highest politico-military leadership should issue a strategic objective that will have a drastic and positive impact on the course or outcome of a war. For example, in the Seven Years War, Secretary of State William Pitt the Elder (1708–1778) had a very clear view of what strategic objectives Britain should pursue. One of the finest British naval thinkers, Admiral Herbert Richmond (1871–1946), wrote that Pitt firmly believed that every undertaking in war, whether political, maritime, or military, must contribute in one way or another toward the attainment of the definitive object. This meant that England must have superiority in a decisive theater. England "must fight where she could be strongest and that was overseas. She must build upon a foundation of the command of the sea." Under Pitt, the Royal Navy at home and overseas was strengthened. The enemy bases were kept under observation. The squadron in the Indian ocean was reinforced. The enemy coast was threatened and his trade stopped. A strong army was sent to North America to capture Louisburg."[24] The British naval strategic objective in the Seven Years' War was to maintain a superior enough force at home that even the united fleets of France and Spain could never be masters of the Channel, to maintain at all times a powerful Western Squadron, and "to maintain a force in the Bay of Gibraltar as may be sufficient to cover that garrison, to watch the Spanish movements and to keep open the communications with Minorca."[25]

The political leadership might determine a clear strategic objective, but a subordinate naval commander might either hesitate or fail to act timely. For example, in the Austro-Italian War of 1866, the Italian Navy commander, Admiral Carlo Pellion Persano (1806–1883), received an order on 8 June directing him to "sweep the enemy from the Adriatic, and to attack and blockade them wherever he should find them."[26] On 20 June, Italian Navy Minister Agostino Depretis directed Persano to sail from Tarent to Ancona. Seven days later, Persano had an opportunity to attack the Austrian fleet, which approached Ancona, but failed to act timely. His lack of action undermined the morale of his fleet. Persano clearly misrepresented his orders by implying that he was not to risk the fleet. Therefore, he could see no advantage to be gained from pursuing the Austrians.[27] For Persano, searching for and destroying the enemy fleet was apparently a strange idea. After receiving several evasive messages from Persano, on 15 July, Depretis made a trip to Ancona to force his reluctant admiral to finally act on his orders or be relieved. Yet after meeting with Persano and chief of staff of the fleet, he changed his previous orders and directed Persano to assault the fortifications on the island of Lissa (Vis today) and then land several thousand troops. The Italians apparently never considered what the Austrian response to their attack on Lissa would be.[28] The next day, Persano reluctantly sailed out from Ancona with his squadron and halfheartedly attacked Austrian shore fortifications on Lissa.[29] In the midst of that attack, the Austrian squadron arrived. In the ensuing battle, Persano was decisively beaten by an inferior but better led and trained fleet. The government made a major error by not adhering to its initial and sound strategic decision of seeking the destruction of the enemy fleet.

Sometimes the political leadership assigns a mistaken strategic objective to a subordinate naval operational commander. For example, in October 1884, during the Sino-French War (August 1884–April 1885), the French government directed Admiral Anatole-Amédée-Prosper Courbet (1827–1885) to conduct the useless and difficult blockade of Formosa.[30] In other cases, it might happen that a naval commander does not receive any strategic objective at all from the government. For example, in April 1898, the Spanish government ordered Admiral Pascal Cervera y Topete (1839–1909) to proceed to the Caribbean but without giving him any objective. Hence, Cervera did not know what to do once he arrived in the Caribbean – only that Spain was at war with the United States.[31] Likewise, the U.S. Navy Department failed to send any instructions to Commodore George Dewey (1837–1917), Commander of the Asiatic Squadron (later Admiral of the Navy).[32]

In general, political and military strategic objectives determine whether war will be predominantly offensive, defensive, or a combination of these. In the littorals, this problem is compounded because the situation on the land front largely determines whether one's naval forces will be strategically on the offensive or defensive. Normally, a side on the strategic offensive on land and having a stronger navy would try to obtain and maintain sea control at the strategic level, while the weaker side on land would be forced onto the strategic defensive at sea.

Clausewitz insisted that defense (in land warfare) is a stronger form of fighting than attack. The attack requires a superiority of one's forces over the defender. In general, the weaker the motives for action, the more will they be overlaid and neutralized by the disparity between attack and defense.[33] Clausewitz's dictum that "attack [is] the weaker and defense the stronger form of war" is not fully applicable to naval warfare (or to air warfare).[34] For one thing, the stronger navy has to be on the offensive if it aims to obtain and then maintain sea control in a given part of a theater. Likewise, exercising sea control consists of a series of offensive actions. For example, a stronger side must be on the offensive to search for and destroy or neutralize the enemy fleet, blockade the enemy's coast or a strait/narrows, attack enemy installations/facilities on the coast, and conduct amphibious landings.[35] However, a stronger side at sea would conduct a combination of offensive and defensive actions and measures in antisubmarine warfare (ASW), in mine countermeasures (MCM), and in the defense and protection of maritime trade.

Most naval classical thinkers have asserted that a navy must be strategically on the offensive. Some of them went to the extreme and absolutized the importance of the offensive, while others recognized the need for the navies conduct defensive tasks too. For example, Rear Admiral Alfred T. Mahan (1840–1914) contended that a navy must be used in offensive action, both tactically and strategically. He rejected the navy's role in defense of the coast because the latter is "a defensive factor while the navy is the offensive factor."[36] By defending ports, one's naval forces lock up offensive strength in a defensive effort. Such an employment is also injurious to the morale and skill of seamen. By "giving up the offensive, the Navy gives up its proper sphere."[37] Mahan insisted that any proposal to employ "a navy as an instrument of pure passive defense is found faulty upon partial examination and these various results all proceed to the one fundamental fact that the distinguishing feature of naval force is mobility while that of passive defense is immobility."[38]

Castex had similar views on strategic offensive to Mahan's. He wrote that "whoever wants to defeat the enemy fleet through combat must necessarily take the offensive without concern for its inherent risks. We need to concentrate as many forces as possible on the principal objective so as to have every possible advantage." In his view, only the offensive can definitively break the equilibrium to produce a decision. This decisive character is the virtue of "genuine offensive and only offensive capable of bringing about decisions are worthy of the name."[39]

Clausewitz observed that (in land warfare) "defense is not an absolute state of waiting and repulse" and that it always includes "pronounced elements of offensive." He pointed out that at the strategic level, there is a "constant alternation and combination of attack and defense." Clausewitz wrote that "it follows that every attack has to take into account the defense that is necessarily inherent in it."[40] Napoleon I said that "the whole art of war consists in a well reasoned and strictly judicious defensive followed by audacious and rapid attacks."[41]

Clausewitz's and Napoleon I's views are also largely applicable to naval warfare. Castex recognized that in some situations, even an offensive plan must provide for the possibility of conducting a defensive in a certain part of a maritime theater. Except in a situation where one's naval strength is overwhelming, it is simply impossible to be "superior at a chosen point without being weaker, and therefore on the defensive elsewhere." Defensive is often combined with the offensive in time as well as in space.[42]

Strategic defensive at sea should invariably include elements of the offensive. Hence, disputing sea control encompasses not only offensive actions aimed to attrite the enemy's fleet but also actions aimed to lift the enemy's blockade of one's coast; to defend and protect one's coastal installations/ facilities, naval bases, and ports; and to defend against the enemy's landings.[43] For example, the German High Seas Fleet was tactically on the offensive but strategically on the defensive in the North Sea for most of World War I.

In the aftermath of the attack on Pearl Harbor on 7 December 1941 and until mid-1942, the U.S. Navy was on the strategic defensive. Yet its carrier forces conducted a number of raids against the Japanese island positions in the spring of 1942. For example, in late January, U.S. carrier groups struck the Japanese positions on the islands of Kwajalein, Wotje, Maleolap, and Jaluit. In February, U.S. carrier aircraft attacked the Japanese-held island of Wake and engaged the enemy aircraft some 300 miles east of Rabaul, New Britain. In March, a U.S. carrier group attacked Marcus Island.[44] In the months after the attack on Pearl Harbor, the major part of the actions against the Japanese in the Pacific was conducted by U.S. submarines. They were the only force capable of operating close to the Japanese ports in the home islands and throughout the Japanese-controlled areas in the Pacific. The U.S. submarines attacked Japan's merchant ships carrying the vital supplies of oil, rubber, and other raw materials to Home Islands and bringing reinforcements and supplies to its newly occupied positions.

Normally, a side on the strategic offensive on land and having a strong navy would go strategically on the offensive at sea too. For example, in the Russo-Japanese War of 1904–1905, the Japanese objective was to obtain control of the Yellow Sea and the Sea of Japan. After the defeat of the Russian Far Eastern Squadron, the Japanese assumed the strategic defensive and awaited the arrival of the Russian Second Pacific Squadron, which eventually was decisively beaten in the Battle of Tsushima in May 1905.[45] In the aftermath of the Battle of Stalingrad in January 1943, the Soviet Black Sea Fleet went on the offensive once the ground forces started their long-awaited offensive against the Wehrmacht. Likewise, the Soviet Baltic Fleet went on the offensive after the Soviet forces lifted the siege of Leningrad and began their advance southward along the Baltic coast in September 1944.

In some cases, a weaker side at sea might go on the offensive from the very outset of the hostilities, while the friendly troops would be on offensive in the coastal area. For example, the German Naval Staff operations plans in 1938–1939 for a war in the Baltic were based on the assumption that the Soviet Baltic Fleet would be on the defensive despite its numerical superiority over the German forces deployed in the Baltic. Hence, the Germans decided to go strategically on the offensive in the Baltic. After the start of the German invasion of Soviet Russia on 22 June 1941, the Germans and the Finns blockaded the Gulf of Finland. This blockade was not lifted until September 1944. This success was achieved despite the small forces the Germans had available in the Baltic for most of the war.[46]

A weaker side at sea would be normally strategically on the defensive when facing a much stronger opponent. For example, in the war between Austria and France/Kingdom of Sardinia in 1859, after the Austrian Army invaded Piedmont on 3 May and France entered the war, the Austrian Navy's commander, Archduke Ferdinand Max (1832–1867), assembled his best ships at the major naval base of Pola (Pula today). The remainder of his small fleet was deployed among the islands in Dalmatia. Some Austrian ships were intentionally sunk at Venice and other harbors to block their entrances to the French squadron. On 2 June, the French declared a blockade of Venice and shortly thereafter also occupied the island of Lussin Piccolo (Mali Lošinj today) to use it as a base for an assault against the mainland coast. However, the war had already been decided on land after the Austrian defeats at Magenta and Solferino.[47]

Generally, a side on the strategic defensive on land would be also strategically on the defensive at sea. For example, the Russians were initially strategically on the offensive in the Crimean War (1853–1856). Their Black Sea Fleet attacked and destroyed the Turkish fleet at Sinope (northern Anatolia) on 30 November 1853. However, they were forced onto the strategic defensive both on land and at sea after the Anglo-French armies (plus their ally Kingdom of Sardinia) and navies started combat operations in 1854 and until the end of war in March 1856.

The Soviets went on the strategic defensive in both the Black Sea and the Baltic theater shortly after the German invasion in June 1941. The Soviet Navy lost almost all its bases in the Baltic and the Black Sea theaters in the first few months after the beginning of the German invasion. The Soviets focused on the defense of the Gulf of Riga and complete closure of the Gulf of Finland from Hanko (Hangö in Swedish) to Odensholm-Reval.[48] Except for occasional forays by its submarines into the open waters of the Baltic, the Soviet Baltic Fleet was on the strategic defensive until the summer of 1944, when the advance of the Red Army along the Baltic coast allowed the fleet to play a more prominent role. Likewise, the Soviet Black Sea Fleet did not shift onto the strategic offensive in the aftermath of the Battle of Stalingrad (Volgograd today) in January–March 1943. The front in southern Russia remained static until September 1943 when the Germans started their major withdrawal from the area.

Sometimes both the weaker and the stronger sides at sea might choose to be on the strategic defensive, although for different reasons. For example, not only the German High Seas Fleet (Hochseeflotte) but also the British Grand Fleet remained on a strategic defensive in the North Sea for most of World War I. The German General Staff was confident that the army could defeat the British Expeditionary Force (B.E.F.) after it landed in France. Therefore, the Germans did not want to risk the High Seas Fleet.[49] The fact that the opposing fleets remained essentially on a strategic defensive throughout the war was probably the main reason for the lack of decisive results in the North Sea for either of the great protagonists.[50]

A navy facing significant naval threats in two adjacent maritime theaters would normally go on the offensive in a theater where the greater threat exists. In other cases, it might take a defensive posture in both theaters. Yet a major part of its forces would be normally deployed in a theater facing the strongest opponent. For example, the Imperial German Navy concentrated its High Seas Fleet in the North Sea to face the British Grand Fleet, while the remaining naval forces were deployed in the Baltic, where they remained strategically on the defensive until 1917.

Generally, a stronger fleet should not be on the defensive both in home waters and overseas. For example, the Royal Navy violated the principle of the offensive during the American Revolutionary War (1775–1783). It remained on the defensive in home waters (which was prudent), but at the same time it tried to defend all the vulnerable points in the Americas. The result was predictable: England lost not only the North American colonies but also much of the West Indies and Minorca (Balearics) in the Mediterranean as well. Even the security of Gibraltar and England itself was endangered by the French. In home waters, too, it was indecision and the defensive-mindedness of the French rather than British actions that saved England from an invasion from across the sea.[51]

Naval strategy also determines the distribution and composition of naval forces among the maritime theaters. The peacetime deployment of naval forces is dictated by the strategic estimate of the situation, and the decision is based upon the national policy and an estimate of the most probable theater of operations in case of war.[52] In general, strategic objectives should be the principal determining factor in selecting main and secondary maritime theaters. The key is to have in the theater of main effort a sufficiently large and capable force able to deal with the "greatest concentrated force which the enemy can bring to bear."[53] At the same time, sufficient forces must be assigned to the theater(s) of secondary effort. It is usually unwise to distribute a fleet equally among the various theaters. For example, both the British and Dutch almost evenly divided their respective fleets between the North Sea/English Channel and the Mediterranean during the First Anglo-Dutch War (1652–1654). Prior to the outbreak of the Russo-Japanese War in 1904, the Imperial Russian Navy made a similar mistake when its fleet was roughly divided between the Baltic Sea and Port Arthur.[54]

Britain was traditionally faced with the problem of how to distribute the Royal Navy so that its source of strength at home is fully preserved while at the same time defending overseas possessions and the free flow of trade to the mother country.[55] The British maintained the "two-power standard" of naval strength between 1770 (when the policy was first enunciated) ad until the end of the nineteenth century. Afterward, this policy became rapidly obsolete because of the steady increase of the strength of the German Navy in the North Sea. A new policy, the "two-power standard with a margin," was declared on 1 March 1904. The British Admiralty then regarded Germany and Russia or France/Russia in combination as the most likely opponents at sea. By 1907, the British planned to obtain at least 10 percent margins in battleships over any of these two combinations. As result of the new policy, the Royal Navy was drastically reorganized in the last decade prior to 1914, and its main strength shifted from the Mediterranean to home waters. The Mediterranean was then a critical link between England and its possessions in the Far East. A fleet based there was usually composed of heavy and fast ships capable of quickly reinforcing the fleet in the English Channel and the North Sea or the fleets in the Indian Ocean and the Far East.[56] In 1904, the Royal Navy reduced its force of battleships in the Mediterranean from twelve to eight. Two years later, an additional two battleships were taken from the Mediterranean and redeployed to the North Sea. Between 1907 and 1912, only four British battleships were deployed in the Mediterranean.[57]

By the spring of 1912, the British Admiralty decided to further reduce the fleet in the Mediterranean because of the need to concentrate as much as possible of the Royal Navy's strength in home waters to meet the German challenge. On 1 May 1912, the British Admiralty announced the establishment of the Home Fleet responsible for the naval defense of home waters. This fleet consisted of three squadrons of 33 battleships in full commission and eight more with nucleus crews. These 41 battleships were believed to be superior to the German 25 battleships ready for war.[58] Under the new scheme, in the Mediterranean were deployed only two to three battle cruisers, a squadron of armored cruisers, one destroyer and submarine flotilla based at Malta and one submarine flotilla based at Alexandria. The rest of the Royal Navy was deployed on colonial duties in the East Indies, Cape of Good Hope, southern Asia and Australia, and the east coast of Americas. The British fleet in the Mediterranean was believed to be large enough in combination with the French Mediterranean fleet (six dreadnoughts and 14 pre-dreadnoughts in commission plus seven dreadnoughts to be completed in 1913–1915) to counter the Austro-Italian combination (17 pre-dreadnoughts and ten dreadnoughts by 1915).[59] The result was that no British battleships, except for a squadron of pre-dreadnoughts temporarily deployed during the Balkan Wars (1912–1913), were deployed in the Mediterranean.[60] The British Admiralty believed that in the event of war with Germany, at least one Mediterranean power would be able to ensure safety of British sea communications in the Mediterranean until the situation in the North Sea was clarified, and that would take several months after the outbreak of hostilities.[61]

Prior to 1914, France also faced the problem of maintaining a strong fleet in the Mediterranean to protect the country's coast and its possessions in North Africa. It had to deal with the threat of the combined Italian and Austro-Hungarian fleets. In September 1912, France moved its Brest squadron (12 pre-dreadnoughts and six armored cruisers) to Toulon to join the Mediterranean Fleet.[62] France was reassured as to the safety of its Channel and Atlantic coasts by the Anglo-French Naval Agreement in February 1913. In the Mediterranean, the French Navy had to protect both shipping lanes to the French colonial possessions and the transport of some 100,000 men to France from North Africa upon mobilization in case of a war with Germany.[63]

In the early 1930s, the French Navy's task was to protect oil supplies in the Mediterranean. The First Squadron in Toulon covered the routes in the Mediterranean. Control of the Marseille-Algiers-Bizerte triangle was considered critical for control of the Western Mediterranean. By the mid-1930s, the French shifted the main theater from the Mediterranean to the Atlantic. Hence, the main route for troop transports shifted from Bizerte-Toulon to Casablanca–French Atlantic Coast. This was the reason for the steady strengthening after 1933 of the Second Squadron based in Brest.[64]

Normally, military/theater strategic objectives determine the theaters of the main and secondary efforts for all the services of the armed forces. However, political, economic, and even psychological factors might persuade the political leadership to make an exception. For example, in World War II, for the U.S. Navy the Pacific was the main theater of war, although the European theater was nominally the theater of main effort for the U.S. armed forces as a whole. An example of mistaken strategic distribution of naval forces was the British strategy during the American Revolutionary War. Instead of deploying the major part of their navy off the coasts of Spain and France, the British tried to defend every outlying post where their flag might be threatened. In the Battle of Chesapeake Bay of 1781, the concentration of the French fleet made possible a victory.[65]

Policy should always dominate strategy. Likewise, maritime strategy must dominate both operational art and naval tactics. Both the political and the military strategic objectives must be in consonance with each other. Any imbalance between these two will cause severe problems in their accomplishment. However, the policy should not be allowed to influence the determination of operational or tactical objectives unless some extraordinary circumstances require it. The objective to be achieved should be clear-cut, and any ambiguity should be avoided. The highest politico-military leadership of the country or of an alliance/coalition bears the responsibility to determine whether naval forces will be on the offensive, defensive, or some combination of these two in the case of the hostilities at sea. This in turn will determine which maritime theater will be the main and which secondary in importance. Accordingly, the overall size of the navy and its distribution among maritime theaters must be in consonance with the strategic objectives to be accomplished in wartime. Hence, the size of a fleet and its force mix in peacetime are pretty good indicators of what probable strategic objectives at sea will be pursued in wartime.

Notes

1 Klaus Goldschmidt, "Grundlagen der Strategie," *Wehrwissenschaftliche Rundschau*, 1 (January 1969), p. 76.
2 Jörg Bahnemann, "Der Begriff der Strategie bei Clausewitz, Moltke und Liddell Hart," *Wehrwissenschaftliche Rundschau*, 1 (January 1968), p. 39.
3 Ash Irwin, *The Levels of War, Operational Art and Campaign Planning* (Camberley, Surrey, England: Strategic and Combat Studies Institute, Occasional Paper No. 5, 1993), p. 6.
4 Hans Hitz, "Taktik und Strategie. Zur Entwicklung kriegswissenschaftlicher Begriffe," *Wehrwissenschaftliche Rundschau*, 11 (November 1956), pp. 617–18.
5 John M. Collins, *Grand Strategy: Principles and Practices* (Annapolis, MD: Naval Institute Press, 1973), p. 5.
6 Headquarters United States Marine Corps, MCDP 1–1, *Strategy* (Washington, DC: U.S. Government Printing Office, 1998), p. 41.
7 Headquarters United States Marine Corps, MCDP 1–1, *Strategy* (Washington, DC: U.S. Government Printing Office, 1998), p. 55.
8 Julian S. Corbett, *Some Principles of Maritime Strategy* (London: Longmans, Green and Co., 1918), p. 12.
9 Cited in Chris Bullock, "A Canadian Naval Strategy for the 21st Century: Constabulary Force or International Player?" Conference of Defence Associations Institute, Third Annual Graduate Student Symposium, 3–4 November 2000, Calgary, Canada, p. 3.
10 Raoul Castex, *Strategic Theories*. Selections translated and edited with an introduction by Eugenia C. Kiesling (Annapolis, MD: Naval Institute Press, 1993), p. 45.
11 Hein-Peter Weyher, *Der Begriff "Seestrategie" und Seine Deutung in den Westlichen Kriegstheorien Des 20. Jahrhunderts* (Hamburg: Führungsakademie der Bundeswehr, July 1967), p. 11.
12 Carl von Clausewitz, *On War*. Edited and translated by Michael Howard and Peter Paret (New York: Alfred A. Knopf, 1993), p. 90.
13 Carl von Clausewitz, *On War*. Edited and translated by Michael Howard and Peter Paret (New York: Alfred A. Knopf, 1993), p. 91.
14 Hein-Peter Weyher, *Der Begriff "Seestrategie" und Seine Deutung in den Westlichen Kriegstheorien Des 20. Jahrhunderts* (Hamburg: Führungsakademi der Bundeswehr, July 1967), p. 4.
15 Otto Groos, *Seekriegslehren im Lichte des Weltkrieges. Ein Buch für den Seemann, Soldaten und Staatsmann* (Berlin: Verlag von E. S. Mittler & Sohn, 1929), p. 22.
16 Otto Groos, *Seekriegslehren im Lichte des Weltkrieges. Ein Buch für den Seemann, Soldaten und Staatsmann* (Berlin: Verlag von E. S. Mittler & Sohn, 1929), p. 23.
17 Otto Groos, *Seekriegslehren im Lichte des Weltkrieges. Ein Buch für den Seemann, Soldaten und Staatsmann* (Berlin: Verlag von E. S. Mittler & Sohn, 1929), p. 23; Hein-Peter Weyher, *Der Begriff "Seestrategie" und Seine Deutung in den Westlichen Kriegstheorien Des 20. Jahrhunderts* (Hamburg: Fuehrungsakademie der Bundeswehr, July 1967), p. 11.
18 Otto Groos, *Seekriegslehren im Lichte des Weltkrieges. Ein Buch für den Seemann, Soldaten und Staatsmann* (Berlin: Verlag von E. S. Mittler & Sohn, 1929), p. 23.
19 Headquarters United States Marine Corps, MCDP 1–1, *Strategy* (Washington, DC: U.S. Government Printing Office, 1998), pp. 44–45.
20 Hein-Peter Weyher, *Der Begriff "Seestrategie" und Seine Deutung in den Westlichen Kriegstheorien Des 20. Jahrhunderts* (Hamburg: Führungsakademie der Bundeswehr, July 1967), p. 8.

21 Hein-Peter Weyher, *Der Begriff "Seestrategie" und Seine Deutung in den Westlichen Kriegstheorien Des 20. Jahrhunderts* (Hamburg: Führungsakademie der Bundeswehr, July 1967), p. 8.

22 B.H. Liddell Hart, "The Objective in War: National Object and Military Aim, A Lecture Delivered at the Naval War College on 24 September 1952," *Naval War College Review* (December 1952), p. 1.

23 T.G.W. Settle, "The Strategic Employment of the Fleet" (Newport, RI: Naval War College, September 18, 1940), p. 9a.

24 Herbert Richmond, *Statesmen and Sea Power* (Oxford: Clarendon Press, first published 1946, reprinted 1947), pp. 134–35.

25 Herbert Richmond, *Statesmen and Sea Power* (Oxford: Clarendon Press, first published 1946, reprinted 1947), p. 142.

26 Gabriel Darrieus, *War on the Sea. Strategy and Tactics.* Translated by Philip R. Alger (Annapolis, MD: United States Naval Institute, 1908), p. 89.

27 Howard Marraro, "Unpublished Documents on the Naval Battle of Lissa (1866)," *The Journal of Modern History*, Vol. 14, No. 3 (September 1942), p. 343; *Iron and Fire. Historical Monograph of the Naval Aspects of European Wars in the Mid 19th Century with Particular Emphasis on the Lissa Campaign*, 9 January 2005, p. 4.; accessed at http://www.aandagames.co.uk/index_htm_files/IF_European_Wars.pdf

28 Howard Marraro, "Unpublished Documents on the Naval Battle of Lissa (1866)," *The Journal of Modern History*, Vol. 14, No. 3 (September 1942), p. 343; *Iron and Fire. Historical Monograph of the Naval Aspects of European Wars in the Mid 19th Century with Particular Emphasis on the Lissa Campaign*, 9 January 2005, pp. 4–5; accessed at http://www.aandagames.co.uk/index_htm_files/IF_Euro pean_Wars.pdf

29 Gabriel Darrieus, *War on the Sea. Strategy and Tactics.* Translated by Philip R. Alger (Annapolis, MD: United States Naval Institute 1908), pp. 89–90.

30 Gabriel Darrieus and René Daveluy, *War on the Sea and Extracts from the Genius of Naval Warfare*, I and II. Translated by Philip R. Alger (Annapolis, MD: The United States Naval Institute, 1920), p. 200.

31 Member of the Staff, *Naval Strategy* (Newport, RI: Naval War College, 24–25 August 1936), p. 7.

32 John D. Hayes, "The Writings of Stephen B. Luce," *Military Affairs*, Vol. 19, No. 4 (Winter 1955), p. 190.

33 Carl von Clausewitz, *On War*. Edited and translated by Michael Howard and Peter Paret (New York/London: Everyman's Library/Alfred A. Knopf, 1993), pp. 94–95.

34 Carl von Clausewitz, *On War*. Edited and translated by Michael Howard and Peter Paret (New York/London: Everyman's Library/Alfred A. Knopf, 1993), pp. 634–35.

35 Alfred Stenzel, *Kriegsführung zur See. Lehre vom Seekriege* (Hannover/Leipzig: Mahnsche Buchhandlung, 1913), p. 96.

36 Cited in Philip A. Crowl, "Alfred Thayer Mahan: The Naval Historian," in Peter Paret, editor, *Makers of Modern Strategy. From Machiavelli to the Nuclear Age* (Princeton, NJ: Princeton University Press, 1986), pp. 458–59.

37 Alfred T. Mahan, *Naval Strategy: Compared and Contrasted with the Principles and Practice of Military Operations on Land* (Boston: Little, Brown, and Company, 1911), p. 153.

38 Alfred T. Mahan, *Naval Strategy Compared and Contrasted with the Principles and Practice of Military Operations on Land* (Boston: Little, Brown, and Company, 1911), p. 132.

39 Raoul Castex, *Strategic Theories*. Selections translated and edited with an introduction by Eugenia C. Kiesling (Annapolis, MD: Naval Institute Press, 1994), pp. 73–74, 312, 316–17.

40 Carl von Clausewitz, *On War*. Edited and translated by Michael Howard and Peter Paret (New York: Alfred A. Knopf, 1993), pp. 634–35.
41 Elwin F. Cutts, *Operations for Securing Command of the Sea Areas*, Part 1 (Newport, RI: Naval War College, 8–9 July 1938), p. 21.
42 Raoul Castex, *Strategic Theories*. Selections translated and edited with an introduction by Eugenia C. Kiesling (Annapolis, MD: Naval Institute Press, 1994), pp. 336–37.
43 Alfred Stenzel, *Kriegsführung zur See. Lehre vom Seekriege* (Hannover/Leipzig: Hahnsche Buchhandlung, 1913), p. 96.
44 Samuel E. Morison, *History of United States Naval Operations in World War II*, Vol. 3: *The Rising Sun in the Pacific, 1931–April 1942* (Boston: Little, Brown and Company, 1959), pp. 263–64, 267–68.
45 M.G. Cook, "Naval Strategy," 2 March 1931, Air Corps Tactical School, Langley Field, VA, 1930–1931, Strategic Plans Division Records, Series, Box 003, Naval Operational Archives, Washington, D.C., p. 8.
46 Michael Salewski, *Die deutsche Seekriegsleitung 1935–1945*, Vol. 1: *1935–1941* (Frankfurt am Main: Bernard & Graefe Verlag für Wehrwesen, 1970), p. 365; ibid., Vol. 2: *1942–1945* (ibid., *1975*), p. 574.
47 Lawrence Sondhaus, *The Habsburg Empire and the Sea: Austrian Naval Policy 1797–1866* (West Lafayette, IN: Purdue University Press, 1989), pp. 191–92.
48 Jürg Meister, *Der Seekrieg in den osteuropaeischen Gewaessern 1941/45* (Munich: J. F. Lehmans Verlag, 1958), p. 11.
49 Ivo N. Lambi, *The Navy and German Power Politics, 1862–1914* (Boston: Allen & Unwin, 1984), p. 422.
50 M.G. Cook, "Naval Strategy," 2 March 1931, Air Corps Tactical School, Langley Field, VA, 1930–1931, Strategic Plans Division Records, Series, Box 003, Naval Operational Archives, Washington, D.C., p. 9.
51 Geoffrey Till, *Maritime Strategy and the Nuclear Age*, 2nd ed. (New York: St. Martin's Press, 1984), p. 116.
52 M.G. Cook, "Naval Strategy," 2 March 1931, Air Corps Tactical School, Langley Field, VA, 1930–1931, Strategic Plans Division Records, Series, Box 003, Naval Operational Archives, Washington, D.C., p. 16.
53 Bernard Brodie, *A Layman's Guide to Naval Strategy* (Princeton, NJ: Princeton University Press, 1942), p. 87.
54 Alfred T. Mahan, *Naval Strategy Compared and Contrasted with the Principles and Practice of Military Operations on Land* (Boston: Little, Brown, and Company, 1919), pp. 115–16.
55 Max Kupfer, "Die strategische Verteilung der Hauptflotten im Hinblick auf ihren Friedens- und Kriegsaufgaben," *Marine Rundschau*, No. 6 (June 1936), p. 291.
56 Max Kupfer, "Die strategische Verteilung der Hauptflotten im Hinblick auf ihren Friedens- und Kriegsaufgaben," *Marine Rundschau*, No. 6 (June 1936), pp. 291–92.
57 Paul G. Halpern, *The Naval War in the Mediterranean 1914–1918* (Annapolis, MD: Naval Institute Press, 1987), pp. 1–2; Arthur J. Marder, *From the Dreadnought to Scapa Flow. The Royal Navy in the Fisher Era, 1904–1919*, Vol. I: *The Road to War, 1904–1914* (London: Oxford University Press, 1961), pp. 123–24.
58 Arthur J. Marder, *From the Dreadnought to Scapa Flow. The Royal Navy in the Fisher Era, 1904–1919*, Vol. I: *The Road to War, 1904–1914* (London: Oxford University Press, 1961), pp. 287–88.
59 Arthur J. Marder, *From the Dreadnought to Scapa Flow. The Royal Navy in the Fisher Era, 1904–1919*, Vol. I: *The Road to War, 1904–1914* (London: Oxford University Press, 1961), p. 288.
60 Paul G. Halpern, *The Naval War in the Mediterranean 1914–1918* (Annapolis, MD: Naval Institute Press, 1987), p. 2.

61 Arthur J. Marder, *From the Dreadnought to Scapa Flow. The Royal Navy in the Fisher Era, 1904–1919,* Vol. I: *The Road to War, 1904–1914* (London: Oxford University Press, 1961), p. 288.

62 Arthur J. Marder, *From the Dreadnought to Scapa Flow. The Royal Navy in the Fisher Era, 1904–1919,* Vol. I: *The Road to War, 1904–1914* (London: Oxford University Press, 1961), pp. 304–05.

63 M.G. Cook, "Naval Strategy," 2 March 1931, Air Corps Tactical School, Langley Field, VA, 1930–1931, Strategic Plans Division Records, Series, Box 003, Naval Operational Archives, Washington, D.C., p. 16.

64 Max Kupfer, "Die strategische Verteilung der Hauptflotten im Hinblick auf ihren Friedens- und Kriegsaufgaben," *Marine Rundschau,* No. 6 (June 1936), p. 295.

65 Bernard Brodie, *A Layman's Guide to Naval Strategy* (Princeton, NJ: Princeton University Press, 1942), p. 87.

2   Sea control

The master of the sea must inevitably be master of the Empire.

Cicero, *Ad Atticus*[1]

Combat employment of one's naval forces and the forces of other services in a maritime theater is aimed to accomplish a certain naval/military objective; otherwise, the entire effort is useless. Almost all aspects of war in general, including war at sea, are directly or indirectly related to the objective to be accomplished.

In broad terms, the main objectives of warfare at sea are sea control, sea denial, basing/deployment area control, and destroying/weakening the enemy's and defending/protecting friendly military-economic potential at sea.

The meaning of the terms "command" and "control" of the sea is not often well understood. A major reason for that is perhaps the very different and sometimes contradictory interpretations of the true meaning of these terms by naval thinkers and their interpreters and followers. Another problem is that term as "command" or "control" of the sea can possibly, directly or indirectly, convey all its variables in terms of the factors of space, time, and force.

The sea as a battlefield

The struggle for sea control cannot be understood without a full comprehending of rather substantial differences in the characteristics of the sea and land area for combat employment of naval and ground forces. About 70 percent of the world's surface is covered by the oceans/seas. The oceans are very large in size. They meet their ultimate boundaries in contact with the land.[2] For example, the Pacific Ocean contains some 64 million square miles, or 46 percent of the world's water surface. It extends for about 8,700 nautical miles (nm) from the east to west along the equator and for 10,860 nm from Panama to the Malay Peninsula. The distance from San Francisco to Yokohama, Japan, is about 3,400 nm. Some 2,100 nm separate San Francisco and Hawaii. The distance from the Panama Canal to Hawaii is about 4,700 nm. Guam is about 3,500 nm away from Hawaii, while Wake is 2,200 nm.[3] The Atlantic Ocean covers an area of 41.1 million square miles and varies in width from about 1,480 nm (between Brazil and Liberia) and 2,600 nm (between the East Coast of the United States and North Africa).

In contrast, enclosed and semi-enclosed seas (popularly called "narrow seas")[4] are much smaller in size. For example, the Baltic Sea covers an area of 163,000 square miles. The Persian (Arabian) Gulf encompasses only some 92,600 square miles.[5] With its 950,000 square miles, the Mediterranean Sea is the largest of all narrow seas. The Mediterranean also encompasses several smaller narrow seas (the Tyrrhenian, the Ionian, the Adriatic, and the Aegean). The Baltic Sea extends along its north–south axis about 920 nm and has an average width a little over 105 nm. The distance between Kiel and Helsinki is about 625 nm; the port of Tallinn (formerly Reval) is only about 220 nm from Stockholm; some 230 nm separate Copenhagen and Rostock. For the North Sea, the British port of Hull is only about 280 nm from the German port of Emden and some 210 nm from Ostend. The German port of Cuxhaven is about 475 nm away from Scapa Flow in the Orkneys. The Persian Gulf is about 535 nm long and between 35 and 190 nm wide.[6] The Mediterranean Sea extends from west to east more than 2,085 nm, while its maximum width is about 870 nm.

An ocean/sea serves as the basis for the employment of one's naval forces against the shore and in the depth of the enemy's territory. It is an area that allows the dispersal and preservation of part of one's military potential. It serves for a network of communications used for free movement of both economic and military goods.[7] A land theater is normally limited to the boundaries of the states in the war.[8] The terrain on land is often full of obstacles of various kinds. In contrast, the sea is flat and generally, except for islands/archipelagoes, free of obstacles. At sea, there are no woods, forests, or mountains in which to hide. Hence, it is much more difficult to move covertly and achieve surprise or to ensure protection against enemy attack, especially from the air. War at sea is also conducted on the surface, in the subsurface, and in the air, while war on land is more two-dimensional. On land, the opposing armies operate in essentially the same area. Because of the many physical obstacles, the movements of the armies are slow. They are also in a certain way predictable.[9] In contrast, the operating areas of naval forces on the open ocean are much greater. The movement of naval forces and the change of dispositions are free and not very predictable. Naval forces also generally move faster than land forces.[10]

Armies are highly dependent on the roads and railroads for their logistical sustainment and bringing up reinforcements. The more the attacker advances into the depth of the enemy's territory, the longer his lines of communication and the more forces need to be detached for their defense and protection. In contrast, naval forces are more self-sufficient, although ships need to be replenished at sea or in ports from time to time.

In a war at sea, there are no fronts, no lines to be held by one side and to be besieged or attacked by the other side. A large body of water cannot be occupied.[11] No part of the ocean/sea can be fenced off, fortified, and defended by itself in the manner in which a land territory can be held by one belligerent even against a superior opponent controlling the adjoining area.[12]

Fighting on land is much more intense than at sea because the opposing forces are in almost continuous contact with each other. The intensity of hatred of the enemy is also generally much higher in land than in naval or air warfare. The pauses in fighting on land are usually much shorter than those in war at sea. Hence, war at sea approximates the absolute form of war in general.[13]

The army can usually control the territory it occupies. In contrast, the fleet cannot remain in the ocean/sea area where it defeats the enemy fleet. Open ocean/sea does not belong to anyone. The ocean/sea cannot be controlled in the same way as the victorious army can claim control of the enemy territory. One of the foremost naval classical thinkers, Julian S. Corbett wrote that one cannot "conquer sea because it is not susceptible of ownership, at least outside of territorial waters. You cannot, as lawyers say, 'reduce it into possession,' because you cannot exclude neutrals from it. . . . [Y]ou cannot subsist your armed forces upon it [command of the sea] as you can upon enemy's territory."[14]

The ocean/sea is a protective shield against any would-be invader. At the same time, the sea is also a "highway" – a means of communications. Characteristics of communications on land and at sea are very different. On land, a highway is usually owned by one or the other side. This is not the case at sea. Sea communications have not only military but also economic and political importance for the belligerents and neutrals alike. Their importance has no parallel on land.[15] In contrast to land, most of the oceans/seas are not an obstacle to transportation.

On the ocean/sea, the interests of the belligerents and neutrals are interwoven. A hostile action by one of the belligerents can damage the interests of the neutrals.[16] One's attack on the enemy's maritime trade often results in losses of commercial shipping by the nations that are not belligerents. Economic pressure on land is felt after victory or the occupation of territory but usually not during the hostilities. In contrast, the economic and political pressure of control of the sea can be felt immediately on both the enemy and neutrals.[17]

Lack of common terms

In the past, several terms were used in referring to one's ability to use the sea for both military and nonmilitary purposes. Perhaps the most commonly used terms were "command of the sea," "control of the sea," and "mastery of the sea." The other synonymous terms used in the past were "dominion of the sea" and "sovereignty of the sea."[18] The concept of command or control of the sea underwent numerous changes in the course of the history of naval warfare. For example, in the ancient era, the main purpose was to obtain control of one's communications and to cut off the enemy's. Because oared vessels had low seaworthiness, they moved mostly close to the coast and during the day. They anchored at night in case they were not able to be beached.[19] Hence, the area controlled by the stronger fleet was small. In the medieval era, the navies generally did not seek a decisive battle to obtain sea dominance but were satisfied to secure shipping routes for the movement of commercial goods and transport of troops.[20] Until the First Anglo-Dutch War (1652–1654), control of the sea was not generally considered to be a prerequisite for defense of maritime shipping or transporting troops and conducting landings on enemy territory. A major change came in the aftermath of that war when it became necessary to assemble main forces in home waters, defeat the enemy fleet first, and then exercise command through blockade, commerce raiding, capturing colonies, and landing on enemy territory.[21]

In the past, command of the sea existed when one side secured the continuous flow of its shipping, cut off the enemy's maritime traffic, and, if necessary, projected power onto the enemy's shore. Yet in a war between two strong opponents, there was no such a thing as complete or full command of the sea.[22] In case of war against a strong opponent at sea, command of the sea on the open ocean has always been incomplete and imperfect. Even if one side obtained control of a major part of an ocean that did not mean control of all the marginal seas, and it meant even less control of adjacent semi-enclosed and enclosed seas. Command of the sea never meant literally securing a certain sea area through the permanent presence of one's fleet. The objective was to, by destroying the opposing fleet, create a situation where one's fleet would not face a serious opposition in executing other missions.[23] Also, it was implied that command of the sea would exist only in time of war.[24]

Naval thinkers and sea control

Perhaps for most naval theoreticians, command of the sea meant control over sea lines of communication. For example, Corbett wrote that the object of naval warfare is "the control of communications and not as in land warfare the conquest of territory; the difference is fundamental." [25] For Corbett, phrases such as "conquest of the water territory" or "making the enemy coast our frontier" were false analogies.[26] Command or control of the sea does not mean that a stronger side can keep a permanent presence in a certain part of a maritime theater.[27] At the same time, one has to deny the enemy to secure his sea communications.[28] Corbett observed that in land warfare, "there are also communications that are ensuring the nation life. They connect points of distribution. The destruction of the enemy forces will not avail for certain unless you have in reserve sufficient force to complete the occupation of his inland communications and principal points of distribution."[29] Corbett noted that maritime communications are not identical to those on land because they have a wider meaning. Although they encompass the fleet lines of supply that correspond in strategic value "not to military lines of supply, but to those internal lines of communications by which the flow of national lines is maintained ashore."[30]

Corbett recognized that in wartime the Royal Navy would be able to control important sea communications only at the decisive places.[31] Because maritime communications are common, one as a rule cannot attack those of the enemy without defending one's own. In military operations on land, the converse is the rule.[32] For Corbett, command of the sea also essentially meant one's ability to move across the sea without significant hindrance or opposition, while at the same time preventing the enemy from doing the same.[33] However, Corbett's understanding of command of the sea was too narrow and also imprecise. Sea communications are only one of many elements of maritime trade. More important, the purpose of obtaining command of the sea even in Corbett's era was not just control of sea communications but encompassed attack on the enemy shore plus political, diplomatic, and morale, and even psychological aspects.

The German vice admiral and one of the leading theoreticians in the interwar years, Wolfgang Wegener (1875–1956) explained that sea mastery (*Seeherrschaft*) means that one's trade flows essentially undisturbed, while the adversary's trade is significantly stopped. For Wegener, if only friendly trade is protected without stopping the enemy's maritime traffic, then this term is essentially meaningless. He wrote that sea mastery does not pertain to the movement of some ships in a limited sea area.[34] Sea mastery does not pertain to the movements of individual steamships that sporadically transit the sea area but to that of many ships that run like a river. A short-term disturbance of a certain sea route is not sea mastery because, as soon disturbance is lifted, the stream of the enemy maritime traffic resumes. Hence, a prerequisite for sea mastery is its *duration* (emphasis added).[35]

Admiral Edward Wegener (son of Wolfgang Wegener) wrote that sea control is a state in a certain sea area in which one's sea traffic flows but not the enemy's. Suppressing the enemy's and maintaining one's own sea traffic comprises what is called "sea control." Hence, sea control is a coin with two sides. Suppressing the enemy's commercial and military sea traffic economically and politically isolates the opponent from overseas. Security of one's sea traffic enables not only commercial use of the sea communications but also military power projection to the entire coast where sea control has been obtained.[36]

Admiral Raoul Castex observed that in a war between two continental states bordering the sea, "mastery of the sea is, at least in theory, no longer even a necessary condition, since the ultimate outcome would depend on the result of the combat between the land armies." Yet "command of the sea will most often have a serious effect on the operations of these armies and it will be useful to the power that holds it."[37] Castex wrote that the main objective of "maritime operations" is to preserve freedom to use communications and to deny the same to the enemy or "at least, not to be entirely excluded by the enemy from their use."[38] He noted that whoever controls sea communications not only preserves his links with overseas but also ensures protection of his coast against the enemy's major actions.[39] Castex observed that the struggle for control of maritime communications cannot be treated as "a separate operation divorced from the rest of the military effort." Yet at the same time it cannot replace the efforts to destroy the enemy fleet.[40]

Castex wrote that control of sea routes has a double meaning: economic and military.[41] In his view, sea mastery cannot be limited to just ensuring the relative security of one's traffic and at the same time preventing the enemy's trade. It means that one's traffic flows almost without a hindrance while the enemy's sea routes are observed and ships searched and captured on the high seas if conditions are favorable, ultimately having a form of traditional blockade.[42] By fully exploiting sea mastery, the effect on war as a whole will be different depending on the situation. When both belligerents are separated by the sea, then obtaining sea mastery would create the necessary preconditions for achieving overwhelming success on land, as the examples of the Crimean War (1854–1856), the Sino-Japanese War (1894–1895), the Spanish-American War (1898), and the Russo-Japanese War (1904–1905) illustrate. On the other hand, sea mastery alone is sufficient in a struggle against an insular power.[43]

Another French naval theorist, Rear Admiral René Daveluy (1863–1939), wrote that many theoreticians claim that the objective of command of the sea is to secure the inviolability of one's coast and to attack the enemy's coast, whereas others "assure us that its role is to destroy commerce." Some other theorists think that command of the sea is aimed to "assure the success of an invasion." He concluded that all these objectives would be achieved by destroying the enemy fleet.[44]

A well-known and influential American theorist, Bernard Brodie (1910–1978), wrote that command of the sea has usually been subject to so many limitations and qualifications that some modern writers balked at use of the term and preferred to use the term "control of communications." He observed that the side that can conduct maritime commerce and stop that of the enemy is said to be in "command of the sea." The first objective of the naval offensive is to establish command in the areas of chief importance.[45] British theoretician Colin Gray (b. 1943) wrote that there is nothing to command at sea because the sea communications are empty. In contrast, land territory can be controlled by establishing garrisons with prepared or no fortifications. For him, command of the sea refers to a more or less geographically extensive and porous working control of the relevant sea routes.[46]

What is sea control?

In the aftermath of World War II, the term "command of the sea" was replaced gradually by the term *sea control*. One of the reasons for this was the perception that the term "command" sounds too absolute in its meaning. Many theorists believe that one cannot really "command" the sea but that a certain sea area could be only "controlled." The term "sea control" is a derivation of the term "control of the sea" used by Admiral Alfred T. Mahan. This term implied that one belligerent in a war at sea was able from the outset or during hostilities to conduct large-scale overseas expeditions.[47] It was also recognized that the advent of new and revolutionary weapons (mines, torpedoes) and platforms (submarine, aircraft) made it difficult, even for a major navy, to obtain full command of the sea for any extended time over a major part of the theater.

The term "sea control" more accurately conveys the reality that in a war between two strong opponents at sea, it is not possible, except in the most limited sense, to completely control the sea for one's use or to completely deny its use to the other side. It implies that one's control of a ocean/sea area is inherently limited in space and time.[48]

The concept of sea control is at the same time both simple and complicated. In its simplest definition, sea control can be described as *one's ability to use a given part of the ocean/sea and associated air (space) for military and nonmilitary purposes and to deny the same to the enemy in a time of open hostilities.* However, this definition does not account for the fact that sea control exists in various states and degrees. Sea control implies the sufficient and extensive control of a major part of a given maritime theater. It does not mean that all hostile ships, submarines, or aircraft are unable to operate. It means only that the enemy does not have significant capabilities to seriously interfere with one's use of the sea for military and nonmilitary purposes. An ocean/sea area may be considered under control when one's naval/air forces can operate freely and conduct seaborne traffic while the enemy cannot do the same except at considerable risk. Control of a specific ocean/sea area requires one's naval forces to exercise that control. At the same time, the weaker opponent is forced to contest control by conducting sporadic actions of limited duration.[49] In a typical narrow sea, if a stronger side obtains sea control, the weaker side could make that control increasingly difficult and ultimately obtain control for itself. Even in the areas where a stronger side at sea possesses substantial degree of control of surface and subsurface, the weaker side can still operate under certain conditions provided that it enjoys air superiority.[50]

Misconceptions

Sea control is often confused with power projection and sea denial. Yet *power projection* is one's capability (and not an objective) to exert influence in peacetime and to secure and exercise sea control in a time of open hostilities. Obviously, the greater the power projection capabilities, the greater the chances would be for securing sea control. Sea control and sea denial are related but far from identical. First, the objectives of a stronger and weaker side are diametrically opposite. A stronger side must gain or obtain something – a *positive object*, while a weaker side must deny or prevent something from happening – a *negative object*. Sea control is inherently an *offensive objective*. In contrast, a weaker side has to go on the strategic defensive and conduct sea denial. However, this does not mean that the weaker side is doomed to be on the defensive at the tactical or even at the operational level of war. Also, the main methods of obtaining and denying sea control differ greatly. Yet the fundamental difference is that sea denial is temporary for a stronger side at sea, whereas a weaker side would be on the strategic defensive for the duration of the war.

It is often believed that sea control already exists in peacetime by virtue of one's naval presence. This ignores the fact that the true meaning of sea control encompasses both the "use of the sea for one's military and nonmilitary purposes" and "denying the same to the enemy." Clearly, in peacetime, any navy, regardless of its size or combat strength, has almost unlimited access to any ocean/sea area. Normally, forward presence of a blue-water navy is conducted with full respect for international treaties and conventions and without violating territorial waters of other countries. Forward deployment of one's naval forces only creates favorable conditions to obtain and then maintain sea control quickly after the start of hostilities.

In time of peace, any navy, regardless of its size and combat potential, possesses only a certain degree of what is arbitrarily called *naval influence* but not sea control. A stronger side does not do anything to deny the weaker side use of the sea for both military and commercial purposes. A weaker side at sea could have a larger naval influence because of the much shorter transit and reaction times than a stronger blue-water navy that must project power over several thousands of miles. In purely physical terms, a naval influence is the sum of one's naval combat potential plus non-naval capabilities (i.e., land-based attack aircraft/bombers, medium- and short-range ballistic missiles). It is also a function of the distances and time required to deploy one's naval forces in time of crisis. The problem is complicated because naval influence also encompasses many hard-to- or impossible-to-measure elements. Hence, it can vary greatly because of very different perceptions and biases on the part of potential opponent(s), friends, and neutrals in a given maritime theater. For example, a weaker regional power at sea might actually have greater naval influence because it is much more aggressive and consistent in pursuing and defending its political and strategic interests in a given theater than an out-of-the-area and stronger naval power.

There are also some views that in a typical narrow sea, such as the Baltic, one's possession of the coast is in itself sufficient to have sea control. However, this is a dangerous delusion. Experience demonstrates that obtaining sea control in the littorals is not possible without participation of strong naval forces. Control of the coast is only one of several prerequisites for obtaining sea control.[51] In the littorals, sea control by one side would greatly facilitate control on land, and the lack of that control would greatly complicate the problem for the other side to obtain a dominant position on land. Sea control is not obtained unless one side or the other has control over both land and sea.[52]

The purpose

In the past, command of the sea referred entirely to control of sea communications, that is, a military-economic purpose. However, properly understood, sea control always had not only economic and military but also political and even psychological purposes. Among other things, sea control facilitates the defense and protection of friendly maritime traffic and denies the same to the enemy. Economic exploitation of sea control can contribute greatly to ultimate victory in a war.[53] A stronger side can move naval and merchant ships through the area in reasonable security. It can interfere with and destroy the enemy's seaborne traffic. It allows the stronger side to transport troops across the sea for the purpose of bringing military pressure to bear directly against the enemy.[54] Sea control also protects the country from an enemy seaborne invasion. For example, England, by controlling four narrow seas washing its shores (the North Sea, the English Channel, the Irish Sea, the Bay of Biscay) and the western Mediterranean, not only secured its seaborne trade from crippling losses but also protected England from seaborne invasions. Supposedly, control of these narrow seas also indirectly protected England's colonies elsewhere.[55]

Sea control creates a prerequisite for the secure transport and sustainment of friendly ground forces in their offensive or defensive operations on the coast. It also greatly facilitates projecting one's power to capture important straits, islands, and parts of the enemy coast. Sea control also allows great flexibility in choosing points of attack within a given maritime theater. For example, during the American Revolutionary War (1775–1783), James Madison (1751–1836) noted in May 1781 that "naval superiority had enabled the enemy (British) to shift the theater of war from one point to another along the coast, wearing down the American forces compelled to march overland."[56] The German rear admiral and noted theorist, Curt von Maltzahn (1849–1930), wrote in 1898 that sea mastery can only create a basis for everything else in the conduct of naval warfare. It cannot decide the outcome of a war. It must be preserved and exploited to force the enemy to make peace.[57]

One's possession of sea control can also exert a strong political pressure on the weaker opponent.[58] By obtaining sea control in a certain part of a maritime theater, the stronger side also exerts considerable political and diplomatic influence on the events on land that sometimes can lead to a drastic shift in political and military alignments. In other cases, a major defeat suffered by a hitherto stronger sea power might cause disproportionately large psychological effects and thereby set in motion a chain of events leading to its eventual decline. For example, the defeat of Athens in its Sicilian expedition in 415–413 BC not only resulted in a large loss of ships and men but had extremely larger and negative effects for Athens. Athens' potential enemies (the Spartans), the anti-Athenian faction in the allied cities, and the Persian satraps in Asia Minor all became convinced that the Athenian dominant position in Greece was on the point of collapse. Hence, they were greatly emboldened to concentrate an attack on her sea power. Athens found itself in a very difficult situation. Its fleet had to be everywhere to guard against all threats, while its weaker enemies at sea were able to choose the places and times of their attacks.[59]

Importance

Command of the sea was the main prerequisite for the rise of many countries or nations since the ancient era. Preponderant sea power played a major role in the ultimate success in war. Yet it was often believed that somehow, sea power, combined with money and diplomacy, could defeat land power. Yet a large army is required to ultimately defeat the enemy army. Such mistaken views were prevalent in England in the medieval era. However, only by creating and sustaining large armies during wars against Louis XIV and Napoleon I (1769–1821) and in World War I was England able to defeat its enemies on land.[60] The importance of having command of the sea was pointed out by British soldier, politician, and explorer Sir Walter Raleigh (1552–1618), who said, "[W]hoever commands the seas, commands the trade of the world; whoever commands the trade of the world, command the riches of the world and consequently the world itself."[61]

The importance of sea control depends on the geostrategic position of a country. Generally, it is much more critical for an insular country like England or Japan than it is for a country occupying a semi-central position such is Germany's or countries that have common land borders. It is also more important if a country, regardless of its maritime position, heavily depends on imports/exports, as was the case with Italy in World War II and the People's Republic of China (PRC) today. Italy survived only because of substantial economic support by Germany. Sea control is also less important for a large and economically self-sufficient country, as was case for Soviet Russia or Nazi Germany (the latter used the economic resources of all of Europe in World War II).[62]

The importance of having sea control is generally much greater for a side that must project its power across the ocean on the opposing shore, as the American Revolutionary War (1775–1783), the Crimean War (1854–1856), the Spanish-American War (1898), and the Falklands/Malvinas War (1982) illustrate. It is also more important for a continental country if war is conducted in a theater far away from the main sources of power, as was the case for Russia in its war with Japan in 1904–1905. This is not generally true in the case of a war between the countries occupying a semi-central position and having common borders, as illustrated by the Franco-Prussian War of 1870–1871 and by the wars in the Baltic and the Black Sea during both world wars. Then, sea control has far less influence on the outcome of war on the land front.[63]

Although sea control contributes to the victory on land, it is by itself not sufficient to win a war. Admiral Horatio Nelson (1758–1805) said about his presence in the Gulf of Genoa (in 1795) that sea control does not win the war.[64] Corbett aptly observed that since humans live on land and not at sea, the outcome of major wars between nations has always been determined on land. Only ground forces can effectively control land areas and force the enemy to acknowledge defeat. Experience gives few examples where a war was conducted solely by the navies. Perhaps the closest examples of purely naval wars were the defeat of the Spanish Armada in 1588 and the First Anglo-Dutch War of 1652–1654.[65]

In the past, command of the sea conferred significant advantages to which there was no counterpart in war on land. The weaker side on land, by having a sea control, not only was able to defend its territory but sometimes went on the offensive and ended the war on favorable terms. In contrast, in a war at sea, the side that lost the ability to dispute the "command" was essentially helpless against the attacks of its enemy and was without much hope of changing the situation. The stronger side that possessed sea control enjoyed almost complete immunity from an invasion across the sea. It was also able to threaten its opponent "with all conceivable forms of attack against his territories."[66]

Command of the sea sometimes played a decisive role on the course and outcome of the war on land as, for example, in the second Persian invasion of Greece (480–479 BC). The Persian King Xerxes I (519–465 BC) abandoned his attempt to subjugate Greece after the decisive Greek naval victory at Salamis in September 480 BC.

Sea control by Carthage had a decisive role on the outcome of the First Punic War (264–241 BC). By the end of sixth century BC, Carthage controlled the northern shore of Africa from Cyrenaica to the Phoenician settlements on the southern and Atlantic shores of Spain, the Balearic Islands, Sardinia, Elba, Malta, and the western end of Sicily. In the struggle for control of Sicily, the Carthaginians were able to throw armies at will. However, the Greeks at times successfully challenged that control because they were skilful sailors and far better sea fighters than the Carthaginians were.[67]

In the Second Punic War (218–201 BC), the most decisive factor for the ultimate victory of Rome over Carthage was its control of the central and western Mediterranean. In 218 BC, Rome possessed control of the Tyrrhenian Sea and the waters along the present-day Riviera as far as the territories of their ally Massilia (Marseilles today). In Sicily, Rome held fortified ports at Panormus (Palermo today), Lilybaeum (Marsala today), and Messana (Messina today). From Sicily, they controlled the coasts of southern Italy and the passage across the Adriatic with an intermediate base at Brundisium (Brindisi today). Carthage had control south of the line northern Spain–Sicily.[68] To win in Italy, Carthage had to obtain command of the Tyrrhenian Sea. Yet the Carthaginian fleet was only able to conduct coastal warfare and transport but not to obtain command of the sea.[69]

The Roman command of the sea in the Second Punic War forced the Carthaginian commander Hannibal Barca (247–183/182 BC) to choose a much longer and more arduous land route in invading Italy. In March 218 BC, Hannibal started his descent into Italy with an army of 50,000 infantry, 6,000 cavalry, and 57 elephants. It took Hannibal about seven months to cross the Pyrenees, advance into southern Transalpine Gaul (today's southern France), cross the Rhône River, and get through the Alps into Italy before snow fell. When he entered Cisalpine Gaul (northern Italy today) in November 218 BC, Hannibal had only 20,000 men and few elephants. Most of his men were lost through desertion and some due sickness.[70] Nevertheless, Hannibal's invasion of Italy was initially an uninterrupted series of successes. He won great victories in the battles of Trebia (December 218 BC), Lake of Trasimene (June 217 BC), and Cannae (August 216 BC). Yet after each victory, Hannibal was left with a diminished force. The only way to bring in fresh troops from either Carthage or Spain was across the sea and that route was closed to Hannibal.[71]

During Hannibal's movement toward northern Italy, command of the sea allowed the Roman army to establish itself north of the Ebro River.[72] The Romans fought only four small and successful naval engagements (two off Lilybaeum, one off the Ebro River and Tarentum each).[73] Thereby they obtained command of the sea north of the coast of Sicily, the Gulf of Lion, and the entire eastern coast of Spain.[74] Rome was able to shift its legions between Italy and Spain, attack and destroy Hannibal's bases in Spain, and intercept his communications. The Roman fleet prevented reinforcements and supplies to reach Hannibal by the sea, from either Spain or Africa or his Macedonian allies.[75] Reinforcements to Hannibal by land were slow and difficult. An army led by Hannibal's brother, Hasdrubal the Bald, was defeated in Cisalpine Gaul at the Battle of Metaurus (Metauro today) River on 23 June 207 BC. Ultimately, the Roman Consul Publius Cornelius Scipio Africanus (236–184/183 BC) first drove the Carthaginians out of Spain and thereby cut Hannibal's' link with its base of operations. He then assembled an expeditionary force to Sicily. Scipio Africanus landed in North Africa and thereby threatened the heart of Carthage. Hannibal was decisively defeated in the Battle of Zama (near Carthage) in October of 202 BC. Subsequently, Carthage was destroyed and became Rome's client state.[76]

Sea control obtained during hostilities has ensured the predominance of the victorious side in peacetime. For example, command of the sea was the key to the control of the major part of the Mediterranean by the Byzantine Empire (c. 330–1453) in the aftermath of the fall of Rome in 476 AD. Byzant's hegemony was first threatened by the Vandals in the fifth century AD. The Emperor Justinian I (482–565 AD) eliminated this threat in the so-called Vandalic War of 533–534 AD. However, Byzantine control of the Mediterranean was challenged with the rising power of the Muslims in the seventh century AD. Byzant first lost control of the Levant and then of North Africa.

Sea power was the single most important reason for the success of Britain and its Prussian ally in the Seven Years' War (1756–1763). Military and naval actions in that first global war took place in Europe, North America, the Caribbean, the West African coast, India, and the Philippines. The war ended with the Treaty of Paris (signed by France, Spain, and Great Britain) and the Treaty of Hubertusburg (signed by Saxony, Prussia, and Austria) in 1763. The greatest winner was Great Britain, which obtained control of New France (in Canada), Spanish Florida, some islands in the Caribbean, Senegal (West Africa), and a superior position over the French trading posts on the Indian subcontinent. These gains would not have been possible without the Royal Navy's superiority at sea over the combined Spanish-French fleet.

In the American Revolutionary War (1775–1783), command of the sea initially gave Britain a tremendous advantage. The British enjoyed mobility denied to the American revolutionaries chiefly dependent on primitive land communications. It allowed the British to capture New York and other important seaports, which afterward were used as bases and havens of refuge for British troops. Without naval power, the revolutionary armies were unable to win decisive victories.[77] Commander-in-Chief (CINC) of the Continental Army, General George Washington (1732–1799), wrote after the battle of Yorktown (19 October 1781) to Marquis de Lafayette (1757–1834) that "no land force can act decisively, unless it is accompanied by a maritime superiority . . . For proof of this we have only to recur to the ease and facility with which the British shifted their ground as advantages were to be obtained at either extremity of the continent, and to their late heavy loss the moment they failed in their naval superiority."[78] Britain's ultimate failure was its inability to exploit its apparently overwhelming advantage on the ocean.[79]

In the French Revolutionary Wars (1792–1802), France defeated first and second coalitions led by Britain. During the Napoleonic Wars (1803–1815), France was victorious against three more coalitions organized by Britain. However, Napoleon I was defeated in a war by a sixth coalition in 1814 and then again by a seventh coalition in 1815. The decisive role in Great Britain's successes was control of the sea obtained by the Royal Navy in European waters. Control of the English Channel prevented the French armies from invading Ireland in 1796 and England in 1803–1805. Britain's ability to raise successive coalitions and sustain its armies on the continent would not have been possible without command of the sea.

Sea control had a major influence on the course of many wars in the nineteenth century. For example, in the War of 1812 between United States and Great Britain, sea control had a large impact on the outcome of the war on land. The American victory on Lake Erie in September 1813 forced an immediate withdrawal of the British army from the Detroit frontier. Afterward, American control of Lake Erie secured control of the West for the duration of war. The American victory in the Battle of Plattsburg (also known as the Battle of Lake Champlain) in September 1812 checked the southward advance of the British army and opened the way for the American counteroffensive against Lower Canada.[80]

In the War of 1812, the British were much more successful in their operations off the U.S. Atlantic seaboard. At the beginning of the war, the Royal Navy was comparatively weak in the American waters. It had an immense strength elsewhere. Although numerically greatly inferior, the American navy fought several highly successful individual ship-vs.-ship actions.[81] However, the Royal Navy swept the entire American commerce from the ocean, at the same time successfully protected British shipping. Its steadily effective naval blockade strangled American commerce at its source. The American Navy was unable after the first weeks of the war to give substantial protection to the country's maritime commerce.[82] The war formally ended with the Treaty of Ghent, signed on 24 December 1814.

In the Mexican-American War (1846–1848), the greatest service that the U.S. Navy provided was command of the Gulf of Mexico. This, in turn, made it possible to transport and land the U.S. Army on Mexico's shore and to cut off Mexico from foreign munitions and other supplies.[83] In the Crimean War (1853–1856) between Russia and the Ottoman Empire and its western allies (France, Great Britain, Kingdom of Sardinia), war at sea was conducted in the Black Sea, the Baltic, the White Sea, and the Sea of Okhotsk. The British and French sea control played a major role in their eventual victory.

Sea control had a major role in the French victory in the war between Austria and France/Kingdom of Sardinia (Second Italian War of Independence) of 1859. The French possessed absolute control of the waters off Italy's western coast. This allowed them and the Kingdom of Sardinia to transport two French army corps plus one division to Genoa and parts of another army corps to Leghorn.[84]

During the American Civil War (1861–1865), the Union Navy had almost undisputed command of the sea. In July 1861, the North established a naval/commercial blockade of the Confederate States' ports.[85] The blockade was established from the Chesapeake Bay to the Mexican border, extending for some 3,500 miles. It was the Union Navy's biggest contribution to the victory of the North.[86] By the end of the first year of the war, the Union Navy obtained control of a number of points on the coast of Virginia, North and South Carolina, Georgia, Florida, and Mississippi. It took three years for the Union armies to make inroads to the positions controlled by the Union Navy.[87] The Union Navy's operations on western rivers secured control of the Mississippi River and its tributaries and thereby isolated the trans-Mississippi Confederacy states. The Union Navy's control of the sea was a major factor in the highly successful cooperation with the army in Chesapeake Bay and Virginia. It also played a large role in support of the Army of Potomac and General George B. McClellan's Peninsula Campaign of spring 1862 and again in support of General Ulysses S. Grant's victorious offensive against Richmond in 1864–1865. The Union's ships covered the army's movement across otherwise impassable terrain and guarded the vital line of water communications to that Army's ultimate source of supplies.[88]

In the War of the Pacific (1879–1884) (the Saltpeter War), Chile faced a defensive alliance of Bolivia and Peru. Geography dictated that both sides had to rely on their naval forces to achieve their respective war objectives. Chile and Peru were separated by a zone of almost uninhabited, arid and very hilly terrain. This, in turn, made it necessary for both sides to obtain an adequate degree of sea control. At the beginning of the hostilities, the naval forces of both belligerents were almost equal. Peru had in service two armored ships, two monitors and two wooden ships. Chile had two armored and four wooden corvettes and two gunboats.[89] In the end, the Chilean Navy emerged victorious. The Peruvian coast was open to an attack from across the sea.[90] On land, the Chilean army defeated the Bolivian army in the Battle of Tacna in May 1880. The Chilean army defeated the Peruvian army in the Battle of Arica in June 1880. It captured the capital Lima in January 1881. Chile and Peru ended hostilities in the Treaty of Ancón, signed in October 1883, and a truce was signed with Bolivia a year later.

In the Spanish-American War of 1898, geography was against Spain. The Spanish naval forces had to operate several thousand miles from their home bases. Puerto Rico, the most easterly Spanish naval depot, lay more than twice as far from Spain as from United States.[91] The U.S. objective was to drive the Spanish forces from Cuba. Hence, it was critical for the Spaniards to control communications between Cuba and mainland Spain. For the Americans, a naval blockade of Cuba was contingent on their command of the Caribbean. This objective could be accomplished only by destroying or immobilizing Spanish naval forces in Cuba's waters.[92]

In the Russo-Japanese War of 1904–1905, the Russians initially attempted to occupy Korea and prevent the Japanese from landing there. To destroy the Japanese fleet and prevent a Japanese landing, a close cooperation between the Russian fleet and the army was a necessity.[93] For the Japanese, command of the Yellow Sea was necessary to successfully land their troops in Korea. Hence, during the night of 8/9 February of 1904, they carried out a surprise torpedo attack on the Russian squadron at Port Arthur. The same day, about 65,000 Japanese troops landed at Chemulpo Bay (Incheon or Inchon today). The Russian fleet suffered great losses and was forced onto the defensive. This, in turn, allowed the Japanese to obtain command of the Yellow Sea and thereby reinforce their army besieging Port Arthur.[94]

During World War I (1914–1918), the Entente powers possessed sea control over the major part of the Atlantic Ocean and the Mediterranean. Sea control was a critical factor that enabled France and Great Britain to transport some 247,000 troops from North Africa and 134,000 from West Africa.[95] Some 2,080,000 troops were also sent from the United States to Europe. About 46 percent of this number were carried on U.S. ships (almost all naval transports).[96] The British and French Navies provided extensive support to the troops operating along the French/Belgian coast. Their role was especially valuable in protecting the transport of British troops across the Channel in the early phase of the war. They also protected the army troops from the German naval raids conducted between Dunkirk and Nieuwpoort.[97] Because of their superiority at sea, the Entente powers were able to use the world's trade in support of their war effort. The longer the war lasted, the stronger the negative effect that was felt by the Central Powers.[98]

The lack of or the inability to obtain control of the sea doomed many military expeditions. For example, in the first Persian invasion of Greece (492–490 BC), the Persians subjugated Thrace and forced Macedonia to become their client state in 492 BC. However, their attempt to extend control to Athens and other Greek states failed because they lost a major part of their fleet in a storm off the coast of Mount Athos. They launched another invasion of Greece, under Datis and Artaphernes in 490 BC, by transporting their army across the Aegean Sea. En route to Attica, they seized Naxos, Eretria (on Euboea), and other island states in the Aegean. Although defeated on land at Marathon in 490 BC, the Persians were able, due to their command of the sea, to reembark part of their force and, by sailing around Cape Sunium, come close enough to capture Athens by surprise. However, the Athenians' swift march overland from Marathon forced the Persians to abandon the Greek coast and return to Asia.[99]

During its war with Napoleonic France in 1805–1810, Sweden's failure to obtain command of the sea allowed its enemies to roam freely along its coast. A combined Russian and French force of about 1,600 men strong had landed on Gotland in May 1808 and then seized Visby, the island's principal port. In the end, a truce was reached; the Franco-Russian force evacuated Gotland, and the Russians agreed to withdraw from the Åland Islands, which they had captured in the winter of 1807 by marching across the ice. A Russian advance to Stockholm was checked by the Swedish and British fleets, although the Swedes had been weakened by the loss of their light coastal forces in the Gulf of Finland.[100]

The lack of sea control would usually force the weaker side to rely on much less efficient and slower land supply routes. For example, in the Russo-Turkish War of 1876–1877, because of the lack of naval forces, the Russians had to send supplies to their army in the Balkans overland to Galatz (Galati today) on the Danube River. The Turkish control of the

Black Sea forced the Russians to use a longer and much more difficult route to descend into the Turkish-controlled Bulgaria. The Turkish command of the sea meant that the Russian attempt to seize Constantinople and to advance in the Caucasus had to be made overland, for there was no possibility to land troops by sea. This led to fierce and costly fighting at Plevna.[101] Although the Russians ultimately defeated the Turks, they would have been probably much more successful if they possessed control of sea communications.[102]

Scale

In theory, sea control can be strategic, operational, and tactical in scale. However, in practical terms, the struggle for sea control is primarily focused on obtaining and maintaining operational and strategic sea control. *Strategic* sea control pertains to the entire maritime theater. Control of a typical narrow sea, such as the Persian (Arabian) Gulf, would amount to *operational* sea control. *Tactical* sea control pertains to control of the ocean/sea area ranging from a naval combat sector (zone) to a maritime area of operations.

Boundaries

In contrast to war on land, the boundaries of one's control at sea cannot be precisely delineated. On the open ocean, these boundaries are very ambiguous, diffuse, and constantly in a state of flux. The situation is somewhat different in an enclosed sea theater because the spatial extent of control of the surface is more or less well-defined. However, the boundaries of control of the subsurface and the air are highly uncertain. Normally, sea control does not encompass the entire ocean/sea. For each side, the most important area to possess control of is the waters adjacent to one's shore. Controlling that part of the ocean/sea makes it possible to keep the free flow of coastal traffic and also to prevent the enemy from carrying out a successful direct attack on one's shore. A major power also has great interest in obtaining control of the ocean/sea area between itself and its allies or between itself and those neutrals upon which it depends for essential war and food supplies. It would also attempt to extend control to those parts of the ocean/sea that are vital to the enemy, not only for the transport of military goods but also for the defense of his territory and the support of his forces on the front. Also, there are focal points, or "foci," of maritime trade that each side would like to control as much as possible.[103]

Relativity

In a war between two strong opponents, neither side will be able to obtain a full and permanent control of the entire maritime theater and all of its three physical mediums or dimensions. The more common situation would be that one or the other side would enjoy control in a certain part of the theater and for a specific purpose. Experience shows that, in a war between two strong opponents, sea control has been in most cases *relative* and *incomplete*. Mahan wrote that "control of the sea does not mean that the enemy's single ships or small squadrons cannot sail out of port, cannot cross more or less frequented tracts of ocean, make harassing descents upon blockaded harbors. Such evasions are possible as history amply showed."[104]

Likewise, Castex wrote that there is no such thing as full command of the sea. Command of the sea "is not absolute but relative, incomplete and imperfect. In spite of crushing superiority, the dominance of communications has never completely prevented his enemy from appearing on the water."[105] Even relative mastery of the sea cannot be exercised at all points of the globe at the same time because even the strongest power lacks sufficient forces. There has never been general control of sea communications but only local control over specific parts of the theater or fewer in number, to a greater or smaller extent, and depending upon one's resources. Sometimes geography and the distribution of fleets shifted local control of the sea to the benefit of the weaker navy.[106] Castex noted that the freedom to use the sea for one's purposes "confers opportunities for coastal raids, captures on the high seas and conditions permitting old-fashioned blockade."[107]

Brodie observed that command has never meant control that was either complete in degree or unbounded in maritime space. It has meant only that the efforts of one belligerent to control sea communications over a certain area have been on the whole successful.[108] One has to bear always in mind that command is always relative and means simply a marked ascendancy in the contest for control.[109] Control of the western Pacific by the Japanese Navy in World War II did not prevent large losses of the Japanese merchant shipping due to Allied submarines. Equally true was that, despite the British command of the sea, the Allies suffered huge losses of merchant shipping in the northern Atlantic.[110]

Degrees

In a war between two strong opponents, sea control is never static but highly dynamic. Changes in the situation occur often and suddenly. This is particularly the case in a typical narrow sea. Depending on the intensity of combat, control of the sea exists in various degrees. Corbett wrote that command of the sea may "exist in various states and degrees, each of which has its special possibilities and limitations."[111] He wrote, "If the object of command of the sea is to control communications, it is obvious it may exist in various degrees. We may be able to control the whole of the common communications as the result of either great initial preponderance or of decisive victory. If we are not sufficiently strong to do this, we may still be able to control some of the communications; that is, our control may be general or local."[112] The German admiral and historian Otto Groos (1882–1970) wrote that sea mastery exist in degrees. It can be partial or complete. It can be limited to a single sea area or extend over the large part of an ocean.[113]

Generally, the degree of sea control depends on the size of the ocean/ sea area, the distance of the operating area from one's basing/deployment area, and the relative numerical/qualitative strength compared to the enemy force. Normally, a much higher degree and longer duration of control is required to ensure the safety of friendly maritime traffic than in conducting amphibious landings on the opposing shore and attacks on enemy coastal installations/facilities. The degree of control is also affected by the uncertainty as to the actual or suspected presence of hostile submarines and mines. This is largely a psychological factor that cannot be anticipated or quantified. The desired degree of sea control is obtained when it is sufficient to accomplish a certain objective.[114]

Spatial extent

A unique feature of sea control is that it exists spatially (also called "state of control") and in all three physical dimensions. There is no counterpart in war on land. The state of control or spatial extent of sea control underwent significant changes since the ancient era. Up to the era of exploration, the scope of sea control was relatively limited because of the short radius and endurance of oared vessels and early sailing ships. It was only after the advent of sailing ships capable of operating in any part of the world's ocean, combined with the vastly increased volume of maritime trade, that control of larger parts of the oceans was required. Command of the sea was then understood in almost absolute terms. There was a need to seek a decisive encounter with the opposing fleet or to prevent the enemy fleet to sail out from its bases and thereby obtain absolute freedom of action.

The spatial extent of sea control depends primarily on size of the ocean/ sea area and its geographic configuration, changes in the correlation of forces, and the course of the operations.[115] It also depends on the physical location of the strategic objective. Obviously, the larger the area, the more difficult it is to obtain an adequate degree of control.

In its spatial extent, sea control can be general or local or combination of these two. Corbett was the first naval theoretician who differentiated between general and local command of the sea. He wrote that if one's forces are not sufficiently superior to those of the enemy or unable to achieve a decisive victory, then "we may still be able to control some of the communications; that is, our control may be general or local."[116] Corbett defined general and permanent control as the one when the enemy cannot "interfere with our maritime trade and overseas operations so seriously as to affect the issue of the war, and that he cannot carry on his own trade and operations except at such risk and hazard as to remove them from the field of practical strategy."[117] In that case, the "enemy can no longer attack one's lines of passage and communications effectively and . . . he cannot use or defend his own."[118] Corbett noted that even general control can never in practice be absolute. In his view, no degree of naval superiority can ensure one's communications against sporadic attacks from detached cruisers or enemy raiding squadrons if they are boldly led and prepared to risk destruction.[119]

In another but broader definition, general sea control pertains to a state in which the stronger side exercises control of a large part of the ocean/ sea without significant challenge from its opponent.[120] However, the latter definition resembles in part of what in generic terms is called "naval (or maritime) superiority." Yet neither of these definitions are quite satisfactory. One difficulty in properly defining the term "general sea control" is that the term "general" has several contradictory meanings in the English language.[121] Perhaps a better definition is that a state of *general sea control* pertains to a loose control of a large part a given maritime theater. Normally, it is possible to obtain control of a relatively large part of the ocean/ sea surface but not the subsurface and air. The extent of general sea control is directly related to the overall ratio of combat potential between belligerents. Normally, general sea control requires that a major part of the enemy fighting force is destroyed or contained. Hence, it does not exist at the beginning of the hostilities at sea but instead sometime after one or the other side is considerably weakened.

In the era of sail and early steam and until the advent of mines, submarines, and aircraft, general control pertained exclusively to control of the surface. In the modern era, general control has been very difficult to obtain in the ocean/sea area within effective range of the enemy land-based aircraft and submarines. General sea control on the open ocean has usually been a decisive factor in a war against an enemy heavily dependent on maritime commerce or vulnerable to naval blockade. However, one's control on the open ocean has rarely, if ever, been complete. For example, during World War II, the Allies possessed general control of the northern Atlantic after 1943 because the Germans did not use their heavy surface ships against Allied shipping. However, this was not the case with control of the subsurface because the U-boats remained a threat.

Today, it is still possible to have general sea control on the open ocean but less so in the peripheral or marginal seas, such as the South China Sea or the East China Sea. Likewise, it would be very hard for a blue-water navy to obtain general sea control in a typical narrow sea such as the Baltic Sea or the Persian (Arabian) Gulf. The reason in both cases is a significant increase in diversity, effective range, precision, and lethality of anti-access/ area denial threats in such sea areas.

In the past, *local sea control* pertained to the sea area near one's bases or ports or to the ability to secure a part of one's sea communications. For example, Carthage lost its naval supremacy in the aftermath of the First Punic War. At the start of the Second Punic War, Carthage had only local command of the sea by maintaining sea communications between North Africa and Spain. However, it lacked general sea control of the western

Mediterranean, which was in Roman hands. This, coupled with lack of control of Sicily and the western part of today's Balkans, forced Hannibal to invade Italy by a much longer and more difficult land route from Spain.[122]

Today, local sea control could be understood as possessing a high degree of control in a specific and relatively small part of a maritime theater. Both the stronger and the weaker sides can exercise local control at the same but in different parts of a theater. However, the difference is that a stronger side would also possess general control while a weaker side would not.

Corbett observed that local control depends on the general situation in a given maritime theater.[123] Local sea control obtained by a stronger side cannot prevent the weaker side from conducting raids or some other offensive action in other parts of a maritime theater. Generally, the objective of a stronger side should be to expand local control to become general control and temporary control to become permanent control. Castex argued that does not mean that the ideal of having general, permanent, and complete sea control is ever possible.[124]

A stronger side needs to obtain local control of a certain ocean/sea area in order to provide support to friendly troops operating on the coast, to conduct amphibious landings, or to destroy the enemy's coastal installations/facilities. For example, the Americans had to obtain control of the northern part of the Caribbean Sea during their operations against Cuba in 1898. Likewise, command of the Yellow Sea was necessary for the Japanese during the Russo-Japanese War of 1904–1905. Obviously, the Japanese never intended to have control of the Baltic.[125] The Germans had to obtain a local control of the Danish Straits and the southern part of the Norwegian Sea during their invasion of Norway in April 1940. The Allies possessed local control of amphibious objective areas during most of their major amphibious landings in the Pacific, Atlantic, and Mediterranean in World War II.

In a major war at sea, a common occurrence is that the stronger side possesses a general control of the major part of an ocean and local control of certain areas within a respective ocean. Yet general control of an ocean does not ensure control of the contiguous narrow seas, as the examples of the Royal Navy during the Seven Years' War, the French Revolutionary Wars, and the Napoleonic Wars illustrate. In World War I, the Entente Powers controlled the surface of every ocean and all the strategically important narrow seas except for the Adriatic, the Black Sea, the Baltic, and the eastern and southeastern rim of the North Sea.[126] The British Grand Fleet possessed control of the northern and southern exits of the North Sea and thereby maintained a distant blockade of Germany. The U-boats and extensive use of mines by the Germans prevented the British from conducting a close blockade. At the same time, the German High Seas Fleet had local control of the Heligoland Bight and effectively controlled the southeastern part of the North Sea. The German bases were within striking distance of the Kattegat, thereby preventing the Grand Fleet from conducting offensive actions within the Baltic in support of Britain's besieged ally, Russia.

During the entire war the Baltic remained essentially a "German lake." Likewise, control of the Adriatic was in the hands of the Austro-Hungarian Navy throughout the entire war.[127]

Sometimes, one side in a narrow sea would obtain general control, but the local control might belong often to a weaker opponent. For example, in World War I, the Germans possessed general control in the western part of the Baltic. However, their control in the eastern and central parts of that sea was in dispute because of the presence of a relatively strong Russian fleet. Likewise, the Germans possessed a general control of the Baltic Sea in 1941–1944. However, they did not have control of the eastern part of the Gulf of Finland. This allowed Soviet submarines to sporadically break through the Finnish-German defenses and operate in the open waters of the Baltic. Control in the central part of the Mediterranean was in dispute in 1940–1943, while Axis' control of the Adriatic, Tyrrhenian, and Aegean seas was never seriously challenged by the Allies until after September 1943.

In the Leyte operation (17 October–25 December 1944), the Allies had general control of the approaches to the Philippines and local control of the Leyte Gulf.[128] However, they did not have control of the Camotes Sea and western approaches to Leyte Island, especially during the night hours and in bad weather. This situation, in turn, allowed the Japanese to bring in fresh troops and materiel to Leyte from nearby islands in the Visayas and Mindanao.[129] The Japanese used mostly barges but also transports, submarine chasers (SCs), and destroyers for carrying troops and materiel. The Allied troops encountered steadily increased Japanese resistance on the ground because of their inability to prevent the flow of troop reinforcements and materiel to Leyte from Luzon and Mindanao and other adjacent islands. When the Allies landed on 20 October, the Japanese had only 16,000 troops on Leyte. By early November, the Japanese brought in some 22,000 combat troops to Leyte and thereby denied the Allies a quick victory. Leyte was not officially declared secured until 25 December 1944. The Japanese landed a total of some 38,000 troops at Ormoc, Leyte. They lost thousands of troops before they reached the shore and some 130,000 tons of shipping.[130] The main reason for the Allied lack of control in the western approaches to Leyte was their lack of ships larger than PT boats and smaller than destroyers and capable of operating in confined waters and also a sufficient number of aircraft fitted with radar to operate at night.[131]

In a typical narrow sea, control of the high seas does not necessarily mean control of the interisland area. A highly indented coast, such as Dalmatia's coast, with many offshore islands greatly reduces the ability to maneuver by naval forces of a stronger side. Their attempt to operate within an island chain could be effectively blocked by mines and coastal missile/gun batteries. They are also very vulnerable to attacks by small surface combatants hiding among the islands. The stronger side can penetrate the interisland positions of a weaker side but only at great risk.[132]

Physical dimensions

The problem of obtaining a satisfactory degree of sea control is greatly complicated by the necessity to control one or all three physical dimensions: surface, subsurface, and air. Obviously, until the end of the era of sail in late nineteenth century, control of the sea meant control of the surface. After the advent of mines, torpedoes, and submarines and aircraft, it was necessary to obtain control of the subsurface and airspace too. The degree of overall control of a given sea area depends on the degree of control of each of the three physical dimensions.[133]

In a war between two strong opponents at sea, it is usually not possible to obtain and maintain control of all three physical dimensions to the same degree and/or for extended times. For example, in World War I, the Entente's control of the surface of the ocean outside the Baltic Sea was almost absolute except for a few occasional enemy cruiser raids.[134] In 1942, the Italian naval forces and aircraft dominated the Adriatic Sea. No British surface ships dared to operate within the Adriatic. Only individual submarines were able to penetrate that area.[135] In the struggle for Guadalcanal (August 1942–February 1943), neither the Japanese nor the Allies had full control of the surface and the air. The Japanese had generally control of the surface during the night, while the Allies controlled both the surface and the air during the daylight hours. In the Falklands/Malvinas War of 1982, during the Battle of San Carlos (21–25 May), the Royal Navy possessed control of the surface because of the passivity of the Argentine Navy. Yet it lacked control of the subsurface around Task Group (TG) 317.8 (Carrier/Battle Group), while control of the air was highly disputed.

Perhaps most critical for ultimate success is control of the surface. Without adequate control of the surface, one's forces will be unable to conduct amphibious landings. Security of one's maritime traffic will be difficult if not impossible to achieve. Control of the surface can pertain to a large ocean/sea area or might be confined to the control of specific waters only. For example, in the Russo-Japanese War of 1904–1905, the Japanese never claimed to have command of the sea generally. They did not make any attempt to stop the Russian fleet using the oceans. Their only objective was to control the waters between Vladivostok and Port Arthur.[136]

In a typical narrow sea, the situation on the surface would greatly depend on the situation in the air and on land. Control of a certain part of the theater would be directly related to the size of one's forces and the duration of their presence.[137]

Control of the subsurface is generally incomplete, uncertain, and tenuous. A successful struggle with enemy submarines requires that a large ocean/sea area be searched. The sheer complexity and variability of the oceanographic/weather conditions considerably affect the work of acoustic sensors. This is especially the case in the littorals. Enemy submarines can exploit the characteristics of the physical environment to avoid detection by blending into the background. The search for submarines is characterized by numerous false alarms. Hence, the detection of enemy submarines requires an enormous amount of time and effort. For the most part, ASW consists of force-on-force encounters. Hence, it takes a long time before the threat posed by enemy submarines is brought down to a satisfactory level. For example, the struggle against German U-boats lasted for more than four years in World War I and for a little less than six years in World War II.

The presence of the enemy mines greatly complicates the task of securing control of the surface. Among other things, the area suspected of being mined must be avoided by one's ships. Mines are one of the greatest threats to the survivability of both naval vessels and commercial shipping. They are in some cases almost the only means available to a weaker opponent at sea to challenge control of a stronger navy. Destroying or neutralizing enemy mines requires a disproportionately larger and more consistent effort, in terms of number of ships, materiel, personnel, and organization, than mining. The search for, neutralization, and destruction of mines are an extremely dangerous, difficult, and nerve-racking effort.

In the modern era, sea control has no meaning unless it is combined with control of the air.[138] Control of the air is even more complicated and elusive than control of the surface. The airspace extends deep over friendly and enemy territories and over the adjacent ocean/sea and upward to altitudes of several hundreds of miles above the earth's surface. Theoretically, there are no geographical boundaries to limit freedom of action for aircraft. Combat in the air occurs at a much higher speed than at sea. Airspace as a physical dimension does not provide inherent advantages to either side in a combat. It does not provide cover to either side.[139]

Castex wrote that air mastery is even more relative than mastery of the sea. The airspace cannot be occupied permanently. Aircraft can dominate a part of the airspace only for the duration of their flight.[140] They cannot remain indefinitely in a given airspace because of high fuel consumption. They must return to a base for refueling and maintenance. A stronger side in the air can never prevent the airplanes of even the weaker side from conducting reconnaissance.[141]

Control of the air is inherently temporary as long as the enemy has the means to contest it. If one side at sea enjoys air superiority, then it can be impossible for the other side to utilize some aspects of sea control for its own purposes. Air superiority over a given sea or ocean area can compensate for those aspects of sea control that naval forces are unable to obtain. Nevertheless, for all its value, air superiority cannot *replace* one's control of the surface and subsurface.[142]

For the first time in history control of the air played a decisive role in the struggle for sea control in World War II. The British learned at heavy cost the critical importance of possessing control of the air in a war at sea as the campaigns in Norway in 1940, Greece/Crete in 1941, Malaya in 1941–1942, and the struggle for control of the central Mediterranean in 1940–1943 show. For example, during the German invasion of Norway (Weserübung Nord) in April–June 1940. The British control of the surface was largely nullified by the German Luftwaffe.

Permanent vs. temporary control

In terms of the factor of time, sea control can be permanent or temporary. A *permanent sea control* exists when the stronger side completely dominates a given theater, either because the other side does not have any means to deny that control or because its fleet has been destroyed. In practice, however, it is more common that the weaker side still has some means at its disposal to challenge the stronger side's control. Corbett wrote that permanent sea control does not mean that the enemy can do nothing but rather that he cannot interfere with one's shipping or amphibious landings in such a way as to seriously affect the course of the war.[143]

Temporary sea control is a condition when one side possesses a high degree of control of the sea but for a limited time. When one side loses the initiative, for whatever reason, the abandonment may be permanent or temporary. The weaker side at sea then usually keeps a major part of its fleet in the bases, avoiding any decisive action at sea. If a weaker enemy succeeds in obtaining superiority in the air, this in itself could be sufficient to allow him the use of the sea for a specific purpose and for a limited time. The lack of sea control for even a relatively short time has doomed many plans for large-scale invasions.

Limited vs. absolute control

In terms of the factor of force, sea control can range from limited to contested/disputed and to absolute. Vice Admiral Phillip Howard Colomb (1831–1899) differentiated between absolute or assured and temporary command of the sea. For him, absolute command of the sea is nothing but the attribute of the nation whose power on the sea is paramount.[144] Corbett wrote that permanent and absolute or unlimited sea control can be obtained only when the enemy fleet is annihilated.[145] He realized that the Royal Navy was unable to have control in all sea areas where British interests were but was able only to have control of important sea communications and to concentrate British forces at the decisive place.[146]

Castex observed that the very term "command of the sea" "gives the impression that its beneficiary enjoys the marvelous privilege of having to himself the immense expanse of the oceans or building a sort of barricade whose keys put in his pocket thus totally banning peacetime users. This is misleading. It is utopian. All the world's fleets collectively would not suffice to achieve it everywhere. Nor would neutrals easily allow themselves to be cut off from trade." Unlike land, a maritime theater is "constantly traveled by strangers to the conflict."[147] Castex wrote that in contrast to war on land, where the combat area is crossed uninterruptedly, this is not the case in war at sea. Sea mastery is not absolute. Even when the stronger side enjoys an overwhelming superiority, it cannot completely prevent its adversary from operating individual ships or even squadrons and inflicting damage. It is true that such actions can never seriously have practical effect on sea mastery.[148] Hence, the term "mastery" appears a little too strong, and perhaps it would be more accurate to say, as the British do, about "control" of sea communications. This term better reflects the reality and at the same time takes into account limitations due to the traffic conducted by the neutrals.[149]

Limited sea control (or conditional or working control) exists when one side has a high degree of freedom to act, whereas the other side operates at high risk. It cannot be quantified but expressed only in very broad terms. In a case where absolute control cannot be obtained, the stronger side would usually try to secure temporary control of limited sea or ocean areas for conducting operations necessary to the successful progress of the war on land.

The state of limited sea control is usually the consequence of the drastic shift in the operational or strategic situation when the initiative passes from one side to the other. The side that has lost the initiative, however, still may be strong enough to inflict significant losses on the stronger side. Limited sea control is inherently transitory and, hence, unstable.[150] In that case, the side without control may still be able to deploy one type of ship without undue risks, while other types of ships operate at high or unacceptable risks. For example, in World War I, the Royal Navy held command of the North Sea only as far as battleships were concerned. Yet the Germans effectively employed their battle cruisers, light cruisers, destroyers, and U-boats. Hence, no matter how tight the blockade was, the Royal Navy still had to provide direct defense for Allied shipping and to defend the coastline behind the blockading line.

In theory, *absolute sea control* exists if one side enjoys superiority over its opponent in a major part of or the entire maritime theater. This was difficult to achieve even prior to the advent of submarine and aircraft. Mahan explained that in the Second Punic War, Rome had absolute control the sea basin between Italy, Sicily, and Spain – the Tyrrhenian and Sardinian seas. The seacoast from the Ebro to the Tiber was the mostly friendly. In the fourth year of war (after the Battle of Cannae), Syracuse abandoned its alliance with Rome. Revolt then spread throughout Sicily. Macedonia entered into an offensive alliance with Hannibal. Despite these challenges, at no time did the Romans cease to control the Tyrrhenian Sea. The Roman ships sailed undisturbed from Italy to Spain. In the Adriatic, the Romans established a naval station at Brundisium (Brindisi today) and maintained a naval squadron there to prevent Macedonians from controlling that sea. Not a single Macedonian soldier ever set foot in Italy.[151] The Romans controlled the sea area north from Tarragona in Spain to Lilybaeum, at the west end of Sicily, then round the north coast of Sicily through the Strait of Messina and then southward to Syracuse, and from there to Brindisi. This control lasted throughout the entire Second Punic War. Although it did not prevent raids against the Roman-controlled coast, it prevented Carthaginians from having secure sea communications with Hannibal's army in Italy.[152]

Yet Mahan was not entirely correct in his claims that the Romans possessed absolute command in a major part of the western Mediterranean. The Carthaginian raids were not as insignificant as he implied. For example, Carthaginian commander Bomilcar landed at Locri in Bruttium (Calabria today) with 4,000 Numidian cavalrymen and 40 elephants in 215 BC. In 209 BC, a Carthaginian fleet descended on Liguria and destroyed the city of Genua (Genoa today).[153]

Absolute control of large ocean/sea areas cannot be achieved in terms of either space or time in the presence of an undefeated and strong opponent. For example, in most of the British-French wars until the late eighteenth century, command of the seas was usually in dispute. During the American Revolutionary War (1775–1783), the Royal Navy was distinctly inferior in strength in America's waters due to dissipation of its available strength. Britain was forced to contemplate going onto a naval strategic defensive.[154] Occasionally, one side could enjoy absolute command of the sea, as Britain did during the Boer War of 1898–1902, when the rebels had no navy whatsoever.

In the modern era, absolute sea control means, in practice, that one's forces operate without major opposition while the enemy forces cannot operate at all. The objective is to obtain sea control of the entire theater or the major part of the theater, so that one can employ one's fleet whenever and wherever required without threat from the enemy. In other words, absolute sea control equates to maritime supremacy or maritime mastery. The weaker side then cannot employ its submarines, aircraft, or sometimes even mines.[155]

Absolute control on the open ocean usually means control of the surface and, to some extent, of the air, whereas control of the subsurface is difficult or impossible to obtain. In a typical narrow sea, however, because of its small size and, hence, more favorable space-force ratio, a blue-water navy can possibly obtain almost absolute and permanent control of the sea surface, the airspace, and possibly the subsurface as well. For example, in the Gulf War of 1990–1991, the coalition's naval forces obtained almost absolute control of the northern part of the Persian (Arabian) Gulf on the surface and in the air in the first two weeks of the air offensive in January 1991. Yet, although the Iraqis did not have submarines, they were able to contest control of the subsurface by laying a large number of mines off the Kuwaiti coast.[156]

Uncommanded sea

Rarely discussed is that, in a war between two strong opponents on the open ocean, in major parts of a theater, neither side has sea control and hence a state of "uncommanded sea" might prevail. Corbett contended that a common error is in believing that if one side loses the command of the sea, it passes at once to the other side. In his view, the most common situation in war at sea was that neither side had the command.[157] However, Corbett did not elaborate when such a situation in a war at sea can actually emerge. Obviously, the number of one's large surface combatants, submarines, and carrier- and/or land-based aircraft is rarely adequate to obtain a sufficient degree of control of the ocean's surface. Hence, most of the ocean would not be controlled by either side, or a state of uncommanded sea would exist. This situation usually prevails in the initial phase of a war between two strong opponents separated by an ocean. At that point, either side might lack a significant presence of surface ships or submarines in the ocean as a whole. Also, a state of uncommanded sea would exist in the area beyond the effective range of one's own and the enemy's land-based aircraft. For example, in World War II, most of the Pacific Ocean between the U.S. West Coast and the Japanese Home Islands was not controlled by either the Allies or the Japanese. This situation was very rare in a typical narrow sea, such as the Baltic Sea or the North Sea, because of their small size and short distances.

A state of uncommanded sea usually exists in those parts of an ocean or large narrow sea where contest for sea control is conducted at high intensity, as the examples of the struggle for control of the central Mediterranean in 1940–1943 and Guadalcanal in 1942–1943 illustrate. Then neither side has full control of all three physical dimensions; both are able to use the sea for a specific and limited purpose, and both suffer high losses.[158] Corbett wrote that

> When the command is in dispute the general conditions may give a stable or unstable equilibrium. It may be that the power of neither side preponderates to any appreciable extent. It may be also that the preponderance is with ourselves, or it may be that it lies with the enemy. Such preponderance of course will not depend entirely on actual relative strength, either physical or moral, but will be influenced by the inter-relation of naval positions and the comparative convenience of their situation in regard to the object of the war or campaign. By naval positions we mean, firstly, naval bases and, secondly, the terminals of the greater lines of communication or trade-routes and the focal areas where they tend to converge, as at Finisterre, Gibraltar, Suez, the Cape [of Good Hope], Singapore, and many others.[159]

Brodie explained that disputed control is the one in which neither side can use the sea without excessive cost or where both sides can use the sea, although at some peril. The sea is not commanded but is disputed. He noted that in both world wars, the North Sea was not commanded by either side. This was also true of the Mediterranean in World War II.[160] War at sea and on land has many commonalties but also rather significant differences. They are largely result of the peculiar characteristics of the sea as a medium for combat. Without full knowledge of these differences, it is difficult to understand the characteristics of naval combat. The terms "command of the sea," "sea mastery," "control of the sea," and "sea control" are all too broad and too imprecise. None of them accurately reflects all the complexities of naval warfare. Perhaps it is not so important which of these terms is used as long as it is understood that in a war between two strong opponents on the open ocean, control is usually local, temporary, and limited. A state of uncommanded sea prevails in a large part of the oceanic theater and in those ocean/sea areas where both sides dispute each other's control in all three physical dimensions.

Notes

1 "To Atticus (at Rome) Cumae," 2 May 49 BC, in Marcus Tullius Cicero, *Cicero's Letters to Atticus*, Vol. 2 (London: Forgotten Books, 2012), p. 303.
2 Hermann Roeckel, *Seeräume und Flottenstützpunkte* (Heidelberg/Berlin/Leipzig: Verlagsanstalt Hüthig & Co., 1942), p. 11.
3 Th. Arps, R. Gadow, H. Hesse, and D. Ritter von Niedermayer, *Kleine Wehrgeographie des Weltmeeres* (Berlin: E. S. Mittler & Sohn, 1938), p. 22.
4 The use of the term "narrow seas" had its origins in the claims of the English kings to "sovereignty of the sea" around the British Isles in the thirteenth century; they had possessions in France and directed their admirals to police the "Narrow Seas" – the area of the Strait of Dover and the English Channel; in 1336, King Edward III reportedly referred to his predecessors as "Lords of the English Sea on every side", cited in Wilhelm G. Grewe, *The Epochs of International Law*. Translated by Michael Byers (Berlin/New York: De Gruyter, 2000), p. 131; the first written reference to "narrow seas" was in Christopher Marlowe's play "King Edward II," written in 1590 or 1591; Edward II (1321–1326) reportedly said, "The haughty Dane commands the narrow seas" (pertaining at that time to St. George Channel between Dover and Calais), cited in William Shakespeare, *The Plays of William Shakespeare, First Part of King Henry VI*. Introduction by George Brandes (London: William Heineman, 1904), p. xi.
5 Fariborz Haghshenass, *Iran's Asymmetric Naval Warfare* (Washington, DC: Washington Institute for Near East Policy, September 2008), p. 2.
6 Fariborz Haghshenass, *Iran's Asymmetric Naval Warfare* (Washington, DC: Washington Institute for Near East Policy, September 2008), p. 2.
7 *Uticaj Mora i Posebno Uskog Mora na Vodjenje Rata* (Divulje: Viša Vojnopomorska Akademija, 1964), p. 1.
8 I Skl I Op 30–1 *Grundlagen und Probleme des Seekrieges, Kriegsaufgaben der Marine. Möglichkeiten der Operativen Verwendung der Seekriegsmittel*, November 1940, RM/7–1949, Bundesarchiv-Militärarchiv (BA-MA), Freiburg, i. Br., p. 4.
9 Otto Groos, *Seekriegslehren im Lichte des Weltkrieges. Ein Buch für den Seemann, Soldaten und Staatsmann* (Berlin: Verlag von E. S. Mittler & Sohn, 1929), p. 42.
10 Otto Groos, *Seekriegslehren im Lichte des Weltkrieges. Ein Buch für den Seemann, Soldaten und Staatsmann* (Berlin: Verlag von E. S. Mittler & Sohn, 1929), p. 42.

11 Bernard Brodie, *A Layman's Guide to Naval Strategy* (Princeton, NJ: Princeton University Press, 1942), p. 84.

12 Herbert Rosinski, *The Evolution of Sea Power* (Newport, RI: Naval War College, 1950), p. 5.

13 Spenser Wilkinson, "Strategy in the Navy," *The Morning Post*, August 1909, p. 6; accessed at http://www.clausewitz.com/readings/Wilkinson/WILK.htm.

14 Julian S. Corbett, *Some Principles of Maritime Strategy* (London: Longmans, Green and Co., 1918), p. 79.

15 Otto Groos, *Seekriegslehren im Lichte des Weltkrieges. Ein Buch für den Seemann, Soldaten und Staatsmann* (Berlin: Verlag von E. S. Mittler & Sohn, 1929), p. 43.

16 I Skl I Op 30–1 *Grundlagen und Probleme des Seekrieges, Kriegsaufgaben der Marine. Möglichkeiten der Operativen Verwendung der Seekriegesmittel*, November 1940, RM/7–1949, Bundesarchiv-Militaerarchiv (BA-MA), Freiburg, i. Br., pp. 5, 7.

17 Otto Groos, *Seekriegslehren im Lichte des Weltkrieges. Ein Buch für den Seemann, Soldaten und Staatsmann* (Berlin: Verlag von E. S. Mittler & Sohn, 1929), pp. 43–44.

18 Cited in Cyprian Bridge, *Sea-Power and Other Studies* (London: Smith, Elder & Co., 1910), pp. 73–74.

19 Alexander Meurer, *Seekriegsgeschichte in Umrissen. Seemacht und Seekriege vornehmlich vom 16. Jahrhundert ab* (Leipzig: Verlag v. Hase & Koehler, 1925), p. 93.

20 Nikola Krajnović, *Prevlast Na Moru* (Belgrade: Viša Vojno-Pomorska Akademija, 1 November 1983), p. 3.

21 Alfred Stenzel, *Seekriegsgeschichte in ihren wichtigsten Abschnitten mit Berücksichtigung der Seetaktik*, Part 3: *Von 1600 bis 1720* (Hannover/Leipzig: Hahnsche Buchhandlung, 1909), p. 86.

22 Reginald Bacon and Francis E. McMurtries, *Modern Naval Strategy* (London: Frederick Muller Ltd., 1940), p. 38.

23 Günther Pöschel, "Über die Seeherrschaft (I)," *Militärwesen* (East Berlin), No. 5 (May 1982), p. 41.

24 Cyprian Bridge, *Sea-Power and Other Studies* (London: Smith, Elder & Co., 1910), p. 77.

25 Julian S. Corbett, *Some Principles of Maritime Strategy* (London: Longmans, Green and Co., 1918), p. 80.

26 Julian S. Corbett, *Some Principles of Maritime Strategy* (London: Longmans, Green and Co., 1918), pp. 78–79.

27 Julian S. Corbett, *Some Principles of Maritime Strategy* (London: Longmans, Green and Co., 1918), p. 80.

28 Eric Grove, *The Future of Sea Power* (Annapolis, MD: Naval Institute Press, 1990), p. 12.

29 Julian S. Corbett, *Some Principles of Maritime Strategy* (London: Longmans, Green and Co., 1918), p. 80.

30 Julian S. Corbett, *Some Principles of Maritime Strategy* (London: Longmans, Green and Co., 1918), p. 86.

31 Uwe Dirks, *Waren Grundzüge britischer Seekriegführung bereits vor dem Ersten Weltkrieg den Schriften Corbetts zu entnehmen?* (Hamburg: Führungsakademie der Bundeswehr, 30 October 1979), p. 10.

32 Julian S. Corbett, *Some Principles of Maritime Strategy* (London: Longmans, Green and Co., 1918), p. 86.

33 Eric Grove, *The Future of Sea Power* (Annapolis, MD: Naval Institute Press, 1990), p. 12.

34 "Seeherrschaft und Kreuzerkrieg." Winterarbeit des K.k. Wegener vom Kommando Baubelehrung Kreuzer Hipper, RM 20/1131 Bundesarchiv-Militaerarchiv (BA-MA), Freiburg, i.Br., pp. 1–2.

35 "Seeherrschaft und Kreuzerkrieg," Winterarbeit des K.k. Wegener vom Kommando Baubelehrung Kreuzer Hipper, Undated, RM 20/1131, BA-MA, p. 2.

36 Edward Wegener, "Die Elemente von Seemacht und maritimes Macht," in Dieter Mahncke and Hans-Peter Schwarz, editors, *Seemacht und Aussenpolitik* (Frankfurt am Main: Alfred Metzner Verlag, 1974), p. 27.

37 Cited in Raoul Castex, *Strategic Theories*. Selections translated and edited with an introduction by Eugenia C. Kiesling (Annapolis, MD: Naval Institute Press, 1994), p. 48.

38 Raoul Castex, *Strategic Theories*. Selections translated and edited with an introduction by Eugenia C. Kiesling (Annapolis, MD: Naval Institute Press, 1994), p. 357.

39 Raoul Castex, *Strategic Theories*. Selections translated and edited with an introduction by Eugenia C. Kiesling (Annapolis, MD: Naval Institute Press, 1994), pp. 30, 35.

40 Raoul Castex, *Strategic Theories*, Selections translated and edited with an introduction by Eugenia C. Kiesling (Annapolis, MD: Naval Institute Press, 1994), pp. 359–60.

41 "Deutsche Bearbeitung des Werkes von Castex *Theories Strategiques*," durch Dr. Rosinski, Berlin 1937, RMD 4/853, BA-MA, p. 10.

42 "Deutsche Bearbeitung des Werkes von Castex *Theories Strategiques*," durch Dr. Rosinski, Berlin 1937, RMD 4/853, BA-MA, p. 10.

43 "Deutsche Bearbeitung des Werkes von Castex *Theories Strategiques*," durch Dr. Rosinski, Berlin 1937, RMD 4/853, BA-MA, pp. 11–12.

44 Chapters I to IV, Part III, Vol. I, Naval War College, Extracts from Raoul Castex, *Theories Strategiques*. Translated from French by R. C. Smith and assisted by E. J. Tiernan (Newport, RI: Naval War College, December 1938), p. 3.

45 Bernard Brodie, *A Layman's Guide to Naval Strategy* (Princeton, NJ: Princeton University Press, 1942), pp. 84–85.

46 Colin S. Gray, *The Leverage of Sea Power* (New York: The Free Press, Maxwell MacMillan International, 1992), pp. 9–10.

47 Cyprian Bridge, *Sea-Power and Other Studies* (London: Smith, Elder & Co., 1910), p. 78.

48 Stansfield Turner, "Mission of the U.S. Navy," *Naval War College Review*, March–April 1974, p. 7.

49 Elwin F. Cutts, *Operations for Securing Command of Sea Areas* (Newport, RI: Naval War College, 8–9 July 1938), pp. 8, 4–5.

50 Günther Pöschel, "Über die Seeherrschaft (I)," *Militärwesen* (East Berlin), No. 5 (May 1982), p. 42.

51 *Uticaj Mora I Posebno Uskog Mora Na Vodjenje Rata* (Divulje: Viša Vojno Pomorska Akademija, 1964), p. 7.

52 *Uticaj Mora I Posebno Uskog Mora Na Vodjenje Rata* (Divulje: Viša Vojno Pomorska Akademija, 1964), p. 8.

53 Nikola Krajnović, *Prevlast Na Moru* (Belgrade: Viša Vojno-Pomorska Akademija, 1 November 1983), p. 10.

54 M.G. Cook, "Naval Strategy," 2 March 1931, Air Corps Tactical School, Langley Field, VA, 1930–1931, Strategic Plans Division Records, Series, Box 003, Naval Operational Archives, Washington, D.C., p. 3.

55 Herbert Rosinski, *The Evolution of Sea Power* (Newport, RI: Naval War College, 1950), p. 7.

56 Cited in Harold and Margaret Sprout, *The Rise of American Naval Power, 1776–1918* (Princeton, NJ: Princeton University Press, 1939), p. 13.

57 Freiherr (Curt) von Maltzahn, "Der Kampf gegen die Seeherrschaft," Private acts of vice admiral Kurt Assmann (1935–1943), Militärgeschichtliches Forschungsamt (MGFA)-Documentation Center, 3 March 1961, RM 8/1120, BA-MA, p. 4.

58 Konrad Seemann, *Grundsätze der Seestrategie. Eine Analyse von konstanten und variable Elementen in den Konzeptionen von Seemächte* (Hamburg: Führungsakademie der Bundeswehr, 15 January 1990), p. 13.

59 John F. Charles, "The Anatomy of Athenian Sea Power," *The Classical Journal*, Vol. 42, No. 2 (November 1946), p. 89.

60 Raoul Castex, *More Protiv Kopna*, Vol 1: *Sea Versus Land*. Translated by Hijacint Mundorfer (*Théorie stratégiques*, Vol. 1: *La Mer Contre La Terre*) (Belgrade: Geca Kon AD, 1939), p. 6.

61 Cited in Robert C. Gooding, *Command of the Sea* (Newport, RI: Naval War College, Historical Archives, 1 May 1959), p. 1.

62 Nikola Krajnović, *Prevlast Na Moru* (Belgrade: Viša Vojno-Pomorska Akademija, 1 November 1983), p. 20.

63 Raoul Castex, *Strategic Theories*. Selections translated and edited with an introduction by Eugenia C. Kiesling (Annapolis, MD: Naval Institute Press, 1994), p. 46.

64 Raoul Castex, *Théories Stratégiques*, Vol I: *Généralites sur la stratégie. La mission des forces maritimes. La Conduite des operations* (Paris: Société d'Editions Géographiques Maritimes et Coloniales, 1929). Translated by Ekrem Duric and Boško Ranitović, *Strategijske Teorije*, Vol. I (Belgrade: Vojno-Izdavački Zavod, 1960), p. 102.

65 Alexander Meurer, *Seekriegs-Geschichte in Umrissen. Seemacht und Seekriege vornehmlich vom 16. Jahrhundert* (Leipzig: Verlag von Hase & Koehler, 1925), p. 42.

66 Herbert Rosinski, *The Development of Naval Thought: Essays by Herbert Rosinski* (Newport, RI: Naval War College Press, 1977), p. 6.

67 Arthur MacCartney Shepard, *Sea Power in Ancient History. The Story of the Navies of Classic Greece and Rome* (London: William Heineman Ltd., 1925), pp. 132–33.

68 William L. Rodgers, *Greek and Roman Naval Warfare. A Study of Strategy, Tactics, and Ship Design from Salamis (480 BC) to Actium (31 BC)* (Annapolis, MD: Naval Institute Press, 1964), p. 317.

69 Alexander Meurer, *Seekriegsgeschichte in Umrissen. Seemacht und Seekriege vornehmlich vom 16. Jahrhundert ab* (Leipzig: Verlag v. Hase & Koehler, 1925), p. 111.

70 Paul K. Davis, *Masters of the Battlefield. Great Commanders from the Classical Age to the Napoleonic Era* (London: Oxford University Press, 2013), p. 68.

71 Arthur MacCartney Shepard, *Sea Power in Ancient History. The Story of the Navies of Classic Greece and Rome* (London: William Heinemann Ltd., 1925), p. 170.

72 Alfred T. Mahan, *The Influence of Sea Power upon History 1660–1783* (Boston: Little, Brown, and Company, 1939), p. 15.

73 Arthur MacCartney Shepard, *Sea Power in Ancient History. The Story of the Navies of Classic Greece and Rome* (London: William Heinemann Ltd., 1925), p. 169.

74 Alexander Meurer, *Seekriegsgeschichte in Umrissen. Seemacht und Seekriege vornehmlich vom 16. Jahrhundert ab* (Leipzig: Verlag v. Hase & Koehler, 1925), p. 111.

75 Cited in Arthur MacCartney Shepard, *Sea Power in Ancient History. The Story of the Navies of Classic Greece and Rome* (London: William Heinemann Ltd., 1925), p. 170.

76 Alfred T. Mahan, *Naval Strategy. Compared and Contrasted with the Principles and Practice of Military Operations on Land* (Boston: Little, Brown, and Company, 1911), p. 59.

77 Cited in Harold and Margaret Sprout, *The Rise of American Naval Power, 1776–1918* (Princeton, NJ: Princeton University Press, 1939), pp. 11–12.

78 Cited in Harold and Margaret Sprout, *The Rise of American Naval Power, 1776–1918* (Princeton, NJ: Princeton University Press, 1939), p. 13.

79 Cited in Harold and Margaret Sprout, *The Rise of American Naval Power, 1776–1918* (Princeton, NJ: Princeton University Press, 1939), pp. 11–12.

80 Harold and Margaret Sprout, *The Rise of American Naval Power 1776–1918* (Princeton, NJ: Princeton University Press, 1939), p. 75.

81 Harold and Margaret Sprout, *The Rise of American Naval Power 1776–1918* (Princeton, NJ: Princeton University Press, 1939), p. 76.

82 Harold and Margaret Sprout, *The Rise of American Naval Power 1776–1918* (Princeton, NJ: Princeton University Press, 1939), p. 79.

83 Harold and Margaret Sprout, *The Rise of American Naval Power, 1776–1918* (Princeton, NJ: Princeton University Press, 1939), p. 135.

84 Raoul Castex, *Théories Stratégiques*, Vol. I: *Généralites sur la stratégie. La mission des forces maritimes. La Conduite des operations* (Paris: Société d'Editions Géographiques Maritimes et Coloniales, 1929). Translated by Ekrem Đurić and Boško Ranitović, *Strategijske Teorije*, Vol. I (Belgrade: Vojno-Izdavački Zavod, 1960), p. 108.

85 Harold and Margaret Sprout, *The Rise of American Naval Power, 1776–1918* (Princeton, NJ: Princeton University Press, 1939), p. 160.

86 Harold and Margaret Sprout, *The Rise of American Naval Power 1776–1918* (Princeton, NJ: Princeton University Press, 1939), p. 154.

87 Otto Groos, *Seekriegslehren im Lichte des Weltkrieges. Ein Buch für den Seemann, Soldaten und Staatsmann* (Berlin: Verlag von E. S. Mittler & Sohn, 1929), p. 45.

88 Harold M. Sprout and Margaret T. Sprout, *The Rise of American Sea Power 1776–1918* (Princeton, NJ: Princeton University Press, 1939), p. 155.

89 Gabriel Darrieus, *War on the Sea. Strategy and Tactics* (Annapolis, MD: United States Naval Institute, 1908), p. 94.

90 Donald E. Worcester, "Naval Strategy of the Pacific," *Journal of Inter-American Studies*, Vol. 5, No. 1 (January 1963), p. 36.

91 Harold and Margaret Sprout, *The Rise of American Naval Power, 1776–1918* (Princeton, NJ: Princeton University Press, 1939), p. 233.

92 Harold and Margaret Sprout, *The Rise of American Naval Power, 1776–1918* (Princeton, NJ: Princeton University Press, 1939), p. 232.

93 Günther Pöschel, *Die Rolle und Bedeutung der Seeherrschaft in Vergangenheit und Gegenwart. Analyse der theoretischen Aussagen zum Begriff der Seeherrschaft* (Dresden: Militärakademie Friedrich Engels, 1978). p. 32.

94 Günther Pöschel, *Die Rolle und Bedeutung der Seeherrschaft in Vergangenheit und Gegenwart. Analyse der theoretischen Aussagen zum Begriff der Seeherrschaft* (Dresden: Militärakademie Friedrich Engels, 1978). pp. 33–34.

95 Peter Handel-Mazzetti, "Einfluss der Seemacht auf den Grossen Krieg," *Militärwissenschaftliche Mitteilungen*, No. 7 (July 1934), p. 551.

96 Alan Westcott, editor, *American Sea Power Since 1775* (New York: J.B. Lippincott Company, 1947), p. 232.

97 Henry Newbolt, *History of the Great War Based on Official Documents. Naval Operations*, Vol. 5: *From April. 1917 to the End of the War* (London: Longmans, Green 1931), pp. 223–24.

98 Peter Handel-Mazzetti, "Einfluss der Seemacht auf den Grossen Krieg," *Militärwissenschaftliche Mitteilungen*, No. 7 (July 1934), p. 551.

99 Cited in Arthur MacCartney Shepard, *Sea Power in Ancient History. The Story of the Navies of Classic Greece and Rome* (London: William Heineman Ltd., 1925), pp. 47–48.

100 David Woodward, *The Russians at Sea: History of the Russian Navy* (New York: Frederick A. Praeger, 1966), p. 77.

101 David Woodward, *The Russians at Sea: History of the Russian Navy* (New York: Frederick A. Praeger, 1966), p. 112.

102 Raoul Castex, *Théories Stratégiques*, Vol. I: *Généralites sur la stratégie. La mission des forces maritimes. La Conduite des operations* (Paris: Société d'Editions

Géographiques Maritimes et Coloniales, 1929). Translated by Ekrem Đurić and Boško Ranitović, *Strategijske Teorije*, Vol. I (Belgrade: Vojno-Izdavački Zavod, 1960), p. 107.

103 Elwin F. Cutts, *Operations for Securing Command of the Sea Areas*, Part 1 (Newport, RI: Naval War College, 8–9 July 1938), p. 4.

104 Cyprian Bridge, *Sea-Power and Other Studies* (London: Smith, Elder & Co., 1910), p. 78.

105 Raoul Castex, *Strategic Theories*. Selections translated and edited with an introduction by Eugenia C. Kiesling (Annapolis, MD: Naval Institute Press, 1994), p. 53.

106 Raoul Castex, *Strategic Theories*. Selections translated and edited with an introduction by Eugenia C. Kiesling (Annapolis, MD: Naval Institute Press, 1994), p. 55.

107 Raoul Castex, *Strategic Theories*. Selections translated and edited with an introduction by Eugenia C. Kiesling (Annapolis, MD: Naval Institute Press, 1994), p. 41.

108 Bernard Brodie, *A Layman's Guide to Naval Strategy* (Princeton, NJ: Princeton University Press, 1942), p. 84.

109 Bernard Brodie, *A Layman's Guide to Naval Strategy* (Princeton, NJ: Princeton University Press, 1942), p. 85.

110 Bernard Brodie, *A Layman's Guide to Naval Strategy* (Princeton, NJ: Princeton University Press, 1942), p. 84.

111 Julian S. Corbett, *Some Principles of Maritime Strategy* (London: Longmans, Green and Co., 1918), p. 90.

112 Julian S. Corbett, *Some Principles of Maritime Strategy* (London: Longmans, Green and Co., 1918), p. 90.

113 Otto Groos, *Seekriegslehren im Lichte des Weltkrieges. Ein Buch für den Seemann, Soldaten und Staatsmann* (Berlin: Verlag von E. S. Mittler & Sohn, 1929), p. 51.

114 Nikola Krajnović, *Prevlast Na Moru* (Belgrade: Viša Vojno-Pomorska Akademija, 1 November 1983), p. 14.

115 Nikola Krajnović, *Prevlast Na Moru* (Belgrade: Viša Vojno-Pomorska Akademija, 1 November 1983), p. 13.

116 Julian S. Corbett, *Some Principles of Maritime Strategy* (London: Longmans, Green and Co., 1918), p. 90.

117 Julian S. Corbett, *Some Principles of Maritime Strategy* (London: Longmans, Green and Co., 1918), pp. 90–91.

118 Julian S. Corbett, *Some Principles of Maritime Strategy* (London: Longmans, Green and Co., 1918), p. 91.

119 Julian S. Corbett, *Some Principles of Maritime Strategy* (London: Longmans, Green and Co., 1918), pp. 90–91

120 Günther Pöschel, "Über die Seeherrschaft (II)," *Militärwesen* (East Berlin), No. 6 (June 1982), p. 72.

121 Its meanings include "completely or almost universal," "prevalent," "widespread," "local," and "partial" or "sectional"; Elisabeth J. Jewell, editor, *The Oxford Desk Dictionary and Thesaurus*, 2nd ed. (New York: Spark Publishers, 2007), p. 334.

122 E.T. Salmon, "The Strategy of the Second Punic War," *Greece & Rome*, Vol. 7, No. 2 (October 1960), p. 132.

123 Julian S. Corbett, *Some Principles of Maritime Strategy* (London: Longmans, Green and Co., 1918), pp. 90–91.

124 Raoul Castex, *Théories Stratégiques*, Vol. I: *Généralites sur la stratégie. La mission des forces maritimes. La Conduite des operations* (Paris: Société d'Editions Géographiques Maritimes et Coloniales, 1929). Translated by Ekrem Đurić and Boško Ranitović, *Strategijske Teorije*, Vol. I (Belgrade: Vojno-Izdavački Zavod, 1960), p. 119.

125 Raoul Castex, *Théories Stratégiques*, Vol. I: *Généralites sur la stratégie. La mission des forces maritimes. La Conduite des operations* (Paris: Société d'Editions Géographiques Maritimes et Coloniales, 1929). Translated by Ekrem Đurić

and Boško Ranitović, *Strategijske Teorije*, Vol. I (Belgrade: Vojno-Izdavački Zavod, 1960), pp. 118–19.

126 Harold M. Sprout and Margaret T. Sprout, *The Rise of American Naval Power 1776–1918* (Princeton, NJ: Princeton University Press, 1939), pp. 351–52.

127 M.G. Cook, "Naval Strategy," 2 March 1931, Air Corps Tactical School, Langley Field, VA, 1930–1931, Strategic Plans Division Records, Series, Box 003, Naval Operational Archives, Washington, D.C., p. 12.

128 M. Hamlin Cannon, *United States Army in World War II: The War in the Pacific, Leyte: The Return to the Philippines* (Washington, DC: Office of the Chief of Military History, Department of the Army, 1954), pp. 101–02; USSBS Interrogation No. 506, Major General Toshio Nishimura, Lieutenant Colonel Matsumae, Commander Otani, Tonosuke, Folder G-44, Box 9, Record Group 23, *World War II, Battle Evaluation Group, 1946–1956*, Naval Historical Collection, Naval War College, Newport, RI. pp. 6, 2, 8; Charles R. Anderson, *Leyte* (Washington, DC: U.S. Government Printing Office, CMH Pub 72–27, 1994), p. 30; Edward J. Drea, *MacArthur's Ultra. Codebreaking and the War Against Japan, 1942–1945* (Lawrence: University Press of Kansas, 1991), p. 178.

129 Milan Vego, *The Battle for Leyte, 1944: Allied and Japanese Plans, Preparations, and Execution* (Annapolis, MD: Naval Institute Press, 2006), p. 352.

130 Milan Vego, *The Battle for Leyte, 1944. Allied and Japanese Plans, Preparations, and Execution* (Annapolis, MD: Naval Institute Press, 2006), pp. 180, 303, 330.

131 Milan Vego, *The Battle for Leyte, 1944: Allied and Japanese Plans, Preparations, and Execution* (Annapolis, MD: Naval Institute Press, 2006), pp. 323, 315, 352.

132 Bogislav Pantović and Delimir Kolec, "Značaj razuđenosti obale i naseljenosti otoka u koncepciji opštenarodne odbrane i društvene samozaštite na jadranskom pomorskom vojištu," *Mornarički Glasnik*, No. 5 (September–October 1981), pp. 608–09.

133 Günther Pöschel, "Über die Seeherrschaft (I)," *Militärwesen* (East Berlin), No. 5 (May 1982), p. 42.

134 Department of Operations, *Naval Strategy* (Newport, RI: Naval War College, August 1936), p. 44.

135 Betrachtung über dies seestrategische und militärische Lage im Mittelmeer nach dem Stand vom 10.1.1942, RM 7/235, I Skl Teil C XV, Deutsche Kriegführung im Mittelmeer Januar 1942–Dezember 1942, BA-MA, p. 26.

136 Reginald Bacon and Francis E. McMurtries, *Modern Naval Strategy* (London: Frederick Muller Ltd., 1940), p. 38.

137 Ante Paić, "Komandovanje na pomorskom vojištu (operativni aspekti)," *Mornarički Glasnik*, No. 3 (May–June 1973), p. 373.

138 Nikola Krajnović, *Prevlast Na Moru* (Belgrade: Viša Vojno-Pomorska Akademija, 1 November 1983), p. 16.

139 John R. Carter, *Airpower and the Cult of the Offensive* (Maxwell AFB, Montgomery, AL: Air University Press, October 1998), p. 13.

140 Andrew Lambert and Arthur C. Williamson, *The Dynamics of Air Power*, 1st ed. (London: Her Majesty's Stationery Office for Royal Air Force Staff College, Bracknell, 1996), p. 11.

141 Raoul Castex, *Strategic Theories*. Selections translated and edited with an introduction by Eugenia C. Kiesling (Annapolis, MD: Naval Institute Press, 1993), p. 58.

142 Günther Pöschel, "Über die Seeherrschaft (I)," *Militärwesen* (East Berlin), No. 5 (May 1982), p. 43.

143 Julian S. Corbett, *Some Principles of Maritime Strategy* (London: Longmans, Green and Co., 1918), p. 91.

144 Cyprian Bridge, *Sea-Power and Other Studies* (London: Smith, Elder & Co., 1910), p. 77.

145 Uwe Dirks, *Waren Grundzüge britischer Seekriegführung bereits vor dem Ersten Weltkrieg den Schriften Corbetts zu entnehmen?* (Hamburg: Führungsakademie der Bundeswehr, 30 October 1979), p. 9.

146 Uwe Dirks, *Waren Grundzüge britischer Seekriegführung bereits vor dem Ersten Weltkrieg den Schriften Corbetts zu entnehmen?* (Hamburg: Führungsakademie der Bundeswehr, 30 October 1979), p. 10.

147 Raoul Castex, *Strategic Theories*. Selections translated and edited with an introduction by Eugenia C. Kiesling (Annapolis, MD: Naval Institute Press, 1994), p. 53; Deutsche Bearbeitung des Werkes von Castex *Theories Strategiques*, durch Dr. Rosinski, Berlin 1937, RMD 4/853, BA-MA, pp. 12–13.

148 Deutsche Bearbeitung des Werkes von Castex *Theories Strategiques*, durch Dr. Rosinski, Berlin 1937, RMD 4/853, BA-MA, p. 13.

149 Deutsche Bearbeitung des Werkes von Castex *Theories Strategiques*, durch Dr. Rosinski, Berlin 1937, RMD 4/853, BA-MA, p. 13.

150 Günther Pöschel, "Über die Seeherrschaft (II)," *Militärwesen* (East Berlin), No. 6 (June 1982), pp. 71–72.

151 Alfred T. Mahan, *The Influence of Sea Power upon History 1660–1783* (Boston: Little, Brown, and Company, 1939), p. 16.

152 Alfred T. Mahan, *The Influence of Sea Power upon History 1660–1783* (Boston: Little, Brown, and Company, 1939), p. 17.

153 Arthur MacCartney Shepard, *Sea Power in Ancient History. The Story of the Navies of Classic Greece and Rome* (London: William Heineman Ltd., 1925), p. 170.

154 Department of Operations, *Naval Strategy* (Newport, RI: Naval War College, August 1936), pp. 43–44.

155 Uwe Dirks, *Waren Grundzüge britischer Seekriegführung bereits vor dem Ersten Weltkrieg den Schriften Corbetts zu entnehmen?* (Hamburg: Führungsakademie der Bundeswehr, 30 October 1979), p. 9.

156 "MCM in the Gulf – More Information Comes to Light," *NAVINT, The International Naval Newsletter* (London), Vol. 3, No. 8 (26 April 1991), p. 1.

157 Julian S. Corbett, *Some Principles of Maritime Strategy* (London: Longmans, Green, 1918), p. 77.

158 Nikola Krajnović, *Prevlast Na Moru* (Belgrade: Viša Vojno-Pomorska Akademija, 1 November 1983), p. 3.

159 Julian S. Corbett, *Some Principles of Maritime Strategy* (London: Longmans, Green and Co., 1918), pp. 91–92.

160 Bernard Brodie, *A Layman's Guide to Naval Strategy* (Princeton, NJ: Princeton University Press, 1942), pp. 84–85.

3 Obtaining and maintaining sea control

Obtaining or securing sea control is the first and most critical step in the struggle for sea control. This phase ends with accomplishing a given operational or strategic objective. Afterward, energetic efforts must be made to maintain the desired degree of sea control through the destruction or containment of the remaining enemy forces. Expressed differently, maintaining sea control is aimed to consolidate operational or strategic success. The final phase is exercising sea control or exploiting that operational or strategic success. Perhaps it cannot be adequately emphasized that these three phases are not rigidly separated from one another in terms of the factors of space and time. Boundaries separating one phase from the other are highly elusive and difficult to precisely identify. Many actions that normally predominate in the phase of exercising control very often would be initiated as soon as a certain degree of sea control is obtained. For example, a commercial blockade would normally be initiated simultaneously with a naval blockade, although it is a part of the phase in exercising control.

Ideally, sea control should be obtained shortly after hostilities begin. Hence, to obtain the desired degrees of control in a selected strategic area, it is necessary to be strategically on the offensive. At the beginning of a war between two strong opponents, each side would normally go on the strategic offensive. However, such a situation would not last for too long because one or the other side would suffer some significant losses and then be forced to shift to a strategic defense and conduct sea denial. The belligerent "who sustains the strongest offensive will force his enemy to take up the defensive, and thus determine the location of the principal theater and active strategic area."[1] Sometimes only one belligerent will be on the offensive, while the other assumes a strategically defensive posture.

Control of a particular ocean/sea area is desirable in proportion to its usefulness in accomplishing one's ultimate strategic or operational objective. Normally, destruction of the enemy's naval forces is the most direct and effective means for obtaining control of operationally or strategically important areas.[2] Deploying the stronger fleet does not of itself ensure control of a sea or ocean area because the fleet must extend its influence over the area by actually operating in it.[3] The struggle to obtain sea control would normally precede the solution of one's main naval tasks in a given sea or ocean theater. Usually, one's naval forces would obtain and maintain control only in those sea or ocean areas where they can project the greater strength and when this strength is so readily available that control would not too often be disturbed by the adversary.[4] If one's fleet remains in port, its existence may constitute a potential threat to the other, but it would not actually enter into contest for sea control.[5] One's naval forces are valuable in a contest for sea control only to the extent that they can operate against the enemy's naval forces.

Prerequisites

Experience shows that ultimate success in the struggle for sea control is enhanced greatly by fulfilling a number of preconditions or prerequisites. Perhaps the most critical prerequisites are as follows: favorable maritime strategic position, favorable base of operations and adequate number of naval/air bases, balanced forces, numerical/qualitative superiority, sound naval theory and naval doctrine/training, the closest of cooperation among services (jointness), offensive spirit, basing/deployment area control, and information superiority. Obviously, no navy can possible have all these pre-requisites at their highest value. Yet all-out efforts should be made already in peacetime to achieve the optimal balance among them. Experience shows that once the hostilities start, it is virtually impossible to remedy one's shortcomings in the fleet's numerical strength and composition and in the lack of sound naval theory, doctrine, combat training, and offensive spirit.

War at sea cannot be conducted without some geographic positions from which one's forces are deployed or redeployed. Normally, each side would initially employ its forces by using the existing geographic positions. In the course of the hostilities, each side would try to improve its existing positions and acquire new and more favorable ones. In the littorals, it would be also necessary to obtain control of both the sea and adjacent land areas.[6]

Naval classical thinkers have repeatedly highlighted the great importance of maritime positions in the struggle for sea control. For example, Admiral Mahan wrote that control of the sea could not be obtained without pos-sessing some positions, especially in the disputed ocean/sea areas, impor-tant routes, and straits/channels.[7] He observed that the strategic value of any place depends upon three principal conditions: its position, or, more exactly, the situation; its military strength, offensive or defensive; and the resources of the place itself and of the surrounding country. Mahan empha-sized that it is "power plus position that constitutes an advantage over power without position; or, more instructively, equations of force are composed of power and position in varying degrees, surplus in one tending to compen-sate for deficiency in the other."[8]

Admiral Wegener was a strong advocate of the need to possess or obtain a favorable strategic geographic position to successfully prosecute war at sea. He wrote that offensive naval strategy can have no other objective than attaining a geographical position from which to initiate the struggle for the commercial arteries of maritime traffic.[9] Yet Wegener absolutized the importance of geography in the development of naval strategy. He wrote that "naval strategy extends over wide areas and cannot – without denigrating itself – be held back in check at territorial frontiers that accidentally have been drawn upon geographical charts in the course of history."[10]

In terms of their potential or actual military importance, strategic, operational, and tactical positions are differentiated.[11] These distinctions are a matter not of a location but, more important, of the factor of force. Obviously, the larger the military importance of a position, the larger the force that has to be used in order to control or defend it. And the higher the military value of a maritime position, the more critical it is to capture, defend, control, or neutralize it.

A strategic position is described as the one that can potentially have a decisive influence on the course and even outcome of a war. In strategic terms, a country or territory can occupy an insular, peninsular, or semi-central strategic position in regard to the adjacent ocean and/or seas. England provides perhaps the best example of the great advantages offered by an insular position for the conduct of naval warfare. The 600-mile-long British Isles extend from the Strait of Dover to the Northern Passage (between Shetlands and Norway). Mahan observed that the British Isles exercise a type of control of the North Sea similar to the control that the island of Cuba has over the Gulf of Mexico. Their defensive value is the same.[12]

England enjoyed a much more favorable maritime position in wars with its enemies on the Continent in the seventeenth and eighteenth centuries. England then faced on one hand Holland and the northern powers and on the other France. The British fleet concentrated in the Downs (the roadstead between North and South Foreland in southern England) and even off the French naval base of Brest, occupying interior positions. Thus, England was able to interpose its fleet against either one of the enemies that tried to pass through the Channel to effect junction with their ally.[13] The British position in the English Channel facilitated the safety of the British trade in the southwestern approaches and the North Sea. It also served as a shield against an invasion of Ireland or England. The British fleet was able to operate offensively in the sea areas fronting Western Europe, while the vast open spaces of the Atlantic Ocean protected England's rear. For example, in the first three Anglo-Dutch Wars (1652–1654, 1665–1667, 1672–1674) (the Fourth Anglo-Dutch War was in 1780–1784), no Dutch merchant ship could reach port without traversing the English Channel and thereby being exposed to British attack. The British ships could observe Dutch naval movements while at same time geography denied the same opportunity to the Dutch ships.[14] In World War I, the main British trade routes in the Atlantic were beyond easy reach of the German fleet deployed in the North Sea. In contrast, the German routes could easily be cut off, either in the English Channel or off Scotland.[15]

A country having a longer frontier on the sea than on the land is said to occupy strategically a semi-isolated or peninsular position. A peninsula offers a double base of operations for naval forces. A disadvantage is that one's naval strength is fragmented because ships must be divided between two bases of operations. One's naval vessels operate from an exterior position while aircraft enjoy the advantages of a central position. A peninsular position offers many advantages to the defender in countering possible amphibious landings because his troops operate from a central position and along very short lines of operation. Yet a strong opponent with substantial amphibious capabilities could simultaneously threaten both coasts of a peninsula with an invasion. For example, the Korean Peninsula dominates all the sea and air routes between Japan and Manchuria, as well as the sea routes from the Yellow Sea to and from the Sea of Japan. Within the Mediterranean, Italy's mainland enjoys a commanding geostrategic position in the central Mediterranean. One leg of the Apennine peninsula faces the Messina Strait, while the other leg borders the Strait of Otranto, the only exit from the Adriatic Sea.

A country, located on the rim of a continental landmass and bordering one or more seas/oceans, occupies a semi-central position. For example, Russia borders one ocean (the Arctic) and three seas (the Baltic, the Black Sea, and the Sea of Okhotsk). The seas are separated from one another by intervening continental landmass and very large distances. In the Russo-Japanese war of 1904–1905, Russia's position in the Far East was highly unfavorable compared to that of Japan. The two territories in Russia's dispute with Japan, the Liaotung (Liaodong today) Peninsula (southeastern Manchuria) and Korea were isolated at the end of primitive lines of communication. This problem was compounded because the two large Russian naval bases, Port Arthur and Vladivostok, were separated from each other by the intervening landmass and the Korea Strait controlled by the Japanese. To defeat Japan, the Russians would have had to invade the Home Islands, while for the Japanese it was sufficient to seize Korea and the Liaotung Peninsula and thereby accomplish their primary war objective.

France occupies a semi-central position in regard to its Atlantic seaboard and the western Mediterranean. In its many wars with Great Britain, the French Navy was at a great disadvantage because its squadrons at Toulon and Brest were separated by the intervening Iberian Peninsula and long distances (about 1,800 nm). This problem was complicated by the fact that the Royal Navy had a permanent fleet presence in the Mediterranean and after 1704 controlled the strategically important Strait of Gibraltar. In almost all the wars with England, the French sent their Toulon squadron to the English Channel via the Strait of Gibraltar. However, the long distances between Toulon and Brest caused delays or gave the British an opportunity to interfere with the junction of the Toulon and Brest squadrons. If the Toulon squadron was delayed, then the Brest squadron had to fight the British fleet alone.

The chances of success in the struggle for sea control are considerably improved by having a favorably located *base of operation* and an adequate number of well developed naval/air bases. The length and directional orientation of a base of operations are directly related to the country's maritime strategic position. A good base of operations should provide a favorable position for both offense and defense. The distances between one's base of operations and prospective operating areas play a critical role in the military effectiveness of those forces. A base of operations should provide multiple short lines of operation, thereby allowing greater freedom of action.[16] In general, a longer base of operations enables the deployment of larger forces and the use of multiple lines of operation. It forces the defender to divide his forces because of uncertainty over which line of operations the attacker is going to use.[17] For example, in World War I, a string of naval and air bases along the eastern coast of England and Scotland, from the Strait of Dover to Scapa Flow, formed a long base of operations, providing many advantages for the Royal Navy in thwarting any attempt by the German High Seas Fleet to break out of its narrow confines in the North Sea. The British position at Scapa Flow dominated not only sea communications between the Danish Straits and the North Atlantic but at the same time protected the British Isles against possible German invasion. It also allowed a link between forces based at Scapa Flow and those protecting British transports in the Channel. Britain blockaded Germany just by virtue of its geographic position.[18]

Generally, the shorter the base, the smaller the basing area and the easier it is for the enemy force to envelop it. A short base of operations also has fewer but more closely spaced lines of operations.[19] For example, in World War I, the German High Seas Fleet was unable to project its power beyond the confines of the North Sea because of its rather short base of operations and the fact that the Entente's forces controlled both sea exits.

A fleet cannot sustain its strength unless it possesses an adequate number of favorably located naval/air bases. Bases are the principal centers of all naval and air activity in a given sea area. Seizing, controlling, and protecting one's bases are important elements of naval strategy in all eras. In general, the possession of a large number of bases offers significant advantages for deployment, maneuver, and redeployment of one's naval forces and for the use of the most suitable bases for their deployment and redeployment.

In general, the closer a base lies to the prospective theater of operations, the higher is its military/naval value. For example, in 1914, the British selected bases along the country's east coast that allowed the Royal Navy to control both the northern and southern exits from the North Sea. Thus, the Grand Fleet based in Scapa Flow (the Orkneys) held the control of the Northern Passage while forces based at Harwich secured control of the southern part of the North Sea.

During most of the eighteenth century, England lacked a sufficient number of bases and ships to protect its interests in the Mediterranean. Its principal bases in home waters were Plymouth and Portsmouth, while for France and Spain, the principal bases were Brest, Ferrol, and Cádiz. Within the Mediterranean, the British had only one base at Port Mahón in Minorca while the Spaniards and the French had two large bases at Cartagena and Toulon, respectively. However, Port Mahón served for purely defensive purposes because Britain was unable to spare any squadron to be deployed in the Mediterranean. Likewise, the British did not have sufficient forces to base at Gibraltar. Because their main focus was on the English Channel, they only sporadically sent supplies for the garrison at Gibraltar.[20] This situation was improved in 1794 when the island of Corsica, after a revolt against the French rule and supported by the British fleet, became a British protectorate. The British selected San Fiorenzo Bay (near the northern tip of Corsica) as the main anchorage for their fleet. This base was some 100 miles away from both Nice and Genoa. Leghorn and Tuscany ports were only 60 miles from Cape Coros (at the northern tip of Corsica). All trade routes with northern Italy had to pass close to Corsica.[21] However, this situation radically changed in September 1796 when the Corsican Parliament, with French assistance, overthrew the unpopular British protectorate. At the same time, the British position in the Mediterranean steadily deteriorated because of the rapid advance of French troops under Napoleon Bonaparte down the Italian peninsula in the summer of 1796. The ports in Tuscany, Naples, and the Papal States were closed to British ships. Former British ally Spain became openly hostile. The British interests in the Mediterranean suffered a severe blow with the loss of access to Leghorn. In addition, Naples withdrew from the coalition and concluded an alliance with France. Piedmont had already yielded Savoy and Nice to France.[22]

A base located too far away from one's main territory is often a source of grave weakness in time of war because of the great difficulties required to secure its defense against the enemy on land. For example, the Russians chose Port Arthur in 1899 as a large base for their fleet. Although the port was ice-free, its links with Russia's Far Eastern ports were long, exposed, and vulnerable to being cut off in case of war with Japan. Moreover, Port Arthur lacked facilities to support more than a part of the Russian Far Eastern Squadron.[23] This, in turn, forced the Russians to divide their available forces into the Vladivostok and Port Arthur squadrons.[24] When the Russians tried to obtain a more favorably located base in the Korea Strait in 1899, the Japanese threatened war. Russia was not ready to fight and was forced to accept an unfavorable position brought upon itself by the acquisition of Port Arthur.[25]

A lack of good bases adversely affects the employment of one's fleet in the struggle for sea control. For example, Britain lacked permanent bases during its rise as a Mediterranean power in the late seventeenth and first decades of the eighteenth centuries. Command of the Mediterranean was impossible without a permanent base for the British fleet. Such a base would have stores of all kinds and in ample quantities and at continuous disposal of the fleet. It had to be also controlled by Britain and "not be dependent on the whims of another power." The British selected the Spanish port of Cádiz, some 60 miles northwest of the Strait of Gibraltar. Its possession would allow for a base in the winter for the British fleet operating in the Mediterranean. In the War of the Spanish Succession (1701–1714), the British and Dutch attempted but ultimately failed in August–September 1702 to capture Cádiz. Until Lisbon became available as a base in 1703, the Anglo-Dutch fleets were able to remain in the Mediterranean only during three summer months. Gibraltar was captured in August 1704 and successfully held against the Spanish-French attack.[26] Afterward, it became the single most important British naval base in the Mediterranean.

Sometimes the value of certain naval bases could be greatly reduced because of the drastic changes in a naval situation. For example, in the first decade of the twentieth century, the growing strength of the German Navy made naval bases in the southern part of England (Chatham, Sheerness, Portsmouth, Plymouth, and Pembroke) unfavorably located for use by the Royal Navy for its actions in the North Sea. In 1914, the Royal Navy had in the North Sea a single first-class base at Rosyth and a second-class base at Cromarty.[27] The only naval anchorage of any importance was at Harwich, and others such as Hartlepool, and Aberdeen were essentially defended commercial ports. Rosyth in the Firth of Forth was selected as the main naval base for the entire fleet to conduct a close blockade in case of a war with Germany. However, after the Grand Fleet adopted a distant blockade of the High Seas Fleet, that required the selection of new bases that were located closer to the North Sea's northern exit. Hence, Invergordon in the Moray Firth and the Scapa Flow were selected as bases for the major part of the Grand Fleet.[28]

The value of a naval basing area or of clusters of airfields is greatly diminished when located close to the land frontier of a potential opponent at sea. For example, the Austro-Hungarian base in Pola was only about 75 miles away from the country's border with Italy. The value of Trieste as a fleet base was even less than that of Pola because it was situated only several miles from the Austro-Italian border.

An advanced base is established either permanently or temporarily near the prospective theater of operations but in either case should be within supplying distance from a major naval base. For example, the use of Elliot Island group, some 60 miles away from the Russian base at Port Arthur, by the Japanese in the Russo-Japanese War of 1904–1905 impressed naval opinion in England to use less frequented but spacious bases such as Scapa Flow and Cromarty Firth as advanced bases.[29]

In 1914–1918, a large British base at Malta and the French bases at Toulon and Bizerte proved to be of little operational significance because they were too far from the main scene of actions in the eastern Mediterranean. Hence, the British and French navies captured control of several islands off the entrance to the Dardanelles and turned them into advanced bases. The Greek harbor on Mudros was used for supplies, while Soudha Bay (Crete) and Famagusta (Cyprus) opened up for the Entente Powers after the Greek King Constantine I in June 1917 fled the country and Greece changed its pro-German foreign policy posture. Afterward, the ports of Corfu and Cephalonia in the Ionian Sea were used as advanced naval bases.[30]

The number of airfields in the coastal area considerably affects one's ability to attack or to defend both naval forces and troops on the ground. The physical control of airfields or of positions where the airfields could be built significantly speeds up and later strengthens the hold on a specific sea or ocean area.

Success in the struggle for sea control requires a balanced composition of one's naval forces. This means that they should be capable of operating successfully in all types of operating areas, from the open ocean to inshore waters. Potential threats and the physical characteristics of the operating area should be the determining factors in planning the overall size of one's battle force and the optimal size and type of surface combatants/submarines. The small size and corresponding short distances in many enclosed sea theaters, combined with their shallow water, make a difficult operating area for aircraft carriers, large surface combatants, and nuclear-powered attack submarines (SSNs). Their effective employment is even more difficult in a narrow sea with a larger number of offshore islands and islets.

A blue-water navy has to project its power across vast ocean distances and to operate close to the coasts of the world's continents or littorals. Obviously, large surface combatants such as aircraft carriers, cruisers, and SSNs could sail in a typical narrow sea. However, their speed and maneuverability must be drastically reduced when operating in confined and shallow waters and off a coast endowed with many islands or archipelagos. Additionally, because of their large size and relatively low maneuverability, large surface combatants are potentially highly vulnerable to concentrated attacks from the surface, subsurface, and air. The enemy would usually make much more of an effort to destroy a large ship, such as cruiser or destroyer, than a small surface combatant. Moreover, major surface combatants are increasingly vulnerable to antiship cruise missiles (ASCMs) launched by aircraft or small surface combatants, to conventionally powered attack submarines (SSKs), to smart mines, and to coastal missile batteries. Additional risks are posed by swarms of small boats. Large ships are costly and cannot be built in large numbers and quickly. The risks of operating highly capable but also highly expensive platforms outweigh the potential benefits.

As in a war on the open ocean, success in littoral warfare requires the employment of diverse naval combat arms. By employing diverse platforms in combination, the deficiencies of each are compensated by the strength of others. Hence, a single type of surface combatant, no matter how advanced, is not a panacea for lacking forces optimally suited for operations in the littorals. Moreover, combat arms/branches of air forces, the army/marines, and special operations forces should be employed in the littorals. AIP (air independent propulsion) SSKs, light frigates (FFLs), large corvettes, multipurpose corvettes, and fast attack craft are obviously much better suited for combat in littoral waters than their much larger counterparts. They are also much less expensive and can be built or acquired in larger numbers.

A blue-water navy should have a relatively large number of small surface combatants and submarines to maintain sea control. Forces optimally suited for employment in the littorals should be organized in what can be arbitrarily called "littoral combat groups" (LCGs). Such a group would also include shipborne and/or land-based multipurpose helicopters, diverse unmanned vehicles (surface, subsurface, aerial), and special operations teams. In some cases, ground forces and coastal missile/gun batteries can also be employed in support of LCGs. Each LCG should be tailored for a particular mission, such as for obtaining or denying sea control, attack on the enemy's maritime trade, and the defense/protection of friendly maritime trade. For an out-of-the-area navy, such as the U.S. Navy, LCGs have to be supported by a much more powerful force of "distant cover and support." Such a force could be composed of the carrier strike groups (CSGs), expeditionary strike groups (ESGs), surface action groups (SAGs), and SSNs, plus the U.S. Air Force's attack aircraft/heavy bombers.

The successful outcome of the struggle for sea control requires not only on qualitative but also on numerical superiority. The main factors in determining the number, size, and type of ships/submarines to be permanently based in a given maritime theater are as follows: potential threats at sea; distance and transit time from the home bases to the prospective operating area; the number of ships to be forwardly deployed and those under repair at any given time; the availability and security of naval/air bases and their relative positions to the enemy; characteristics of the operating environment; type of missions and their duration; and the potential contribution of the allies/coalition partners. Normally, there is a great advantage to being numerically stronger than your opponent. Nowhere is this truer than at the operational and strategic levels of war. It is also often forgotten that a navy needs a large number of ships not only to obtain but also to maintain control of the sea.

Moreover, many information warfare (IW) enthusiasts firmly believe that relatively small and rapidly deployable forces are capable of accomplishing missions that would otherwise require a large massed force. Supposedly, substituting information and effects for mass would reduce the need to concentrate one's forces within specific geographical locations. This, in turn, would increase the tempo and speed of movement throughout the battle space, complicating the enemy's targeting problems.[31] In the early 2000s, network-centric warfare enthusiasts repeatedly asserted that "netting" geographically widely dispersed forces, combined with shared situational awareness and speed of communications, would allow much smaller forces to defeat much larger enemy forces – and quickly.[32] These assertions are largely unsupported with empirical evidence. Yet the gain in one's combat power due to information technologies is extremely hard to express in meaningful terms. Information is not something tangible as, for example, traditional firepower and mobility. It is just one of the many elements that the commander would use to reach a sound decision. Having complete information does not necessarily mean being more informed. What is needed is not more information but more orientation.[33] Using more and more knowledge means collecting more and more information. The result will be too much information, integrated poorly or not at all.[34]

In general, the larger the numbers of ships, the higher the probability of a successful operation. At some point, sheer numbers are simply overwhelming, regardless of skills, morale and discipline, soundness of doctrine, and quality of combat training and state of combat readiness of one's naval forces. In many examples, a numerically superior force was a decisive factor in achieving a victory over a better armed, trained, and led but numerically smaller force. Whenever possible, overwhelming force should be used at a decisive place and time.[35] There is no such a thing as being too strong if the objective is to achieve a quick and decisive victory. In practice, this means one should "mass" one's forces in the sector of main effort and assign relatively weak forces to the sectors of secondary effort.[36] Today, a force does not necessarily need to be physically massed, but one should create a mass effect at a decisive place and time. It is the successful application of overwhelming force that will seize the initiative from the enemy and defeat him.

Experience shows that success in the struggle for sea control is very difficult to achieve without having a comprehensive theory developed in peacetime. Naval theory should describe both the offensive and defensive aspects of warfare at sea and their mutual relationship. Its broader framework is provided by a general theory of war. One of its main purposes is to provide a much broader and deeper understanding of the entire spectrum of warfare at sea. A sound naval theory consists of two main components: (1) common features derived from the history of naval warfare; (2) the character of the future war at sea. Both of these components should be mutually supporting; overemphasizing one or the other would invariably result in an unsound naval theory. Perhaps the single greatest problem is to develop naval theory predominantly or exclusively based on the new and largely unproven technologies. Although the character of the future war at sea is heavily affected by technological advances, international security environment, demography, and law of the sea – to name a few – also exert strong influences.

Sea control cannot be successful without a sound naval/joint doctrine and a high level of combat training. In general, the main purpose of a doctrine is to provide a military organization with a common philosophy, a common language, a common purpose, and unity of effort. Sound doctrine is the key tool in having a common operational or tactical outlook and common vocabulary; otherwise, mission command cannot be successfully applied. Doctrine can help considerably in bonding a service to its sister services and to its alliance and coalition partners.

Doctrine is a bridge between theory and practice. It translates theoretical ideas into doctrinal principles. These principles are then used to devise tactics, techniques, and procedures.[37] A sound doctrine should take fully into account current and projected technological advances. However, it should never be predominantly or, even worse, exclusively based either on theory or on technology.

Naval doctrine for the operational level of war should be the primary document guiding one's naval/maritime forces for obtaining and maintaining sea control. Properly written, it should describe in some detail the employment of naval forces in major naval/joint operations and as part of a maritime/littoral campaign. In other words, it should be focused on the employment of the numbered/theater fleets at the operational level of war. A sound doctrine should include methods of the combat employment of naval/joint forces, tenets of command organization and leadership, operational decision making and planning/execution, and supporting functions (intelligence, information operations, logistics, and protection).

A sound operational doctrine should encompass several different operational concepts. Each them should be aimed at accomplishing an operational objective through the conduct of a major naval/joint operation. Specifically, a sound operational concept for obtaining/maintaining sea control should be based on the proper assessment of the operating area and the realistic vision of the future war at sea. It should describe, in broad and simple terms, how one's forces should be deployed, employed, and sustained in the course of accomplishing their respective operational objectives. It should not directly refer to a specific potential enemy or ocean/sea area in which one's operational concept will be applied in case of the hostilities.

In general, an operational concept should be flexible so as to allow creative ways in the employment of one's naval/maritime forces in the case of a sudden change in the operational situation. It should ensure speed of action and surprise. It should pose a threat to the enemy from multiple physical mediums (sea, air, and land) and thereby considerably limit his options. It should also provide for operational deception and thereby greatly enhance the chances of surprising the enemy. It should integrate both offensive and defensive cyberwar capabilities.

In the past, the navies played almost an exclusive role in obtaining and maintaining sea control. This is not the case today. Sea control cannot be accomplished without the closest cooperation with other services – jointness. The employment of multiservice or joint forces offers several major advantages. Among other things, the naval/maritime operational commander has more options in employing the employment of subordinate forces. The enemy is put at a great disadvantage by facing a multidimensional threat for which he might not have an effective counter. Joint forces allow a creative operational commander to combine their diverse but complementary capabilities in asymmetrical as well as symmetrical ways and to generate greater impact than the sum of the individual parts.[38] For example, missile-armed surface combatants can attack a variety of targets on the enemy coast, while land-based aircraft can strike enemy warships and merchant ships at sea or in their bases/ports. Friendly ground forces can capture enemy naval bases/ports and airfields and thereby greatly facilitate the task of obtaining sea control.

Generally, a symmetric employment of one's forces requires substantial numerical superiority and/or much more advanced weapons to achieve success and minimize friendly losses or casualties. In contrast, the employment of dissimilar forces can be extremely lethal. Sometimes friendly ground troops might be called upon to capture some objectives on or off the enemy-held coast that are of little or no significance for the army but are critical to the naval forces' ability to obtain and maintain sea control. The long range, high speed, and lethality of modern aircraft allow them to operate not only over adjacent narrow seas but also over the major part of an ocean. Land-based aircraft generally have a long range and can carry a large payload of weapons. They can also generate a larger number of sorties within a given time frame than carrier-based aircraft can. They have great flexibility in attacking enemy's warships and merchant ships when operating from a central position. An exterior position with numerous air bases allows the attacker to shift sectors of the main effort on very short notice.

The joint employment two or more services also has some disadvantages. Among other things, command and control (C2) of major naval/joint operations is more complex than in the employment of single-service forces. The different service cultures and doctrines might lead to misunderstanding and make cooperation more difficult. Other problems include the parochialism of services, personal incompatibility (or even animosities) among high commanders, operation security, and interoperability. The use of communications is more complex because of different types of systems and procedures used by various services. This is an especially difficult problem in employing multinational forces. Forces' deployment and logistics also pose much greater challenges than the employment of single-service forces. Information flow within a multiservice or multinational force is also generally much slower than if only a single-service force is used.

Offensive action is one of the main requirements in the successful employment of one's forces to obtain and maintain sea control. Having numerical superiority cannot by itself secure control of a given ocean/sea area. One's naval forces must present an existential threat to the enemy. This means actually operating in the area that needs to be eventually controlled. Keeping one's naval forces predominantly in their bases/ports as a so-called fortress fleet was an obsession in the past by the Russians. It invariably led to numerous disasters. A navy would never "discharge its full obligations except through active and persistent operations at sea." Command of the sea is not secured until the ability of the "enemy naval forces to operate in that area is nullified."[39]

To obtain the initiative at the beginning of the hostilities at sea, the stronger side should attempt to destroy the major part of the enemy's forces in a surprise attack. Afterward, to retain the initiative, one's forces must be continuously on the offensive. The offensive not only ensures freedom of action but also enhances the morale of one's forces and depresses that of the enemy. The initiative depends largely upon leadership exercised throughout the chain of command. Slackness in following up victory often has the most decisive influence upon the results of the war's outcome, both on land and at sea.[40]

Aggressiveness means determined action by one's forces to seize and hold the initiative and to inflict maximum damage on the enemy with all available forces. Aggressive actions are necessary to accomplish decisive results. Experience shows that excessive boldness has usually been less costly than passivity. Any military action poses risks. Hence, it is always necessary to decide between possible loss from inaction and the risk of action. Ability to obtain the initiative at the outset of a war is the result mainly of careful preparation beforehand.

Historically, passivity on the part of a stronger side has allowed a weaker side to obtain sea control by default. For example, in the Crimean War (1854–1856), the Russians were extremely passive in the Baltic despite their numerical superiority. They had a fleet of twenty-seven ships of the line with smaller craft, including fifty to sixty gunboats, whereas the British squadron consisted of only nine steamships of the line and six sailing ships of the line.[41]

In 1781, a combined Franco-Spanish fleet boxed in the British Channel fleet of fifty ships in the undefended Bay of Torbay. It inflicted a crushing defeat on the British fleet. However, its commander lacked the will to fight. He sailed away on a minor enterprise.[42] In another example, had Admiral Heihachirō Tōgō (1848–1934) been prepared to risk a full-scale attack at dawn to take advantage of the confusion caused by his night torpedo attack, there can be little doubt that a decisive Japanese naval victory could have been secured in the first day of the Russo-Japanese War on 8 February 1904. The local Russian superiority was largely illusory; since the loss of the battleship *Petropavlovsk* (on 13 April 1904) and the death of Admiral Stephan O. Makaroff (1849–1904), the offensive spirit necessary to make even the defensive role of a fleet-in-being credible had gone out of the Russian fleet. Its effective units lay idle in Port Arthur under the uninspiring Admiral Wilgelm Vitgeft (1847–1904).[43]

A stronger force distinctly lacking the offensive spirit usually pursues defensive strategic objectives. Inactivity or passivity on the part of a stronger fleet often allows an inferior force to accomplish its objective. For example, in World War I, the Italian Navy, although numerically superior to the

Austro-Hungarian Navy, remained passive in the Adriatic for most of the war.[44] The Italian Navy's missions, after the country entered the war on the side of the Entente powers in May 1915, were as follows: to keep the fleet ready to engage the Austro-Hungarian fleet; to protect the Italian coast against enemy raids by using mines, torpedo craft, small submarines, armored trains, and light cruiser-destroyer squadrons; and to establish an effective watch in the Strait of Otranto to deny its passage to Austro-Hungarian U-boats.[45] In the first four months of the war, the Austrians, at a price of only two U-boats and a few aircraft, inflicted large losses on the Italian fleet (sinking two cruisers, one destroyer, two torpedo craft, three submarines, and two dirigibles, in addition to damaging one British light cruiser). At one point, the Italian heavy ships were not allowed to leave their bases. During the remainder of war, every place of any importance upon the Adriatic coast of Italy was made to feel the presence of the Austro-Hungarian ships or aircraft. The Italian fleet rarely intervened to stop these raids.[46]

Likewise, in 1940, the Italian Navy's surface fleet limited its role to defend the country's coast and to protect the sea routes to Libya. The Italian Naval Staff (Supermarina) envisaged offensive actions only in the eastern Mediterranean, while a defensive posture would be taken in the western and central Mediterranean.[47] The German Naval Staff, in contrast, believed that it was in Italy's interest to concentrate actions by all services to neutralize British dominance in the eastern Mediterranean. Specifically, this meant providing mutual support in blockading the British Mediterranean Fleet, capturing Egypt, and eliminating British influence in Palestine and Turkey. The Germans also believed that the reduction of the British position in the Mediterranean was a key prerequisite for the successful outcome of the war at sea. Both the German Naval Staff and the Supreme Command of the Wehrmacht considered Suez/Egypt and Gibraltar to be the strategic pillars in the Mediterranean. The Germans also tried very hard to persuade the Italians to take a more offensive posture and thus change the situation in the Mediterranean in favor of the Axis. However, all these attempts remained unsuccessful.[48]

The struggle for sea control in the littorals cannot be successful unless an adequate degree of basing/deployment area control exists. Another objective is to put the enemy under constant pressure and tie up his forces in a certain sea area, thereby creating conditions to change the operational situation to one's advantage. Optimally, all the elements for basing/deployment area control should be established in peacetime. They should be an integral part of theater-wide or operational protection in a given maritime theater. Operational protection is inherently one of the responsibilities of a theater or operational commander. Basing/deployment area control is obtained, then maintained, and, if possible, extended during the hostilities at sea.

Basing/deployment area control is accomplished through the series of related defensive and offensive tactical actions on the surface, in the subsurface, in the air, and on land. The principal actions are reconnaissance/surveillance of the coastal area and adjacent ocean/sea; defense of the coast and naval bases/airfields and ports in particular; territorial air defense, antisubmarine defense in the coastal waters; anti–combat craft defense; defense against enemy combat swimmers/commandos; defensive mining of the bases/ports and selected parts of the coastal waters; defensive and offensive mine countermeasures (MCM); defense against terrorist acts and enemy raids; defense and protection of the coastal installations/facilities; and defense against weapons of mass destruction (WMDs). Offensive actions encompass strikes or attacks against enemy surface combatants threatening one's naval/air bases and ports and installations/and facilities on the coast. Protection of one's basing and deployment areas is significantly enhanced by defensive/offensive information warfare, cover/concealment, countering enemy reconnaissance/surveillance, and cover and concealment.

In the information era, the struggle for sea control must be accompanied from the very beginning by all-out efforts to obtain or deny information superiority. This should be an integral part of the operational concept for obtaining/maintaining sea control. In general, information dominance can be described as one's ability to make quick and sound decisions, assisted by technical capabilities in collecting, processing, and disseminating an uninterrupted flow of information while at the same time exploiting or denying an enemy's ability to do the same. The struggle for control of cyberspace is very similar to the struggle for sea control. It is simply a myth – and dangerous one – that one could achieve full and absolute control of the cyberspace for any length of time. That control is inherently relative, incomplete, and highly tenuous. It is in a constant state of flux. A weaker side at sea might in fact have a greater ability to achieve information dominance than its stronger opponent; the opposite could be also true. Because the extent of the cyberspace is essentially limitless, one cannot achieve general or local control as in the struggle for sea control. Like sea control, one's control of the cyberspace can be permanent or temporary. In theory, a *permanent control* of the cyberspace exists when the stronger side dominates the EM spectrum for the duration of the war. However, this is probably not achievable in a war between two strong opponents. The more likely outcome is a temporary control of the cyberspace. Such a situation is highly unstable. The advantage can be shifted rapidly from one side to the other.

In theory, control of cyberspace can vary from limited to absolute. A *limited control* of cyberspace pertains to one's ability use it for only a certain purpose. This means that the stronger side is successful in destroying or neutralizing some key elements of the enemy cyberspace capabilities. In practice, an absolute control of cyberspace in a war between two strong opponents is not achievable. Normally, a state of disputed or contested control of the cyberspace would exist in the struggle between two strong opponents. It is less than absolute control and more than limited control.

This situation would be characterized by rapid and sudden changes in the situation in cyberspace.

Central vs. exterior positions

The initial geographic positions occupied by the opposing sides in a war at sea significantly affect their deployment and combat employment. Generally, one's forces can operate from either a central or an exterior position or combination of these two. The mutual positions of naval/air bases, the length and directional orientation of the base of operations, and the type of platforms of the opposing positions largely determine whether one's forces would operate from a central or an exterior position. A force operating from a position interposed between hostile forces is said to occupy a *central* (or *interior*) *position*. Such a force operates along shorter and divergent lines of operation. Hence, it can concentrate more quickly at a selected point within its effective striking range than a hostile force moving along the periphery. A central position has the additional advantage that the enemy cannot easily concentrate against one's forces.[49]

Mahan generally agreed with a well-known and highly influential military theoretician General Antoine-Henry Jomini (1779–1869) on the inherent value of the central position and interior lines of operation but with some caveats. For him, a central position was a contributory, not the principal element of a situation. Mahan explained that an interior position would "enable you to get there sooner but with that its advantage ends." Such "a position does not give also the most men needed to complete the familiar aphorism. The position in itself gives no large numbers, and when left it serves only the defensive purpose of a refuge, a base of supplies, lines of communication. A central position cannot be carried to the field or as reinforcement."[50] In Mahan's view, the central position enjoyed by England, vis-à-vis its continental rivals, was its main advantage. Operating from a central position, it is possible to mount a naval offensive along interior lines outward from the center. It enables the attacker to keep his enemy separated and therefore inferior by concentration against one unit while holding the other in check.[51] Mahan was correct in stating that a central position is of little use if the enemy on both sides is stronger than one's forces are.

In general, by operating from a central position, one's force can defeat the hostile forces and obtain local superiority before other hostile forces can intervene at the threatened area.[52] For example, during World War I, the Royal Navy, by concentrating superior forces in home waters, controlled the oceanic supply lines to and from the northern and western coasts of Europe. The British Grand Fleet, by its disposition in the Firth of Forth, occupied in operational terms a central position in case the High Seas Fleet tried to move either to the northern exit or south past the Texel-Yarmouth line. Likewise, the High Seas Fleet, by occupying a central position between the North Sea and the Baltic, prevented the Grand Fleet from operating in the Baltic Sea.

In World War II, the Japanese-controlled Philippines and Netherlands East Indies (NEI) strategically occupied a central position in the western Pacific. The centrally located island of Luzon dominated the eastern approaches from the Pacific Ocean to the South China Sea. Likewise, the Japanese control of the islands Java, Timor, and Sumatra provided them with a central position in using their air and naval forces against any enemy force approaching the archipelago from the south or west.

A force occupies an *exterior* (or *flanking*) *position* when it operates along the periphery of the enemy's center. Such a position de facto corresponds to a strategic flanking position. A force operating from such a position can move against one or both of the enemy's flanks. It can also threaten or carry out surprise attacks from multiple directions against diverse points on the enemy's periphery. The exterior position allows one's forces to draw the opposing force away from its assigned physical objective. A force operating from an exterior position can threaten or attack from multiple directions or axes. However, to be successful, forces operating from the exterior position have to usually numerically larger and more mobile than the hostile forces opposed to them.

Concentration vs. dispersal

The first step in obtaining sea control is deploying sufficient forces to deal with the greatest concentrated force that the enemy can bring to bear.[53] Concentration is aimed at ensuring a rapid concentration of any of the two or more parts of one's naval forces within a given ocean/sea area. The principal objective should be to force the enemy to divide his forces and thereby give an opportunity to defeat him in detail. However, such methods of forces' concentration are unlikely to be successful in a war betweeen two strong opponents at sea. Among other things, naval forces today are numerically much smaller than they were in the past. They could be dispersed over a relatively larger part of the ocean but still be able to operate within the mutually supporting distances. Yet the situation in an enclosed sea theater, such as the Persian (Arabian) Gulf or the Baltic, is very much different. Because of the smallness of the area and the short distances in such theaters, the forces of both opponents will be relatively concentrated. Each opponent's movements and whereabouts will be hard to conceal from the other side.

In the past, the need to have a fleet concentrated was almost absolutized. For example, Admiral Mahan insisted that a fleet should never be divided and that victory at sea is possible only by fleet concentration.[54] He wrote that fleet concentration "sums up in itself all other factors, the entire alphabet of military efficiency in war."[55] In his view, whether one is engaged "in a strategic deployment or tactical maneuver, the correct course of action is to distribute one's force as to be superior to the enemy in one quarter, while holding the enemy in check in other quarters long enough to allow one's main attack to reach its full result." He also wrote that the "essential underlying idea [of concentration] is that of mutual support; that the entire force . . . is acting in such way that each part is relieved by the others of a part of its own burden."[56] Mahan firmly believed that a fleet should never be divided. If the concentrated fire of the battle fleet is the principal means by which naval power is to be asserted, the preferred target of such fire is the enemy fleet.[57]

In contrast, Corbett observed that a war cannot be successful unless one takes high but prudent risks, and the greatest and most effective of such risks is a division or dispersal of one's fleet. Corbett asserted that the idea of massing as a virtue in itself is bred in peace, not in war. He insisted that the wars at sea are won by what he called "strategical" combinations, which as a rule entail at least apparent dispersal. They can be achieved only by taking risks, and the greatest and most effective of these is division. The war experience shows that, without division, no strategical combinations are possible. A division is bad only when it is pushed beyond the limits of well knit deployment. In distinguishing between concentration and mass, he wrote that the "essential feature of strategic deployment which contemplates dispersal with a view to a choice of combinations is flexibility and free movement. One's forces should be so dispersed that they conceal one's intentions and at the same time allow flexibility in countering enemy movements."[58] In his view, it is wrong to put one's fleet in a position that would prevent it from "falling back to its strategic center when it is encountered by a superior force." Such retreats would always depend on the skill and resources of the opposing commanders and on the weather. However, such risks must be taken. Those who risk nothing rarely accomplish anything. The idea of division is essential, as is the idea of concentration.[59]

Corbett believed (erroneously) that a country must have the means for ending the war in a single blow. This, in turn, requires superiority both on land and at sea. It may be said that the concentration of the weaker determines that of the stronger. Yet the opposite is not true.[60] Daveluy noted that the general naval concentration of one side would usually lead the other side to concentrate too. For example, in the Anglo-Dutch Wars, the fleets of both sides assembled in a narrow part of the theater. The Dutch had to concentrate to cover the frontier. By massing their fleet in the North Sea, they also covered at the same time the country's land territory and the point of convergence of the Dutch convoys. England was forced to act in the same way. It had to cover the estuary of the Thames River and to protect its greatest naval base at Chatham.[61] Daveluy wrote that dividing up one's naval forces must be done judiciously. To compel the enemy to divide, each separate fraction must by its strength and its position constitute a threat, the different fractions and their positions must constitute a threat, and the different fractions must not be so close together as to enable a single enemy force to look after them.[62]

Normally, it is a bad thing to divide one's force when one enjoys a great numerical superiority. For example, the Russians in their war with Japan in 1904–1905 made a mistake by dividing their fleet in the Far East into two squadrons, one based in Port Arthur and another in Vladivostok. This in turn made it difficult, if not impossible, for the Russians to concentrate both squadrons to fight a decisive battle with the Japanese fleet. However, sometimes the division of forces might be caused by the mistakes of statesmen or by circumstances developing during the war. For example, the German Navy in World War I was forced to deploy its fleet in both the North Sea and the Baltic because the country stumbled into fighting the war on two fronts.

In some cases, the concentration of forces may be the fruit of calculated dispersion. Two fleets, for example, can act in conjunction from widely separated bases with far greater certainty than is possible for armies. Thus, the variety of combinations is usually much higher at sea than on the land, and a variety of combinations is in constant opposition to the central mass.

Normally, one's forces should not be divided into too many force elements. It is even worse if they operate beyond their effective mutual distances; the exception is if each force is superior in strength to any enemy force it might encounter. In several notable cases, the Imperial Japanese Navy (IJN) misapplied the principle of mass and economy of effort. For example, the Japanese prepared and executed extremely complicated plans and fragmented their forces in the Port Moresby-Solomons operation (that led to the Battle of the Coral Sea) in May 1942, in the Midway-Aleutians operation in June 1942 (that led to the Battle of Midway), and in the naval defense of the Philippines in October 1944 (*Sho-1* Plan). Not surprisingly, all three operations ended in the Japanese defeats.

Obtaining control

Obviously, at the beginning of the hostilities, each belligerent possesses control of only the basing and deployment areas. In the modern era, this control has been extended to a greater distance because of the presence of mines, submarines, and aircraft.[63] In a war between two strong opponents, as each fleet commences its deployment into those parts of the sea that are initially the most important, it would start to gradually extend its control over additional ocean/sea areas. Once the opposing naval forces come into contact, the struggle for sea control would begin.[64] Both sides would then try to have control of the ocean/sea area separating their respective basing/deployment areas.[65] The full struggle for command would take place only in a part of the theater most important for each side. Normally, neither belligerent would try to obtain command in the areas where success is unlikely or might be too costly.[66]

To make a certain ocean/sea area more secure, the stronger side should be able to concentrate timely enough strength to prevent serious damage to its forces and positions. This would require, in turn, that essential units are deployed at such distances and in such directions to concentrate superior strength prior to the arrival of the hostile force.[67] From time to time, one side can have sea control over a given area for a considerable period, while at other times neither side has control.[68]

Sea control cannot be obtained quickly unless the weaker side reacts operationally or strategically. This can be achieved by attacking a physical objective that the other side considers critically important for the successful outcome of the war. These might include geographic positions such as strait/narrows or an island, endangering the success of operations by the enemy ground forces in the littoral area, or cutting off his seaborne traffic.[69] An attempt to capture an important position or the threat to cut off seaborne traffic completely would usually force the enemy to react strongly and thereby provide an opportunity to destroy a major part of his naval/air forces. The results of such actions would be control of the certain ocean/sea area. However, the selection of such objectives is not simple. One or the other side might not select an objective that their opponent considers vital. Yet a decisive encounter with the enemy forces might occur even though vital points have not been attacked. Very often, pride, prestige, false evaluation of the enemy power and capabilities, unsound strategic ideas or dispositions, or even chance and luck may play a major role.[70]

The strategic situation on the open ocean will considerably influence the situation in the adjacent peripheral or narrow seas. A stronger side might obtain a larger degree of control on the open ocean, but its control closer to the continental landmass would be greatly reduced or even nonexistent. The weaker side in a typical narrow sea would enjoy some advantage over the blue-water navy because of better reconnaissance/surveillance of the area, shorter lines of operation and supplies, and good opportunities to repair ships and evacuate personnel. Moreover, the weaker opponent can employ not only naval forces but also land-based aircraft and coastal missile/gun batteries in denying the stronger side full control of the surface and air in the area contiguous to the coast. Then, the presence of naval forces of a stronger side in an area under enemy control would be probably sporadic. In a typical narrow sea, a sufficient degree of sea control would be obtained after one's forces obtain control of all three physical dimensions and part of the coast. In some cases, it might be possible that one's forces could obtain sea control even when the enemy controls the coastal area, provided that his forces are so weakened that they do not represent a serious threat.[71]

Sea control on the open ocean cannot be isolated from sea control in the littorals and narrow seas in particular. This is especially the case where land and sea boundaries of the two opponents are contiguous.[72] In strategic terms, obtaining or losing sea control on the open ocean would normally have an indirect effect on the situation on land. This effect is far more direct and immediate in an enclosed sea theater where, in many cases, the loss of sea control might even considerably affect the outcome of the war as a whole. The opposite is also true; obtaining or losing sea control in the littorals is considerably affected by the course of events in the war on land.[73] In contrast to the open ocean, sea control in a typical narrow sea cannot be usually obtained and then maintained without the closest cooperation among all the services. Even when the navy is the principal force, it should be directly or indirectly supported by the other services.[74]

Sea control obtained in part of or the entire theater should facilitate accomplishing one's objectives on land. One's naval forces accomplish this through continuous actions in support of the coastal flank of friendly ground forces. The main purpose would be to neutralize the enemy's forces from operating within a specific ocean/sea area. If successful, such actions would make it possible to release considerable friendly ground troops for their employment in the sector of main effort. The lack of one's sea control on the army flank would otherwise require significant defensive forces on the coast. Also, by exercising sea control, the enemy would be able to inflict high losses on friendly forces. This in turn could endanger the overall objective of a major ground operation. Obtaining and maintaining sea control is the first, the most important, and the most effective way of providing support to friendly ground forces on the coast.[75]

The struggle for sea control in a typical narrow sea cannot be separated from the one fought in the airspace over the sea surface and adjacent littoral area. The struggle for air superiority in a typical narrow sea is most closely linked to the war on land. Both naval and air forces should take part in the struggle for sea control. Because of the short distances, the effectiveness of air strikes against enemy ships and forces and installations/facilities on the coast is considerably higher in a typical narrow sea than on the open ocean. Land-based aircraft can fly more sorties within a given time frame than can carrier-based aircraft on the open ocean. In a narrow sea with many offshore islands and islets, land-based aircraft can strike from bases flanking the transit routes of the enemy ships. They can be quickly deployed and redeployed from one base to another or from one part of the theater to another. The small size of narrow seas also allows "rolling" employment of fixed-wing aircraft and helicopters. Aircraft represent a constant threat to the survivability of all ships but especially to one's surface forces. The threat of continuous strikes from the air could completely paralyze one's naval forces.[76]

Land- and/or carrier-based aircraft are the principal means to obtain control of the surface and perhaps even subsurface in the littorals. When obtained, such control is usually local and temporary, as the examples from World War II and some regional wars fought since 1945 illustrate. Because of the increased range, endurance, and speeds of modern aircraft, the ever larger sea and ocean areas have become the area of employment of naval forces and land-based aircraft. Today, no part of any narrow seas is free from observation and attack from the air. One's naval forces can conduct sustained actions only when one's forces control the airspace.

In early 1943, the situation in the central Solomons was similar to that which had prevailed around Guadalcanal in the latter part of 1942. Allied control of the air was so complete that the Japanese did not dare to use their surface forces in daylight. During the night, however, the waters of New Georgia were hotly contested. The Japanese then repeatedly tried to run reinforcements, while Allied cruisers and destroyers tried to intercept them.[77] By mid-1943, Allied forces stood poised and ready to resume their offensive in the Solomons archipelago. Although the Allies possessed air superiority in the area, they lacked well-placed and sufficient airfields in the island group. For this, it was necessary to seize the islands northwest of Guadalcanal so that fighters could accompany bombers sent to attack key Japanese positions around Rabaul in New Britain. The Japanese, in contrast, possessed an excellent chain of airfields stretching south from New Britain to New Georgia and west to Lae, Salamaua, Madang, and Wewak on the northern coast of New Guinea. It was then obvious to the Allies that control of the air over Rabaul could never be obtained until the Japanese had been driven from at least some of these positions.[78] The success of the Allies' neutralization of Rabaul from September 1943 through April 1944 was predicated on obtaining local air superiority.[79]

In some cases, a multitude of offshore islands spread over a relatively large area allows one's forces to obtain sea control by using predominantly land-based aircraft supported with either naval surface forces or ground troops or both. For example, after seizing Crete in May 1941, the Germans rapidly extended their hold over the Aegean by occupying the key islands in the archipelago. They also reinforced the Italian-held garrisons in the area. Not only was the Aegean virtually closed to Allied shipping, but the Germans and Italians also made good use of island bases in attacking British convoys in the Eastern Mediterranean. German U-boats and Italian submarines regularly used harbors in the Aegean, while their light forces and aircraft protected the Axis's coastal and interregional traffic.

Main methods

In operational terms, the main methods for obtaining sea control are as follows:

- Destruction of the enemy forces
- Containment of the enemy forces
- Choke point control
- Capturing important enemy positions and basing areas.

Destruction of the enemy forces can be achieved by a decisive action at sea or against enemy forces at their bases and by weakening enemy forces over time. The enemy forces are "contained" by a combination of naval blockade, posing a threat to critical positions/areas, and strategic diversions.[80] A stronger side at sea could exercise choke point control by containing the enemy naval forces/commercial shipping within an enclosed or semi-enclosed theater by using the existing control or by capturing one/ both shores of one or several straits. A stronger side can contain the enemy force by deploying its naval forces and aircraft at the outer approaches to the enemy-controlled choke point(s). Another rarely discussed method of obtaining sea control is by capturing selected points or areas on the mainland coast or offshore islands/archipelagoes and enemy naval bases/airfields in the littoral area.

Maintaining control

Once a sufficient degree of control is obtained, it must be maintained; otherwise, it would be weakened and might even be lost to a strong and offensively minded enemy.[81] Slackness in following up victory has often been the most negative influence upon a war's outcome at sea.[82] There have been many examples of successful offensives failing to achieve decisive results because of the failure to inflict a total defeat on a badly beaten and disorganized enemy.

Methods used for obtaining sea control are largely used in maintaining that control. However, the intensity of one's efforts in this phase of the struggle for sea control is usually generally less than in obtaining control. Under certain conditions, the stronger side would execute the tasks of obtaining and maintaining sea control in short sequence or even simultaneously.[83]

In maintaining control of the sea, the stronger side should concentrate enough of its strength to ensure that the remaining enemy forces cannot present a serious threat to its forces. Otherwise, it would not have any other option but to exercise control over a smaller part of the ocean/sea area. A stronger side should always be able to concentrate enough strength to drive enemy forces out of that particular ocean/sea area.[84]

An effective control of an ocean/sea area might require considerable dispersion of the available strength of a stronger side at sea. In a war on the open ocean, a stronger side would deploy highly capable forces far from their home bases to maintain the desired degree of sea control. This problem is much easier in the littorals, where smaller and less capable platforms could be effectively used in maintaining sea control.

Notes

1 T.G.W. Settle, *The Strategic Employment of the Fleet* (Newport, RI: Staff Presentation, Naval War College, September 18, 1940), p. 9.
2 Elwin F. Cutts, "Operations for Securing Command of Sea Areas" (Newport, RI: Naval War College, 8–9 July 1938), p. 46.
3 R.K. Turner, *Backgrounds of Naval Strategy* (lecture delivered before the Marine Corps Schools, Quantico, VA., 16 February 1938), Folder 2038, Box 76, Publications,

Record Group (RG)-4, Naval Historical Collection, Archives, U.S. Naval War College, Newport, RI, p. 5.

4 R.K. Turner, *Backgrounds of Naval Strategy* (lecture delivered before the Marine Corps Schools, Quantico, VA., 16 February 1938), Folder 2038, Box 76, Publications, Record Group (RG)-4, Naval Historical Collection, Archives, U.S. Naval War College, Newport, RI, p. 6.

5 Elwin F. Cutts, "Operations for Securing Command of Sea Areas" (Newport, RI: Naval War College, 8–9 July 1938), p. 5.

6 Raoul Castex, *More Protiv Kopna*, Vol. 1. Translated by Hijacint Mundorfer (*Théórie Stratégiques*, Vol. 1: *La Mer Contre La Terre*) (Belgrade: Geca Kon AD, 1939), p. 12.

7 Günther Pöschel, *Die Rolle und Bedeutung der Seeherrschaft in Vergangenheit und Gegenwart. Analyse der theoretischen Aussagen zum Begriff der Seeherrschaft* (Dresden: Militärakademie Friedrich Engels, Schriften der Militärakademie, Heft 165, 1978), p. 82.

8 Alfred T. Mahan, *Naval Strategy Compared and Contrasted with the Principles and Practice of Military Operations on Land* (Boston: Little, Brown, and Company, 1919), p. 134.

9 Wolfgang Wegener, *The Naval Strategy of the World War*. Translated and with an Introduction and Notes by Holger H. Herwig (Annapolis, MD: Naval Institute Press, 1989), p. 30.

10 Wolfgang Wegener, *The Naval Strategy of the World War*. Translated and with an Introduction and Notes by Holger H. Herwig (Annapolis, MD: Naval Institute Press, 1989), p. 31.

11 Antoine Henri de Jomini differentiated between what he called "strategic" and "tactical" positions. The first were those taken for some time and intended to cover a much greater portion of the front of operation than tactical positions used for the actual battle Antoine-Henri de Jomini, *The Art of War*. Translated by G.H. Mendel and W.P. Craighill (Westport, CT: Greenwood Press Publishers, 1971; originally published Philadelphia: J.P. Lippincott & Co., 1862), p. 97.

12 Mahan, *Naval Strategy Compared and Contrasted with the Principles and Practice of Military Operations on Land* (Boston: Little, Brown, and Company, 1919), p. 129.

13 Alfred T. Mahan, *The Influence of Sea Power upon History 1660–1783* (Boston: Little, Brown, and Company, 1939), p. 30.

14 Rene Daveluy, *The Genius of Naval Warfare*, Vol. I: *Strategy* (Annapolis, MD: The United States Naval Institute 1910), pp. 53–54.

15 Wolfgang Wegener, *The Naval Strategy of the World War*. Translated by Holger H. Herwig (Annapolis, MD: Naval Institute Press, 1989), pp. 16–18.

16 Colmar von der Goltz, *Kriegsführung. Kurze Lehre ihrer wichtigsten Grundsätze und Formen* (Berlin: R.v. Decker's Verlag, 1895), pp. 70, 64.

17 G. J. Fiebeger, *Elements of Strategy* (West Point, NY: United States Military Academy Press, 1910), pp. 12–14.

18 Otto Groos, *Seekriegslehren im Lichte des Weltkrieges. Ein Buch für den Seemann, Soldaten und Staatsmann* (Berlin: Verlag von E. S. Mittler & Sohn, 1929), p. 52.

19 Colmar von der Goltz, *The Conduct of War: A Short Treatise on Its Most Important Branches and Guiding Rules*. Translated by G. F. Leverson (London: Kegan, Paul, Trench, Truebner, 1908), p. 106.

20 Alfred T. Mahan, *The Influence of Sea Power upon History 1660–1783* (Boston: Little, Brown, and Company, 1939), p. 515.

21 Alfred T. Mahan, *Influence of Sea Power upon the French Revolution and Empire, 1793–1812*, Vol. I, 8th ed. (Boston: Little, Brown, and Company, 1897), pp. 186–87.

22 C.J. Marcus, *The Age of Nelson. The Royal Navy in the Age of Its Greatest Power and Glory 1793–1815* (New York: Viking Press, 1971), p. 71.
23 Donald Macintyre, *Sea Power in the Pacific. A History from the 16th Century to the Present Day* (London: Military Book Society, 1972), pp. 130–31.
24 Alfred T. Mahan, *Naval Strategy Compared and Contrasted with the Principles and Practice of Military Operations on Land* (Boston: Little, Brown, and Company, 1919), p. 188.
25 David Woodward, *The Russians at Sea. A History of the Russian Navy* (New York: Frederick A. Praeger, Publishers, 1966), pp. 120–21; Macintyre, *Sea Power in the Pacific. A History from the 16th Century to the Present Day* (London: Military Book Society, 1972), pp. 126–27.
26 Herbert Richmond, *Statesmen and Sea Power* (Oxford: Clarendon Press, first published 1946, reprinted 1947), p. 74.
27 M.G. Cook, "Naval Strategy," 2 March 1931, Air Corps Tactical School, Langley Field, VA, 1930–1931, Strategic Plans Division Records, Series, Box 003, Naval Operational Archives, Washington, D.C., p. 18; Stephen B. Luce, "The Navy and Its Needs," *The North American Review*, Vol. 193, No. 665 (April 1911), p. 497.
28 James Stewart, "The Evolution of Naval Bases in the British Isles," *Proceedings*, No. 7 (July 1957), p. 757.
29 Julian S. Corbett, *Naval Operations*, Vol. 1: *To the Battle of Falkland, December 1914* (London: Longmans, Green and Co., 1920), p. 4.
30 Walter Gadow, "Flottenstützpunkte," *Militärwissenschaftliche Rundschau*, No. 4 (April 1936), p. 519.
31 Arthur K. Cebrowski, *Military Transformation Strategic Approach* (Washington, DC: Office of Force Transformation, December 2003), p. 32.
32 Aldo Borge, *The Challenges and Limitations of "Network Centric Warfare" – The Initial Views of an NCW Skeptic* (Barton: Australian Strategic Policy Institute, 17 September 2003), p. 6.
33 Dieter Stockfisch, "Im Spannungsfeld zwischen Technologiefortschritt und Führungsverständniss. Auftragstaktik," *Marineforum*, 12 (December 1996), p. 12.
34 Norbert Bolz, "Wirklichkeit Ohne Gewähr," *Der Spiegel*, 26 June 2000, pp. 130–31.
35 Cited in Azar Gat, *A History of Military Thought from the Enlightenment to the Cold War* (Oxford: Oxford University Press, 2001), p. 118.
36 Arbeitspapier, *Operative Führung* (Hamburg: Führungsakademie der Bundeswehr, August 1992), p. 18.
37 John E. Schlott, *Operational Vision: The Way Means Reach the End* (Fort Leavenworth, KS: School of Advanced Military Studies, United States Army Command and General Staff College, 12 May 1992), p. 21.
38 Michael C. Vitale, "Jointness by Design, Not Accident," *Joint Force Quarterly*, Autumn 1995, p. 27.
39 Elwin F. Cutts, *Operations for Securing Command of the Sea Areas*, Part 1 (Newport, RI: Naval War College, 8–9 July 1938), p. 5.
40 Russell Grenfell, *The Art of the Admiral* (London: Faber & Faber Ltd., 1937), p. 183.
41 David Woodward, *The Russians at Sea. A History of the Russian Navy* (New York: F. A. Praeger, 1966), p. 104.
42 Elwin F. Cutts, *Operations for Securing Command of the Sea Areas*, Part 1 (Newport, RI: Naval War College, 8–9 July 1938), p. 25.
43 Donald Macintyre, *Sea Power in the Pacific. A History from the 16th Century to the Present Day* (London: Military Book Society, 1972), pp. 141, 150.
44 Arthur J. Marder, *From the Dreadnought to Scapa Flow: The Royal Navy in the Fisher Era, 1914–1919*, Vol. II: *The War Years: To the Eve of Jutland* (London: Oxford University Press, 1965), p. 330.
45 Arthur Marder, *From the Dreadnought to Scapa Flow. The Royal Navy in the Fisher Era, 1914–1919*, Vol. II: *The War Years: To The Eve of Jutland* (London: Her Majesty's Stationary Office, 1965), p. 330.

46 Arthur Marder, *From the Dreadnought to Scapa Flow. The Royal Navy in the Fisher Era, 1914–1919*, Vol. II: *The War Years: To the Eve of Jutland* (London: Her Majesty's Stationary Office, 1965), p. 332.

47 S.W.C. Pack, *Sea Power in the Mediterranean. A History from the Seventeenth Century to the Present Day* (London: Arthur Barker Ltd., 1971) p. 181; Michael Salewski, *Die deutsche Seekriegsleitung 1935–1945*, Vol. 1: *1935–1941* (Munich: Bern and Graefe, 1970–1975), pp. 228, 341.

48 Michael Salewski, *Die deutsche Seekriegsleitung 1935–1945*, Vol. 1: *1935–1941* (Munich: Bern and Graefe, 1970–1975), pp. 294–95, 297, 324.

49 Rudolf Heinstein, *Zur Strategie des Mehrfrontenkrieges. Das Problem der "inneren und ausseren Linien" dargestellt am Beispiel des Ersten Weltkrieges* (Hamburg: Führungsakademie der Bundeswehr, 10 November 1975), p. 6; Antoine Henri de Jomini, *The Art of War* (London: Greenhill Books, reprinted 1992), p. 331.

50 Alfred T. Mahan, *Naval Strategy Compared and Contrasted with the Principles and Practice of Military Operations on Land* (Boston: Little, Brown, and Company, 1911), pp. 31–32, 55, 53.

51 Cited in Philip A. Crowl, "Alfred Thayer Mahan: The Naval Historian," in Peter Paret, editor, *Makers of Modern Strategy. From Machiavelli to the Nuclear Age* (Princeton, NJ: Princeton University Press, 1986), pp. 457–58.

52 Rudolf Heinstein, *Zur Strategie des Mehrfrontenkrieges. Das Problem der "inneren und ausseren Linien" dargestellt am Beispiel des Ersten Weltkrieges* (Hamburg: Führungsakademie der Bundeswehr, 10 November 1975), p. 6.

53 Bernard Brodie, *A Layman's Guide to Naval Strategy* (Princeton, NJ: Princeton University Press, 1942), p. 87.

54 Barry M. Gough, "Maritime Strategy: The Legacies of Mahan and Corbett as Philosophers of Sea Power," *RUSI Journal* (Winter 1988), p. 56.

55 Philip A. Crowl, "Alfred Thayer Mahan: The Naval Historian," in Peter Paret, editor, *Makers of Modern Strategy. From Machiavelli to the Nuclear Age* (Princeton, NJ: Princeton University Press, 1986), p. 457.

56 T.G.W. Settle, "The Strategic Employment of the Fleet" (Newport, RI: Staff Presentation, Naval War College, September 18, 1940), p. 18.

57 Cited in Philip A. Crowl, "Alfred Thayer Mahan: The Naval Historian," in Peter Paret, editor, *Makers of Modern Strategy. From Machiavelli to the Nuclear Age* (Princeton, NJ: Princeton University Press, 1986), p. 458.

58 Julian S. Corbett, *Some Principles of Maritime Strategy* (London: Longmans, Green and Co., 1918), pp. 120, 115–16.

59 Julian S. Corbett, *Some Principles of Maritime Strategy* (London: Longmans, Green and Co., 1918), pp. 117, 120.

60 Rene Daveluy, *The Genius of Naval Warfare*. Vol. I: *Strategy* (Annapolis, MD: The United States Naval Institute 1910), pp. 28–29.

61 Cited in Rene Daveluy, *The Genius of Naval Warfare*, Vol. I: *Strategy* (Annapolis, MD: The United States Naval Institute, 1910), pp. 26–27.

62 Rene Daveluy, *The Genius of Naval Warfare*, Vol I: *Strategy* (Annapolis,. MD: The United States Naval Institute, 1910), p. 30.

63 Staff Presentation, "Operations in Sea Areas Under Command, Part 1" (Newport, RI: Naval War College, July 17, 1941), pp. 4–5.

64 Elwin F. Cutts, *Operations for Securing Command of the Sea Areas*, Part 1 (Newport, RI: Naval War College, 8–9 July 1938), p. 8.

65 Elwin F. Cutts, *Operations for Securing Command of Sea Areas*, Part 1 (Newport, RI: Naval War College, 8–9 July 1938), p. 4.

66 Elwin F. Cutts, *Operations for Securing Command of the Sea Areas*, Part 1 (Newport, RI: Naval War College, 8–9 July 1938), pp. 8–9.

67 Elwin F. Cutts, *Operations for Securing Command of the Sea Areas*, Part 1 (Newport, RI: Naval War College, 8–9 July 1938), p. 10.

68 Elwin F. Cutts, *Operations for Securing Command of the Sea Areas*, Part 1 (Newport, RI: Naval War College, 8–9 July 1938), p. 8.
69 T.G.W. Settle, *The Strategic Employment of the Fleet* (Newport, RI: Staff Presentation, Naval War College, September 18, 1940), p. 16.
70 T.G.W. Settle, *The Strategic Employment of the Fleet* (Newport, RI: Staff Presentation, Naval War College, September 18, 1940), p. 16.
71 Günther Pöschel, "Über die Seeherrschaft (III)," *Militärwesen*, No. 8 (August 1982), p. 58.
72 Günther Pöschel, "Über die Seeherrschaft (II)," *Militärwesen* (East Berlin), No. 6 (June 1982), p. 74.
73 Günther Pöschel, "Über die Seeherrschaft (I)," *Militärwesen* (East Berlin), No. 5 (May 1982), p. 41.
74 Günther Pöschel, "Über die Seeherrschaft (I)," *Militärwesen* (East Berlin), No. 5 (May 1982), pp. 41, 45.
75 Günther Pöschel, "Über die Seeherrschaft (III)," *Militärwesen*, No. 8 (August 1982), pp. 57–58.
76 Günther Pöschel, "Über die Seeherrschaft (III)," *Militärwesen* No. 8 (August 1982), p. 59.
77 Stephen W. Roskill, *The War at Sea 1939–1945*, Vol. III: *The Offensive*, Part I, *1st June 1943–31st May 1944* (London: Her Majesty's Stationery Office, 1960), p. 229.
78 Stephen W. Roskill, *The War at Sea 1939–1945*, Vol. III: *The Offensive*, Part I, *1st June 1943–31st May 1944* (London: Her Majesty's Stationery Office, 1960), p. 223.
79 Donald Macintyre, *Sea Power in the Pacific. A History from the 16th Century to the Present* (London: Military Book Society, 1972), p. 160.
80 Staff Presentation, *Operations in Sea Areas under Command*, Part 1 (Newport, RI: Naval War College, July 17, 1941), p. 2.
81 Günther Pöschel, "Über die Seeherrschaft (I)," *Militärwesen* (East Berlin), No. 5 (May 1982), p. 42.
82 Russell Grenfell, *The Art of the Admiral* (London: Faber & Faber Ltd., 1937), p. 183.
83 Günther Pöschel, *Die Rolle und Bedeutung der Seeherrschaft in Vergangenheit und Gegenwart. Analyse der theoretischen Aussagen zum Begriff der Seeherrschaft* (Dresden: Militärakademie "Friedrich Engels," Schriften der Militärakademie, Heft 165, 1978), p. 123.
84 Elwin F. Cutts, *Operations for Securing Command of the Sea* (Newport, RI: Naval War College, 8–9 July 1938), p. 9.

4 Destroying the enemy's forces by a decisive action at sea

The destruction of the enemy's naval forces could be accomplished by a decisive action or their weakening over time. Normally, these two methods are used in combination. The most effective but also most difficult method is by engaging a major part of the enemy forces at sea and/or their bases and destroying them in a short and decisive action. A decisive action should be optimally executed at the beginning of the hostilities at sea. Until the advent of submarines and aircraft, control of the sea was obtained by destroying enemy surface ships. Today, this objective is more difficult to accomplish because control of the surface could be disputed also by enemy submarines, aircraft, and mines.

In the past, a *decisive naval battle* was considered the principal method of employment of naval forces to obtain control of the sea. A decisive naval battle was understood as a clash between major parts of the opposing fleets that results in such damage to one side that it drastically changes naval situation.[1] Still, what mattered the most were not initial intent and the losses inflicted on the opposing fleet or one's losses but whether the ultimate objective was actually accomplished. Sometimes one side inflicted larger losses in materiel and personnel, but that did not necessarily mean that the ultimate objective was accomplished; the opposite was also true. In several notable cases, the results of a decisive naval battle were inconclusive, but one side was able to accomplish its ultimate objective. In a war between two numerically weak fleets, the loss of even a single or a few ships might have a decisive effect on the course of a war at sea, as the example of the War of the Pacific between Chile and Peru/Bolivia (1879–1883) shows.[2]

Naval classical thinkers emphasized the critical importance of a decisive naval battle for obtaining control of the sea. Mahan was perhaps the most consistent and strongest believer in the absolute importance of a decisive battle. He claimed that control of the sea's communications could be obtained only through "decisive battle."[3] Mahan stressed that the "fleet's destruction is an essential prerequisite for the conquest of the enemy's territory and attack on his commerce.[4] The same result would be achieved, though less conclusively and less permanently if the enemy fleet is reduced to inactivity by the immediate presence of a superior force."[5] Similarly,

Admiral Philip Howard Colomb (1831–1899) believed that ". . . it serves no purpose to try to obtain the mastery of the sea by any means than by battle and this is so serious that no other objective can be put in comparison with it."[6]

Castex agreed with Mahan that the enemy "fleet must be defeated in order to obtain command of the sea." He observed that one's actions should be directed against the enemy fleet because its destruction "will very probably irreparably compromise the rest of the enemy's organization." The best method of disposing of the enemy fleet is to wage a decisive naval battle. In case the enemy chooses to "shut himself up in a port," then he should be tightly blockaded in order to prevent his escape or ". . . to force him to do battle as soon as possible if he does."[7] After having dealt with the enemy fleet, the stronger fleet can exercise command of the sea. Yet Castex also cautioned that the stronger fleet should not exercise command of the sea prematurely because that might undermine the freedom of action essential to the destruction of the enemy fleet.[8]

French Navy captain and well-known theoretician René Daveluy (1863–1939) emphasized that to "reduce an enemy to impotence it is necessary to disarm it, that is to say, destroy the established force which is a guarantee of its power. The necessity of attacking the established force of an enemy leads directly to battle."[9] Another French Navy captain, Gabriel Darrieus (1859–1931), wrote that to consider the fleet of the enemy as the principal force that must be destroyed or reduced to impotence is to fulfill most surely the object of the war.[10]

A well-known and influential British theorist, Admiral Herbert Richmond (1871–1946), wrote that the "the first and fundamental step toward gaining the command of the sea is always the destruction of the massed forces of the enemy. If these forces are unwilling to fight, the possibility exists of putting the enemy in the dilemma of either fighting at what may appear to him as a disadvantage or of sacrificing some essential element in his national economy, trade, a vital position, or the assistance of an ally."[11]

In contrast to Mahan and other classical naval thinkers, Corbett contended that to obtain command, it is not always necessary to fight a decisive naval battle. He wrote that "under certain conditions, it may not be the primary function of the fleet to seek out the enemy's fleet and destroy it, because general command may be in dispute, while local command may be with us, and political or military considerations may demand for us an operation for which such local command is sufficient, and which cannot be delayed until we have obtained a complete decision."[12] However, Corbett erred because one cannot obtain local control of the sea without destroying at least a part of the enemy fleet. A stronger side should also avoid the state of disputed, or contested, control. Experience shows that, as in a war on land or in the air, the best way to proceed is in most cases to focus one's efforts on destroying the strongest part of the enemy forces – or the enemy's operational center of gravity. Once this is successfully accomplished, a stronger side would not have great difficulties in accomplishing other operational tasks. Corbett also noted that as long as the weaker fleet remains in existence, it will try to avoid a major clash with its superior opponent.[13] This is probably true. But, again, a stronger side should not just accept that situation without trying to entice or lure a weaker side into a major clash.

Corbett also emphasized difficulties in seeking a decisive battle. He wrote that in land warfare, it is possible to specify with some precision the limits and direction of the enemy movements because they are determined by roads and physical obstacles. This is not the case at sea. In Corbett's view, "seeking to strike out at the enemy at sea the chance is greater that we would miss him.[14] However, experience shows that only a few decisive naval battles have taken place far from the shore. Hence, it was very rare that the opposing fleets did not locate the whereabouts of each other.

In the seventeenth century, opposing fleets fought major battles with a large number of ships of the line. For example, in the First Anglo-Dutch War (1652–1654), each side in a battle had on average some 70 to 120 ships. However, with the increased size, seaworthiness, and greater effectiveness of guns, fleets became numerically smaller. For example, in the Battle of Trafalgar in October 1805, the British had only 27 ships of the line against the Franco-Spanish fleet of 33 ships of the line. The ships of the line were the mainstay of the battle fleets in 1652, as they were in 1805. Yet their lethality was, of course, far less than that of first-rate ships of the line in Nelson's times.[15]

In the era of the oar/sail, a large number of major naval battles were fought. By the eighteenth century, the number of major battles in a war was progressively reduced because the ships of the line became larger, and hence it took much longer time to build them than it did in the seventeenth century. Normally, a decisive naval battle was fought in a single day and lasted for only a few hours. However, in several notable examples, decisive results were achieved by fighting a series of successive minor tactical actions spread over two or more days and sometimes over a relatively large part of a given maritime theater. For example, the British victory over the Spanish Armada in 1588 was achieved through a series of small-scale clashes conducted over seven days in the English Channel. Afterward, a large number of the Spanish ships wrecked in stormy weather while rounding Scotland and Ireland.

In the era of oar/sail, relatively few ships were sunk in major naval battles; most of them were captured. For example, the first three Anglo-Dutch Wars (1652–1654; 1665–1667; 1672–1674; the Fourth Anglo-Dutch War was in 1780–1784) were perhaps the bloodiest of all naval wars; not many ships of the line were sunk, but great damage was inflicted, on both sides, to the masts and riggings and personnel. Only a few commanders, notably Dutch Admiral Michiel Adriaanszoon de Ruyter (1607–1676) and the Danish Admiral Niels Juel (1629–1697), inflicted disproportionate losses on their enemies. In most cases, major parts of the opposing fleets escaped to fight again.[16]

Prior to the era of steam, only relatively few major naval battles were "decisive," that is, either resulting in the destruction of a major part of the enemy fleet or having decisive results on the course and outcome of war at sea or on land. Yet in several cases, a decisive naval battle had a major impact on the course or even outcome of the war on land. In a few notable cases, as, for example, the battles of Salamis in 480 BC and Actium in 31 BC, it has changed world history. However, the decisiveness of a major naval battle apparently declined in the medieval era. As the Anglo-Dutch Wars show, a strong opponent was able to relatively quickly reconstitute its navy and then resume struggle for disputing command of the sea. In the War of Grand Alliance, 1688–1697, naval battles became less decisive than they were in the Anglo-Dutch Wars. Although the French Navy had a combined strength of the British and the Dutch navies, it missed every opportunity to achieve a decisive victory.[17]

A major reason for the lack of decisiveness of naval battles was the relatively low effectiveness of the shipboard guns and the rigid application of the line ahead formation. For more than one hundred years, a war at sea had shown the futility of fighting in an unbroken line ahead with van, center, and rear trying to engage the respective parts of the enemy line.[18] One of the reasons for such a profound lack of thinking was the general lack of interest in the theory of naval tactics by many naval officers.[19] Corbett observed that the reason for the sterility of naval tactics in that era was that "unintelligent admirals, pedantically absorbed in preserving their formation, contented themselves with fighting ship to ship and trying to manoeuvre for a concentration on part of their adversaries' line." He claimed that the system of engaging two battle lines was fully adopted in the Battle of Texel in 1665 (fought on 13 June). It replaced the older system of fighting in groups of ships.[20]

The situation gradually changed for the better in the late eighteenth century when some aggressive and very innovative commanders, specifically British admirals Edward Hawke (1705–1781), Samuel Hood (1724–1816), John Jervis (1735–1823), Adam Duncan (1731–1804), and above all Horatio Nelson (1758–1805), introduced tactical innovations that allowed for far more decisive results. They used maneuver to achieve local concentration and attack exposed parts of the enemy fleet.[21]

In fact, it was a Scottish landlubber and amateur scientist, John Clerk of Eldin, who, in his book *Essay on Naval Tactics, Systematical and Historical* (written in 1779 and published in 1782), gave an answer on how to improve tactics of the battle line. Clerk analyzed fighting instructions and concluded that the Royal Navy's naval tactics were all wrong.[22] He pointed out that during the Anglo-Dutch Wars, naval instructions were much improved but that they were " . . . admirably fitted for fighting in narrow seas, where these battles were fought but not for bringing on an action with a fleet of French ships, unwilling to stand a shock, having sea room to range in at pleasure, and desirous to plays off maneuvers of defence, long studied with the greatest attention."[23] Clerk argued that decisive action can be fought only by concentrating superior forces on weaker forces. In other words, decisive victories could be won only by close, concentrated fighting. Yet his book met with derision by admirals, who believed that they cannot be taught by an amateur.[24] According to some sources, Nelson read Clerk's book.[25] In fact, the commanding officer (CO) of Admiral Nelson's flagship *Victory*, Captain (later Vice Admiral) Thomas M. Hardy (1769–1839), stated that

> Lord Nelson, read Mr. Clerk's works with great attention and frequently expressed his approbation of them in the fullest manner. He also recommended all the captains to read them with attention and said that many good things might be taken from them. He most approved of the attack from to-windward, and considered that breaking through the enemy's line as absolutely necessary to obtain a great victory.[26]

Major changes in the way of how to fight war at sea had its origins in the English Navy (renamed the Royal Navy in 1660). During the Anglo-Dutch Wars a belief took hold in the English Navy that, in a war at sea, one's efforts should be focused on the enemy fleet, not on maritime trade, and thereby on destroying the enemy's power of resistance. Such warfare required the effective use of state-owned ships specialized for war with as little as possible assistance from privately owned ships.[27] It required discipline, fleet tactics, and a navy of warships to make war in the modern sense of the term.[28] The experience in combat led the Royal Navy to adopt the first Articles of War that provided statutory regulations regarding the Royal Navy's crews. The first fighting instructions were issued in 1678. They were revised several times (in 1688, 1690, 1695, and 1702) to allow more initiative on the part of subordinate commanders.[29] The first Permanent Sailing and Fighting Instructions was issued in 1703 during the War of Spanish Succession (1701–1714). They were for the first time used in the naval battle of Málaga on 24 August 1704 and with slight modifications until 1783.[30]

The first three Anglo-Dutch Wars had a major influence on the evolution of the concept of the control of the sea. In the First Anglo-Dutch War (1652–1654), the British attacked the Dutch convoys and blockaded the Dutch coast. Naval battles came as result of one side or the other trying to protect a convoy or making a way free for the convoy.[31] Reportedly, the Dutch Admiral Maarten Tromp (1598–1653) was the first who realized in 1653 the best way to protect a large convoy is to obtain command of the sea.

In the Second Anglo-Dutch War (1665–1667), the Dutch partially stopped their maritime traffic. Both sides tried to obtain command of the sea. Only afterward they would attack maritime trade and blockade the enemy coast. In the Third Anglo-Dutch War (1672–1674), the British and the French attempted to threaten Holland with seaborne invasion in addition to land invasion. A defender was much more under threat than in the previous wars. The struggle for control of the sea in the intervening waters was much more important than in the previous wars. The Anglo-French fleet had to transport and land an invasion army. The Dutch were forced on the defensive because they had a smaller fleet. Hence, they had to make greater efforts to obtain sea control.[32]

Corbett wrote that the English focus of fighting a decisive action in the First Anglo-Dutch War was carried to the extreme. Not much thought was given to exercising control of the sea. Also, the British emphasis on offensive action was the main cause for neglecting the need to sustain combat by bringing in fresh reinforcements. Hence, the British Navy suffered from exhaustion. After the battle, its fleet had to return to its home bases. In some major naval battles, the British inflicted larger losses on the enemy fleet but either failed or were unable to pursue the Dutch fleet. This, in turn, gave the Dutch sufficient freedom of action not only to secure their maritime trade but also to deliver severe blows on British trade.[33] The question was how to induce the Dutch to fight a decisive action. To seek the enemy off his coast and thereby force him to leave his protected bases would not lead to a decisive action. One way was to attack the enemy maritime traffic instead of carrying out sporadic attacks. An effort to stop completely the enemy trade but far away from his coast led to a major naval battle, as the example of the Four Days' Battle in June 1666 illustrates. In the Seven Years' War, Admiral George Anson (1697–1762) tried for two years to secure a decision by seeking out the enemy fleet. Yet he failed, and the British fleet was exhausted.[34]

In a war between two strong opponents, a single or even several major naval battles did not necessarily secure absolute and permanent control of the sea. As the example of the first three Anglo-Dutch Wars illustrate, a strong opponent was able to relatively quickly reconstitute its fleet and then resume the struggle for disputing command of the sea. Sometimes, a weaker fleet was still able to challenge the presence of the stronger fleet even after suffering a major defeat. But even when a weaker fleet was kept under observation, it did not follow that a stronger fleet had secured undisputed control of the sea. An active and energetic enemy, operating from a long coastline endowed with numerous harbors, invariably would take the opportunity to launch attacks and cause a diversion of one's efforts.[35] For example, the Royal Navy, after its great victory in the Battle of Trafalgar in October 1805, still faced the threat posed by the remaining French/Spanish naval forces. Between November 1805 and June 1815, some 87 warships were sunk or captured by the enemy. Also, the victory at Trafalgar did not negate the need to escort merchant ships.[36] In another example, Admiral Heihachirō Tōgō (1848–1934) had to keep close watch on the movements of the remaining Russian ships based at Port Arthur and Vladivostok after his decisive victory at Tsushima in May 1905. The experience also shows that decisive victories at sea were largely wasted if the remnants of the enemy fleet were left at large or if not followed by an invasion of enemy-held territories.

In the era of oar/sail and the early era of steam, most major battles that turned out to have a "decisive" result occurred when one or both sides were carrying out missions that are today considered part of exercising sea control. Most major battles that had decisive results took place while one of the fleets provided cover for or attempted to prevent a large landing, supported army troops operating in the coastal area, protected/attacked a large convoy, or imposed/lifted a naval blockade. In contrast, attacks aimed to destroy an enemy fleet in its anchorage/port did not happen by an accident. Also planned were major battles aimed to prevent an enemy large-scale seaborne invasion, as the Battle of Trafalgar in October 1805 illustrates.

In the era of sail, a large number of major battles between the opposing surface ships took place because of the need to *defend/attack convoys of merchant shipping*. This was especially the case during the first three Anglo-Dutch Wars. For example, in the inconclusive battle off Plymouth on 26 August 1652, both the British and the Dutch claimed victory. Admiral Michiel de Ruyter commanded 30 warships while the British General-at-Sea George Ayscue (ca. 1616–1671) had 40 large warships, eight smaller and four fireships. The Dutch lost more people, but the British fleet suffered more damage. In the aftermath of the battle, Ayscue sailed for Plymouth while de Ruyter assembled the convoy and sailed home.[37]

In the Battle of Kentish Knock on 8 October 1652, the Dutch fleet of 64 warships led by Admirals de Ruyter and Johan de Witt (1625–1672) engaged some 68 British warships under General-at-sea Robert Blake (1598–1657). This battle took place in the areas between Dunkirk and Nieuwpoort.[38] The British claimed to have captured two Dutch warships, and one was burned at no losses for themselves. The Dutch sources claimed 600 dead and wounded and heavy damages to the British ships. De Witt wanted to resume the fight the next day, but a war council decided against doing so because of damages on other Dutch ships. The next day (9 October), the British attempted to pursue the Dutch fleet but abandoned the chase because of the shallows close to the Dutch coast. De Witt's attempt to secure the Dutch maritime trade by attack on the enemy naval force failed. In the aftermath of the battle, the British had greater control of the English Channel.[39]

One of the most decisive naval battles of the First Anglo-Dutch War was fought off Dungeness on 10 December 1652. Because of their victory in the Battle at Kentish Knock, the British expected (wrongly) that the Dutch would not be able to repair their damages and would not reappear at sea. In the meantime, a small English squadron in the Mediterranean was worsted by the Dutch squadron, and the English Mediterranean trade became wholly unprotected. Hence, the British detached some 20 ships to the Mediterranean. This proved to be a big mistake.[40] On 9 December, Blake, with only 37 warships and some small craft, was at Dover when Admiral Tromp, with a fleet of 73 warships plus small craft and fireships, left a 300-ship convoy off the Flemish coast and appeared near Goodwin-Sands.[41] Both fleets clashed the next day at Dungeness. Blake lost five warships (two were captured and three sunk), while Dutch lost only a single ship. For some reason, Tromp did not try to pursue and complete the destruction of the enemy fleet. Such energetic warfare was unknown to him. He was mainly concerned with the safety of the convoy and was satisfied with partial success in the battle.[42]

After the battle off Dungeness, control of the English Channel was for a few weeks in Dutch hands.[43] The English ships were driven into the Thames Estuary. The port of London was closed. The British trade in the Channel was brought to a standstill. The lessons of dividing a fleet were not lost on the British. Afterward, they focused their efforts on defeating the enemy main body, and their Dutch opponents did the same. The Dutch concluded that their fleet should not escort large convoys in the Channel and narrow seas in the presence of a strong British fleet. As for the British, they put all their energies into strengthening their navy and on maintaining superiority in the decisive area.[44]

The situation changed for the better for the British in the aftermath of their victory in the three-day Battle of Portland on 28 February–2 March 1653. This was one of the most decisive battles aimed to protect a large convoy. It encompassed the sea area from Portland to Cap Gris-Nez. The British had ready some 70 warships, many of them newly built. This fleet was under the command of three generals-at-sea: Robert Blake (2598–1657), Richard Deane (1610–1653), and George Monck (1608–1670). Admiral Maarten Tromp (1598–1653) had some 80 ships. Tromp also had the problem of protecting a 250-ship convoy.[45] The Dutch acknowledged the loss of three ships sunk, one captured, and several others burned. The British losses were a single ship sunk and several others, including three or four large warships, damaged. The Dutch had 1,500–2,000 men killed, while the British had some 2,000 dead and wounded.[46] Both sides had large personnel losses.[47] On the last day of the battle, on 1 March near the Isle of Wight, the British captured two Dutch warships and 10 to 12 merchant ships. Many ships that subsequently left the convoy were captured by the British. On 2 March, more Dutch ships were destroyed or captured. By the end of the day, both fleets were near Cap Gris-Nez.[48] The Dutch losses in these three days of fighting were about a dozen warships while the British lost only a single ship.[49] Other sources claimed that the Dutch lost only four warships and 30 merchant vessels; the rest of the convoy managed to escape.[50] The result of this battle was unfavorable for the Dutch because the British fleet obtained control of the Channel.

In the aftermath of the victory at Outer Gabbard in 2-3 June 1653, Oliver Cromwell (Lord Protector of England, Scotland and Ireland) demanded the loss of Holland's sovereignty as the price for peace. The Dutch were unwilling to accept that demand and raised a new fleet to lift the British blockade of their coast. On 8 August 1653, Admiral Tromp with 90 ships came to fight Monck with 100 ships at Katwijk. Tromp was joined the next day by a squadron under de Witt from Texel in the vicinity of Scheveningen. The Dutch penetrated the British blockading line, and in the subsequent mêlée both fleets suffered great losses. The Dutch lost 12 to 13 ships, 500 killed, 700 wounded, plus 700 captured. The British had half of the Dutch losses in ships. Monck won a big victory, but he was unable to conduct a pursuit. He had to leave for England to reconstitute his forces and thereby was forced to lift the blockade of the Dutch coast. This was then used by the Dutch to bring in a large convoy from the Sund and Norway.[51]

Several decisive battles resulted in obtaining local control of the sea, although initially the main purpose was to *support a landing on a hostile shore*. For example, the Battle of Mylae (Milazzo today) in 260 BC during the First Punic War (264–241 BC) took place when the Roman fleet of some 130 ships led by Second Consul Gaius Duilius was on its way to land troops in Sicily. The Roman fleet was opposed by the Carthaginian fleet of some 120–130 ships under Hannibal Gisco (c. 300-290–258 BC).[52] The Carthaginians were overly confident in their better seamanship and had contempt for the Romans as sailors. The Romans were using for the first time the *corvus*, a boarding device that allowed them to transform the fight at sea into land combat. They were successful in grappling some 50 Carthaginian ships, while the remainder of the Carthaginian fleet escaped. Duilius did not pursue the Carthaginians but instead sailed to the western tip of Sicily, where he landed troops just in time to relieve Segesta (Calatafimi-Segesta, southeast of today's Trapani), which was under siege by the Carthaginian commander Hamilcar Barca (ca. 275–228 BC).[53] Afterward, First Consul Lucius Cornelius Scipio (b. ca. 300 BC) landed on Corsica and captured the city of Aléria and expelled the Carthaginians. In 258 BC, Second Consul Gaius Sulpicius Paterculus made several successful attacks on the African coast.[54]

In the Battle of Cape Ecnomus (Poggio di Sant'Angelo, Licata, Sicily, today) in 256 BC, the Roman fleet achieved a decisive victory. Despite vastly exaggerated claims, both the Roman and the Carthaginian fleets probably did not include more than 100 ships.[55] The Carthaginians lost some 30 ships, and 64 other ships were captured, while the Romans lost only 24 ships. The Carthaginian fleet left the area while the Roman fleet returned to Sicily to rest its crews, repair the ships, and repair as many as possible captured enemy ships.[56] After few days of refit on Sicily, the Romans resumed sailing and landed their army on the coast of Africa. However, they were not particularly successful on land. After few years, the Carthaginians restored their strength.[57]

The Battle at Actium on 2 September 31 BC during the Roman Civil War (32–30 BC) between the two leaders of the Second Triumvirate, Gaius

Octavius (Octavian) and Marcus Antonius (Mark Antony) (the third triumvir was Aemilius Lepidus) had a decisive effect on the subsequent history of Rome and Western Civilization. Antony (83–30 BC) was assigned to rule Rome's eastern provinces including Ptolomaic Egypt, ruled by Queen Cleopatra. His military and naval resources were drawn from Asia Minor, Syria, and Egypt. However, he had to leave a strong occupation force in these territories (four legions in Cyrenaica, four in Egypt, and three in Syria). Antony depended on the sea for supplying his army in Epirus. He was unable to carry the war to Italy without possessing control of the sea.[58] His army of about 100,000 men marched from Macedonia to the shore of the Gulf of Ambracia (also known as the Gulf of Arta).[59] Antony's fleet consisted of about 800 ships, including 500 warships (200 were provided by Cleopatra).[60] He embarked some 20,000 legionaries onboard his ships and burned all the ships for which he lacked personnel.[61]

Octavian's naval commander, Marcus Vipsanius Agrippa commanded some 230 beaked ships and 30 unbeaked. The majority of his ships were triremes and quadriremes. Many were light, swift galleys – *liburnae* (built by the Dalmatian pirates).[62]

In the ensuing battle, Antony lost some 200 ships while about 5,000 men were killed. Cleopatra and Antony fled the scene of battle with about 60 ships. Afterward, the opposing armies faced each other for one week before terms of surrender were agreed. After Antony's legions in Cyrenaica and Syria heard about the defeat in the battle of Actium, they went over to Octavian. It took Octavian another year before he invaded Egypt and finally defeated Antony.[63]

Octavian's victory in the battle at Actium transformed the Mediterranean into a Roman lake and established *Pax Romana* on both land and sea.[64] It secured the unity of the Roman Empire for some three hundred years[65] and saved the Roman Empire from probable dissolution. For the first time in history, a single people held absolute sway over the entire Mediterranean.[66]

One of the most important decisive naval battles in history was the British defeat of the Spanish Armada in 1588. The strategic objective of the Spanish King Phillip II (1527–1598) was to overthrow Queen Elizabeth I (1533–1603) and the Tudor dynasty and rule England by force. The main reason for Phillip II's decision to invade was to stop England's interference and subsidies to rebels in the Spanish possessions in the Low Countries, principally the Dutch provinces[67] and thereby stop English interference in the Spanish Netherlands. The Spanish King Phillip II directed the commander of the expedition, Duke Medina Sidonia (1550–1615), to sail up to the Thames Estuary and then to cover a landing on English soil of about 17,000 men [led by General Alexander Farnese, Duke of Parma (1635–1689)], deployed in Flanders. Medina Sidonia would be involved in combat only if Farnese's troops could not be landed without enemy opposition.[68]

The Spaniards assembled a large fleet to cover the projected invasion of England. When it sailed out from La Coruña on 23 July 1588, Medina

Sidonia had under his command 137 warships and 27,500 men (including 7,000 seamen and 17,000 soldiers), plus some 60 cargo vessels with 6,000 men.[69] The Armada included 20 galleons, four galleasses and galleys each, 44 armed merchantmen, 23 transports, and 35 smaller vessels.[70] The British fleet consisted of 197 ships (including 23 ships that voluntarily joined during the fight) with about 16,000 men.[71]

After many delays, the powerful armada approached the western entrance to the English Channel. The British main fleet was then deployed at Plymouth while one squadron was at the Thames Estuary. The first clashes between the British ships and the Armada took place off Plymouth and Portland on 21 and 22–23 July, respectively. Yet Medina Sidonia continued to sail up the Channel and anchored off Calais.[72] On 29 July, the largest battle took place near the small port of Gravelines in the Flanders. The Spanish losses were very heavy. By the nightfall of 29 July, they lost 11 ships and 3 ships sunk from English gunfire that evening plus 8 ships lost from other causes. A large number of the Spanish ships were heavily damaged. The Spaniards had much larger personnel losses than the British: 600 dead and 800 wounded. The British losses were only 50–100 dead. The Armada never recovered from the losses it suffered from the English guns in the Battle of Gravelines.[73]

In the aftermath, Medina Sidonia was unable to make a junction with the army in Flanders and effectively gave control of the Channel to the British fleet. The British ships went home to replenish stores, fearing another Spanish attempt to land. Because the return route to Spain via the Channel was blocked, Medina Sidonia decided to take advantage of the southerly wind and return home by sailing through the Channel, across the North Sea, and then around Scotland and Ireland. However, he lost some 50 ships in a heavy weather while rounding Scotland and Ireland.[74] The remaining 65 ships, with some 10,000 starved and fever-stricken men, reached home waters by the end of September.[75] The total Spanish losses in personnel were very heavy – some 20,000 dead.[76] The British victory led eventually to the collapse of the Spanish power.[77] It restored the strategic initiative to England. It led England to create a large maritime empire and ultimately acquire the status of world power. Also, the defeat of the Spanish Armada led to the rise of Dutch sea power.[78]

In the Battle of Solebay (also called the Battle of Southwold Bay) on 7 June 1672 (during the Third Anglo-Dutch War), the Dutch Admiral Michiel Adriaenszoon de Ruyter (1607–1676) defeated a combined Anglo-Dutch fleet and thereby prevented the landing of an invasion army and broke up England's attempt to blockade the Dutch coast.[79] The Anglo-French fleet under the Duke of York, consisting of 71 ships (45 English and 26 French), faced the Dutch fleet of 61 ships led by Admiral Michiel de Ruyter. The allies also had 16 small ships, 35 transports, and two dozen fireships, while the Dutch fleet had 14 small ships, 22 transports, and three dozen fireships. The Anglo-French ships carried 5,100 guns and 33,000 men while the Dutch ships had 4,500 guns and 21,000 men. In addition, the allies had some 2,000 soldiers ready for embarkation at Dunkirk.[80] In the ensuing battle, the British lost four and the Dutch only two ships.[81] Yet both sides suffered heavy losses in personnel: 2,500 killed and wounded on board the English ships, while Dutch losses were about 2,000 killed and wounded. Both sides claimed victory. However, de Ruyter was a clear victor. He remained another night in the vicinity of the enemy fleet and left the area on the second night without being pursued.[82]

In two battles off Schooneveldt (near the Scheldt River Estuary) on 7 June and 14 June 1673, the Dutch fleet under de Ruyter engaged a much stronger combined Anglo-French fleet commanded by Prince Rupert of the Rhine (1619–1682). The Dutch fleet had some 64 ships and about 14,700 men. The Anglo-French fleet consisted of 86 ships and some 24,300 men. The first battle ended inconclusively; the Dutch lost a single ship while the allies lost two. Both sides suffered almost equal damage.[83] The second battle was also inconclusive; neither side lost ships.[84] However, a dozen of the British ships suffered heavy damage, while the Dutch had only a few ships damaged. The British lost nearly 2,000 men while Dutch losses were half that many. As a result, the allies had to abandon their plan for landing in the United Provinces. Also, the route for the arrival of a large Dutch convoy became open.[85] This dual naval battle is considered a Dutch victory.[86] De Ruyter obtained control of the sea for the next six to seven weeks. He was able to keep scouting ships close to the British coast, while his main fleet was at anchor at Schooneveldt. He also sent a squadron of 28 ships to reconnoiter the Thames Estuary. On 3 July 1673, he left his anchorage with the entire fleet to demonstrate to the British that the Dutch held command of the sea and was not destroyed, as the rumors were then circulated in England and Europe.[87]

During the War of the Grand Alliance, the French fleet was preparing to transport a Franco-Irish army to Ireland to restore James II to the English throne.[88] The plan was that Admiral Anne-Hilarion de Costentin, Count de Tourville (1642–1701) would command some 50–60 ships of the line (13 of these would come from Toulon). However, the Toulon squadron under Admiral Victor-Marie D'Estrees (1660–1737) never arrived.[89] Tourville had available only 44 ships of the line. Yet he received a direct order from Louis XIV that he had to engage the enemy regardless of the size the enemy force.[90] To prevent invasion, the Anglo-Dutch fleet of 82 ships engaged Tourville's squadron near Cape Barfleur on 29 May 1692.[91] The battle was tactically inconclusive. The French did not lose any ships, although they suffered heavy damages.[92] In the battle off La Hague on 2 June, some 99 Anglo-Dutch ships of the line engaged 44 French ships. In the initial clash, neither side lost a single ship. It was only during the four-day-long retreat that Tourville lost some 15 ships of the line.[93] The British pursued the withdrawing French fleet all the way to Cherbourg.[94] In the aftermath, the Anglo-Dutch fleet controlled the Channel. However, except for some minor actions, the Anglo-Dutch fleet was generally passive.[95]

The main reasons for the French defeat were the rigid orders issued by King Louis XIV and the execution of those orders by Tourville.[96] Although the French replaced the lost ships of the line, far more important was the psychological effect of the defeat on the French king, the Navy, and population at large. The public was accustomed to the glories and successes of Louis XIV.[97] In the aftermath of the Cape Barfleur/La Hague battles, the French radically changed their strategy. They gave up on the employment of their navy against the enemy fleet and focused on the war against the enemy maritime commerce. For the next five years, the French Navy mostly conducted commerce raiding (*guerre de course*, "war of the chase") against the allies.[98] As result, it decayed as a combat force. Mahan wrote that the main reason was not defeat at Cape Barfleur/La Hague but the exhaustion of France and the great cost of the continental wars.[99] Admiral Richmond wrote that the French losses were not greater than what the allies suffered in the battle of Beachy Head. However, the allies with their greater resources could recover from their defeat, while the French, lacking such resources, could not. The French fleet continued to operate at sea, but attempts to regain control of the Channel were abandoned.[100]

One of the most decisive naval battles in the era of sail was the Battle of Trafalgar on 20 October 1805, fought to indirectly prevent an enemy landing. The British Admiral Horatio Nelson's 27 ships of the line met and decisively defeated 33 Franco-Spanish ships of the line (15 were Spanish), led by Admiral Pierre-Charles Villeneuve (1763–1806). The British objective was to prevent the Franco-Spanish fleet from reaching Brest and then cover the then widely believed Napoleon I's intent to invade England. Although the British lost no ships, many of their ships were badly damaged. Their casualties were about 1,700. The British captured 14 enemy ships while 11 ships withdrew to Cádiz, where they were promptly blockaded by Admiral Cuthbert Collingwood (1748–1810).[101] Four surviving French ships of the line were captured on 4 November. The Franco-Spanish casualties were 2,600 dead and 7,000 prisoners (including Admiral Villeneuve).[102]

Victory at Trafalgar freed England from further threats of invasion, secured its naval predominance, and offered the prospect of more energetic efforts in the war on land. However, that was not immediately known because of Napoleon I's decisive victories at Ulm in October and at Austerlitz in December 1805. It was only later that the British forces took a conspicuous part in the Peninsular Campaign and elsewhere.[103]

Many influential historians believed that the defeat of the Franco-Spanish fleet at Trafalgar ruined Napoleon I's plan to invade England. However, Napoleon I had decided even before Villeneuve arrived in Cádiz in August 1805 to move his army against the Austrians (which eventually led to the siege of Ulm and the surrender of some 27,000 Austrian troops on 19 October 1805).[104] Mahan wrote, "Trafalgar was not only the greatest and most momentous victory won either by land or by seas during the whole Revolutionary War . . . No victory and no series of victories of Napoleon produced the same effect on Europe. . . . A generation passed after Trafalgar before France again seriously threatened England at sea." For Napoleon I, the prospect of defeating the British Navy vanished. In Mahan's view, the defeat at Trafalgar forced Napoleon I either to impose his rule on all Europe or to abandon the hope of conquering Great Britain. Hence, he tried to compel every state on the continent to exclude British commerce and thereby exhaust the British resources if it continued the war.[105] Napoleon I issued the Berlin Decrees on 21 November 1806, which imposed a Continental Blockade against all trade with Britain. They were followed by the Milan Decrees in December 1807. The blockade stretched from Spain to Russia. The ultimate objective was to weaken Great Britain and force it to accept peace.[106]

A well-known and highly influential British general and theoretician, J.F.C. Fuller (1878–1966), asserted that Nelson's victory in the Battle of Trafalgar on 20 October 1805 had a profound effect. Among other things, it shattered forever Napoleon I's dream of an invasion of England. It allowed England to become an undisputed master of the oceans that eventually led to *Pax Britannica*. Without Trafalgar, there would be no victory in the Peninsular War (1807–1814), and it is "hard to believe that there would ever have been a Waterloo.[107]

In the Battle of Lissa on 20 July 1866, a weaker but much better led and trained Austrian fleet defeated the Italian fleet and thereby obtained command of the Adriatic. The original intent of the Austrians was to prevent the Italians from landing and capturing the critically important island of Lissa (Vis today) in the central Adriatic. Italian Admiral Carlo Pellion di Persano (1806–1883) commanded a force consisting of 12 modern ironclads (totaling 46,000 tons), and 23 wooden ships (frigates, gunboats, dispatch vessels, and transports totaling 28,000 tons).[108] However, instead of focusing on the destruction of the incoming enemy fleet and thereby obtaining sea control, he unwisely engaged shore batteries as a preliminary to the landing ashore. Persano was surprised by the sudden appearance of the Austrian squadron under Admiral Wilhelm von Tegetthoff (1827–1871).[109] The Austrian squadron was greatly inferior to the Italians in the number of modern ships and guns. Its total tonnage was some 47,000 tons. It consisted of seven screw frigates (totaling 27,000 tons), seven screw wooden frigates, one steam-powered two-decker, and nine gunboats (totaling 20,000 tons).[110] Tegetthoff realized before departing the Fasana roadstead in Pola (Pula today) on 19 July that the only way to achieve victory was to use some unorthodox method of engaging the enemy fleet.[111] In the ensuing clash that quickly became a mêlée, the Austrians rammed and sunk two Italian ironclads while two other ships were heavily damaged. The Italians also had 38 officers and 574 men killed and 40 wounded, plus 19 captured. The Austrian losses were only one steam-powered two-decker damaged, 38 dead, and 138 wounded. However, Tegetthoff was unable to pursue the enemy fleet because his ships were slower.[112] The Italians had forgotten that the true strength of a fleet resided not in excellence of weapons alone but also

in the training and quality of personnel. The Italian fleet lacked organization, discipline, and sea training. Its crews were raw and unskilled in gunnery, and its officers were inexperienced.[113]

The Austrian victory not only determined the question of command in
the Adriatic but also had a highly positive effect for Austria on the peace
settlement. On the same day that the Battle of Lissa was fought, the armistice ended the hostilities between Austria and Prussia on the land front.
The Austrians withdraw to the Isonzo River and thereby left Venice in Italian hands. France and Prussia pressured Italy to conclude an armistice on
its own with Austria. Yet the Italian Prime Minister Bettino Ricasoli refused
the call and insisted on obtaining "natural" frontiers for Italy. These
included the direct cession of Venice and the South Tyrol and a guarantee that Italian interests in Istria would be respected. However, the Italian
government ignored the fact that Tegetthoff had won command of the sea
and that the Austro-Prussian armistice had strengthened Vienna's hand.[114]
On 12 August 1866, Austria and Italy signed an armistice at Cormons. The
peace treaty was signed on 3 October 1866. Although Austria was forced to
cede Venice to Italy, it was able to retain control of the rest of the Adriatic
coast.[115]

The Battle of the Yalu River on 17 September 1894 was the largest naval
engagement of the Sino-Japanese War of 1894–1895. It ended in a decisive Japanese victory. The battle was the result of the Chinese landing of
some 5,000 troops at the estuary of the Yalu River on 16 September. The
transports were escorted by Chinese warships.[116] The Chinese squadron
consisted of 14 ships (two armorclads, four cruisers, six protected cruisers,
two corvettes and torpedo boats each), while the Japanese squadron was
composed of 12 ships (three armorclads, seven protected cruisers and one
corvette, plus one gunboat and transport each).[117] The Chinese losses were
heavy: five ships sunk and three damaged. The Japanese had only four ships
damaged. The Chinese crews fought bravely but lacked skills. Perhaps the
most important effect of the battle was that the Chinese fighting spirit had
been broken.[118] In the aftermath of the battle, the Chinese fleet withdrew
to Lueshunkou for repairs and then to Weihaiwei. The Japanese did not
attempt to pursue the Chinese ships. The Chinese fleet was later destroyed
in the Battle of Weihaiwei on 20 January–12 February 1895.

Some decisive naval battles were fought to recapture an important position and/or to *prevent further enemy conquest*, as was the Battle of Lepanto
on 7 October 1571 in the Gulf of Corinth, the Ionian Sea. The Christian
fleet of the Holy League, composed of Venice, Spain, Sardinia, Genoa, and
the Papal States, plus several other Italian states under the command of
the Hapsburg Prince Don John of Austria (1547–1578), inflicted a heavy
defeat on the Ottoman fleet. Venice's objective was to destroy the Turkish
fleet and thereby regain Cyprus (lost in 1570). Spain was not particularly
interested in the Mediterranean commerce because its interests were primarily in Peru and Mexico. However, the Spaniards wanted the Turks to be

crushed so that they would not threaten its possessions in Italy (Kingdom of Sardinia) and the Spanish commerce in the Mediterranean.[119] On 7 October, the Christian fleet consisted of 108 Venetian and 81 Spanish galleys, along with 32 galleys provided by the pope and other smaller states, plus six Venetian galleasses.[120] The Christian ships carried 84,000 men, including 20,000 soldiers. The Turkish fleet under Sufi Ali Pasha (d. 1571) consisted of 210 galleys with about 75,000 men (50,000 sailors and 25,000 soldiers).[121] The Turks had the numerical superiority, but their perhaps greatest advantage was psychological. The Ottoman armies and fleets were the terror of Europe. Nevertheless, the Christian ships were better armed and their soldiers better armed and protected.[122]

In the ensuing Battle at Lepanto (Naupaktos or Nafpaktos today) on the northern coast of the Gulf of Corinth, the Christian fleet inflicted huge losses on the Ottoman fleet. The Turkish losses were heavy: 107 galleys were captured, and 80 burned and sunk.[123] They had 25,000 men killed and 3,500 captured. About 15,000 slaves (12,000 were Christians) were liberated.[124] Only about 60 Turkish ships, with 10,000–12,000 men, escaped.[125] The Christians lost only 13 ships, but about 7,700 men (4,800 Venetians, 2,000 Spaniards, and 800 Papalini) were killed in combat, and about 8,000 were wounded.[126] Defeat in the Battle of Lepanto was a major blow to the Turkish sultan Selim II's prestige.[127] The Christian victory saved the Venetian-controlled islands of Corfu and Zante in the Ionian Sea and most of Dalmatia from Turkish conquest.[128]

A relatively large number of major naval battles were fought to *provide support to the army* operating in the coastal area. For example, one of the most decisive naval battles in history, the Battle of Salamis in August (or September) 480 BC, was aimed to cut off the Persian army's retreat from mainland Greece. In the Second Persian Invasion of Greece (480–479 BC), King Xerxes I (519–465 BC) led an army of only about 20,000.[129] The Persians had about 1,000 ships and the Greeks 367 ships.[130] Athens and its allies (Sparta and Corinth) The battle was conducted over three days and coincided with the land battle at Thermopylae.[131] The Persians lost about 200 and the Greeks about 40 ships.[132]

In the aftermath of the Battle of Salamis, the morale of the Persians was broken. The Phoenician contingent, terrified of harsh treatment and the reproaches of Xerxes I, slipped their cables secretly at night and sailed for home.[133] In 479 BC, the Greeks won a great victory at Mycale (east of the island of Samos) on or about 27 August 479 BC by destroying the remnants of the Persian fleet.[134] The Battle of Salamis ended all Persian attempts to conquer Greece. It essentially saved the Greek and Western Civilization and thereby changed the history of the world.

In the Peloponnesian War (431–404 BC), Sparta's commander Lysander (d. 395 BC), with an inferior force, captured all but nine (some sources say 20) out of 180 ships of the Athenian fleet off the mouth of the Aegospotami River (across from the Hellespont) in 405 BC. The battle lasted about one hour.[135] This victory allowed the Spartans to advance to Athens and force the Athenians to surrender in April 404 BC.

During the First Punic War (264–241 BC), in the battle of the Aegetes Islands (near Lilybaeum) in 242 BC, the Romans inflicted a heavy defeat on the hitherto much more successful Carthaginians. The Romans did not decide until 243 BC to build a fleet. Afterward, they constructed some 200 quinqueremes.[136] The Carthaginians assembled a fleet of some 250 ships and sent it to Sicily. The Romans proved to be much superior in seamanship than were the Carthaginians. They sunk some 50 enemy ships and captured another 70.[137] They also taking some 10,000 prisoners.[138] Their own losses were 30 ships sunk and 50 crippled. Many Carthaginian ships escaped, and the Romans were unable to pursue them.[139] This naval battle decided the outcome of the struggle on Sicily. The Carthaginian army under Hamilcar Barca and the few strongholds left in Sicily were utterly isolated. The Romans starved the Punic garrisons on Sicily. Both Rome and Carthage were exhausted. However, it was Carthage that sued for peace.[140] Carthage was forced to evacuate Sicily. Afterward, the Romans were masters of both the sea and land.[141] Carthage lacked either the will or resources to restore its previous naval dominance.[142]

The Battle of Naoluchus (at the northwestern tip of Sicily, some ten miles from Messina), on 29 or 30 August 36 BC, had a decisive effect in the civil war between Octavian [later emperor Augustus (63 BC–AD 14)] and Sextus Pompey (67 –35 BC), which was also called the "Sicilian Revolt" (44–36 BC).[143] Octavian's fleet, led by Agrippa (64/63–12 BC), defeated the fleet led by Sextus Pompey. Octavian landed three legions on Sicily, and these forces were supplied by the sea. Pompey's position became desperate, and he assembled some 280 ships at Messana. Agrippa's fleet consisted of some 130 vs. Pompey's 150–160 ships. Pompey's fleet was predominantly composed of smaller and faster ships that were better suited for fighting pirates. Agrippa won a decisive victory. He lost only three ships, while Pompey lost 28 ships, 17 ships escaped, and the remainder were captured.[144] Pompey escaped to Messana and then fled to the east, ending Pompey's resistance to the Second Triumvirate.

The outcome of the American Revolutionary War (1775–1783) was essentially decided by the British defeat and subsequent surrender of some 8,000 British troops under General Charles Cornwallis (1738–1805) in the Siege of Yorktown on 19 September 1781. This defeat was not militarily catastrophic but had an enormous political and psychological impact. Among other things, it fatally undermined Parliament's confidence in the British government.[145] The French fleet under Admiral François Joseph Paul de Grasse (1722–1788) made a major contribution to that victory in the Battle of the Chesapeake (or Virginia Capes) on 5 September 1781. This battle was a result of an agreement between General George Washington and the French General Jean-Baptiste Donatien de Vimeur de Rochambeau (1725–1807) on 21 May 1781. Both then agreed that the effort of the French West Indies Fleet should be directed against either New York or the Chesapeake.[146] De Rochambeau notified de Grasse that he personally would prefer Chesapeake because the French government refused to provide force for the siege of New York. By 15 August, the allied generals knew that de Grasse's fleet would reach Chesapeake. The French governor of Cap Francoise (Cap-Haïtien today) spared a force of 3,500 men upon the condition that the Spanish squadron would anchor at the place that de Grasse had procured. The governor also raised money for the Americans from the governor of Havana. De Grasse arrived at Lynnhaven within the Chesapeake (near Cape Henry) on 30 August. He had 28 ships of the line. On 25 August, the French squadron of eight ships of the line led by Commodore Jacques-Melchior Saint-Laurent, Count de Barras (1719–1793) sailed out of Newport, Rhode Island, to join de Grasse.[147]

Some 2,500 American troops under Washington and 4,000 French troops under de Rochambeau crossed the Hudson River on 24 August and then continued their advance toward the head of the Chesapeake Bay. Their objective was to defeat the British troops under Cornwallis.[148] After he heard about de Grasse's departure, British Admiral George Brydges Rodney (1718–1792), then in the West Indies, sent 14 ships of the line under Admiral Samuel Hood (1724–1816) to the North American waters. Because of his illness, Rodney left the West Indies for England. Hood reached Chesapeake Bay three days before de Grasse did. After reconnoitering the Chesapeake Bay and finding it empty, he sailed to New York, where he met five ships of the line under Admiral Thomas Graves (1725–1802), who as a senior officer took command of the entire force. Graves left for Chesapeake Bay on 31 August. He hoped to intercept de Barras before he joined de Grasse.[149] De Grasse, expecting de Barras to arrive, remained outside Chesapeake Bay for five days without taking any action against the British fleet.[150]

On 5 September, Graves appeared with 19 ships of the line in the vicinity of Cape Henry. Graves was surprised not to find the enemy fleet in Chesapeake Bay.[151] He believed that de Grasse had 14 ships of the line. However, de Grasse had under his command 24 ships of the line. That same day, de Grasse received a request from George Washington to support his troops on the move from Philadelphia to Virginia. De Grasse assigned seven ships of the line to that task but wanted to wait on the return of his boats before deploying them. In the meantime, de Grasse received information about appearance of the British fleet.[152]

In the ensuing clash, only Graves' van and center became heavily engaged; yet de Grasse extricated his ships and returned to the Chesapeake Bay.[153] Graves left the scene of action for New York with 18 ships of the line in order to repair damaged ships. The British lost some 90 men killed and 246 men wounded. The French losses were about 200 men.[154] Graves failed to bring badly needed reinforcements to Cornwallis. The lack of naval support made Cornwallis's end inevitable.[155] On 14 September, de Grasse transported American and French troops to the proximity of Yorktown, where they joined with troops of Gilbert du Motier, Marquis de Lafayette (1757–1834). By 28 September, Yorktown was completely encircled by the American and French troops. De Grasse remained in the area until 5 November, when he left for West Indies.[156]

De Grasse suffered eventual defeat in the Battle of Saints (between Dominica and Guadalupe) on 12 April 1782. His fleet of 29 ships of the line met 34 British ships of the line under Rodney and Hood. Seven French ships were captured, including the flagship. Within a week two, more ships were captured. However, this great British victory came too late to affect the outcome of the American Revolutionary War.[157]

Some major battles have taken place when a weaker side tried to either *prevent the establishment of, or lift the existing naval blockade* by a stronger side. For example, in the Third Anglo-Dutch War, the Battle of Lowestoft on 13 June 1665 was fought because the Dutch tried to prevent a second blockade of their coast by the British. The British fleet of some 110 ships under the Duke of York inflicted a heavy defeat on the Dutch fleet under Jacob van Wassenaer Obdam.[158] The Dutch lost some 17 ships and 4,000 men while the British lost only two ships and 800 men. Yet the Duke of York, for some reason, failed to pursue the withdrawing Dutch ships.[159]

The British victory in the Battle of Cape of St. Vincent on 14 February 1797 allowed the subsequent blockade of the Spanish fleet. The British fleet of 15 ships of the line plus five frigates and two smaller ships under Admiral John Jervis encountered the Spanish fleet of 24 ships of the line, seven frigates plus one brig and four armed merchantmen led by Admiral José de Córdoba y Ramos (1732–1815) on the way to Cádiz. The Spanish fleet had passed the Strait of Gibraltar on 5 February 1797.[160] Its task was first to cover a convoy carrying quicksilver and then to join the French squadron at Brest for the planned invasion of England.[161] However, because of unfavorable winds, Córdoba's squadron was pushed much farther into the Atlantic than intended. As result, it was unable to reach Cádiz before it was intercepted by the British fleet. In the ensuing clash, the British captured four ships of the line, including two three-deckers.[162] Some ten Spanish and five British ships of the line were heavily damaged. The Spanish had 260 dead and 350 wounded. The British losses were only 73 dead and about 400 wounded.[163] Jervis did not pursue the beaten enemy. He was not a commander who would take a substantial risk for a doubtful further gain. In the aftermath of the battle, Jervis imposed a blockade on Cádiz.[164] The Spanish fleet at Cádiz remained blockaded until the Treaty of Amiens in March 1802.

Only relatively few decisive naval battles were planned from the outset to *obtain control of the sea.* For example, at the beginning of the Hundred Years' War (1337–1453), the British obtained command of the "narrow sea" (the English Channel) after decisively defeating the French fleet in the Battle of Sluys (on the inlet between west Flanders and Zeeland) (also called the Battle of l'Ecluse). In 1338, the French King Phillip VI started hostilities at sea. Two years later, the British King Edward III declared himself king of

France. He wanted to start new conquests, although he did not have a navy. Hence, he demanded from various parts of England that all ships 100 tons and larger to be in his service. Edward III also planned to have a strong army to be transported to the port Sluys, near Damme in Flanders. He put some 200 ships to sea on 22 June 1340. The next day, this force was joined by some 50 ships. The French fleet of some 400 ships (only 190 were large ships) appeared at Blankenberge, about 10 nm west of Sluys.[165] In the battle on 24 June, the French fleet suffered a major defeat, and the British suffered no losses. This battle was decisive because the British for the first time obtained one of four narrow seas washing their shores.[166]

The Battle of Outer Gabbard (also known the Battle of North Foreland) on 2-3 June 1653 was fought primarily for control of the English Channel and the North Sea. It was the bloodiest and greatest battle of the entire First Anglo-Dutch War (1652–1654).[167] On 11 June, the English fleet, led by General-at-Sea George Monck (1608–1670), was anchored at Yarmouth, and the Dutch fleet under de Ruyter was some 12 nm northeast at North Foreland. Monck left the anchorage and moved to a position some 15 nm southwest of Oxfordness and just outside of Gabbard Sand.[168] On 12 June, the Dutch fleet under overall command of Admiral Tromp consisted of 98 ships and eight fireships. The British fleet had 105 warships, including five fireships and some 30 armed merchantmen with 16,550 men and 3,840 guns.[169] For the first time, almost the entire fleet of both sides faced each other.[170] The encounters took place along the entire length of the English Channel and ended at Nieuwpoort, Flanders. In the battle at North Foreland-Nieuwpoort, on 12 and 18 June, the Dutch offered strong resistance. By the end of the day, Monck received reinforcements of 18 ships. A much larger clash took place on 13 June. Tromp was forced to move closer to the Dutch coast because of the shortage of ammunition on board many of his ships. There was panic on board the Dutch ships.[171]

In the three days of clashes, the British inflicted heavy losses on the Dutch fleet: 11 warships (including six sunk and two burned) and 1,350 prisoners. They did not lose a single ship but had some 120 killed and 236 wounded.[172] The British were not able to destroy larger part of the enemy fleet because they had to break off the fight due to the coming darkness and waters that were becoming too shallow for their large ships. This allowed the Dutch fleet to reach its ports the next morning,[173] having withdrawn in great disarray. The British exploited their victory by establishing a close blockade of the Dutch coast from Nieuwpoort to Texel.[174]

The British defeat in the Four Days' Battle on 1–4 June 1666 (during the Second Anglo-Dutch War) allowed the Dutch to obtain control of the English Channel and close the mouth of the Thames to trade.[175] It was the longest and most difficult and bitter naval battle of the first three Anglo-Dutch Wars.[176] The British objective was to destroy the Dutch naval power before it became much stronger. Another objective was to end Dutch commerce raiding against English trade. The British fleet of about 80 ships was commanded by Monck. Prior to the battle, the British king Charles II was mistakenly informed that the French squadron was on its way to join the Dutch fleet. In what proved to be a costly mistake, he divided the fleet by detaching some 20 ships under Prince Rupert of the Rhine westward to meet the French while the remainder under Monck went eastward to meet the Dutch.[177] The Dutch fleet of about 100 ships was led by one of the best commanders in the Anglo-Dutch Wars, Admiral Michiel de Ruyter.[178] He had to start battle without waiting on the arrival of the Duke of Beaufort.[179] The battle commenced off the Northforeland coast with an English attack. In the ensuing engagement, some 20 British ships were lost. The British also had 5,000 killed and wounded and 3,000 prisoners. The Dutch losses were only four ships and 2,000–2,500 men.[180] The arrival of Dutch reinforcements led Monck to withdraw to the Thames Estuary. So did Prince Rupert with his squadron (delayed by bad weather), on 3 June. The next day, de Ruyter blockaded the Thames Estuary.[181] Although the Dutch achieved a great victory, they were unable to exploit it by destroying the remnants of the enemy fleet. The Dutch fought valiantly, but in contrast to the British they lacked discipline.[182] Mahan wrote that the British defeat was largely due to dividing their fleet.[183]

In the War of Grand Alliance, the French achieved their greatest naval victory in the Battle of Beachy Head (the Battle of Bévéziers for the French) on 10 July 1690. The French fleet of 70 ships was lead by Admiral Tourville. The combined Anglo-Dutch fleet of 56 ships was under the command of Admiral Arthur Herbert (Lord Torrington) (1648–1716).[184] The battle took place some 12 nm south of Beachy Head (near Eastburne, East Sussex).[185] The French objective was to destroy British and Dutch power at sea.[186] The battle was a mêlée, in which the French did not lose a single ship. The English gave allied losses as only eight ships. Yet out of 22 ships, only three remained operational; all were heavily damaged.[187] Tourville was able to capture a number of the damaged allied vessels.[188] However, he made a big mistake in ordering a pursuit but not general chase. The reason was that he wanted to keep his line ahead formation, so his pursuit was very sluggish. This allowed the Anglo-Dutch fleet to escape to the Thames Estuary.[189] The Battle of Beachy Head was a great victory but it was not decisive because Tourville failed to consolidate his combat success.[190] In the aftermath, the French had for some ten weeks unopposed control of the English Channel. Tourville's victory did not have any influence on the land war in Ireland (where King James II wanted to ultimately regain the British throne).[191] Both Tourville and Herbert were dimissed because their respectvie governments found their peformance wanting.

In the Russo-Japanese War of 1904–1905, the Japanese fleet under Admiral Heihachirō Tōgō inflicted a crushing defeat on the Russian Baltic Squadron under Admiral Zinovy P. Rozhdestvensky (1848–1909) in the Battle of Tsushima on 27–28 May 1905. As a result, the Japanese obtained full control of the Yellow Sea.[192] The Japanese had two main divisions with a total of four battleships and eight armored cruisers backed by 16 light cruisers organized in four divisions.[193] The Russian squadron consisted of twelve 13,600-ton battleships organized in three divisions, one small battleship, three armored cruisers, one squadron of four smaller cruisers, four scouting cruisers, and nine destroyers.[194] The Japanese also had a great speed advantage: 15 vs. 9 knots.[195] The Russian losses were heavy; 21 ships sunk, including six battleships, 4,500 men killed, plus, 5,920 captured. Only one cruiser and two destroyers escaped and reached Vladivostok. The Japanese lost only three torpedo boats. Not a single Japanese ship was heavily damaged.[196] The Japanese had about 120 men killed and 583 wounded.[197] The main reason for the Russian defeat was the poor training and morale of their officers and crews. The Russians had not learned that the most important thing in winning victory in naval combat is spirit and decisiveness.[198]

The largest naval action of World War I was the Battle of Jutland (Battle of the Skagerrak for the Germans) on 31 May–01 June 1916. The original German operation plan developed by Admiral Reinhard Scheer (1863–1928), the commander of the German High Seas Fleet (*Hochseeflotte*) and his staff, envisaged bombarding Sunderland and thereby triggering a strong British reaction. Scheer planned to deploy two battle squadrons, a scouting force, and the rest of the torpedo boat flotillas southwest of Dogger Bank and Flamborough. On 13 May, a decision was made to delay execution of the plan from the 17 to 23 May.[199] Both sides intended to engage only one part of the enemy fleet. Despite an unfavorable tactical position, the Germans hoped to inflict greater losses than the enemy could inflict on their fleet.[200]

The final German operation plan envisaged the major part of the High Seas Fleet sailing out from Wilhelmshaven at about midnight on 30 May and then proceeding northward, staying well off the Danish coast, and arriving the next afternoon off the western entrance to the Skagerrak. Afterward, Vice Admiral Franz von Hipper (1863–1932) with his battle cruisers would head north and advertise his presence by steaming very close to the Norwegian coast in broad daylight. Scheer would sail about 50 miles to the rear but out of sight of shore. Scheer was confident that as soon as the British learned the whereabouts of Hipper's battle cruisers, they would send their battle cruisers on a high-speed dash across the North Sea to cut off Hipper's retreat to his home base. Scheer's plan was to attack the enemy battle cruisers jointly with Hipper's force the next morning.

By coincidence, Admiral John Jellicoe (1859–1935) also planned a sortie with his Grand Fleet to the Skagerrak area on 1 June 1916. His main objective was to lure the High Seas Fleet to the north and fight a general fleet action.[201] Specifically, he intended to send one battle squadron with two light squadrons off Skagen, with two squadrons of light cruisers to advance through Kattegat to the northern exits of the Great Belt and Sund, thereby enticing the Germans to use strong forces to counterattack. The other battle squadrons and battle cruisers, deployed in the vicinity of Horns Reef and

Fischer Bank, would join the battle.[202] As it turned out, Scheer sortied one day earlier than Jellicoe planned.[203]

Scheer's fleet consisted of 16 dreadnoughts, six pre-dreadnoughts, five battle cruisers, 11 light cruisers, and 61 destroyers. Admiral Jellicoe commanded a fleet consisting of 28 dreadnoughts, nine battle cruisers, 26 light and eight armored cruisers, 78 destroyers, and one seaplane carrier and minelayer each.[204]

The Battle of Jutland was the first and last clash of battle fleets in World War I. This battle came closest to what can be considered as a general fleet action. It also had many elements of a modern major fleet-vs.-fleet operation. It consisted of several major and smaller encounters between the opposing fleets. Neither fleet was able to deliver a crippling blow to the other. Several encounters ended inconclusively. The Germans won a tactical victory by destroying 14 British ships (three battle cruisers, three armored cruisers, eight destroyers/torpedo boats) and killing 6,100 men (out of 60,000). The German losses were 11 ships (one pre-dreadnought battleship, one battle cruiser, four light cruisers, and five destroyers/torpedo boats) and about 2,550 men killed (out of 36,000).[205] However, despite larger losses, the British achieved an operational victory.[206] The situation in the North Sea remained the same as it was prior to the battle.

Since World War I, a major fleet-vs.-fleet operation aimed at *destroying an enemy fleet at sea or its base* replaced a decisive naval battle as the quickest and most effective – but most difficult – method to establish sea control. Major naval operations are invariably planned and conducted when decisive results must be accomplished in the shortest time possible and with the least loss for one's forces.[207] They are especially critical for one's success in the initial phase of a war. Yet major fleet-vs.-fleet operations are to some extent less "decisive" than were some decisive naval battles.

In World War II, most fleet-vs.-fleet encounters took place when one fleet provided a distant cover and support to a major convoy or amphibious force or when the stronger fleet used the threat of an amphibious landing to lure a weaker fleet into a decisive battle. For example, the Japanese Port Moresby–Solomons operation was a major offensive naval/joint operation aimed to capture Port Moresby, New Guinea. For the Allies, in contrast, the Battle of the Coral Sea (4–8 May 1942) was a major defensive naval/joint operation aimed at preventing the Japanese from landing at Port Moresby. Both the U.S. and Australian naval forces and land-based aircraft took part. The Japanese inflicted larger losses on the Allies than they suffered and hence won a clear tactical victory; however, the Japanese failed to achieve the ultimate objective of their operation, and hence the Allies won an operational victory. All losses on both sides were caused by air strikes. The Japanese sank one fleet oiler and destroyer each and so heavily damaged a U.S. fast carrier that it had to be sunk. The Japanese lost only one small carrier and a few small ships at Tulagi, Guadalcanal. They also lost 69 aircraft (12 fighters, 27 dive bombers, and 30 torpedo bombers) and 1,074 men; the Allies lost

66 aircraft and 543 men.[208] One Japanese fleet carrier was heavily damaged and was unable to rejoin the fleet for two months. The losses of planes on another carrier were not replaced until 12 June 1942. So neither of these two fleet carriers took part in the main carrier action off Midway.[209]

Although the way to Port Moresby was open, the Japanese carrier force withdrew from the Coral Sea. The landing on Port Moresby was delayed until July 1942. However, because of the defeat in the Battle of Midway in June 1942, the capture of Port Moresby from the sea was abandoned.[210] The Japanese eventually decided to seize Port Moresby by a much more difficult land route over the 11,000- to 13,000-foot Owen Stanley Range. They made two unsuccessful attempts to advance on Port Moresby, the last one starting in January 1943. After suffering high losses of a large convoy bound for Lae in the Bismarck Sea on 1–3 March 1943, they abandoned all offensive operations in eastern New Guinea.[211]

The Japanese Midway-Aleutians operation (popularly known as the Battle for Midway) represented a turning point in the Pacific War 1941–1945. The primary objective of the CINC of the Japanese Combined Fleet, Admiral Isoroku Yamamoto (1884–1943), was to "lure" the U.S. Pacific Fleet into fighting a decisive battle and thereby to secure Japan's defensive perimeter in Pacific. Yamamoto hoped that a landing on the island of Midway would lead the U.S. Pacific Fleet to react by deploying its fast carrier forces. In the ensuing encounter, the Imperial Japanese Navy (IJN) suffered the greatest defeat in its proud history. After June 1942, Japan was forced onto the strategic defensive and was never able to regain the initiative until its unconditional surrender in August 1944. The Japanese losses in the Midway operation were extremely high. They lost four front line carriers, 253 aircraft, and one heavy cruiser. In addition, one heavy cruiser was heavily damaged, and one destroyer suffered moderate damages, while one battleship, destroyer, and oiler each suffered slight damages. Other sources claim that the Japanese lost 332 aircraft, including 280 that went down with the carriers.[212] Yet some 150 Japanese pilots were saved. The Japanese lost about 3,500 men. In contrast, the U.S. had only 92 officers and 215 men killed. However, three U.S. carrier air groups were decimated.[213] The U.S. losses in aircraft were heavy, 147 of them being shot down.[214]

One of the most decisive defeats suffered by the IJN in the Pacific War came during the Battle of the Philippine Sea on 19–20 June 1944. This clash of the opposing carrier forces came as a result of the Japanese execution of the plan in defense of the central Pacific (codenamed the A-Go Operation). This operation started on 13 June as a reaction to the U.S. invasion of the southern Marianas (Operation FORAGER). The entire operation lasted about ten days. The U.S. Pacific Fleet possessed superiority in the numbers and quality of ships and aircraft. It had a larger number of fast carriers (seven vs. five) and light carriers (eight vs. four).[215] The Japanese were numerically grossly inferior in carrier-based aircraft (473 vs. 956). They had 43 vs. 65 U.S. floatplanes.[216] The U.S. Task Force 58 also had a greater number of battleships (seven vs. five), light cruisers (13 vs. two), and destroyers (63 vs. 28) than the Japanese First Mobile Force had. The Japanese had a larger number only of heavy cruisers (11 vs. 8).[217] In mid-June 1944, about 880 U.S. Marine, Navy, and Army aircraft were based in the Marshalls and Gilberts.[218] The Japanese had available some 630 land-based naval aircraft.[219]

The Japanese were strategically on the defensive, but the A-Go Operation was a major offensive fleet-vs.-fleet operation. In contrast, the U.S. was strategically on the offensive with a major amphibious landing. The engagement between the opposing carriers forces on 19–20 June resulted in a decisive victory for the Fifth Fleet. The U.S. claimed that the Japanese lost 476 planes and 445 aviators. However, their fighting strength was emasculated because so many pilots were lost.[220] The Fifth Fleet failed to complete the destruction of the much weakened enemy force, which escaped to fight another day. Out of nine carriers, six Japanese carriers survived.

In the Leyte operation, the main objective of the Allied naval forces was to provide both close and distant cover to the Allied forces that landed on Leyte on 20 October. The invasion of Leyte was the first Allied major amphibious operation in the new Philippines campaign that would end with the liberation of the entire archipelago less than a year later. By October 1944 the Allied forces had cut off Japan from its vital sources of raw materials in the so-called Southern Resources Area. From their bases on Luzon, Allied airpower was able to neutralize the enemy airpower on Formosa (Taiwan).[221] The Philippines were also used as a base for preparing the final Allied assault on the Home Islands. Although the Japanese were strategically on the defensive, the IJN planned a major fleet-vs.-fleet operation aimed to prevent the Allies from obtaining a foothold on Leyte and in the central Philippines. Between 24 and 27 October, four major naval battles were fought: the Battle in the Sibuyan Sea on 24 October, the Battle of Surigao Strait on 24–25 October, the Battle off Samar on 25 October, and the Battle of Cape Engano on 25 October. In addition, numerous tactical actions on the surface, in the subsurface, and in the air took place in Philippine waters. The IJN lost all four battles. In all, the Japanese lost three battleships, four carriers, ten cruisers, and nine destroyers, totaling 306,000 tons. The Allies lost one light and two escort carriers, two destroyers, and one destroyer escort, for 37,000 tons.[222] In the aftermath, the IJN ceased to pose any serious threat to Allied control of the sea. The IJN's defeat sealed the fate of the defenders on Leyte and thereby created the preconditions for the eventual Allied invasion of Luzon. It also significantly affected Japan's ability to prosecute the war because all the links with the Southern Resources Area and the Home Islands were cut.

In a major fleet-vs.-fleet operation off Matapan on 27–29 March 1941, the Italians suffered a major defeat at the hands of the British Mediterranean Fleet. The Italian force, composed of one battleship, six heavy and two light cruisers, and 13 destroyers, sailed out on 26 March 1941 to attack British convoys bound for Greece in the area south of Crete. The entire operation would be supported by the German X Air Corps. The British obtained accurate and timely information on the impending action by decoding German orders to the Luftwaffe's X Air Corps. A strong British force sailed out to intercept the Italian fleet, and in the ensuing battle on 28–29 March, three Italian heavy cruisers and two destroyers were sunk, while one battleship, heavy cruiser, and destroyer each were damaged. The German X Air Corps' attacks on the British ships were unsuccessful.[223] This victory led to a temporary Allied control of the surface in the central part of the Mediterranean.

In some cases, a stronger side has conducted a major naval operation aimed to obtain sea control and also to exercise that control at the same time. For example, in the aftermath of their successful attack on Pearl Harbor, the Japanese began planning to deploy their fast carrier force into the Indian Ocean. Instead of capturing Ceylon, Admiral Yamamoto made a decision on 14 February 1942 to carry out a raid in the Bay of Bengal. The Japanese planners expected the British fleet to interfere with their invasion of the Andamans and Burma. The Japanese carrier force would operate east of Ceylon and wait on a favorable opportunity to launch a surprise attack on Ceylon and the British Eastern Fleet. As part of the preparations, the Combined Fleet conducted war games on 20–22 February. The Japanese planners intended to accomplish two main objectives: (1) destroy the British Eastern Fleet (believed to consist of two carriers two battleships, three heavy cruisers, four to seven light cruisers, and a number of destroyers); and (2) destroy the British air strength near the Bay of Bengal, (believed to consist of some 300 aircraft).[224] The Japanese secondary objectives were to attack shipping and port installations on Ceylon and enemy shipping in the Bay of Bengal.

The Japanese striking force assigned to destroy the British Eastern Fleet was led by Vice Admiral Chūichi Nagumo (1887–1944). He commanded a force of six fast carriers accompanied by four battleships, two heavy cruisers, and one light cruiser, plus nine destroyers.[225] This was the same carrier force that attacked Pearl Harbor. The Japanese carriers had some 300 aircraft onboard, and their pilots were well trained and combat experienced. The Japanese assigned another force consisting of one light carrier, six cruisers and eight destroyers to sweep British shipping in the Bay of Bengal.[226]

The British naval forces in the Indian Ocean looked formidable on paper. However, they were grossly inferior to their Japanese opponents. Vice Admiral James Somerville (1882–1949), who took command of the British Eastern Fleet on 27 March, upon receiving reports on the impending Japanese attack on Ceylon, divided his fleet two days later into two groups: Force A (two carriers, four cruisers, and six destroyers) and Force B (four battleships, one carrier, three cruisers, and seven destroyers (including one Dutch cruiser and destroyer each). In addition, seven British submarines were deployed in the Indian Ocean.[227] On 31 March, Somerville concentrated his fleet south of Ceylon.[228] The single biggest weakness of the Eastern Fleet was its air component. Only 57 strike aircraft and three dozen fighters were available. Also, there was an inadequate number of the land-based long-range reconnaissance aircraft.[229]

The British received a steady stream of reports about the strength and the movements of the Japanese forces in the area.[230] Intelligence reports indicated that the attack on Colombo and Trincomalee was to be expected on or about 1 April. On 31 March, a new intelligence report indicated (as Somerville also suspected) that the enemy attack would be made next day.[231]

The Japanese carrier striking force entered the Indian Ocean on 31 March. As planned, it carried out a series of carrier strikes on the ships and installations in Colombo. From 6 to 8 April, Nagumo directed a search for the British Eastern Fleet's main body southeast of Ceylon. However, Somerville's main body was far west of Ceylon. Hence, the Japanese searches were (fortunately for the British) unsuccessful. On 8 April, the Japanese carriers struck Trincomalee. After detecting Nagumo's force, the British ordered all ships to leave Trincomalee. Nevertheless, many of the ships were attacked at sea.[232]

In the meantime, the British Admiralty concluded that that there was little security against air or surface attacks at their naval base at Ceylon or at Addu Atoll (the southernmost atoll in the Maldives) used by the Eastern Fleet. The British battle fleet was slow, outgunned, and had short endurance. It was a liability if it remained in the area of Ceylon. Hence, a decision was made on 8 April to move Force B to Kilindini (part of port of Mombasa), Kenya; Force A at Addu Atoll was directed on 9 April to Bombay (Mumbai today) to operate in the Arabian Sea. For all practical purposes, the Allies temporarily abandoned the Indian Ocean.[233]

After the raid on Trincomalee, the Japanese carrier striking force left the Indian Ocean for Japan to prepare for the planned attack on Midway.[234] The results of the raid to the Bay of Bengal were very favorable to the attackers. At the loss of only 17 aircraft, the Japanese sank one British carrier, two heavy cruisers, two destroyers, one corvette, and one armed cruiser. They also damaged 31 merchant ships of 153,600 tons, plus seven transports. However, the Japanese failed to accomplish their main objective because the British Eastern Fleet escaped.[235] Their single biggest mistake was trying to accomplish several objectives almost simultaneously and thereby fragmenting their formidable strength. A more promising course of action for the Japanese would have been to focus most of their efforts in destroying or substantially weakening the enemy's greatest critical strength, the British carrier force—or the enemy's "operational center of gravity." Afterward, they would have obtained almost undisputed control of the Indian Ocean.

In a war between coastal navies or between a blue-water navy and a small coastal navy, it might be possible to obtain sea control by planning and executing a series of quick and decisive tactical actions. For example, in the 20-day Yom Kippur/Ramadan War of 1973, from the first day of hostilities, the Israelis seized the initiative and inflicted heavy losses on their enemies. In the Battle of Latakia on the night of 6/7 October, a group of five Israeli missile craft sunk three Syrian missile craft and one torpedo craft and minesweeper each.[236] A naval battle between six Israeli missile craft and Egyptian missile craft took place off Damietta-Baltim (off the Egyptian coast) on the night of 8/9 October. In the ensuing exchange, the Israelis sunk three Egyptian missile craft, while one was heavily damaged and subsequently destroyed by artillery fire.[237] These victories drastically changed the operational situation at sea to the Israeli advantage. The Israelis essentially obtained control of those parts of the eastern Mediterranean declared by Syria and Egypt as war zones.[238]

A blue-water navy can obtain a large degree of control of the surface relatively quickly through a series of tactical actions in case of a war with very weak opponent at sea. For example, in the Gulf War I (1990–1991), the U.S. Navy/Coalition aircraft conducted a number of strikes against the Iraqi navy on 22–24 January, destroying two minelayers, one oiler (serving as a scouting ship), two patrol craft, and one hovercraft. On 29 January, in the engagement off Bubiyan Island, U.S. and British missile-armed helicopters and ground attack aircraft destroyed four and ran aground 14 patrol craft carrying commandos probably to take part in the Iraqi attack on Kafji; in a separate incident, a British helicopter destroyed a large patrol craft.[239] A day later, U.S. and British helicopters and ground attack aircraft attacked a force consisting of one former Kuwaiti patrol craft and three Iraqi amphibious craft and one minesweeper; all ships suffered various degrees of damage. In another encounter, a force of eight combat craft, including some missile craft, were attacked by U.S. ground attack aircraft in the northern part of the gulf; four craft were sunk and three damaged.[240] The end result of these small-scale tactical actions was that the U.S./Coalition forces obtained control of the northern part of the Persian (Arabian) Gulf.

Traditionally, the decisive naval battle, aimed at destroying a major part of the enemy fleet, was the principal method used in the era of oar/sail and until the turn of the twentieth century. However, experience shows that relatively few major naval battles resulted in the annihilation of destruction of a major part of the enemy fleet. Very often, the far more important results were not losses in materiel and personnel but the military, political, economic, and even psychological effects of such battles. After World War I, major fleet-vs.-fleet operations emerged as the main method of combat employment to a destroy major part of the enemy fleet and thereby obtain control of the sea. In contrast to a decisive naval battle, major fleet-vs.-fleet operations are fought in all three physical dimensions: on the surface, in the subsurface, and in the air. In relatively few cases, decisive naval battles and major fleet-vs.-fleet operations were planned from the outset to obtain sea control. That came as a result of one's fleet providing cover or preventing a major enemy landing or in providing cover for a large convoy. Although major fleet-vs.-fleet operations have not been conducted since World War II, they still remain the optimal method of combat employment of maritime forces to destroy a major part of the enemy's naval forces at sea. In the absence of two blue-water opponents and in a war between a blue-water and small coastal navy or between two numerically smaller coastal navies, a series of successive tactical actions might be decisive and achieve sea control relatively quickly. Such tactical actions should be optimally planned and carried out at the beginning of the hostilities at sea.

Notes

1 Staff Presentation, "Operations for Securing Command of Sea Areas," Part II (Continued) and Part III (Newport, RI: Naval War College, July 1941), Box 31, Strategic Plans Division Records, NWC Presentation Studies, etc. (Series II-B), Naval . . . Panama, Naval Historical Collection, Naval War College, Newport, RI, p. 4.
2 Gabriel Darrieus, *War on the Sea. Strategy and Tactics* (Annapolis, MD: United States Naval Institute, 1908), p. 95.
3 Barry M. Gough, "Maritime Strategy: The Legacies of Mahan and Corbett as Philosophers of Sea Power," *RUSI Journal* (Winter 1988), p. 56.
4 Cited in Chapter III, Part III, Vol. I, Naval War College, Extracts from Raoul Castex, *Théories Stratégiques*. Translated from French by R.C. Smith and assisted by E.J. Tiernan (Newport, RI: Naval War College, December 1938), p. 2.
5 Alfred T. Mahan, *Naval Strategy Compared and Contrasted with the Principles and Practice of Military Operations on Land* (Boston: Little, Brown, and Company, 1911), p. 176.
6 Cited in Chapters I–IV, Part III, Vol. I, Naval War College, Extracts from Raoul Castex, *Théories Stratégiques*. Translated from French by R.C. Smith and assisted by E.J. Tiernan (Newport, RI: Naval War College, December 1938), p. 3.
7 Raoul Castex, *Strategic Theories*. Selections translated and edited with an introduction by Eugenia C. Kiesling (Annapolis, MD: Naval Institute Press, 1993), pp. 72–74, 359.
8 Raoul Castex, *Strategic Theories*. Selections translated and edited with an introduction by Eugenia C. Kiesling (Annapolis, MD: Naval Institute Press, 1993), pp. 72–74, 359.
9 Chapters I–IV, Part III, Vol. I, Naval War College, Extracts from Raoul Castex, *Théories Stratégiques*. Translated from French by R.C. Smith and assisted by E.J. Tiernan (Newport, RI: Naval War College, December 1938), p. 3.
10 Chapters I –IV, Part III, Vol. I, Naval War College, Extracts from Raoul Castex, *Théories Stratégiques*. Translated from French by R.C. Smith and assisted by E.J. Tiernan (Newport, RI: Naval War College, December 1938), pp. 3–4.
11 Herbert Richmond, *Statesmen and Sea Power* (Oxford: Clarendon Press, first published 1946, reprinted 1947), p. 67.
12 Cited in Barry M. Gough, "Maritime Strategy: The Legacies of Mahan and Corbett as Philosophers of sea Power," *RUSI Journal* (Winter 1988), p. 59.
13 Barry M. Gough, "Maritime Strategy: The Legacies of Mahan and Corbett as Philosophers of Sea Power," *RUSI Journal* (Winter 1988), p. 59.
14 Julian S. Corbett, *Some Principles of Maritime Strategy* (London: Longmans, Green and Co., 1918), p. 142–43.
15 William Oliver Stevens and Allan Westcott, *A History of Sea Power* (New York: Doubleday, Doran & Company, Inc., 1942), p. 137.

16 William D. O'Neill, *Technology and Naval War* (Washington, DC: Department of Defense, November 1981, reprinted 1996, 2000), p. 5; accessed at http://www.analysis.williamdoneil.com/Technology%20&%20Naval%20War.pdf

17 William Oliver Stevens and Allan Westcott, *A History of Sea Power* (New York: Doubleday, Doran & Company, Inc., 1942), pp. 152–53.

18 William Oliver Stevens and Allan Westcott, *A History of Sea Power* (New York: Doubleday, Doran & Company, Inc., 1942), pp. 162–63.

19 William Oliver Stevens and Allan Westcott, *A History of Sea Power* (New York: Doubleday, Doran & Company, Inc., 1942), p. 162.

20 Julian S. Corbett, *England in the Mediterranean. A Study of the Rise and Influence of British Power Within the Straits, 1603–1713*, Vol. II (London: Longmans, Green and Co., 1904), p. 268.

21 William D. O'Neill, *Technology and Naval War* (Washington, DC: Department of Defense, November 1981, reprinted 1996, 2000), p. 5; accessed at http://www.analysis.williamdoneil.com/Technology%20&%20Naval%20War.pdf

22 William Oliver Stevens and Allan Westcott, *A History of Sea Power* (New York: Doubleday, Doran & Company, Inc., 1942), p. 162.

23 "A Civilian Critic," extract from the Introduction to *An Essay on Naval Tactics, Systematical and Historical*, by J. Clerk of Eldin, printed in 1782, in H.W. Hodges and E.A. Hughes, editors, *Select Naval Documents* (Cambridge: Cambridge University Press, 1922, reprinted by the Cornell University Library Digital Collections, 2015), p. 170.

24 William Oliver Stevens and Allan Westcott, *A History of Sea Power* (New York: Doubleday, Doran & Company, Inc., 1942), pp. 162–63.

25 Alfred Stenzel, *Seekriegsgeschichte in ihren wichtigsten Abschnitten mit Beruecksichtigung der Seetaktik*, Part 4: *Von 1720 bis 1850* (Hannover/Leipzig: Hahnsche Buchhandlung, 1911), p. 12.

26 Nelson's View of Clerk of Eldin, T.M. Hardy (CO of "Victory") to Sir J.D. Thomson, 5 May 1806, in H.W. Hodges and E.A. Hughes, editors, *Select Naval Documents* (Cambridge: Cambridge University Press, 1922, reprinted by the Cornell University Library Digital Collections, 2015), pp. 171–72.

27 Julian S. Corbett, *Some Principles of Maritime Strategy* (London: Longmans, Green and Co., 1918), p. 109.

28 Julian S. Corbett, *Some Principles of Maritime Strategy* (London: Longmans, Green and Co., 1918), p. 110.

29 James J. Tritten and Luigi Donolo, *A Doctrine Reader* (Newport, RI: Naval War College, Newport Paper # 9, December 1995), p. 4.

30 Julian S. Corbett, editor, *Fighting Instructions, 1530–1816* (London: Publications of the Navy Records Society, Vol. XXIX, 1905, produced by Bibliothèque Nationale de France, Paris, reprinted September 15, 2005), p. 115.

31 Rudolph Rittmeyer, *Seekrieg und Seekriegswesen in ihrer weltgeschichtlichen Entwicklung mit besonderen Berücksichtigung der grossen Seekrieg XVII und XVIII Jahrhunderts*, Vol. I: *Von den Anfängen bis 1740* (Berlin: Ernst Siegfried Mittler und Sohn, 1907), p. 357.

32 Rudolph Rittmeyer, *Seekrieg und Seekriegswesen in ihrer weltgeschichtlichen Entwicklung mit besonderen Beruecksichtigung der grossen Seekrieg XVII und XVIII Jahrhunderts*, Vol. I: *Von den Anfaengen bis 1740* (Berlin: Ernst Siegfried Mittler und Sohn, 1907), p. 357.

33 Julian S. Corbett, *Some Principles of Maritime Strategy* (London: Longmans, Green and Co., 1918), p. 110.

34 Julian S. Corbett, *Some Principles of Maritime Strategy* (London: Longmans, Green and Co., 1918), pp. 160–61.

35 M.G. Cook, "Naval Strategy," 2 March 1931, Air Corps Tactical School, Langley Field, VA, 1930–1931, Strategic Plans Division Records, Series, Box 003, Naval Operational Archives, Washington, D.C., p. 11.

36 Jan S. Breemer, *The Burden of Trafalgar. Decisive Battle and Naval Strategic Expectations on the Eve of the First World War* (Newport, RI: Naval War College Press, Newport Paper #6, October 1993), p. 27.

37 Rudolph Rittmeyer, *Seekrieg und Seekriegswesen in ihrer weltgeschichtlichen Entwicklung mit besonderen Berücksichtigung der grossen Seekrieg XVII und XVIII Jahrhunderts*, Vol. II: *Von 1739–1793* (Berlin: Ernst Siegfried Mittler und Sohn, 1911), pp. 206–07.

38 Rudolph Rittmeyer, *Seekrieg und Seekriegswesen in ihrer weltgeschichtlichen Entwicklung mit besonderen Berücksichtigung der grossen Seekrieg XVII und XVIII Jahrhunderts*, Vol. II: *Von 1739–1793* (Berlin: Ernst Siegfried Mittler und Sohn, 1911), p. 209.

39 Rudolph Rittmeyer, *Seekrieg und Seekriegswesen in ihrer weltgeschichtlichen Entwicklung mit besonderen Berücksichtigung der grossen Seekrieg XVII und XVIII Jahrhunderts*, Vol. II: *Von 1739–1793* (Berlin: Ernst Siegfried Mittler und Sohn, 1911), p. 211.

40 Herbert Richmond, *Statesmen and Sea Power* (Oxford: Clarendon Press, first published 1946, reprinted 1947), p. 40.

41 Rudolph Rittmeyer, *Seekrieg und Seekriegswesen in ihrer weltgeschichtlichen Entwicklung mit besonderen Berücksichtigung der grossen Seekrieg XVII und XVIII Jahrhunderts*, Vol. II: *Von 1739–1793* (Berlin: Ernst Siegfried Mittler und Sohn, 1911), p. 212; other sources cited that Tromp had 85 ships and Blake no more than 42 Herbert Richmond, *Statesmen and Sea Power* (Oxford: Clarendon Press, first published 1946, reprinted 1947), p. 41.

42 Rudolph Rittmeyer, *Seekrieg und Seekriegswesen in ihrer weltgeschichtlichen Entwicklung mit besonderen Berücksichtigung der grossen Seekrieg XVII und XVIII Jahrhunderts*, Vol. II: *Von 1739–1793* (Berlin: Ernst Siegfried Mittler und Sohn, 1911), p. 213.

43 Rudolph Rittmeyer, *Seekrieg und Seekriegswesen in ihrer weltgeschichtlichen Entwicklung mit besonderen Berücksichtigung der grossen Seekrieg XVII und XVIII Jahrhunderts*, Vol. II: *Von 1739–1793* (Berlin: Ernst Siegfried Mittler und Sohn, 1911), p. 214.

44 Herbert Richmond, *Statesmen and Sea Power* (Oxford: Clarendon Press, first published 1946, reprinted 1947), p. 41.

45 Rudolph Rittmeyer, *Seekrieg und Seekriegswesen in ihrer weltgeschichtlichen Entwicklung mit besonderen Berücksichtigung der grossen Seekrieg XVII und XVIII Jahrhunderts*, Vol. II: *Von 1739–1793* (Berlin: Ernst Siegfried Mittler und Sohn, 1911), pp. 214–15.

46 Alfred Stenzel, *Seekriegsgeschichte in ihren wichtigsten Abschnitten mit Berücksichtigung der Seetaktik*, Part 3: *Von 1600 bis 1720* (Hannover/Leipzig: Hahnsche Buchhandlung, 1910), p. 68.

47 Rudolph Rittmeyer, *Seekrieg und Seekriegswesen in ihrer weltgeschichtlichen Entwicklung mit besonderen Berücksichtigung der grossen Seekrieg XVII und XVIII Jahrhunderts*, Vol. II: *Von 1739–1793* (Berlin: Ernst Siegfried Mittler und Sohn, 1911), p. 217.

48 Rudolph Rittmeyer, *Seekrieg und Seekriegswesen in ihrer weltgeschichtlichen Entwicklung mit besonderen Berücksichtigung der grossen Seekrieg XVII und XVIII Jahrhunderts*, Vol. II: *Von 1739–1793* (Berlin: Ernst Siegfried Mittler und Sohn, 1911), p. 218.

49 Rudolph Rittmeyer, *Seekrieg und Seekriegswesen in ihrer weltgeschichtlichen Entwicklung mit besonderen Berücksichtigung der grossen Seekrieg XVII und XVIII Jahrhunderts*, Vol. II: *Von 1739–1793* (Berlin: Ernst Siegfried Mittler und Sohn, 1911), p. 218.

50 Jacques Mordal, *25 Centuries of Sea Warfare* (London: Abbey Library, 1959), p. 73.

51 Alexander Meurer, *Seekriegsgeschichte in umrissen. Seemacht und Seekriege vornehmlich vom 16. Jahrhundert ab* (Leipzig: Verlag v. Hase & Koehler, 1925), p. 188.

52 Alfred Stenzel, *Seekriegsgeschichte in ihren wichtigsten Abschnitten mit Berücksichti- gung der Seetaktik*, Part 2: *Von 400 vor Christen bis 1600 nach Christen* (Hannover/ Leipzig: Hahnsche Buchhandlung, 1909), p. 18.

53 Alfred Stenzel, *Seekriegsgeschichte in ihren wichtigsten Abschnitten mit Berücksichti- gung der Seetaktik*, Part 2: *Von 400 vor Christen bis 1600 nach Christen* (Hannover/ Leipzig: Hahnsche Buchhandlung, 1909), pp. 20–21.

54 Arthur MacCartney Shepard, *Sea Power in Ancient History. The Story of the Navies of Classic Greece and Rome* (London: William Heineman Ltd., 1925), p. 146–48.

55 Adrian Goldsworthy, *The Punic Wars* (London: Cassell & Co, 2001), p. 111.

56 Adrian Goldsworthy, *The Punic Wars* (London: Cassell & Co, 2001), p. 114.

57 Arthur MacCartney Shepard, *Sea Power in Ancient History. The Story of the Navies of Classic Greece and Rome* (London: William Heineman Ltd., 1925), p. 152–53.

58 Alfred Stenzel, *Seekriegsgeschichte in ihren wichtigsten Abschnitten mit Berücksichti- gung der Seetaktik*, Part 2: *Von 400 vor Christen bis 1600 nach Christen* (Hannover/ Leipzig: Hahnsche Buchhandlung, 1909), p. 94.

59 John D. Grainger, *Hellenistic & Roman Naval Wars 336–31 BC* (Barnsley, South Yorkshire: Pen & Sword Maritime, 2011), p. 181.

60 John D. Grainger, *Hellenistic & Roman Naval Wars 336–31 BC* (Barnsley, South Yorkshire: Pen & Sword Maritime, 2011), p. 181.

61 Alexander Meurer, *Seekriegsgeschichte in umrissen. Seemacht und Seekriege vornehm- lich vom 16. Jahrhundert ab* (Leipzig: Verlag v. Hase & Koehler, 1925), p. 115.

62 William Ledyard Rodgers, *Greek and Roman Naval Warfare. A Study of Strategy, Tactics and Ship Design from Salamis (480 B.C.) to Actium (31 B.C.)* (Annapolis, MD: Naval Institute Press, 1937, 1964), p. 522.

63 John D. Grainger, *Hellenistic & Roman Naval Wars 336–31 BC* (Barnsley, South Yorkshire: Pen & Sword Maritime, 2011), pp. 183–84.

64 Arthur MacCartney Shepard, *Sea Power in Ancient History. The Story of the Navies of Classic Greece and Rome* (London: William Heineman Ltd., 1925), p. 222.

65 William Ledyard Rodgers, *Greek and Roman Naval Warfare. A Study of Strategy, Tactics and Ship Design from Salamis (480 B.C.) to Actium (31 B.C.)* (Annapolis, MD: Naval Institute Press, 1937, 1964), p. 534.

66 Arthur MacCartney Shepard, *Sea Power in Ancient History. The Story of the Navies of Classic Greece and Rome* (London: William Heinemann Ltd., 1925), p. 222; Andrew C. Hess, "The Battle of Lepanto and Its Place in Mediterranean His- tory," *Past & Present*, No. 57 (November 1972), p. 62.

67 Michael Lewis, *The Spanish Armada* (New York: Thomas Y. Crowell Company, 1968), pp. 32–33.

68 Alexander Meurer, *Seekriegsgeschichte in umrissen. Seemacht und Seekriege vornehm- lich vom 16. Jahrhundert ab* (Leipzig: Verlag v. Hase & Koehler, 1925), p. 163.

69 William Ledyard Rodgers, *Naval Warfare Under Oars. A Study of Strategy, Tactics and Ship Design* (Annapolis, MD: Naval Institute Press, 1940, 1967), p. 275.

70 R. Ernest Dupuy and Trevor N. Dupuy, *The Encyclopedia of Military History from 3500 B.C. to the Present*, 2nd rev. ed. (New York: Harper & Row, Publishers, 1986), p. 466.

71 Out of this total, the Queen's navy numbered 24 vessels and 13,470 tons with some 6,700 men William Ledyard Rodgers, *Naval Warfare Under Oars. A Study of Strategy, Tactics and Ship Design* (Annapolis, MD: Naval Institute Press, 1940, 1967), p. 288; Alexander Meurer, *Seekriegsgeschichte in umrissen. Seemacht und Seekriege vornehmlich vom 16. Jahrhundert ab* (Leipzig: Verlag v. Hase & Koehler, 1925), p. 141.

72 Alexander Meurer, *Seekriegsgeschichte in umrissen. Seemacht und Seekriege vornehm- lich vom 16. Jahrhundert ab* (Leipzig: Verlag v. Hase & Koehler, 1925), p. 163.

73 Michael Lewis, *The Spanish Armada* (New York: T. Y. Crowell Co., 1968), pp. 166–67.

74 Jan S. Breemer, *The Burden of Trafalgar. Decisive Battle and Naval Strategic Expectations on the Eve of the First World War* (Newport, RI: Naval War College Press, Newport Paper #6, October 1993), p. 9.

75 Alexander Meurer, *Seekriegsgeschichte in umrissen. Seemacht und Seekriege vornehmlich vom 16. Jahrhundert ab* (Leipzig: Verlag v. Hase & Koehler, 1925), pp. 165–66; other sources claim that out of 130 Spanish ships, 67 were lost (the English sunk or captured 15 ships; 19 ships were wrecked on the Scottish or the Irish coast; the fate of the 33 other ships was unknown); R. Ernest Dupuy and Trevor N. Dupuy, *The Encyclopedia of Military History from 3500 B.C. to the Present*, 2nd rev. ed. (New York: Harper & Row, Publishers, 1986), p. 467.

76 William Oliver Stevens and Allan Westcott, *A History of Sea Power* (New York: Doubleday, Doran & Company, Inc., 1942), p. 122.

77 Alexander Meurer, *Seekriegsgeschichte in umrissen. Seemacht und Seekriege vornehmlich vom 16. Jahrhundert ab* (Leipzig: Verlag v. Hase & Koehler, 1925), p. 166.

78 Cited in Jan S. Breemer, *The Burden of Trafalgar. Decisive Battle and Naval Strategic Expectations on the Eve of the First World War* (Newport, RI: Naval War College Press, Newport Paper #6, October 1993), p. 8.

79 R. Ernest Dupuy and Trevor N. Dupuy, *The Encyclopedia of Military History from 3500 B.C. to the Present*, 2nd rev. ed. (New York: Harper & Row, Publishers, 1986), p. 558.

80 Alfred Stenzel, *Seekriegsgeschichte in ihren wichtigsten Abschnitten mit Berücksichtigung der Seetaktik*, Part 3: *Von 1600 bis 1720* (Hannover/Leipzig: Hahnsche Buchhandlung, 1910), p. 205.

81 Rudolph Rittmeyer, *Seekrieg und Seekriegswesen in ihrer weltgeschichtlichen Entwicklung mit besonderen Berücksichtigung der grossen Seekrieg XVII und XVIII Jahrhunderts*, Vol. I: *Von den Anfaengen bis 1740* (Berlin: Ernst Siegfried Mittler und Sohn, 1907), p. 329.

82 Alfred Stenzel, *Seekriegsgeschichte in ihren wichtigsten Abschnitten mit Berücksichtigung der Seetaktik*, Part 3: *Von 1600 bis 1720* (Hannover/Leipzig: Hahnsche Buchhandlung, 1910), p. 209; Rudolph Rittmeyer, *Seekrieg und Seekriegswesen in ihrer weltgeschichtlichen Entwicklung mit besonderen Berücksichtigung der grossen Seekrieg XVII und XVIII Jahrhunderts*, Vol. I: *Von den Anfaengen bis 1740* (Berlin: Ernst Siegfried Mittler und Sohn, 1907), p. 329.

83 Rudolph Rittmeyer, *Seekrieg und Seekriegswesen in ihrer weltgeschichtlichen Entwicklung mit besonderen Berücksichtigung der grossen Seekrieg XVII und XVIII Jahrhunderts*, Vol. I: *Von den Anfaengen bis 1740* (Berlin: Ernst Siegfried Mittler und Sohn, 1907), p. 338.

84 Rudolph Rittmeyer, *Seekrieg und Seekriegswesen in ihrer weltgeschichtlichen Entwicklung mit besonderen Berücksichtigung der grossen Seekrieg XVII und XVIII Jahrhunderts*, Vol. I: *Von den Anfaengen bis 1740* (Berlin: Ernst Siegfried Mittler und Sohn, 1907), p. 340.

85 Alfred Stenzel, *Seekriegsgeschichte in ihren wichtigsten Abschnitten mit Berücksichtigung der Seetaktik*, Part 3: *Von 1600 bis 1720* (Hannover/Leipzig: Hahnsche Buchhandlung, 1910), p. 226.

86 Rudolph Rittmeyer, *Seekrieg und Seekriegswesen in ihrer weltgeschichtlichen Entwicklung mit besonderen Berücksichtigung der grossen Seekrieg XVII und XVIII Jahrhunderts*, Vol. I: *Von den Anfaengen bis 1740* (Berlin: Ernst Siegfried Mittler und Sohn, 1907), p. 338.

87 Alfred Stenzel, *Seekriegsgeschichte in ihren wichtigsten Abschnitten mit Berücksichtigung der Seetaktik*, Part 3: *Von 1600 bis 1720* (Hannover/Leipzig: Hahnsche Buchhandlung, 1910), p. 222.

88 Alfred T. Mahan, *The Influence of Sea Power upon History 1660–1783* (Boston: Little, Brown, and Company, 1939), pp. 188–89.

89 Rene Daveluy, *The Genius of Naval Warfare*, Vol. I: *Strategy* (Annapolis, MD: United States Naval Institute 1910), p. 51.

90   Alfred T. Mahan, *The Influence of Sea Power upon History 1660–1783* (Boston: Little, Brown, and Company, 1939), pp. 188–89.

91   Alfred Stenzel, *Seekriegsgeschichte in ihren wichtigsten Abschnitten mit Berücksichtigung der Seetaktik*, Part 3: *Von 1600 bis 1720* (Hannover/Leipzig: Hahnsche Buchhandlung, 1910), p. 362.

92   Alfred Stenzel, *Seekriegsgeschichte in ihren wichtigsten Abschnitten mit Berücksichtigung der Seetaktik*, Part 3: *Von 1600 bis 1720* (Hannover/Leipzig: Hahnsche Buchhandlung, 1910), p. 362.

93   William Oliver Stevens and Allan Westcott, *A History of Sea Power* (New York: Doubleday, Doran & Company, Inc., 1942), p. 154.

94   Alfred Stenzel, *Seekriegsgeschichte in ihren wichtigsten Abschnitten mit Berücksichtigung der Seetaktik*, Part 3: *Von 1600 bis 1720* (Hannover/Leipzig: Hahnsche Buchhandlung, 1910), p. 364.

95   Rudolph Rittmeyer, *Seekrieg und Seekriegswesen in ihrer weltgeschichtlichen Entwicklung mit besonderen Berücksichtigung der grossen Seekrieg XVII und XVIII Jahrhunderts*, Vol. I: *Von den Anfaengen bis 1740* (Berlin: Ernst Siegfried Mittler und Sohn, 1907), pp. 455.

96   Alfred Stenzel, *Seekriegsgeschichte in ihren wichtigsten Abschnitten mit Berücksichtigung der Seetaktik*, Part 3: *Von 1600 bis 1720* (Hannover/Leipzig: Hahnsche Buchhandlung, 1910), p. 364.

97   Alfred T. Mahan, *The Influence of Sea Power upon History 1660–1783* (Boston: Little, Brown, and Company, 1939), p. 191; Rudolph Rittmeyer, *Seekrieg und Seekriegswesen in ihrer weltgeschichtlichen Entwicklung mit besonderen Berücksichtigung der grossen Seekrieg XVII und XVIII Jahrhunderts*, Vol. I: *Von den Anfaengen bis 1740* (Berlin: Ernst Siegfried Mittler und Sohn, 1907), pp. 454–55.

98   Alfred Stenzel, *Seekriegsgeschichte in ihren wichtigsten Abschnitten mit Berücksichtigung der Seetaktik*, Part 3: *Von 1600 bis 1720* (Hannover/Leipzig: Hahnsche Buchhandlung, 1910), p. 366.

99   Alfred T. Mahan, *The Influence of Sea Power upon History 1660–1783* (Boston: Little, Brown, and Company, 1939), p. 191.

100 Herbert Richmond, *Statesmen and Sea Power* (Oxford: Clarendon Press, first published 1946, reprinted 1947), p. 69.

101 Alexander Meurer, *Seekriegsgeschichte in umrissen. Seemacht und Seekriege vornehmlich vom 16. Jahrhundert ab* (Leipzig: Verlag v. Hase & Koehler, 1925), p. 344.

102 Jan S. Breemer, *The Burden of Trafalgar. Decisive Battle and Naval Strategic Expectations on the Eve of the First World War* (Newport, RI: Naval War College Press, Newport Paper #6, October 1993), p. 24.

103 William Oliver Stevens and Allan Westcott, *A History of Sea Power* (New York: Doubleday, Doran & Company, Inc., 1942), p. 238.

104 Alfred T. Mahan, *Influence of Sea Power upon the French Revolution and Empire, 1793–1812*, Vol. II, 8th ed. (Boston: Little, Brown, and Company, 1897), p. 196; Jan S. Breemer, *The Burden of Trafalgar. Decisive Battle and Naval Strategic Expectations on the Eve of the First World War* (Newport, RI: Naval War College Press, Newport Paper #6, October 1993), p. 29.

105 Alfred T. Mahan, *Influence of Sea Power upon the French Revolution and Empire, 1793–1812*, Vol. II, 8th ed. (Boston: Little, Brown, and Company, 1897), p. 196.

106 Silvia Marzagalli, "Napoleon's Continental Blockade. An Effective Substitute to Naval Weakness?" in Bruce A. Elleman and S.C.M. Paine, editors, *Naval Blockades and Seapower. Strategies and Counterstrategies, 1805–2005* (London/New York: Routledge, 2006), p. 25.

107 Cited in Jan S. Breemer, *The Burden of Trafalgar. Decisive Battle and Naval Strategic Expectations on the Eve of the First World War* (Newport, RI: Naval War College Press, Newport Paper #6, October 1993), p. 6.

108 William Oliver Stevens and Allan Westcott, *A History of Sea Power* (New York: Doubleday, Doran & Company, Inc., 1942), pp. 261–62; Gabriel Darrieus, *War*

on the Sea. Strategy and Tactics (Annapolis, MD: United States Naval Institute, 1908), pp. 89, 91.

109 M.G. Cook, "Naval Strategy," 2 March 1931, Air Corps Tactical School, Langley Field, VA, 1930–1931, Strategic Plans Division Records, Series, Box 003, Naval Operational Archives, Washington, D.C., p. 4.

110 William Oliver Stevens and Allan Westcott, *A History of Sea Power* (New York: Doubleday, Doran & Company, Inc., 1942), pp. 256–57, 261–62; Gabriel Darrieus, *War on the Sea. Strategy and Tactics* (Annapolis, MD: United States Naval Institute, 1908), pp. 89, 91.

111 Hans Hugo Sokol, *Des Kaisers Seemacht 1848–1914. Die k.k. oesterreichische Kriegsmarine* (Vienna: Amalthea, 2002), pp. 75–76.

112 Hans Hugo Sokol, *Des Kaisers Seemacht 1848–1914. Die k.k. oesterreichische Kriegsmarine* (Vienna: Amalthea, 2002), p. 80.

113 Stephen B. Luce, "Naval Warfare Under modern Conditions," *The North American Review*, Vol. 162, No. 470 (January 1896), p. 71.

114 Lawrence Sondhaus, *The Habsburg Empire and the Sea* (West Lafayette, IN: Purdue University Press, 1989), p. 257.

115 Hans Hugo Sokol, *Des Kaisers Seemacht 1848–1914. Die k.k. oesterreichische Kriegsmarine* (Vienna: Amalthea, 2002), pp. 83–84.

116 William Oliver Stevens and Allan Westcott, *A History of Sea Power* (New York: Doubleday, Doran & Company, Inc., 1942), p. 263.

117 William Oliver Stevens and Allan Westcott, *A History of Sea Power* (New York: Doubleday, Doran & Company, Inc., 1942), p. 264; Giuseppe Fioravanzo, *A History of Naval Thought*, translated by Arthur W. Holst (Annapolis, MD: Naval Institute Press, 1979), p. 146.

118 William Oliver Stevens and Allan Westcott, *A History of Sea Power* (New York: Doubleday, Doran & Company, Inc., 1942), p. 268.

119 William Ledyard Rodgers, *Naval Warfare Under Oars. A Study of Strategy, Tactics and Ship Design* (Annapolis, MD: Naval Institute Press, 1940, 1967), p. 167.

120 R. Ernest Dupuy and Trevor N. Dupuy, *The Encyclopedia of Military History from 3500 B.C. to the Present*, 2nd rev. ed. (New York: Harper & Row, Publishers, 1986), p. 502; other sources claim 205 ships, including six galleasses, and 80,000 men (including 20,000 soldiers) Alfred Stenzel, *Seekriegsgeschichte in ihren wichtigsten Abschnitten mit Berücksichtigung der Seetaktik*, Part 2: *Von 400 vor Christen bis 1600 nach Christen* (Hannover/Leipzig: Hahnsche Buchhandlung, 1909), p. 137.

121 William Ledyard Rodgers, *Naval Warfare Under Oars. A Study of Strategy, Tactics and Ship Design* (Annapolis, MD: Naval Institute Press, 1940, 1967), p. 186; other sources claimed a total number of 88,000, including 16,000 soldiers R. Ernest Dupuy and Trevor N. Dupuy, *The Encyclopedia of Military History from 3500 B.C. to the Present*, 2nd rev. ed. (New York: Harper & Row, Publishers, 1986), p. 502.

122 William Ledyard Rodgers, *Naval Warfare Under Oars. A Study of Strategy, Tactics and Ship Design* (Annapolis, MD: Naval Institute Press, 1940, 1967), p. 187.

123 Alfred Stenzel, *Seekriegsgeschichte in ihren wichtigsten Abschnitten mit Berücksichtigung der Seetaktik*, Part 2: *Von 400 vor Christen bis 1600 nach Christen* (Hannover/Leipzig: Hahnsche Buchhandlung, 1909), p. 140; other sources claim that the Turkish losses were 53 ships sunk and some 117 galleys and 13 galliots captured R. Ernest Dupuy and Trevor N. Dupuy, *The Encyclopedia of Military History from 3500 B.C. to the Present*, 2nd rev. ed. (New York: Harper & Row, Publishers, 1986), p. 503; Giuseppe Fioravanzo, *A History of Naval Thought*, translated by Arthur W. Holst (Annapolis, MD: Naval Institute Press, 1979), p. 65.

124 Alfred Stenzel, *Seekriegsgeschichte in ihren wichtigsten Abschnitten mit Berücksichtigung der Seetaktik*, Part 2: *Von 400 vor Christen bis 1600 nach Christen* (Hannover/Leipzig: Hahnsche Buchhandlung, 1909), p. 140.

125   William Ledyard Rodgers, *Naval Warfare Under Oars. A Study of Strategy, Tactics and Ship Design* (Annapolis, MD: Naval Institute Press, 1940, 1967), p. 212.

126   William Ledyard Rodgers, *Naval Warfare Under Oars. A Study of Strategy, Tactics and Ship Design* (Annapolis, MD: Naval Institute Press, 1940, 1967), p. 212; R. Ernest Dupuy and Trevor N. Dupuy, *The Encyclopedia of Military History from 3500 B.C. to the Present*, 2nd rev. ed. (New York: Harper & Row, Publishers, 1986), p. 503.

127   Andrew C. Hess, "The Battle of Lepanto and Its Place in Mediterranean History," *Past & Present*, No. 57 (November 1972), p. 62.

128   Frederic C. Lane, *Venice. A Maritime Republic* (Baltimore, MD: Johns Hopkins Press, 1973), p. 248.

129   Alexander Meurer, *Seekriegsgeschichte in umrissen. Seemacht und Seekriege vornehmlich vom 16. Jahrhundert ab* (Leipzig: Verlag v. Hase & Koehler, 1925), p. 101.

130   Pierre Ducrey, *Warfare in Ancient Greece.* Translated by Janet Lloyd (New York: Schocken Books, 1986), p. 187. Herodotus cited highly inflated figures of 1,207 triremes and 3,000 penteconters, triconters, light boats manned with 481,400 sailors of subjected peoples (mostly Phoenicians, Lycians, Cilicians, and Egyptians) and 36,120 Persian marines Arthur MacCartney Shepard, *Sea Power in Ancient History. The Story of the Navies of Classic Greece and Rome* (London: William Heineman Ltd., 1925), p. 48; other sources claimed that the Greek fleet consisted of about 375 ships and 80,000 men, while the Persians had 600–700 ships and 120,000 men Reginald Custance, *War at Sea. Modern Theory and Ancient Practice* (Edinburgh/London: William Blackwood and Sons, 1919), p. 14.

131   John Warry, *Warfare in the Classical World* (New York: Barnes & Noble, 1998), p. 43.

132   Jacques Mordal, *25 Centuries of Sea Warfare,* Translated by Len Ortzen (London: Abbey Library, 1959), p. 8.

133   Arthur MacCartney Shepard, *Sea Power in Ancient History. The Story of the Navies of Classic Greece and Rome* (London: William Heineman, Ltd., 1925), pp. 65–66.

134   Jacques Mordal, *25 Centuries of Sea Warfare,* Translated by Len Ortzen (London: Abbey Library, 1959), p. 8.

135   William L. Rodgers, *Greek and Roman Naval Warfare. A Study of Strategy, Tactics, and Ship Design from Salamis (480 B.C.) to Actium (31 B.C.)* (Annapolis, MD: Naval Institute Press, 1964), p. 191.

136   Adrian Goldsworthy, *The Punic Wars* (London: Cassell & Co, 2001), p. 122.

137   Adrian Goldsworthy, *The Punic Wars* (London: Cassell & Co, 2001), pp 124–25.

138   Arthur MacCartney Shepard, *Sea Power in Ancient History. The Story of the Navies of Classic Greece and Rome* (London: William Heineman Ltd., 1925), pp. 166–67.

139   Adrian Goldsworthy, *The Punic Wars* (London: Cassell & Co, 2001), p. 125.

140   Adrian Goldsworthy, *The Punic Wars* (London: Cassell & Co, 2001), pp. 125–26.

141   Arthur MacCartney Shepard, *Sea Power in Ancient History. The Story of the Navies of Classic Greece and Rome* (London: William Heineman Ltd., 1925), pp. 166–67.

142   Adrian Goldsworthy, *The Punic Wars* (London: Cassell & Co, 2001), pp. 125–26.

143   William Ledyard Rodgers, *Greek and Roman Naval Warfare. A Study of Strategy, Tactics and Ship Design from Salamis (480 B.C.) to Actium (31 B.C.)* (Annapolis, MD: Naval Institute Press, 1937, 1964), p. 511.

144   William Ledyard Rodgers, *Greek and Roman Naval Warfare. A Study of Strategy, Tactics and Ship Design from Salamis (480 B.C.) to Actium (31 B.C.)* (Annapolis, MD: Naval Institute Press, 1937, 1964), pp. 511–12.

145   N.A.M. Rodger, *The Command of the Ocean. A Naval History of Britain, 1649–1815* (New York/London: W. W. Norton & Company, 2004), pp. 352–53.

146   Alfred T. Mahan, *The Influence of Sea Power upon History 1660–1783* (Boston: Little, Brown, and Company, 1939), p. 387.

147 Alfred T. Mahan, *The Influence of Sea Power upon History 1660–1783* (Boston: Little, Brown, and Company, 1939), pp. 388–89.

148 Alfred T. Mahan, *The Influence of Sea Power upon History 1660–1783* (Boston: Little, Brown, and Company, 1939), p. 389.

149 Alfred T. Mahan, *The Influence of Sea Power upon History 1660–1783* (Boston: Little, Brown, and Company, 1939), p. 389; Alfred Stenzel, *Seekriegsgeschichte in ihren wichtigsten Abschnitten met Berücksichtigung der Seetaktik*, Part 4: *Von 1720 bis 1850* (Hannover/Leipzig: Hahnsche Buchhandlung, 1911), p. 177.

150 Alfred T. Mahan, *The Influence of Sea Power upon History 1660–1783* (Boston: Little, Brown, and Company, 1939), pp. 389–90.

151 Alfred T. Mahan, *The Influence of Sea Power upon History 1660–1783* (Boston: Little, Brown, and Company, 1939), pp. 389–90.

152 Rudolph Rittmeyer, *Seekrieg und Seekriegswesen in ihrer weltgeschichtlichen Entwicklung mit besonderen Berücksichtigung der grossen Seekrieg XVII und XVIII Jahrhunderts*, Vol. II: *Von 1739–1793* (Berlin: Ernst Siegfried Mittler und Sohn, 1911), pp. 337–38.

153 N.A.M. Rodger, *The Command of the Ocean. A Naval History of Britain, 1649–1815* (New York/London: W. W. Norton & Company, 2004), p. 352.

154 Alfred Stenzel, *Seekriegsgeschichte in ihren wichtigsten Abschnitten mit Berücksichtigung der Seetaktik*, Part 4: *Von 1720 bis 1850* (Hannover/Leipzig: Hahnsche Buchhandlung, 1911), p. 177.

155 Alfred T. Mahan, *The Influence of Sea Power upon History 1660–1783* (Boston: Little, Brown, and Company, 1939), pp. 389–90.

156 Alfred Stenzel, *Seekriegsgeschichte in ihren wichtigsten Abschnitten mit Berücksichtigung der Seetaktik*, Part 4: *Von 1720 bis 1850* (Hannover/Leipzig: Hahnsche Buchhandlung, 1911), p. 177.

157 R. Ernest Dupuy and Trevor N. Dupuy, *The Encyclopedia of Military History from 3500 B.C. to the Present*, 2nd rev. ed. (New York: Harper & Row, Publishers, 1986), p. 724.

158 Alfred Stenzel, *Seekriegsgeschichte in ihren wichtigsten Abschnitten mit Berücksichtigung der Seetaktik*, Part 3: *Von 1600 bis 1720* (Hannover/Leipzig: Hahnsche Buchhandlung, 1910), p. 152.

159 Alfred Stenzel, *Seekriegsgeschichte in ihren wichtigsten Abschnitten mit Berücksichtigung der Seetaktik*, Part 3: *Von 1600 bis 1720* (Hannover/Leipzig: Hahnsche Buchhandlung, 1910), p. 156.

160 Alfred T. Mahan, *Influence of Sea Power upon the French Revolution and Empire, 1793–1812*, Vol. I, 8th ed. (Boston: Little, Brown, and Company, 1897), p. 221.

161 N.A.M. Rodger, *The Command of the Ocean. A Naval History of Britain, 1649–1815* (New York/London: W.W. Norton & Company, 2004), p. 438.

162 Alfred T. Mahan, *Influence of Sea Power upon the French Revolution and Empire, 1793–1812*, Vol. I, 8th ed. (Boston: Little, Brown, and Company, 1897), p. 229.

163 Alfred Stenzel, *Seekriegsgeschichte in ihren wichtigsten Abschnitten mit Berücksichtigung der Seetaktik*, Part 4: *Von 1720 bis 1850* (Hannover/Leipzig: Hahnsche Buchhandlung, 1911), p. 240.

164 Alfred T. Mahan, *Influence of Sea Power upon the French Revolution and Empire, 1793–1812*, Vol. I, 8th ed. (Boston: Little, Brown, and Company, 1897), p. 229.

165 Alfred Stenzel, *Seekriegsgeschichte in ihren wichtigsten Abschnitten mit Berücksichtigung der Seetaktik*, Part 2: *Von 400 vor Christen bis 1600 nach Christen* (Hannover/Leipzig: Hahnsche Buchhandlung, 1909), p. 178.

166 Alfred Stenzel, *Seekriegsgeschichte in ihren wichtigsten Abschnitten mit Berücksichtigung der Seetaktik*, Part 2: *Von 400 vor Christen bis 1600 nach Christen* (Hannover/Leipzig: Hahnsche Buchhandlung, 1909), pp. 180–81.

167 R. Ernest Dupuy and Trevor N. Dupuy, *The Encyclopedia of Military History from 3500 B.C. to the Present*, 2nd rev. ed. (New York: Harper & Row, Publishers, 1986), p. 555.

168 Rudolph Rittmeyer, *Seekrieg und Seekriegswesen in ihrer weltgeschichtlichen Entwicklung mit besonderen Berücksichtigung der grossen Seekrieg XVII und XVIII Jahrhunderts*, Vol. II: *Von 1739–1793* (Berlin: Ernst Siegfried Mittler und Sohn, 1911), p. 220.

169 Rudolph Rittmeyer, *Seekrieg und Seekriegswesen in ihrer weltgeschichtlichen Entwicklung mit besonderen Berücksichtigung der grossen Seekrieg XVII und XVIII Jahrhunderts*, Vol. II: *Von 1739–1793* (Berlin: Ernst Siegfried Mittler und Sohn, 1911), p. 221; Alfred Stenzel, *Seekriegsgeschichte in ihren wichtigsten Abschnitten mit Berücksichtigung der Seetaktik*, Part 3: *Von 1600 bis 1720* (Hannover/Leipzig: Hahnsche Buchhandlung, 1910), p. 74.

170 Rudolph Rittmeyer, *Seekrieg und Seekriegswesen in ihrer weltgeschichtlichen Entwicklung mit besonderen Berücksichtigung der grossen Seekrieg XVII und XVIII Jahrhunderts*, Vol. II: *Von 1739–1793* (Berlin: Ernst Siegfried Mittler und Sohn, 1911), p. 220.

171 Rudolph Rittmeyer, *Seekrieg und Seekriegswesen in ihrer weltgeschichtlichen Entwicklung mit besonderen Berücksichtigung der grossen Seekrieg XVII und XVIII Jahrhunderts*, Vol. II: *Von 1739–1793* (Berlin: Ernst Siegfried Mittler und Sohn, 1911), p. 223.

172 Rudolph Rittmeyer, *Seekrieg und Seekriegswesen in ihrer weltgeschichtlichen Entwicklung mit besonderen Berücksichtigung der grossen Seekrieg XVII und XVIII Jahrhunderts*, Vol. II: *Von 1739–1793* (Berlin: Ernst Siegfried Mittler und Sohn, 1911), p. 224.

173 Rudolph Rittmeyer, *Seekrieg und Seekriegswesen in ihrer weltgeschichtlichen Entwicklung mit besonderen Berücksichtigung der grossen Seekrieg XVII und XVIII Jahrhunderts*, Vol. II: *Von 1739–1793* (Berlin: Ernst Siegfried Mittler und Sohn, 1911), p. 223.

174 Alexander Meurer, *Seekriegsgeschichte in umrissen. Seemacht und Seekriege vornehmlich vom 16. Jahrhundert ab* (Leipzig: Verlag v. Hase & Koehler, 1925), p. 188.

175 Alfred T. Mahan, *The Influence of Sea Power upon History 1660–1783* (Boston: Little, Brown, and Company, 1939), p. 125.

176 Alexander Meurer, *Seekriegsgeschichte in umrissen. Seemacht und Seekriege vornehmlich vom 16. Jahrhundert ab* (Leipzig: Verlag v. Hase & Koehler, 1925), p. 201.

177 Alfred T. Mahan, *The Influence of Sea Power upon History 1660–1783* (Boston: Little, Brown, and Company, 1939), p. 118.

178 Alfred T. Mahan, *The Influence of Sea Power upon History 1660–1783* (Boston: Little, Brown, and Company, 1939), p. 125.

179 Rene Daveluy, *The Genius of Naval Warfare*, Vol. I: *Strategy* (Annapolis, MD: United States Naval Institute, 1910), p. 51.

180 Alfred T. Mahan, *The Influence of Sea Power upon History 1660–1783* (Boston: Little, Brown, and Company, 1939), p. 125; Alfred Stenzel, *Seekriegsgeschichte in ihren wichtigsten Abschnitten mit Berücksichtigung der Seetaktik*, Part 3: *Von 1600 bis 1720* (Hannover/Leipzig: Hahnsche Buchhandlung, 1910), p. 168.

181 R. Ernest Dupuy and Trevor N. Dupuy, *The Encyclopedia of Military History from 3500 B.C. to the Present*, 2nd rev. ed. (New York: Harper & Row, Publishers, 1986), p. 557.

182 Rudolph Rittmeyer, *Seekrieg und Seekriegswesen in ihrer weltgeschichtlichen Entwicklung mit besonderen Berücksichtigung der grossen Seekrieg XVII und XVIII Jahrhunderts*, Vol. I: *Von den Anfängen bis 1740* (Berlin: Ernst Siegfried Mittler und Sohn, 1907), p. 282.

183 Alfred T. Mahan, *The Influence of Sea Power upon History 1660–1783* (Boston: Little, Brown, and Company, 1939), p. 125.

184 Alfred T. Mahan, *The Influence of Sea Power upon History 1660–1783* (Boston: Little, Brown, and Company, 1939), p. 182.

185 Alfred Stenzel, *Seekriegsgeschichte in ihren wichtigsten Abschnitten mit Berücksichtigung der Seetaktik*, Part 3: *Von 1600 bis 1720* (Hannover/Leipzig: Hahnsche Buchhandlung, 1910), p. 351.

186 Alfred Stenzel, *Seekriegsgeschichte in ihren wichtigsten Abschnitten mit Berücksichtigung der Seetaktik*, Part 3: *Von 1600 bis 1720* (Hannover/Leipzig: Hahnsche Buchhandlung, 1910), p. 351.

187 Alfred Stenzel, *Seekriegsgeschichte in ihren wichtigsten Abschnitten mit Berücksichtigung der Seetaktik*, Part 3: *Von 1600 bis 1720* (Hannover/Leipzig: Hahnsche Buchhandlung, 1910), p. 351.

188 Rudolph Rittmeyer, *Seekrieg und Seekriegswesen in ihrer weltgeschichtlichen Entwicklung mit besonderen Berücksichtigung der grossen Seekrieg XVII und XVIII Jahrhunderts*, Vol. I: *Von den Anfängen bis 1740* (Berlin: Ernst Siegfried Mittler und Sohn, 1907), p. 439.

189 Alfred T. Mahan, *The Influence of Sea Power upon History 1660–1783* (Boston: Little, Brown, and Company, 1939), p. 184.

190 Rudolph Rittmeyer, *Seekrieg und Seekriegswesen in ihrer weltgeschichtlichen Entwicklung mit besonderen Berücksichtigung der grossen Seekrieg XVII und XVIII Jahrhunderts*, Vol. I: *Von den Anfaengen bis 1740* (Berlin: Ernst Siegfried Mittler und Sohn, 1907), pp. 439–40.

191 Rudolph Rittmeyer, *Seekrieg und Seekriegswesen in ihrer weltgeschichtlichen Entwicklung mit besonderen Berücksichtigung der grossen Seekrieg XVII und XVIII Jahrhunderts*, Vol. I: *Von den Anfaengen bis 1740* (Berlin: Ernst Siegfried Mittler und Sohn, 1907), p. 440.

192 Department of Operations, *Naval Strategy* (Newport, RI: U.S. Naval War College, August 1936), p. 43.

193 William Oliver Stevens and Allan Westcott, *A History of Sea Power* (New York: Doubleday, Doran & Company, Inc., 1942), pp. 295, 297.

194 William Oliver Stevens and Allan Westcott, *A History of Sea Power* (New York: Doubleday, Doran & Company, Inc., 1942), p. 295.

195 William Oliver Stevens and Allan Westcott, *A History of Sea Power* (New York: Doubleday, Doran & Company, Inc., 1942), p. 300.

196 Julian S. Corbett, *Maritime Operations in the Russo-Japanese War 1904–1905* (Annapolis, MD: Naval Institute Press/Newport, RI: Naval War College Press, 1994), p. 333; William Oliver Stevens and Allan Westcott, *A History of Sea Power* (New York: Doubleday, Doran & Company, Inc., 1942), p. 301.

197 Alexander Meurer, *Seekriegsgeschichte in umrissen. Seemacht und Seekriege vornehmlich vom 16. Jahrhundert ab* (Leipzig: Verlag v. Hase & Koehler, 1925), p. 403; Julian S. Corbett, *Maritime Operations in the Russo-Japanese War 1904–1905* (Annapolis, MD: Naval Institute Press/Newport, RI: Naval War College Press, 1994), p. 333.

198 Alexander Meurer, *Seekriegsgeschichte in umrissen. Seemacht und Seekriege vornehmlich vom 16. Jahrhundert ab* (Leipzig: Verlag v. Hase & Koehler, 1925), p. 403.

199 Otto Groos, editor, *Der Krieg in der Nordsee*, Vol. 5: *Von Januar bis Juni 1916* (Berlin: Verlag von E.S. Mittler & Sohn, 1925), pp. 189–90.

200 Herbert Schottelius and Wilhelm Deist, editors, *Marine und Marinepolitik im kaiserlichen Deutschland 1871–1914* (Düsseldorf: Droste Verlag, 1972), p. 238.

201 Keith Yates, *Flawed Victory: Jutland 1916* (Annapolis, Md.: Naval Institute Press, 2000), pp. 118–19.

202 Otto Groos, *Seekriegslehren im Lichte des Weltkrieges. Ein Buch für den Seemann, Soldaten und Staatsmann* (Berlin: Verlag von E.S. Mittler & Sohn, 1929), p. 70.

203 Keith Yates, *Flawed Victory: Jutland 1916* (Annapolis, Md.: Naval Institute Press, 2000), pp. 118–19.

204 Arthur J. Marder, *From Dreadnought to Scapa Flow. The Royal Navy in the Fisher Era*, Vol. III: *Jutland and After (My 1916–December 1916)* (London: Oxford University Press, 1966), pp. 37, 39.

205 Geoffrey Bennett, *Naval Battles of the First World War* (New York: Scribner's, 1968), p. 242.

206 Arthur J. Marder, *From Dreadnought to Scapa Flow. The Royal Navy in the Fisher Era*, Vol. III: *Jutland and After (May 1916–December 1916)* (London: Oxford University Press, 1966), p. 205.

207 H. Engelmann, "Die Sicherstellung von Seeoperationen," *Militärwesen* (East Berlin), 3 (March 1980), p. 69; S. Filonov, "Morskaya Operatsiya," *Morskoy Sbornik* (Moscow), 10 (October 1977), p. 24.

208 Samuel E. Morison, *History of United States Naval Operations in World War II*, Vol. IV: *Coral Sea, Midway and Submarine Operations, May 1942–August 1942* (Boston: Little, Brown and Company, 1984), p. 113.

209 Samuel E. Morison, *History of United States Naval Operations in World War II*, Vol. IV: *Coral Sea, Midway and Submarine Operations, May 1942–August 1942* (Boston: Little, Brown and Company, 1984), p. 63.

210 Ministry of Defence (Navy), *War with Japan*, Vol. II: *Defensive Phase* (London: Her Majesty's Stationery Office, 1995), p. 146.

211 Ministry of Defence (Navy), *War with Japan*, Vol. III: *The Campaigns in the Solomons and New Guinea* (London: Her Majesty Stationery Office, 1995), pp. 135–37.

212 Mitsuo Fuchida and Masatake Okumiya, *Midway: The Battle That Doomed Japan* (Annapolis, MD: United States Naval Institute, 1955), p. 250.

213 Ministry of Defence (Navy), *War with Japan*, Vol. II: *Defensive Phase* (London: Her Majesty Stationery Office, 1995), p. 164.

214 Mitsuo Fuchida and Masatake Okumiya, *Midway: The Battle That Doomed Japan* (Annapolis, MD: United States Naval Institute, 1955), p. 249.

215 Samuel Eliot Morison, *History of United States Naval Operations in World War II*, Vol. XIII: *New Guinea and the Marianas, March 1944–August 1944* (Boston: Little, Brown and Company, 1953), p. 233.

216 Samuel Eliot Morison, *History of United States Naval Operations in World War II*, Vol. XIII: *New Guinea and the Marianas, March 1944–August 1944* (Boston: Little, Brown and Company, 1953), p. 233.

217 Samuel Eliot Morison, *History of United States Naval Operations in World War II*, Vol. XIII: *New Guinea and the Marianas, March 1944–August 1944* (Boston: Little, Brown and Company, 1953), p. 233.

218 United States Strategic Bombing Survey (Pacific), Naval Analysis Division, *The Campaigns of the Pacific War* (Washington, DC: United States Government Printing Office, 1946), p. 235.

219 Barrett Tillman, *Clash of the Carriers. The True Story of the Marianas Turkey Shoot of World War II* (New York: New American Library, Caliber, 2005), p. 102.

220 Thomas B. Buell, *The Quiet Warrior. A Biography of Admiral Raymond A. Spruance* (Annapolis, MD: Naval Institute Press, 1987), p. 303.

221 The island was named after *Ilha Formosa*, meaning "Beautiful Island," by the Portuguese in 1544 when their ships transited the Taiwan Strait on their way to Japan. The name "Taiwan" is of Chinese origin. Both names are alternately used here.

222 Elmer B. Potter, *Bull Halsey* (Annapolis, MD: Naval Institute Press, 1985), p. 306.

223 Jürgen Rohwer and Gerhard Hümmelchen, *Chronology of the War at Sea 1939–1945. The Naval History of World War II*, 2nd rev. ed. (Annapolis, MD: Naval Institute Press, 1992), p. 56.

224 Toshikazu Ohmae, "Japanese Operations in the Indian Ocean," in David C. Evans, editor, *The Japanese Navy in World War II. In the Words of Former Japanese Naval Officers*, 2nd ed. (Annapolis, MD: Naval Institute Press, 1986), pp. 109–10.

225 Jürgen Rohwer and Gerhard Hümmelchen, *Chronology of the War At Sea 1939–1945*, 2nd rev. exp. ed. (Annapolis, MD: Naval Institute Press 1992), p. 131.

226 Stephen W. Roskill, *History of the Second World War, The War at Sea*, Vol. II: *The Period of Balance* (London: Her Majesty's Stationery Office, 1956), p. 24.

227 Stephen W. Roskill, *History of the Second World War, The War at Sea*, Vol. II: *The Period of Balance* (London: Her Majesty's Stationery Office, 1956), p. 23.

228 Jürgen Rohwer and Gerhard Hümmelchen, *Chronology of the War at Sea 1939–1945*, 2nd, rev. exp. ed. (Annapolis, MD: Naval Institute Press, 1992), p. 132.

229 Stephen W. Roskill, *History of the Second World War, The War at Sea*, Vol. II: *The Period of Balance* (London: Her Majesty's Stationery Office, 1956), p. 23.

230 Ministry of Defence (Navy), *War with Japan*, Vol. II: *Defensive Phase* (London: Her Majesty Stationery Office, 1995), p. 128.

231 Stephen W. Roskill, *History of the Second World War, The War at Sea*, Vol. II: *The Period of Balance* (London: Her Majesty's Stationery Office, 1956), pp. 25–26.

232 Stephen W. Roskill, *History of the Second World War, The War at Sea*, Vol. II: *The Period of Balance* (London: Her Majesty's Stationery Office, 1956), pp. 27–28.

233 Ministry of Defence (Navy), *War with Japan*, Vol. II: *Defensive Phase* (London: Her Majesty Stationery Office, 1995), p. 130.

234 Stephen W. Roskill, *History of the Second World War, The War at Sea*, Vol. II: *The Period of Balance* (London: Her Majesty's Stationery Office, 1956), p. 30.

235 Toshikazu Ohmae, "Japanese Operations in the Indian Ocean," Shigeru Fukudome, and "The Hawaii Operation," in David C. Evans, editor, *The Japanese Navy in World War II. In the Words of Former Japanese Naval Officers*, 2nd ed. (Annapolis, MD: Naval Institute Press, 1986), p. 113.

236 Walter Jablonsky, "Die Seekriegführung im vierten Nahostkrieg," *Marine Rundschau*, No. 11 (November 1974), p. 654.

237 Benyamin Telem, "Die israelischen FK-Schnellboote im Yom-Kippur-Krieg," *Marine Rundschau*, No. 10 (October 1978), p. 640.

238 Walter Jablonsky, "Die Seekriegführung im vierten Nahostkrieg," *Marine Rundschau*, No. 11 (November 1974), p. 653.

239 Hartmut Zehrer, editor, *Der Golfkonflikt. Dokumentation, Analyse und Bewertung aus militärischer Sicht* (Herford/Bonn: Verlag E. S. Mittler & Sohn, 1992), p. 197.

240 Hartmut Zehrer, editor, *Der Golfkonflikt. Dokumentation, Analyse und Bewertung aus militärischer Sicht* (Herford/Bonn: Verlag E. S. Mittler & Sohn, 1992), pp. 197–98.

5 Destroying the enemy's forces by a decisive action at their bases

Attacks on the enemy fleet in its base has played a prominent role since the ancient era. Generally, the main purpose was to attack and destroy or damage as many as possible of enemy warships and merchant vessels. The situation in which a stronger fleet attacked enemy bases or anchorages varied greatly. Sometimes an attack was planned against the enemy fleet at its main base. At other times the enemy fleet took refuge in a fortified base and declined to accept battle.[1] In most cases in the era of oar/sail, attacks on the enemy fleet at a base or anchorage were conducted by numerically smaller forces and hence were not decisive. However, there were some notable exceptions to this, such as the examples of the British attacks on the French fleet at Quiberon Bay in November 1759 and at Aboukir Bay in August 1798.

Experience shows that in destroying the enemy naval force at its base(s), two main methods can be used: (1) penetration of the base's defenses and (2) attacks beyond the effective range of the enemy's defense. Prior to the advent of submarines and aircraft, attacks on the enemy fleet in its anchorage/port were primarily conducted by surface ships. Their attacks were sometimes combined with attacks by army troops from the land side. Only with the advent of aircraft was it possible to launch attacks beyond the effective range of the enemy defenses. Today, surface combatants and attack submarines armed with long range land attack cruise missiles (LACMs) can also be used in attacking enemy ships in their bases/ports.

In the past, a stronger side attacked the enemy fleet at its base or anchorage, blocking its exit. Another method used was to penetrate a port or anchorage and then sink or burn enemy naval vessels and/or merchant ships. With only few exceptions, such attacks results in relatively small losses of the weaker fleet. For example, the Athenians' defeat in the Battle of Syracuse in September 413 BC during the Peloponnesian War (431–404 BC) started its decline as a sea power. The political objective in its Sicilian Expedition (415–413 BC) was formally to support cities that had applied to Athens for help against other cities. However, the Athenians' real objective was to conquer Sicily. Alcibiades (450–404 BC) was appointed commander of the expedition, and the Athenian fleet assembled at Corcyra in June 415 BC.

It consisted of 134 triremes and at least 40 transports, 30 merchant ships, and 100 small vessels. The army comprised about 11,500 men, with the major part of the troops provided by Athens' allies.[2] In the second Battle of Syracuse on 28 August–13 September 414 BC, more than 200 Athenian triremes were destroyed, together with their highly trained and skilled crews. The Athenians lost some 60,000 men. The Athenian fleet that fought in Sicily simply ceased to exist.[3] This battle changed the course of the Peloponnesian War. To reach a decision by land, Athens would have had to raise an army large enough to defeat the Sparta-led Peloponnesian League. Yet that was beyond Athens' power. The League built up its naval strength, ultimately dooming the Athenian Navy and thereby leading to Athens' defeat.[4]

During the First Punic War (264–241 BC), in the siege of Lilybaeum in 249 BC, the Romans suffered a great defeat. Out of some 220 Roman ships only about 30 escaped; 97 ships were sunk, and another 93 were captured, as were some 20,000 Roman sailors. The Punic fleet under Adherbal suffered only minor losses. The Roman commander, Consul Publius Claudius (d. 249/246 BC), was recalled to Rome and forced to quit his command.[5] Carthage again controlled the sea. The Romans stopped building fleets and for five years practically abandoned the water. They had only enough ships to transport troops and occasionally fight pirates. Their main interest turned to land.[6]

On 19–23 June 1667, Admiral Michiel de Ruyter sailed into the Thames Estuary and penetrated (despite unfavorable winds) with 64 ships, 20 craft, and 15 fireships as far as Gravesend, within some 20 miles of London. At Gravesend, he destroyed some 20 merchant ships and ten to 12 warships,[7] captured Sheerness, and destroyed the arsenal nearby.[8] He burned three ships of the line and carried off to Holland the flagship of General-at-sea Robert Blake.[9] The Dutch kept control of the entrance to the Thames until the end of June.[10] This raid was considered the most shameful incident in English naval history.[11] Although the British losses in ships destroyed were not significant, the effect of this bold action was highly adverse for Britain. De Ruyter's defeat coincided with the Great Fire of London, which burned down the areas most affected by the Great Plague (brought under control in 1666). This led king Charles II to consent to peace with the Netherlands, and on 31 June 1667 the Peace of Breda was signed.[12]

The Battle of Quiberon Bay (near St. Nazaire) (known as Bataille des Cardinaux by the French) on 20 November 1759 was the most decisive battle of the Seven Years' War (1756–1763). The British fleet, led by Admiral Edward Hawke, defeated the French fleet under Marchal Louis de Brienne de Conflans d'Armentières (1711–1774). The reason for this battle was the British determination to prevent the French invasion of Britain. The main French invading force of some 15,000 or 20,000 men (depending on the source), intended to land in Scotland, was assembled at Morbihan, Quiberon Bay. A smaller army detachment was assembled at Ostend and would land at the Thames Estuary. Another smaller army contingent at Dunkirk would land in Ireland. The French plan was to join the Brest and Toulon squadrons at Morbihan Bay to cover the landing in Scotland.[13]

The original French plan envisaged that only five ships of the line plus some smaller vessels would cover the landing force for Scotland. However, de Conflans insisted that the entire fleet should be used for supporting the landing. French Minister of Marine Nicolas René Berryer (1703–1762) believed that de Conflans was not a skillful enough tactician to ensure that the troops' arrival at the Clyde River (Scotland) without seeking a decisive encounter. Hence, in his view, it would be better to fight a general action prior to departure of the troops. The troop transports were therefore assembled not at Brest but in ports southward as far as the Loire Estuary.[14]

Instead of in July, the invading force was not ready until November 1759. The French Brest squadron consisted of 22 ships of the line. The Toulon squadron of 12 ships of the line was intercepted by the British fleet of 13 ships of the line under Admiral Edward Boscawen (1711–1761) in the Strait of Gibraltar on 18 August 1759 and was almost completely destroyed. A small detachment from that squadron fled to Lagos (southern Portugal), but the British followed it and eventually destroyed it even though it was in a neutral place.[15]

On 14 November, de Conflans finally sailed. Hawke, who was forced to go to Torbay because of heavy weather, went out to the sea on 12 November. He came back with 27 ships of the line to station off Brest, only to learn that the French fleet had sailed southward, bound for Quiberon Bay.[16] Hawke also had a blockading squadron of four 50-gun ships. He sailed to Quiberon Bay, hoping that he would arrive there first and force the enemy to take a position between his squadron and the beaches some six miles to leeward.[17] The Quiberon Bay anchorage has a large number of islands and dangerous reefs. Hence, de Conflans believed it impossible that the British would follow him. Hawke believed the opposite: where French ships can sail, British ships can sail too.[18] Hawke was a skillful seaman and was not deterred by the navigational difficulties. He also realized that, if the French led the way, they would act partially as his pilots. Hawke was convinced that his officers were better trained and more skillful than the French because of their experience in blockading duties.[19]

Nothing went according to de Conflans' plans. Hawke arrived at Quiberon Bay on 20 November. The British attack was carried out in heavy weather and under extremely difficult navigatory conditions. The ensuing battle pitted ship against ship.[20] The British lost only two ships of the line (that went aground), 50 men killed and some 250 wounded. The French losses were much higher; three ships of the line were sunk, one captured, and two burned. In addition, eight ships of the line escaped to Rochefort and seven others, plus some frigates, to the mouth of the Vilaine River. They were as good as being lost.[21] Two ships of the line, plus frigates, at Vilaine escaped in January 1761; two more got out in November 1761; and the last ship of the line escaped in April 1762.[22]

The Battle at Quiberon Bay had a decisive impact on the further course of the war at sea. With the destruction of the Brest squadron, the French hopes to invade England simply vanished.[23] The French Navy in the Atlantic was paralyzed for the remainder of the war. The British fleet was able to operate freely against the French and later also Spanish colonies.[24] France lost all links with its colonies. In 1760, Montreal was lost to the British, and then followed the loss of the islands in West Indies (Guadeloupe, Dominica, and Martinique).[25]

A classic example of a single annihilating blow against an enemy fleet at its base prior to the advent of aircraft was the British attack on the French fleet anchored at Aboukir Bay (some 20 miles northeast of Alexandria) on 1–3 August 1798. Rear Admiral Horatio Nelson, with 13 ships of the line (plus one fourth-rate ship of the line and sloop each), attacked and literally annihilated the French fleet of 13 ships of the line and four frigates under Admiral Francois-Paul Brueys d'Aigalliers (1753–1798). The French believed that their fleet was well protected by the shoals and batteries of Aboukir Island and that it would be impossible for the British ships to pass inside their line. The French also enjoyed a substantial superiority in the number of guns and manpower.[26] The speed and ferocity of the British attack took the French by surprise. Many French sailors were on duty ashore and thereby unprepared for an immediate action.[27] The French losses were heavy. The British destroyed two ships of the line, and nine others were captured. The French losses also included two frigates plus several smaller vessels. About 1,700 French sailors were killed and 1,500 wounded (this included 1,000 captured), plus 2,000 others captured.[28] The British losses were 218 killed and 678 wounded.[29] Mahan wrote that Nelson gave a most brilliant example of grand tactics, "the art of making good combinations preliminary to battles as well as during their progress."[30]

The French fleet was not only defeated but destroyed, cutting off Napoleon Bonaparte from the homeland. The French did not have any other fleet available to support his plans in the Middle East.[31] This catastrophic event eventually had far-reaching and negative consequences for Napoleon's fortunes in Egypt.[32] His Mameluk enemies were not completely destroyed. Napoleon was unable to receive reinforcements because the British had control of the Mediterranean. Napoleon still achieved some other victories in Egypt, including the Battle of Aboukir on 25 July 1799. However, he left Egypt and on 9 October 1799 landed in France.[33] The French presence in Egypt ended with the British invasion of Egypt in October 1800. The British troops and the Ottoman Army captured Cairo on 27 June 1801. Eventually, the remaining 30,000 French troops in the Nile Valley surrendered on 30 August 1801. They were evacuated from Egypt under the terms of the Treaty of Amiens on 1 October 1801, which ended the War of the Second Coalition against France.[34]

The political consequences of the French defeat at Aboukir Bay were significant. England restored its dominance in the Mediterranean, and its political influence was greatly increased. It came in close and constant touch with Russia.[35] On 9 September 1798, the (Sublime) Porte (central government of the Ottoman Empire) declared war on France.[36] The Kingdom of Naples and the Tsarist Russia also joined the British-led coalition. The Russo-Turkish fleet entered the Mediterranean and proceeded to eject the French from Corfù and Dalmatia; Malta was then closely watched. Port Mahón on Minorca was captured by a British contingent based in Gibraltar. A new lease on life was given to England's lucrative trade with Turkey.[37] The French threat to the approaches to India was dissipated. Napoleon I's dreams of an eastern empire were demolished.[38]

During the Greek War for Independence (1821–1829), three major European powers – Britain, France, and Russia – sided with the Greek rebels. After receiving reports that the combined Ottoman-Egpytian fleet planed to attack the Greek island of Hydra (between Saronic and Argolic Gulfs, the Aegean Sea), the Anglo French force under the British Vice Admiral Edward Codrington (1770–1851) anchored in a single line at Navarino (Pylos today) on the southwestern coast of the Peloponnesus) on 10 September 1827. A prolonged truce followed. The Russian fleet joined the allies on 11 October. Seven days afterward, the Allies demanded that the Turks must conclude negotiations before the winter. They entered Navarino Bay. Some 11 Anglo-French ships and 16 other ships faced seven Turkish ships and 58 smaller vessels. In the ensuing gunnery duel, the Turks lost one ship of the line, 34 frigates and corvettes, and the best of the Turkish officer corps. After their fleet was destroyed, the Turks were unable to move their troops by sea. However, the Turkish troops offered stubborn resistance until November 1828 when the French troops finally captured the last Turkish strongpoint in Morea. The Russian Black Sea Fleet supported their army's advance to Varna, Bulgaria., and a blockade of the Turkish coast in the Black Sea and the Mediterranean followed.[39]

On the night of 8/9 February 1904, the Japanese carried out a surprise attack against the Russian squadron anchored at Port Arthur without a declaration of war (Japan formally declared war on 10 February). Port Arthur was unsuitable as a base for major ships. It was not deepened to allow major ships to sail into and out of it except during high tide. It was separated from the other large Russian naval base in the Pacific, Vladivostok, by some 1,100 miles. The state of the Russian fleet in the Far East was abysmal. On the Russian ships, training in gunnery and navigation was grossly neglected for many years. Reportedly, it took up to 22 hours to move the fleet out of Port Arthur.[40]

The Russian fleet in the Far East consisted of seven battleships and five protected cruisers with escorts.[41] The Russians anchored its fleet in the roadstead outside the harbor (so as to take less time to sail out), making them more vulnerable to an enemy attack.[42] In the northernmost line were five battleships; in the middle line were two other battleships, plus three cruisers; and in the southernmost line were three more cruisers with the duty ship. Two Russian destroyers were patrolling some 20 miles out of the base. The Japanese knew that the Russian fleet had returned from an exercise off Dalny, Talienwan Bay (some 45 miles away from Port Arthur, in the Yellow Sea) and was unlikely to sail out in a day or two.[43]

Admiral Heihachirō Tōgō's force consisted of six battleships, five armored cruisers, some 15 destroyers, and 20 torpedo boats.[44] The Japanese fleet was about 60 miles away, anchored at an advanced base established on the Elliot islands.[45] The attack was carried out by the Japanese destroyers. Despite ideal conditions for a surprise attack, the results were relatively poor. Out of the 16 torpedoes fired, all but three either missed or failed to explode. Still, two Russian battleships and one large cruiser were torpedoed and put out of commission. The Russians had some 150 killed and the Japanese 132. Both fleets had many ships heavily damaged. However, the Japanese had many dry-docking facilities available, whereas the Russians had only one small dock at Port Arthur, plus one incomplete.[46] With the raid, the Japanese secured numerical superiority on the first day of the war. On the next day, Tōgō was able to destroy the remaining Russian battleships. However, he chose instead to engage in the ineffective shelling of the Port Arthur.[47]

Theoretically, a naval base/port could be *penetrated* by surface ships, submarines, and special forces. In the past, surface ships were largely used in penetrating enemy naval base/ports and anchorages. Such actions could be decisive if a large enough number of enemy ships were destroyed. Penetration of naval bases is usually very difficult because the approach of one's forces is hard to conceal. One's forces are also operating within the effective range of the enemy's defenses on the coast.

After the advent of aircraft, attacks by a stronger side against the enemy fleet at its bases were much more decisive. A stronger side at sea can plan and execute a major operation aimed at destroying or neutralizing a major part of the enemy's fleet at its bases. Not only enemy ships but airfields and other facilities/installations should be destroyed. Such major naval operations could be conducted either at the opening of the hostilities, when neither side possesses sea control, or during the hostilities when control is contested. Generally, a major naval/joint operation against the enemy fleet at its bases is difficult to organize and execute. The advantages are usually with the defender. To attack successfully the major part of the enemy fleet in its base, it is not necessary to have numerical superiority. For example, in World War II the majority of attacks against the enemy fleet at its bases were conducted with small forces. Hence, they did not have decisive results. Such attacks were part of one's efforts to destroy enemy naval/air forces over time.

Experience shows that the best results against the enemy fleet at its bases have been achieved by conducting air strikes from beyond the effective range of the enemy's defenses. Such strikes could be conducted by carriers and/or land-based bombers and attack aircraft. For example, the British attack on the major Italian naval base at Tarent (Taranto) on 11–12 November 1940 (Operation JUDGMENT) was conducted over a contested sea.

Taranto is some 320 miles away from Malta. The inner harbor, Mar Piccolo, is almost entirely landlocked except for a narrow channel. It allowed entrance to cruisers and smaller ships but not to battleships. The outer harbor, Mar Grande, was used by the battleships and was protected by a long breakwater.[48]

The original British plan envisaged two carriers (*Illustrious, Eagle*) attacking the Italian ships at Tarent on 21 October. By mid-October 1940, both carriers completed a series of exercises, including night flying, and were considered ready for the operation. However, because of a fire on board one carrier (*Illustrious*), the operation was delayed. The final date for the execution of Operation JUDGMENT was fixed for 11 November. The planners hoped to take advantage of the expected confusion among the Italians because several other actions by the British forces would take place at the same time. Operation JUDGMENT was part of the MB8 operation to be carried out between 4 and 14 November. This larger effort would include the movement of a convoy (MW3) from Egypt to Malta and Soudha Bay, Crete, and another convoy (AN6) from Egypt to the Aegean, plus movement of Force F from Gibraltar to Alexandria (Operation COAT). Force F, consisting of one battleship (*Barham*), two cruisers (*Berwick, Glasgow*), plus three destroyers, would disembark troops at Malta. At the same time, Force H would sail from Malta to Egypt (Operation CRACK), in conjunction with the passage of one monitor and destroyer each from Malta to Soudha Bay. Another convoy (AS5) would sail from the Aegean to Egypt, while two cruisers (*Ajax, Sydney*) would sail from Port Said to Soudha Bay with troops and equipment, and one cruiser (*Orion*) would carry RAF stores and personnel from Port Said to Piraeus and Soudha Bay.[49]

As planned, in the evening of 11 November, one aircraft carrier (*Illustrious*), with 21 aircraft and accompanying escort ships, launched a two-wave air attack against the Italian ships at Tarent from a distance of about 180 miles. The attackers achieved complete surprise.[50] One Italian battleship (*Littorio*) was hit with three torpedoes, while two others (*Duilio, Cavour*) received one hit each. Out of 60 bombs dropped, some 25 percent failed to explode (including those that hit one cruiser and destroyer each, plus two fleet auxiliaries). The bombs that did go off caused fires in the dockyard and at the seaplane base. The attack left the Italian Navy with only two battleships in service (*Vittorio Veneto, Giulio Cesare*).[51] All but two British aircraft returned safely to their carriers.[52] In the aftermath, the Allies had temporary control of the surface in the central Mediterranean.

The Japanese surprise attack on Pearl Harbor on 7 December 1941 was carried out at the very outset of the hostilities. The operational objective of the attack was to destroy the major part of the U.S. Pacific Fleet to prevent it from interfering with the Japanese invasion of the Philippines. Navy Minister Admiral Shigetarō Shimada (1883–1976), was strongly against the plan to attack Pearl Harbor. He wanted the United States to commit the first act of war and thereby enable Japan to declare war. Shimada wanted Japan to declare war only on Britain and The Netherlands.[53] However, he was overruled. The Japanese attack force consisted of six fast carriers screened by the 1st Destroyer Squadron (four destroyers) and support force of 3rd Battleship Division, plus 8th Cruiser Division. The remainder of the attacking force consisted of a Patrol Force (three I-class submarines), the Supply Force (ten oilers), plus the Midway Bombardment Unit (7th Destroyer Division).[54] The Japanese plan envisaged that the first attacking force would arrive at a point some 230 nm north of Z point (26° N; 158° W, some 275 miles north of Pearl Harbor) at 0130 on X-Day, while the second attack unit would reach a position about 200 nm north of Z point at 0245 on X-Day.[55] This operation was unique because the Japanese objective was to prevent the possible interference by the U.S. Pacific Fleet in the invasion of the Philippines. The only force that could have possibly prevented the Japanese from occupying the Philippines was not the Asiatic Fleet in the Philippines but the U.S. battle fleet in Hawaii.[56] However, that fleet was more than 5,000 miles away from the Philippines. It did not pose any immediate threat to the Japanese forces intended to invade the Philippine islands.

The Japanese carried out a two-wave attack on Pearl Harbor with total of 350 aircraft. Some 190 aircraft took part in the first wave and 161 aircraft in the second wave. In the attack, three battleships (*Arizona, California, West Virginia*) were sunk, one battleship (*Oklahoma*) was capsized, one battleship (*Nevada*) was heavily damaged, and three others (*Maryland, Pennsylvania, Tennessee*) were damaged. Also, two heavy cruisers (*Helena, Raleigh*) were heavily damaged, and another cruiser (*Honolulu*) was damaged). Other losses included three destroyers heavily damaged, one repair ship heavily damaged, one minelayer sunk, one seaplane tender damaged, and one target ship capsized.[57] The U.S. losses were over 2,000 officers and men killed and 710 wounded. The Army and Marine Corps had 327 men killed and 433 wounded. [58] The Japanese lost some 30 aircraft in the attack.[59] In military terms, the Japanese attackers accomplished an operational objective; they temporarily crippled the U.S. Pacific Fleet's battle line. However, they did not destroy the fast carriers, which were by fortunate coincidence at sea and not in Pearl Harbor, nor did they destroy the critically important shore installations. The U.S. carriers were, in fact, the true operational center of gravity for the Japanese, not the battleships. But the political and psychological consequences of the attack on Pearl Harbor were extremely negative for the Japanese. Their unprovoked attack on U.S. soil made the American people determined to prosecute war until the unconditional surrender of Japan.

In other cases, attacks against the enemy fleet could be conducted when its naval base is also besieged by one's ground forces. For example, in the first phase of their invasion of Soviet Russia, the Germans tried to seize Leningrad (St. Petersburg today) from the landside. The aim was to destroy the heavy surface ships of the Soviet Baltic Fleet bottled up in the Leningrad-Kronshtadt area. The First Air Fleet (Luftflotte 1), responsible for cooperation with the Army Group North, assigned one squadron of its Ju-87 Stuka dive bombers specially adapted to carry a single 2,200-pound bomb to attack ships. The first attack between 16 and 19 September 1941 failed, but more success was achieved on 21 September when heavy damages were inflicted on one battleship, which subsequently sunk. The same day, the German bombers damaged another battleship and one heavy cruiser, while one destroyer was sunk. On 23 September, the Luftwaffe's aircraft sunk one Soviet destroyer and submarine each, capsized one destroyer, and damaged two heavy cruisers, two destroyers, one submarine tender, one submarine, and one torpedo craft.[60]

In April 1942, the Germans launched a major air operation (Operation EISSTOSS) to eliminate the remnants of the Soviet Baltic Fleet. The First Air Fleet received an order on 26 February to prepare an attack to destroy all the enemy ships in the Gulf of Finland (one battleship, two heavy cruisers, and one minelaying cruiser). The German plan also envisaged support from the siege artillery of the 18th Army Corps.[61] The operation, executed by the I Air Corps, started on 4 April when 95 Ju-87s/-88 bombers attacked enemy surface ships, while 37 He-111 aircraft suppressed Soviet air defenses. Fighter protection was provided by about 60 Me-109s. In another attack with about 30 He-111s on the night of 4–5 April, one Soviet battleship, four cruisers, and one destroyer were heavily damaged while one minelaying cruiser, one destroyer, and one training ship were slightly damaged.[62] In the series of attacks carried out on 24 April, (Operation GÖTZ VON BERLICH-INGEN), the German bombers attacked enemy ships and shore facilities, but only one Soviet cruiser suffered further damage. Despite many efforts, the Germans failed in their stated objective to destroy the Soviet surface fleet bottled up in the Gulf of Finland.[63] Moreover, the Soviet warships continued to provide fire support to the defenders on the Leningrad front and the Oranienbaum beachhead.[64]

Air strikes against enemy naval bases in an enclosed sea, such as the Persian (Arabian) Gulf, could be far more effective than those mounted from the open ocean because of the much shorter distances and the larger number of land-based aircraft that can be used. Such strikes can be conducted with high intensity and repeated at short intervals. In some instances, not only fixed-wing aircraft but also missile-armed helicopters can be effectively employed. For example, between 25 and 28 January 1991, U.S./Coalition forces aircraft attacked Iraqi ships based in Umm Qasr, Bubiyan Channel, and the Port of Kuwait. One Iraqi minelayer, two patrol craft, and one transport were sunk in these attacks.[65] In another action on 4 February, the U.S./Coalition aircraft attacked the Iraqi naval base Al Kalia and disabled two missile craft. Helicopters from a U.S. frigate engaged four Iraqi patrol craft off the Maradin Island; one of them was sunk and another damaged.[66] These strikes in combination with actions of surface ships resulted in control of the northern part of the Persian (Arabian) Gulf for the U.S./Coalition forces.

Nuclear-powered attack submarines (SSNs), modern conventionally powered attack submarines (SSKs), land- and carrier-based aircraft, and surface ships armed with long-range antiship cruise missiles/land attack cruise missiles (ASCMs/LACMs) are the most effective platforms for destroying enemy ships. For example, in the first few days after the start of the air offensive against Iraq on 17 January 1991, U.S. carrier-based aircraft and SSNs deployed in the Arabian Gulf and the Red Sea repeatedly struck Iraqi naval installations near Umm Qasr and Basra with "smart" bombs and Tomahawk missiles.[67]

For the immediate future, it is unlikely that major fleet-vs.-fleet operations will be conducted on the open ocean. A more likely scenario of a war either between the navies of riparian states in an enclosed or semi-enclosed sea or between a blue-water navy and one operating in the littorals. Optimally, a stronger side at sea should, from the beginning of hostilities, focus on destroying the enemy naval forces and aircraft in naval/air bases and ports by conducting massive and almost simultaneous attacks and strikes, using all naval combat arms and air forces. These actions should be complemented by destroying enemy naval forces at sea and aircraft.

Notes

1 A.C. Davidonis, "Harbor Forcing Operations," *Military Affairs*, Vol. 8, No. 2 (Summer 1944), p. 81.
2 Reginald Custance, *War at Sea. Modern Theory and Ancient Practice* (Edinburgh/London: William Blackwood and Sons, 1919), pp. 66–67.
3 Arthur MacCartney Shepard, *Sea Power in Ancient History. The Story of the Navies of Classic Greece and Rome* (London: William Heineman Ltd., 1925), pp. 107–08.
4 Reginald Custance, *War at Sea. Modern Theory and Ancient Practice* (Edinburgh/London: William Blackwood and Sons, 1919), p. 77; R. Ernest Dupuy and Trevor N. Dupuy, *The Encyclopedia of Military History from 3500 B.C. to the Present*, 2nd rev. ed. (New York: Harper & Row, Publishers, 1986), p. 557.
5 Arthur MacCartney Shepard, *Sea Power in Ancient History. The Story of the Navies of Classic Greece and Rome* (London: William Heineman Ltd., 1925), p. 161.
6 Arthur MacCartney Shepard, *Sea Power in Ancient History. The Story of the Navies of Classic Greece and Rome* (London: William Heineman Ltd., 1925), p. 163.
7 Alfred Stenzel, *Seekriegsgeschichte in ihren wichtigsten Abschnitten mit Berücksichtigung der Seetaktik*, Part 3: *Von 1600 bis 1720* (Hannover/Leipzig: Hahnsche Buchhandlung, 1909), pp. 176–77.
8 Rudolph Rittmeyer, *Seekrieg und Seekriegswesen in ihrer weltgeschichtlichen Entwicklung mit besonderen Berücksichtigung der grossen Seekrieg XVII und XVIII Jahrhunderts*, Vol I: *Von den Anfaengen bis 1740* (Berlin: Ernst Siegfried Mittler und Sohn, 1907), p. 292.
9 Geoffrey Callender, *The Naval Side of British History* (Boston: Little, Brown, and Company, 1924), p. 117.
10 Alfred T. Mahan, *The Influence of Sea Power upon History 1660–1783* (Boston: Little, Brown, and Company, 1939), p. 132.
11 Geoffrey Callender, *The Naval Side of British History* (Boston: Little, Brown, and Company, 1924), p. 117.
12 Alfred T. Mahan, *The Influence of Sea Power upon History 1660–1783* (Boston: Little, Brown, and Company, 1939), p. 132.

13 Alexander Meurer, *Seekriegsgeschichte in umrissen. Seemacht und Seekriege vornehm-lich vom 16. Jahrhundert ab* (Leipzig: Verlag v. Hase & Koehler, 1925), pp. 273–74.

14 Alfred T. Mahan, *The Influence of Sea Power upon History 1660–1783* (Boston: Lit-tle, Brown, and Company, 1939), p. 300.

15 Alexander Meurer, *Seekriegsgeschichte in Umrissen. Seemacht und Seekriege vornehm-lich vom 16. Jahrhundert ab* (Leipzig: Verlag v. Hase & Koehler, 1925), p. 275.

16 Alfred T. Mahan, *The Influence of Sea Power upon History 1660–1783* (Boston: Lit-tle, Brown, and Company, 1939), p. 301.

17 Alfred T. Mahan, *The Influence of Sea Power upon History 1660–1783* (Boston: Lit-tle, Brown, and Company, 1939), p. 302.

18 Alexander Meurer, *Seekriegsgeschichte in Umrissen. Seemacht und Seekriege vornehm-lich vom 16. Jahrhundert ab* (Leipzig: Verlag v. Hase & Koehler, 1925), p. 275.

19 Alfred T. Mahan, *The Influence of Sea Power upon History 1660–1783* (Boston: Lit-tle, Brown, and Company, 1939), p. 302.

20 Alexander Meurer, *Seekriegsgeschichte in Umrissen. Seemacht und Seekriege vornehm-lich vom 16. Jahrhundert ab* (Leipzig: Verlag v. Hase & Koehler, 1925), p. 276.

21 Rudolph Rittmeyer, *Seekrieg und Seekriegswesen in ihrer weltgeschichtlichen Entwick-lung mit besonderen Berücksichtigung der grossen Seekrieg XVII und XVIII Jahrhunderts*, Vol. II: *Von 1739–1793* (Berlin: Ernst Siegfried Mittler und Sohn, 1911), p. 159.

22 Alfred T. Mahan, *The Influence of Sea Power upon History 1660–1783* (Boston: Lit-tle, Brown, and Company, 1939), p. 303; Rudolph Rittmeyer, *Seekrieg und Seekriegs-wesen in ihrer weltgeschichtlichen Entwicklung mit besonderen Berücksichtigung der grossen Seekrieg XVII und XVIII Jahrhunderts*, Vol II: *Von 1739–1793* (Berlin: Ernst Siegfried Mittler und Sohn, 1911), p. 159.

23 Alexander Meurer, *Seekriegsgeschichte in umrissen. Seemacht und Seekriege vornehm-lich vom 16. Jahrhundert ab* (Leipzig: Verlag v. Hase & Koehler, 1925), p. 276.

24 Rudolph Rittmeyer, *Seekrieg und Seekriegswesen in ihrer weltgeschichtlichen Entwick-lung mit besonderen Berücksichtigung der grossen Seekrieg XVII und XVIII Jahrhun-derts*, Vol II: *Von 1739–1793* (Berlin: Ernst Siegfried Mittler und Sohn, 1911), p. 159.

25 Alexander Meurer, *Seekriegsgeschichte in umrissen. Seemacht und Seekriege vornehm-lich vom 16. Jahrhundert ab* (Leipzig: Verlag v. Hase & Koehler, 1925), p. 276.

26 C.J. Marcus, *The Age of Nelson. The Royal Navy in the Age of Its Greatest Power and Glory 1793–1815* (New York: Viking Press, 1971), p. 132.

27 C.J. Marcus, *The Age of Nelson. The Royal Navy in the Age of Its Greatest Power and Glory 1793–1815* (New York: Viking Press, 1971), p. 133.

28 Alfred Stenzel, *Seekriegsgeschichte in ihren wichtigsten Abschnitten mit Berücksichti-gung der Seetaktik*, Part 4: *Von 1720 bis 1850* (Hannover/Leipzig: Hahnsche Buch-handlung, 1911), p. 252.

29 Alfred Stenzel, *Seekriegsgeschichte in ihren wichtigsten Abschnitten mit Berücksichti-gung der Seetaktik*, Part 4: *Von 1720 bis 1850* (Hannover/Leipzig: Hahnsche Buch-handlung, 1911), p. 253.

30 Alfred T. Mahan, *The Influence of Sea Power upon History 1660–1783* (Boston: Lit-tle, Brown, and Company, 1939), p. 10.

31 Alfred Stenzel, *Seekriegsgeschichte in ihren wichtigsten Abschnitten mit Berücksichti-gung der Seetaktik*, Part 4: *Von 1720 bis 1850* (Hannover/Leipzig: Hahnsche Buch-handlung, 1911), p. 254.

32 David G. Chandler, *The Campaigns of Napoleon* (New York: Scribner, 1966), p. 217.

33 David G. Chandler, *The Campaigns of Napoleon* (New York: Scribner, 1966), p. 245.

34 David G. Chandler, *The Campaigns of Napoleon* (New York: Scribner, 1966), p. 245.

35 C.J. Marcus, *The Age of Nelson. The Royal Navy in the Age of Its Greatest Power and Glory 1793–1815* (New York: Viking Press, 1971), p. 141.

36 Alexander Meurer, *Seekriegsgeschichte in Umrissen. Seemacht und Seekriege vornehm-lich vom 16. Jahrhundert ab* (Leipzig: Verlag v. Hase & Koehler, 1925), p. 334.
37 C.J. Marcus, *The Age of Nelson. The Royal Navy in the Age of Its Greatest Power and Glory 1793–1815* (New York: Viking Press, 1971), p. 141; Herbert Richmond, *Statesmen and Sea Power* (Oxford: Clarendon Press, first published 1946, reprinted 1947), p. 198.
38 C.J. Marcus, *The Age of Nelson. The Royal Navy in the Age of Its Greatest Power and Glory 1793–1815* (New York: Viking Press, 1971), p. 141.
39 Richard Harding, *Seapower and Naval Warfare 1650-1830* (Annapolis, MD: Naval Institute Press, 1999), pp. 278-79.
40 Donald W. Mitchell, "Admiral Makarov: Attack! Attack! Attack!" *United States Naval Proceedings*, July 1965, pp. 64–65.
41 Richard Connaughton, *Rising Sun and Tumbling Bear. Russia's War with Japan* (London: Cassell, 2003), p. 46.
42 Richard Connaughton, *Rising Sun and Tumbling Bear. Russia's War with Japan* (London: Cassell, 2003), p. 44.
43 Richard Connaughton, *Rising Sun and Tumbling Bear. Russia's War with Japan* (London: Cassell, 2003), p. 46
44 Richard Connaughton, *Rising Sun and Tumbling Bear. Russia's War with Japan* (London: Cassell, 2003), p. 50.
45 Richard Connaughton, *Rising Sun and Tumbling Bear. Russia's War with Japan* (London: Cassell, 2003), p. 46.
46 Richard Connaughton, *Rising Sun and Tumbling Bear. Russia's War with Japan* (London: Cassell, 2003), p. 50.
47 Alexander Meurer, *Seekriegsgeschichte in umrissen. Seemacht und Seekriege vornehm-lich vom 16. Jahrhundert ab* (Leipzig: Verlag v. Hase & Koehler, 1925), pp. 392–93.
48 Angelo N. Carravagio, "The Attack at Taranto. Tactical Success, Operational Failure," *Naval War College Review*, Vol. 59, No. 3 (Summer 2006), p. 198.
49 Angelo N. Carravagio, "The Attack at Taranto. Tactical Success, Operational Failure," *Naval War College Review*, Vol. 59, No. 3 (Summer 2006), p. 110.
50 Stephen W. Roskill, *The War at Sea*, Vol. I: *The Defensive* (London: Her Majesty's Stationery Office, 1954), pp. 300–01; Rohwer and Hümmelchen, *Chronology of the War at Sea 1939–1945. The Naval History of World War II* (Annapolis, MD: Naval Institute Press, 2005), p. 41.
51 Angelo N. Carravagio, "The Attack at Taranto. Tactical Success, Operational Failure," *Naval War College Review*, Vol. 59, No. 3 (Summer 2006), p. 112.
52 Stephen W. Roskill, *The War at Sea*, Vol. I: *The Defensive* (London: Her Majesty's Stationery Office, 1954), pp. 300–01; Rohwer and Hümmelchen, *Chronology of the War at Sea 1939–1945. The Naval History of World War II* (Annapolis, MD: Naval Institute Press, 2005), p. 41.
53 Shigeru Fukudome, "The Hawaii Operation," in David C. Evans, editor, *The Japanese Navy in World War II. In the Words of Former Japanese Naval Officers*, 2nd ed. (Annapolis, MD: Naval Institute Press, 1986), p. 6.
54 "Pearl Harbor Operations: General Outline of Orders and Plans," in Donald M. Goldstein and Katherine V. Dillon, *The Pearl Harbor Papers. Inside the Japanese Plans* (Washington, DC: Brassey's, 1993), p. 98.
55 "Pearl Harbor Operations: General Outline of Orders and Plans," in Donald M. Goldstein and Katherine V. Dillon, *The Pearl Harbor Papers. Inside the Japanese Plans* (Washington, DC: Brassey's, 1993), p. 100; Samuel E. Morison, *History of United States Naval Operations in World War II*, Vol. III: *The Rising Sun in the Pacific, 1931–April 1942* (Boston, MA: Little, Brown and Company, 1959), p. 93.
56 On 8 December 1941, the Asiatic Fleet was deployed as follows: at Manila/Olon-gapo (4 destroyers, 13 submarines, 3 submarines tenders, 6 gunboats, 2 sea-plane tenders with 33 planes, 5 minesweepers, 2 tankers, 3 salvage vessels/tugs, 1 floating dock); elsewhere in the Philippines (1 heavy cruiser, 1 light cruiser, 2

submarines; 2 seaplane tenders with 8 planes, 1 station ship); at Tarakan, Borneo (1 light cruiser, 5 destroyers); and at Balikpapan, Borneo (4 destroyers, 1 destroyer tender) Samuel E. Morison, *History of United States Naval Operations in World War II*, Vol. III: *The Rising Sun in the Pacific, 1931–April 1942* (Boston, MA: Little, Brown and Company, 1959), pp. 158–60.

57 Ministry of Defence (Navy), *War with Japan*, Vol. II: *Defensive Phase* (London: Her Majesty's Stationery Office, 1995), pp. 21–22.

58 Samuel E. Morison, *The Two-Ocean War. A Short History of the United States Navy in the Second World War* (Boston: Little. Brown and Company, 1963), p. 67.

59 Ministry of Defence (Navy), *War with Japan*, Vol. II: *Defensive Phase* (London: Her Majesty's Stationery Office, 1995), p. 22.

60 Jürgen Rohwer, "Der Minenkrieg im Finnischen Meerbusen, Part II: September–November 1941," *Marine Rundschau*, No. 2 (February 1967), pp. 97–100.

61 Gerhard Hümmelchen, "Unternehmen 'Eisstoss'—Der Angriff der Luftflotte 1 gegen die russischen Ostseeflotte im April 1942," *Marine Rundschau*, No. 4 (April 1959), pp. 226, 229.

62 The plan of attack envisaged the following priority of targets: battleship, *Kirov*-class cruisers, the half-completed former German heavy cruiser *Lützow*, and a minelaying cruiser; Rohwer and Hümmelchen, *Chronology of the War at Sea 1939–1945. The Naval History of World War II* (Annapolis, MD: Naval Institute Press, 2005), p. 134.

63 Between 4 and 30 April 1942, about 600 aircraft, including 162 Stukas, attacked a variety of ships in the Leningrad-Kronshtadt area, resulting in a loss of 29 German aircraft Hümmelchen "Unternehmen 'Eisstoss'—Der Angriff der Luftflotte 1 gegen die russischen Ostseeflotte im April 1942," *Marine Rundschau*, No. 4 (April 1959), pp. 231–32.

64 Friedrich Ruge, *The Soviets as Naval Opponents 1941–1945* (Annapolis, MD: Naval Institute Press, 1979), p. 24.

65 Albert Lord and Klaus Tappeser, "Rolle und Beitrag der Seestreitkraefte," in Hartmut Zehrer, editor, *Der Golfkonflikt. Dokumentation, Analyse und Bewertung aus militaerischer Sicht* (Herford/Bonn: Verlag E. S. Mittler & Sohn, 1992), p. 197.

66 Albert Lord and Klaus Tappeser, "Rolle und Beitrag der Seestreitkraefte," in Hartmut Zehrer, editor, *Der Golfkonflikt. Dokumentation, Analyse und Bewertung aus militaerischer Sicht* (Herford/Bonn: Verlag E. S. Mittler & Sohn, 1992) p. 198.

67 Edward J. Marolda and Robert J. Schneller, *Shield and Sword: The United States Navy and the Persian Gulf War* (Washington, DC: Naval Historical Center, 1998), pp. 181–82.

6   Destroying the enemy's forces over time

A stronger side would ideally start hostilities by mounting a major fleet-vs.-fleet operation, thereby destroying a major part of the enemy's naval forces. Afterward, such operations would not be conducted very often. Most of the actions during a war at sea would be tactical in size and aimed to destroy individual enemy platforms or their groups in their bases/ports and at sea. The aim would be to reduce the enemy naval and air strength over time. Also, minor and sometimes major tactical actions would be a predominant method of combat employment of one's naval forces and other services in maintaining sea control.

Weakening the enemy's forces over time should not lead to force-on-force encounters or attrition. This could be avoided today by using long-range and precision weapons such as antiship cruise missiles (ASCMs). Another perhaps even more effective method is to use one's forces asymmetrically, as for example by carrying out long-range attacks and strikes with carrier- and/or land-based aircraft. Also, whenever possible, offensive mining should be extensively used in weakening the enemy's forces over time. Among many advantages, offensive mining is the only form of attrition that usually does not result in losses for friendly forces (unless they accidentally run into mines laid by one's forces). In contrast to a major fleet-vs.-fleet operation, weakening the enemy's strength over time requires much more time and effort. Another disadvantage is that one's naval/air forces might be tied down to a certain sea area and not be employable for other urgent tasks elsewhere.

A weaker side would also try to weaken the enemy's forces over time. But the fundamental difference is that a weaker side has to primarily rely on this method in the employment of its forces for disputing control by a stronger side. It would also have much smaller chances of avoiding a war of attrition than a stronger side.

A stronger side, in its effort to weaken the enemy's strength over time, should concentrate on destroying those enemy forces that pose the greatest potential threat in obtaining/maintaining sea control, that is, large surface combatants, attack submarines, and land-based attack aircraft/bombers, plus their support structures ashore. In the modern era, the great majority of losses in surface combatants, submarines, and aircraft by the weaker side have been the result of numerous attacks and strikes conducted over the course of the entire war.

Destruction of the enemy surface combatants

Traditionally, the principal platforms for destroying enemy surface combatants were surface ships. In the era of the oar/sail, the main method of combat employment was naval battle and attacks on enemy ships at their anchorage. Prior to the sixteenth century, naval battles were nothing more than a series of independent actions by individual ships that ended in a mêlée (confused fights or skirmishes).[1] Guns were used for the first time in the Ryde (Isle of Wight) and Shoreham (West Sussex, England) in 1545 during the Italian War (1542–1546) involving France and Britain. In these two battles, opposing fleets fought for the first time in a line ahead formation. However, the prevalent view then was that the guns were not sufficiently decisive. Hence, one's fleet should fight from the very beginning in a mêlée but in a more orderly fashion than prior to adoption of guns. The other school of thought argued for either massing against a part of the enemy fleet or outflanking it or by breaking through it. This debate went on for 40 years. The Duke of York was relieved for being unsuccessful in the Battle of Lowestoft on 13 June 1665. Monck and Rupert used mêlée tactics in the Four Days Battle on 1–4 June 1666 and were defeated.).[2]

The first three Anglo-Dutch Wars were essentially wars of attrition. A total of 23 major battles [nine in the First, eight in the Second, and four in the Third Anglo-Dutch War (1672–1674), respectively] were fought. For example, seven naval battles were fought within 12 months in the last year of the Second Anglo-Dutch War (1665–1667).[3] Only relatively few were decisive for either side. The battles were bloody and led to extremely high losses of personnel on both sides. For example, one of the most decisive battles aimed at protecting a large convoy was fought between 28 February and 2 March 1653 and spread from Portland to Cap Gris-Nez; in that battle, Dutch Admiral Maarten Tromp suffered larger losses than his British counterpart General-at-Sea Robert Blake.[4] He lost 17 ships and more than 50 merchant ships, while the English lost ten ships.[5] The Dutch had 1,500–2,000 men killed, while the British had some 2,000 dead and wounded.[6]

The Seven Years' War (1756–1763) and the French Revolutionary Wars (1792–1802)/Napoleonic Wars (1803–1815) were largely wars of attrition at sea. In contrast to the Anglo-Dutch Wars, naval battles in the eighteenth century resulted in larger losses of ships while losses in personnel were generally much lower. War at sea in 1914–1918 was also largely a war of attrition. This was especially the case in the North Sea and the Baltic but to a lesser extent in the Adriatic and the Black Sea. During the entire war, the only clash between the opposing battle fleets was the Battle of Jutland on 31 May–1 June 1916.

In World War I, most of the losses of surface ships on both sides occurred as a result of minor tactical actions. For example, the Central Powers lost a total of 413 naval vessels for 451,427 tons.[7] The Imperial German Navy lost 362 ships (including one battleship and battle cruiser each, six cruisers, 17 light cruisers, eight gunboats, 68 torpedo boat destroyers, 55 torpedo boats, and one minelayer) for 362,371 tons. Austria-Hungary lost 23 ships totaling 58,416 tons. This number included three battleships, two light cruisers, three river monitors, four torpedo boat destroyers, four torpedo boats, and seven U-boats. Turkey's losses amounted to 28 ships (including one battleship, two light cruisers, four gunboats, one armored vessel, three torpedo boats destroyers, five torpedo boats, and two minelayers) for 30,640 tons.[8]

In World War II, a relatively large number of major fleet-vs.-fleet operations were conducted. Still, the great majority of losses of surface combatants of all belligerents were the result of attrition warfare. For example, the German Kriegsmarine's total losses in surface ships amounted to 17 large surface combatants (one battleship, two battle cruisers, three pocket battleships, two old battleships, three heavy cruisers, five light cruisers, and one aircraft carrier), as well as some 559 smaller combatants [(45 destroyers, 56 torpedo boats, 146 S-boats, seven armed merchant raiders, 23 minelayers, and 282 minesweeping craft (119 M-boats and 163 R-boats)].[9]

The struggle for control of the Solomons in 1942–1943 is a classic example of attrition warfare at sea and in the air. Between 9 August 1942 and 25 November 1943, 15 major surface actions were fought in the waters around Guadalcanal, New Georgia, and Bougainville. All the battles but three were fought in the night. No fewer than seven naval battles were fought in the struggle for Guadalcanal alone. The Japanese were much better than the Allies in night fighting and in the use of guns and torpedoes in combination. They won or achieved a draw in ten naval battles.[10] A great majority of the naval battles took place during the Japanese attempts to bring in fresh reinforcements and supplies or to bombard the Allied positions on the coast. In the five-month-long struggle for Guadalcanal, the Japanese lost two battleships, three cruisers, 12 destroyers, 16 transports, and more than 100 aircraft.[11] In the entire Solomons campaign, the Japanese losses (including fighting off the New Guinea coast and the Bismarck Archipelago) amounted to two battleships, one small aircraft carrier, three heavy and light cruisers each, and 36 destroyers. In addition, Japanese naval air strength was so severely depleted that fleet aircraft carriers could not be properly manned. A more serious problem for the Japanese was the fact that new construction was unable to make up for the losses. No more battleships or heavy cruisers were built by the Japanese, and no more than half of the lost destroyers were ever replaced.[12] Because most of major actions took place at night, both sides grossly exaggerated their successes. The Japanese believed that they were more successful than they actually were. This, in turn, led them to continue with their efforts in supporting their ground forces and thereby incurring ever larger losses, especially in destroyers. For the Allies, exaggerated reports of their encounters with the Japanese cruisers and destroyers led them to think falsely that they were overcoming their deficiencies in night fighting.[13]

In 1943–1945, the Allied carrier- and land-based heavy bombers repeatedly struck Japanese surface ships, submarines, merchant shipping in their bases/ports, plus shipping-related facilities on the coast. In addition, they destroyed/damaged a large number of enemy aircraft and airfields and air-related facilities. These attacks were part of the Allies' efforts to "shape" the theater or what is in theory called today "operational fires" prior to a major amphibious landing. Their main purpose was either to isolate the area of the pending amphibious landing from the rest of the enemy-controlled territory or to deceive the enemy about the place and time of such a landing. These fires could be conducted in a state of either uncommanded sea or sea in dispute. Hence, destruction of the enemy surface ships, submarines, and land-based aircraft was an integral part of the struggle to obtain and maintain sea control.

In the first six months of 1944, the U.S. carrier forces and land-based aircraft of the U.S. Army Air Corps – based in the Solomons, Central Pacific (CENTPAC), and the Far Eastern Air Force (FEAF) of the Southwest Pacific Area (SWPA) – conducted a series of strikes and raids against Japanese strongpoints, bases, and shipping in the Central Pacific in support of the planned invasions of the Marshalls, Marianas, and western Carolines. The purpose of all these actions was generally to degrade enemy airpower and cut off shipping traffic between the Home Islands, the Southern Resources Area, and naval bases/strongpoints in the central and southern Pacific. On a few occasions, massive strikes by Task Force (TF) 58 and Allied land-based long-range bombers were aimed to isolate the area in which major landings would take place. The strikes by the Allied carrier- and land-based aircraft significantly reduced Japanese air strength in the central and southern Pacific. In one example, on 17 February 1944, TF 58 composed of nine carriers and six battleships plus accompanying cruisers/destroyers, conducted a series of massive strikes against Truk (Chuuk today), the central Carolines (Operation HAILSTONE). They destroyed 168 enemy aircraft at the loss of only five U.S. aircraft.[14] The TF 58 planes sunk some seven warships and damaged nine others.[15] Other sources say that at least 70 Japanese aircraft and about 200,000 tons of merchant shipping were destroyed.[16]

On 30 March and 1 April 1944, TF 58 conducted large-scale air attacks on enemy airfields, shipping, and fleet and air installations at Palau, Yap, Ulithi, and Woleai. The attack on Palau was aimed primarily to destroy enemy naval ships and aircraft and also to mine entrances to the ports. The attacks on Yap, Ulithi, and Woleai were secondary in importance to the attack on Palau. The TF 58 had 11 carriers organized in three task groups. The carrier strikes were supplemented by strikes on enemy bases and long-range searches by aircraft from both the central Pacific and SWPA. U.S. submarines were directed to attack enemy shipping, conduct reconnaissance, and provide lifeguard duties.[17] U.S. carrier aircraft also extensively mined the channels to the Palaus. TF 58 planes sunk and damaged a relatively large number of the enemy ships at Palau and Angaur.[18] On 31 March, one fast carrier group attacked Yap, Ulithi, and Ngulu, and on 2 April all three carrier groups attacked Woleai. Some 150 enemy aircraft were destroyed in the air and on the ground at the loss of only 25 U.S. aircraft.[19]

Prior to the invasion of Leyte, the Allies isolated first the Philippines from other enemy-controlled areas and then Leyte from the rest of the Philippines. In mid-September, the Allies conducted concentrated air strikes against the Ryukyus, Formosa, southern China, the Netherlands East Indies (NEI), and the Philippines. The FEAF and TF 38 started massive attacks against enemy naval bases and airfields, air installations, commercial ports, merchant shipping, and oil refineries. These attacks were conducted with ever increasing intensity and continuously until the beginning of the third week of October. They were very successful: enemy air strength in the Philippines and other adjacent areas was significantly reduced. On 20 September, three carrier groups of TF 38, from a position of about 300 miles east of Manila, carried out a high-speed run to the launching position, some 70 miles east of central Luzon. Throughout the day, the Allied carrier aircraft attacked enemy airfields and shipping in Manila Bay and adjacent areas on the western coast of Luzon. U.S. pilots claimed that, by the end of the day, some 27 freighters, oilers, and transports plus three destroyers were sunk. Because of the approaching typhoon from the north, most of the sweeps and strikes planned for the next day were canceled. On 23 September, all three groups were refueled at a position of about 200 miles east of Samar. The next day, they struck a variety of targets in the Visayas and at Coron Bay, Palawan.[20]

Allied efforts to isolate the Philippines before landing at Leyte were considerably expanded and intensified in October 1944. In addition to the TF-38 fast carrier groups, the Allies extensively employed their land-based heavy and medium bombers from four theater commands to isolate the central Philippines – in particular, the island of Leyte. Allied airpower essentially blockaded all air and sea approaches to the Philippines. The objective was to prevent the arrival of Japanese air reinforcements from the home islands, the Ryukyus, Formosa, or mainland China.

TF 38's primary task was to destroy enemy aircraft, air installations, and shipping on Formosa and the Ryukyus.[21] The initial part of the plan for the strikes against Formosa and the Ryukyus was executed on 9 October, when TF 38's carrier forces struck some 30 airfields/airstrips on Formosa. For the next three days, TF-38's carrier groups attacked airfields in the Ryukyus from a position some 130 miles southeast of the island. Allied aircraft found 60 enemy medium and small merchant vessels and about the same number of luggers (small sailing ships with two or three masts) and other smaller vessels. The attack came as a complete surprise to the Japanese. They had no aircraft there, nor were they prepared to counterattack from bases in southern Kyūshū. The TF 38 aircraft, flying about 1,400 sorties, reportedly took out some 110 enemy aircraft. They also inflicted damage on the city of Naha and nearby airfields.[22]

Between 12 and 14 October, the main weight of TF 38's attacks shifted to enemy aircraft and shipping on Formosa, which might be used as a staging area for reinforcements to the Philippines.[23] On 12 October, TF 38 launched four major strikes from a position some 50 to 90 miles east of Formosa against enemy shipping, airfields, and ground installations on the island. Some 1,380 sorties were flown, and 48 Allied aircraft were lost that day.[24]

In the third week of October, FEAF bombers attacked targets on Mindanao. To prevent the Japanese from using their aircraft based in the NEI, attacks were carried out against the Halmaheras, Moluccas, and Vogelkop Peninsula. Also struck were oil enemy installations on Borneo and numerous targets on Celebes, Timor, Palawan, and the Visayas. At the same time, the bombers of the Northern Solomons Air Command, based at Torokina in Bougainville and Emirau (St. Matthias group) attacked isolated Japanese garrisons on Truk and other islands in the central Carolines. The Allied fighters and bombers flew about 1,000 sorties in October to attack these targets. Farther east, the Central Pacific Air Forces attacked Japanese airfields in the Marshall Islands.[25] On 8–10 October, land-based Army aircraft from the Marianas attacked the Japanese-controlled Volcano (*Kazan Retto*) and Bonin Islands (*Ogasawara Gunto*). Another Allied theater command, the Southeast Asia Command (SEAC), provided support to the Leyte operation by intensifying its ground and air operations in Burma beginning on 5 October. Between 15 and 25 October, Allied aircraft attacked targets in the Bangkok and Rangoon areas.[26] The joint effort of TF-38 aircraft, Seventh Fleet escort carriers, and Army land-based aircraft led to the attainment of almost complete air supremacy over the Philippines by the time the landing at Leyte took place.[27]

In World War II, land-based aircraft were also used on several occasions to attack and destroy enemy large surface combatants at their bases. For example, the British Bomber Command tried repeatedly but ultimately unsuccessfully to destroy two German battle cruisers (*Scharnhorst*, *Gneisenau*) and one heavy cruiser (*Prinz Eugen*) at Brest, Brittany, in 1941–1942. The first attack was carried out by about 110 heavy bombers, mostly Wellingtons, on 30 March 1941.[28] Very little damage was inflicted on the German ships despite the large number of bombers and good weather. More successful was the attack in April. The British bombers attacked in four successive nights hoping to put *Gneisenau* out of commission. Extensive damages were inflicted on the vessel, putting it in dry dock until the end of 1941. Between June 1941 and February 1942, Bomber Command used some 1,800 bombers in bombing these two battle cruisers. They failed in their main propose but inflicted extensive damage on the city of Brest.[29] On 12 February 1942, both battle cruisers and the heavy cruiser finally sailed out from Brest through the Channel and eventually reached Kiel.

The presence of the 58,000-ton (full load) battleship *Tirpitz* in Norway posed a significant threat to Allied convoys to Russia and in the northern Atlantic. It tied down significant forces of the British Home Fleet in northern waters. The British tried repeatedly to destroy *Tirpitz* at its berth in the Norwegian fiords. Between January 1942 and November 1944, a total of 14 attacks (not including three attacks that were canceled or aborted) against the *Tirpitz* were carried out by the Fleet Air Arm (F.A.A.) and the R.A.F.[30] The first major British air attack on the *Tirpitz* was conducted by the F.A.A. with some 40 Barracuda torpedo bombers, escorted by about 80 fighters (Operation TUNGSTEN) at Kåfjord (11 miles west of the town Alta, Altafjord) on 3 April 1944. These aircraft were launched from two fleet and four escort carriers. The German defenses were not well organized. Some 14 bombs (eleven 500-pounders, four 1,600-pounders) hit the Tirpitz. Yet they achieved only minor damage to the *Tirpitz*'s superstructure.[31] On 15 September 1944 (Operation PARAVANE), R.A.F. Bomber Command carried out a series of attacks with about 28 Lancaster bombers (carrying 12,000-lb bombs) on the *Tirpitz* at Kåfjord. They used the Soviet base Yagodnik, near Archangelsk, in mounting the attack and inflicted modest damage on the *Tirpitz*'s bow. This operation was excellently planned and executed. This damage forced the Germans to move the *Tirpitz* from the Altafjord to Tromsø (where it was less vulnerable but at the same time posed a lesser threat to the Allied convoys to Soviet Russia). The Soviets also willingly cooperated.[32] Another attack on the *Tirpitz* was carried out by 38 Lancasters on 29 October (operation OBVIATE) at Tromsø. Because of the low cover over the coast, aiming was poor, resulting in only one near miss. The final attack was carried out by 32 Lancasters on 12 November 1944 (Operation CATECHISM) at the Bay of Hakoybotn, west of Tromsø. This attack was highly successful. The *Tirpitz* was hit with three 12,000-lb bombs and capsized with a large loss of life.[33]

Not only a weaker but also a stronger side at sea can reduce the enemy's naval strength by using unconventional forces such as midget submarines and commandos. For example, the Japanese, as part of their plan to attack Pearl Harbor in December of 1941, envisaged the employment of five midget submarines. Their task was to penetrate the enemy's harbor defense and attack U.S. ships. In the event, only a single submarine penetrated the harbor and fired two torpedoes, but both missed and hit the shore. All five midget submarines were lost.[34]

The Japanese planned a simultaneous raid by midget submarines on the ports of Diego Suarez, Madagascar, and Sydney by the end of May 1942. The Japanese hoped to find some important Allied ships at Sydney. However, on the night of 31 May/1 June, only two Australian cruisers (*Canberra, Adelaide*) and one U.S. heavy cruiser (*Chicago*) were present.[35] The raid on Sydney was carried out by five parent I-class submarines. Four of them carried one two-man A-class midget submarine.[36] They released their midgets off Port Jackson, some 7 nm away from Sydney in the late afternoon on 31 May.

Afterward, all parent submarines took a new position off Port Hacking to retrieve the midget submarines upon completion of their mission. The fifth I-class submarine, carrying one floatplane, reconnoitered Sydney harbor on 28 May. It also conducted reconnaissance of the harbor after the raid, on 2 June.[37] Two midget submarines penetrated the harbor, but one did not and destroyed itself.

One of the midget submarines fired two torpedoes against the cruiser USS *Chicago*. Both torpedoes missed *Chicago* and passed under a Dutch submarine, but one torpedo hit and sunk a converted harbor ferry (HMAS *Kuttabul*), killing 21 sailors.[38] That submarine escaped the pursuit. The second midget was detected and sunk.[39] The parent submarines waited for about a week for the midget submarines return before leaving the area.[40]

On 31 May 1942, two Japanese midget submarines attacked the port of Diego Suarez, then under the British control. A special attack force of five I-class submarines, each carrying one midget submarine, left Penang, Malaya, on 30 May.[41] Their destination was Diego Suarez, where a reconnaissance plane from one I-class submarine observed the 28,000-ton British battleship *Ramillies*. Only two submarines were able to launch their midgets during the evening of 30 May. But this time the Japanese had more success; one of the midget submarines torpedoed *Ramillies* and put it out of action for about a year; the same craft also torpedoed a 7,000-ton British oil tanker (*British Loyalty*). Both midget submarines that took part in the attack were lost.[42]

By April 1943, the Royal Navy created a force of six midget submarines (X-craft).[43] They were used for the first time in combat in September 1943 (Operation SOURCE). An attack force of six submarines, each carrying one X-craft, arrived at Loch Cairnbawn (a sea inlet off Eddrachilis Bay, west coast of Scotland) on 30 August/1 September. From there, they made the more than 1,000-mile transit to the targets of their intended attack. Three X-craft would penetrate the Kåfjord and attacked the *Tirpitz*, while two X-craft would attack *Scharnhorst*; a single X-craft would attack *Lützow* in the nearby Langerfjord.[44]

On 20 September, all but one X-craft were launched by their parent submarines to attack their assigned targets. The four X-craft assigned to attack *Tirpitz* penetrated the fiord on 20/21 September.[45] One of X-craft was successful in releasing its charges causing heavy damages to *Tirpitz*'s machinery, putting it out of action until April.[46] The remaining X-craft all failed in attacking their assigned targets. All six parent submarines returned safely to their base, but no X-craft survived.[47]

During the Yom Kippur/Ramadan War of 1973, Israeli combat divers penetrated Port Said, a major Egyptian port. In the Gulf of Suez, Israeli patrol craft penetrated two Egyptian anchorages and entered the port of Adabia. In the northern part of the Red Sea, Israeli naval commandos penetrated the Port of Hurghada and destroyed – at no losses to themselves – four Egyptian *Komar*-class missile craft deployed in the Red Sea. These attacks forced the Egyptians to remove their remaining missile craft from the base, thereby strengthening the Israeli navy's control of the Gulf of Suez. The repeated raids on the Port of Hurghada also contributed to the slowdown of the flow of oil from the Suez wells to Israel.[48]

Destruction of enemy submarines

Control of the subsurface requires the destruction or neutralization of the threat posed by enemy submarines and other submersible vehicles and mines. This is one of the most critical and yet most difficult and time-consuming tasks in the struggle for obtaining and maintaining sea control. It is largely an offensive, not a defensive aspect of naval warfare.

In the past, ASW was almost solely focused on the defense and protection of one's merchant shipping at sea. Today, SSNs and quiet SSKs pose a great threat not only to one's warships and merchant vessels but also to one's naval bases/ports, coastal installations/facilities, and military and political-economic centers deep in one's country. They also represent a serious threat to one's ground forces deployed in the littorals. Modern submarines are armed with long-range and fast heavy-weight torpedoes (HWTs), antiship cruise missiles (ASCMs), and land-attack cruise missiles (LACMs). The most advanced SSKs, fitted with air-independent propulsion (AIP), have emerged as the primary threat to naval forces operating in the littorals, especially in narrow seas. The emerging threats to one's naval bases and commercial ports are minisubmarines, swimmer delivery vehicles (SDVs), remotely operated vehicles (ROVs), and autonomous underwater vehicles (AUVs).

ASW is an inherently force-to-force, or attritional, type of warfare. The reason is that submarines, unlike surface ships, are not normally employed in large numbers in a given operating area. This is even more pronounced in an enclosed or semi-enclosed sea, where submarines are employed individually. Their employment in groups is relatively rare. ASW requires disproportionately large forces and resources to destroy or neutralize the threat posed by the enemy submarines. Some sources claim that a six-to-one ratio of surface, air, and subsurface platforms is required to deal with a single potentially hostile submarine.[49] ASW is also a very time-consuming task. No single platform or weapon system can be a panacea to such a complex problem as ASW. Hence, success in ASW cannot be achieved without the synchronized employment of diverse naval maneuvering forces and stationary systems. In the littorals, the combat arms of other services, primarily land-based aircraft, should also be employed in combination.

The principal methods of combat employment of ASW forces are tactical actions ranging from patrolling/surveillance, search, and tracking to attacks/strikes and pursuits. The opportunities to conduct decisive operations by planning and executing major naval operations against enemy submarines are rare. The exception would be a war between major naval powers when each would need to attack the enemy's and defend/protect one's own sea-based nuclear deterrent forces. Tactical ASW would be conducted mainly by using forces of a single combat arm, such as surface ships, with their helicopters or submarines or naval aircraft. In contrast, operational and strategic ASW would require the employment of all naval combat arms and the forces of other services. By employing surface combatants, submarines, maritime patrol aircraft (MPA), and helicopters in combination, the advantages of one arm can compensate for the disadvantages of other combat arms.

ASW is invariably conducted as a combination of offensive and defensive actions. Offensive ASW is aimed at destroying or neutralizing the enemy submarines at their basing areas, during their transit to/from their operating areas, and in their operating areas. Offensive ASW is aimed to accomplish control of the subsurface and also indirectly control of the surface. Defensive ASW is aimed to protect naval forces and merchant shipping at sea.

Offensive ASW consists broadly of two mutually supporting components: direct and indirect actions. Direct offensive actions are intended to destroy/neutralize enemy submarines at sea or in their bases, whereas indirect actions aim to destroy/neutralize the enemy submarines' supporting structure ashore. Enemy submarines can be attacked and destroyed during transit from their basing areas to their assigned operating areas by conducting so-called barrier operations. The effectiveness of these operations would depend primarily on the number and diversity of platforms conducting the ASW search, sensor capabilities, the speed of the ASW platforms, environmental conditions, and the length and number of the routes used by enemy submarines. Theoretically, the optimal way to detect enemy submarines during their transit is by patrolling a strait/narrows. The analysis of enemy submarines' deployment routes should include their lengths and required transit times, as well as whether a particular route passes through a strait or narrows. This information would largely determine which ASW forces and methods should be used against enemy submarines.

Submarine transit routes over the open ocean are measured in thousands of miles. It takes many days or even weeks for a submarine to reach its operating area close to the enemy-controlled waters. For example, in World War II, the Germans deployed their U-boats across the Atlantic and off the U.S. East Coast and in the Caribbean, southern Atlantic, and Indian Ocean. The distance from the French U-boat bases to New York is about 3,000 nm; to Charleston, South Carolina, 3,600 nm; and to Trinidad, 3,800 nm. The speed of submarine deployment would affect its time in the operating area.

Modern attack submarines have much higher transit speeds than their predecessors of World War II. Today's SSNs are capable of high sustained speed for very long periods. For example, U.S. SSNs have a rated speed of 20 knots on the surface. Their listed submerged speed is 25–28 knots, but their actual maximum speed is 30–32 knots or even higher. The top submerged speed of many SSKs is not higher than 20 knots. For example, an SSN would need about eight days at submerged speed of 28 knots to transit the some 5,290-nm distance between San Diego and Guam.

During the Battle of the Atlantic (1939–1945), the Allies exerted great efforts to search for, detect, and destroy German U-boats transiting the Bay of Biscay on the way to their operating areas in the northern Atlantic, off the U.S. East Coast, the Caribbean, southern Atlantic, and even the Indian Ocean. Normally, the U-boats transited the Bay of Biscay during the day and dived if sighted by aircraft. Starting in September 1941, British aircraft patrolled the Bay of Biscay, searching for U-boats in transit to and from their bases in occupied France. This was considered an offensive search, as opposed to defensive search in the immediate vicinity of convoys.[50] Allied ASW aircraft were very effective in making life difficult for U-boats transiting the Bay of Biscay. In the air offensive from mid-May to early August 1943, Allied aircraft destroyed 28 U-boats. An additional 17 U-boats were heavily damaged and forced to return to their bases in France. It was a rare occurrence that a surfaced U-boat was not cited by an Allied aircraft.[51]

On the open ocean and in deep water, enemy submarines have much room to act freely. Offensive ASW actions would focus on the search and surveillance of fairly large areas with the suspected presence of enemy submarines. The greatest challenge for ASW today is to detect and destroy enemy submarines in their operating areas on the open ocean before they can launch their long-range ASCMs/LACMs. In contrast, submarines' operating areas in the littorals are much smaller. In a typical narrow sea endowed with many offshore islands or in the archipelagic coast, an enemy submarine can hide and carry out a surprise attack from an ambushing position. At the same time, it would become vulnerable to counterattack because its presence would become known.

The destruction of enemy submarines in their operating areas should be combined with attacks on their bases. The first example of an attack on an enemy submarine base was the British raid against the U-boat bases at Zeebrugge–Ostend, Belgium, on 22–23 April 1918. The main purpose was to deny the use of these two bases for some 40 U-boats. Another objective of the raid was to reduce the threat of German destroyers attacking the Dover Barrage.[52] In the attack on Zeebrugge, the British employed one destroyer and 76 miscellaneous vessels.[53] The simultaneous attempt to block Ostend failed. The plan was similar to the one against Zeebrugge, minus a diversionary attack. Some 146 ships took part in the attack. Another attempt to block the port of Ostend was repeated on 10 May 1918 but also failed.[54] The results of these raids were very disappointing because the main objectives were not accomplished. The Zeebrugge channel was never blocked, and within few days after the raid, the Germans were able to use Zeebrugge as a base for their U-boats.[55] The port of Ostend also resumed its operations.

The first air attacks on submarine bases were conducted in the last year of World War I. In the Adriatic, British aircraft, with some participation by the Italians, conducted constant and intensive attacks on the German and Austro-Hungarian U-boat bases at Pola, Istria, and the Bay of Cattaro in 1918.[56] The Allies also conducted numerous air attacks on German U-boat bases in Flanders in February–April 1918.[57]

With the advent of heavy bombers, it was possible to attack enemy submarine bases from long distances. However, initially, this was not made an integral part of the Allied operational planning. For example, bombing attacks on U-boat bases were not part of British prewar plans. The heavy bombers would be employed primarily for bombing Germany's war industries.[58] Yet World War II changed all that, although only gradually. Initially, German U-boats operated near British ports. When forced to operate on the open ocean and having to pass north of Scotland, they were not only vulnerable but also used much time in transit. All of this dramatically changed after the fall of France in June 1940, when the U-boats started to operate from the French ports in the Bay of Biscay. The use of the bases in France shortened U-boat transit distances to operating areas in the northern Atlantic by some 450 miles.[59] However, the time saved was even more important. When using routes through the Skagerrak and Kattegat and the North Sea on their way to the northern Atlantic, U-boats faced danger from British aircraft and mines and had to sail at night, with escorts, thereby prolonging their transit time. By using bases in the Bay of Biscay, U-boats saved at least one week of sailing time for each sortie.[60]

On 20 October 1942, General Dwight Eisenhower, Commanding General, European Theater of Operations (ETOUSA), issued a directive that the U-boat bunkers and U-boat production facilities were the first and second priorities, respectively.[61] Yet the British Bomber Command had great difficulties shifting its main effort from strategic bombing to attacking the U-boat bases. Because the U-boats were housed in hardened pens, the Allied bombers focused their attacks on the surrounding area with the aim of dislocating U-boat maintenance facilities.[62] As usual, the British bombed by night and the Americans by day. Over the first five months of 1943, some 7,000 bomber sorties were divided between attacks on U-boat building yards in Germany and U-boat bases in France. The night attacks by Bomber Command continued until 16 April 1943, and the daylight attacks by the U.S. bombers went on until July 1943. About 18,000 tons of bombs were dropped on the U-boat pens. The Allied area bombing had unfortunate consequences because it practically destroyed nearby French towns and cities. Moreover, in 1943 alone, the Allies lost 266 heavy bombers in their attacks on the U-boat bases in France.[63]

Allied bombing continued, although on a less intensive scale, until the U-boat bases were captured by the Allies in the fall of 1944. However, the U-boats inside the pens were unaffected by bombing.[64] Despite all the bombings, no German U-boat was ever destroyed in these massive attacks;

not a single shelter was penetrated.[65] Only a single U-boat was damaged in its dock at Lorient in December 1940. The U-boat maintenance capabilities were not seriously affected. Also, the morale effect on the U-boat crews was low because they were housed far away in the countryside.[66]

Allied long-range heavy bombers were more successful in attacking non-hardened U-boat bases in the North Sea, the Baltic, and the Mediterranean. For example, they conducted 15 attacks against German U-boat bases in the Mediterranean, specifically bases at Salamis (Greece), La Spezia and Fiume (Rijeka today) (Italy), and Toulon and Marseille (France). All attacks, except for one in 1941 and two in 1943, were conducted in 1944.[67] These attacks resulted in the loss of a number of U-boats, while many suffered heavy damages. The U.S. heavy bombers claimed to have destroyed 41 U-boats during the entire war.[68]

Indirect offensive actions are aimed at destroying enemy submarines' command and control (C2) nodes, construction/repair yards, submarine research centers, missile/torpedo depots, logistical depots, and communications centers. For example, in the last phase of World War II, the Allies conducted massive attacks with long-range heavy bombers against German U-boat prefabrication and assembly facilities. The Germans assembled some of the new U-boats at the hardened assembly plant Valentin, (between the suburbs of Farge and Rekum) near Bremen. That plant was large enough to allow building three Type XXI boats simultaneously.[69] Prefabricated sections of U-boats were assembled in the three other smaller bunkers on the Weser River (at Bremen, Bremerhaven, and Wilhelmshaven) and then shipped by barges to the Valentin site for final assembly. Allied planners identified some 200 miles of embankments, aqueducts, and canal locks to be vulnerable to bombing.[70] By the beginning of 1943, the emphasis of the U.S. Eighth Air Force shifted to the U-boat yards, and after mid-1943 it shifted again to factories. Yet attacks on the U-boat construction yards were not really effective until the spring of 1945.[71]

In World War I, the Germans lost 178 U-boats at sea; five were destroyed when their bases in Flanders were abandoned and 11 U-boats were lost at the Austro-Hungarian naval base at Cattaro, Dalmatia, after they were ordered to return home. Some 176 U-boats were handed over to the Allies and interned upon the end of the hostilities.[72]

During World War II, the Germans lost 782 U-boats from all causes. With the exception of losses during major U-boat operations against Allied convoys in northern Atlantic in the winter 1942/1943, the great majority of these losses were the result of tactical actions by Allied escorts and aircraft. Almost 300 U-boats were destroyed by the Allied aircraft (246 by the land-based- and 43 by shipborne aircraft), while 47 U-boats were sunk in cooperation between aircraft and surface ships. Allied submarines destroyed 21 U-boats, and 26 U-boats were destroyed by mines laid by aircraft and surface ships.[73] The Italian Navy lost 85 submarines from all causes. Allied surface ships sunk 38 submarines, while aircraft were responsible for sinking or destroying 14 boats; five other submarines were sunk jointly by aircraft and surface ships. Allied submarines sunk 18 of their Italian counterparts.[74] The Imperial Japanese Navy (IJN) lost 130 submarines in the Pacific War (1941–1945). More than 70 boats were destroyed by Allied surface ships. Allied aircraft sunk only 12 Japanese submarines (eight by shipborne and four by land-based aircraft); five other boats were sunk jointly by the Allied surface ships and aircraft. Allied submarines were very successful in ASW, sinking 25 Japanese boats.[75]

The destruction and/or neutralization of submarine communication posts ashore are another critical aspect of the struggle against the enemy submarines. Jamming very low-frequency (VLF)/ultralow-frequency (ULF) communications is technically very difficult. Intercepting and deciphering radio messages between submarines and their command centers ashore are among the most effective methods of narrowing down a search area and finding enemy submarines. This is especially valuable in open-ocean ASW.

Today, one's naval forces, in cooperation with carrier- and land-based aircraft armed with ASCMs/LACMs and smart bombs, could be employed to attack enemy naval bases, including submarine bases, as part of the larger objective of destroying a major part of the enemy fleet, preferably at the beginning of hostilities. They also can conduct raids specifically aimed to destroy submarine basing facilities or to prevent their use by enemy submarines. In addition, tactical ballistic missiles (TBMs) can be effectively used in attacking enemy bases.

As with any complex problem, the diversity of forces and of platforms and sensors/weapons is absolutely necessary for ultimate success in ASW. Not only naval forces but also the combat arms/branches of other services must be employed; otherwise, ultimate success will remain elusive. Moreover, experience shows that the struggle against submarines is hardly possible without the close and smooth cooperation among the military and other branches of government and the scientific community. A successful struggle may also require the support of various government and nongovernment organizations and the public. ASW is conducted with the participation of allies and coalition partners as well.

A typical narrow sea and archipelagic waters pose the greatest challenges for the conduct of ASW. The smallness of the area, the prevalence of shallow water, and the proximity of the landmass greatly affect the employment of submarines and ASW platforms and their weapons/sensors. Because of the great diversity and unpredictability of the physical environment in the littorals, detection, classification, and reliable tracking of the enemy submarines are extremely difficult. Because of the small size of the theater, enclosed or semi-enclosed seas are almost ideal for the deployment of advanced bottom surveillance systems. In general, ASW is largely an art, not a science.

Offensive mining

Mines are the cheapest and probably one of the most effective naval weapons in attriting both naval forces and merchant shipping. All mines, regardless of their design, pose potential threats to the surviv- ability of surface ships and submarines operating in littoral waters shal- lower than 300 feet.[76] They are small, easy to conceal, and generally cheap to acquire.[77] They are an inherently attritional weapon. When used offensively, mines can inflict relatively large losses on enemy sur- face ships and submarines. For example, the British mined large parts of the Heligoland Bight in January 1915. These minefields proved to be very effective because they required considerable effort on the part of the Germans to sweep them. They also forced the Germans to use a much longer route through the Skagerrak for their U-boats. This, in turn, increased their time in transit and thereby reduced their numbers in the operating areas at any given time.[78] Enemy surface combatants and submarines could be also destroyed by laying defensive mine bar- riers in one's controlled waters. Such barriers are usually larger than offensive mine barriers and consist of simpler types of mines. An anti- submarine mine barrier is aimed at destroying hostile submarines or preventing their penetration into one's surface ships' operating area or merchant shipping traffic area or at protecting naval bases and ports. It can be established either close to one's controlled shores or in more dis- tant areas. For example, in World War I, the British laid a defensive mine barrier across the Irish Channel. Not only did the barrier limit freedom of movement for German U-boats, but also ten U-boats were sunk while trying to penetrate the defended area.[79]

Mines played a significant role in the Russo-Japanese War of 1904–1905. The Japanese used mines to block the movements of the Russian ships out of their Port Arthur base.[80] The Russians lost eight warships, including one battleship, to Japanese mines. The Japanese suffered heavier losses; 12 war- ships were sunk from the Russian mines, including two modern and one obsolete battleship.[81]

Mines were for the first time used extensively for both offensive and defensive purposes by all belligerents during World War I. Some 309,000 mines were laid during that conflict.[82] The Central Powers laid 51,900 mines (Germany 45,000, Turkey 900, and Austria-Hungary 6,000 mines). The Entente Powers laid 255,600 mines (Great Britain 129,000, Russia 52,000, United States 57,600, and Italy 12,000, and France 5,000 mines). Neutral powers laid some 1,600 mines (Denmark 1,200, and Norway 400 mines). Out of 132 submarines sunk, 89 were lost to mines. Similarly, out of 78 large surface combatants, 17 were lost to mines, and out of 166 destroyers/torpedo boats, 110 were lost to mines.[83] The Central Powers lost about 130 warships to Allied mines, and their mines caused the loss of 87 enemy warships.[84]

In World War II, the Axis powers and their allies laid 341,500 mines (including 223,000 mines laid by the Germans), while the Allies laid 347,400 mines (United Kingdom 263,400, United States 44,000, and the Soviets 40,000).[85] The British lost 577 ships to the enemy, including 280 warships.[86] The Germans lost 27 of their U-boats to Allied mines.[87] In the Pacific War (1941–1945), the Allies laid some 25,000 mines (21,389 dropped by aircraft). The mines were responsible for sinking or damaging two Japanese battleships, two escort carriers, eight cruisers, 38 destroyers and destroyer escorts, five submarines, and 54 other vessels.[88]

Destroying enemy individual platforms or their groups over time is an integral part of the struggle to obtain and maintain control of the sea. These efforts would require larger forces and much greater effort than in case of major fleet-vs.-fleet operations. The effectiveness of actions to weaken enemy forces over time is usually much greater if not only naval forces but also the forces of other services, particularly land-based aircraft, are part of the overall effort. Expressed differently, one's forces should use both symmetric and asymmetric methods in destroying the enemy's forces over time. A danger exists if weakening of the enemy's forces over time is allowed to degenerate into a war of attrition. The only way to avoid this from happening is by having not only numerical and qualitative superiority and excellently trained and led forces, but, even more importantly, by thinking operationally and not tactically. The enemy must be first out-thought before being outfought.

Notes

1 "The Evolution of Naval Tactics," *Naval Review*, February 1949, p. 1.
2 "The Evolution of Naval Tactics," *Naval Review*, February 1949, p. 2.
3 Alfred Stenzel, *Seekriegsgeschichte in ihren wichtigsten Abschnitten mit Berücksichtigung der Seetaktik*, Part 3: *Von 1600 bis 1720* (Hannover/Leipzig: Hahnsche Buchhandlung, 1910), p. 81.
4 Alexander Meurer, *Seekriegsgeschichte in umrissen. Seemacht und Seekriege vornehmlich vom 16. Jahrhundert ab* (Leipzig: Verlag v. Hase & Koehler, 1925), p. 187.
5 R. Ernest Dupuy and Trevor N. Dupuy, *The Encyclopedia of Military History from 3500 B.C. to the present* (New York: Harper & Row, Publishers, 2nd revised ed., 1986), p. 555.
6 Alfred Stenzel, *Seekriegsgeschichte in ihren wichtigsten Abschnitten mit Berücksichtigung der Seetaktik*, Part 3: *Von 1600 bis 1720* (Hannover/Leipzig: Hahnsche Buchhandlung, 1910), p. 68.
7 Henry Newbolt, *History of the Great War Based on Official Documents, Naval Operations*, Vol. V (London: Longmans, Green and Co., 1931), p. 432.
8 Henry Newbolt, *History of the Great War Based on Official Documents, Naval Operations*, Vol. V (London: Longmans, Green and Co., 1931), p. 432.
9 Stephen W. Roskill, *History of the Second World War, The War at Sea*, Vol. III: *The Offensive* Part II: *1st June 1944–14th August 1945* (London: Her Majesty's Stationery Office, 1961), pp. 457–61.
10 Paul S. Dull, *A Battle History of the Imperial Japanese Navy (1941–1945)* (Annapolis, MD: Naval Institute Press, 1978), p. 295.

11 Raizo Tanaka, "The Struggle for Guadalcanal," in David C. Evans, editor, *The Japanese Navy in World War II. In the Words of Former Japanese Naval Officers*, 2nd ed. (Annapolis, MD: Naval Institute Press, 1986), p. 211.

12 Stephen W. Roskill, *War at Sea 1939–1945*, Vol. III: *The Offensive*, Part 1: *1st June 1943–31st May* (London: Her Majesty's Stationery Office, 1960), p. 231.

13 Samuel E. Morison, *History of United States Naval Operations in World War II*, Vol. VI: *Breaking the Bismarcks Barrier: 22 July 1942–1 May 1944* (Boston: Little, Brown and Company, 1975), pp. 195–96.

14 Bernard D. Cole, "Struggle for the Marianas," *Joint Force Quarterly*, Spring 1995, p. 90; *Robert* J. Crossman, *The Official Chronology of the U.S. Navy in World War II* (Washington, DC: Contemporary History Branch, Naval Historical Center, 1999), p. 446.

15 Specifically, TF 58 aircraft sunk one light cruiser, two destroyers, one auxiliary cruiser, one auxiliary submarine depot ship, one aircraft ferry, 17 transports, four fleet tankers, and one water carrier, auxiliary vessel, Army cargo ship, merchant cargo ship, and motor torpedo boat (MTB) each; two destroyers and submarines each, and one target ship, repair ship, ammunition ship, seaplane tender, and auxiliary submarine chaser (SC) each were damaged Bernard D. Cole, "Struggle for the Marianas," *Joint Force Quarterly*, Spring 1995, p. 90; *Robert* J. Cressman, *The Official Chronology of the U.S. Navy in World War II* (Washington, DC: Contemporary History Branch, Naval Historical Center, 1999), p. 446.

16 Philip A. Crowl, *United States Army in World War II. The War in the Pacific. Campaign in the Marianas* (Washington, DC: Office of the Chief of Military History, Department of the Army, 1960), p. 15.

17 United States Strategic Bombing Survey (Pacific), Naval Analysis Division, *The Campaigns of the Pacific War* (Washington, DC: United Government Printing Office, 1946), p. 207.

18 At Palau they sunk one destroyer, one repair ship, five fleet tankers, one submarine chaser (SC), four auxiliary SCs, one patrol boat, one net layer, one aircraft ferry, five transports, two tankers, two guard boats, one salvage vessel, one torpedo transport/repair ship, five Army cargo ships, and one Army tanker; one SC, net layer, tanker, and army cargo ship each were damaged; at Angaur were sunk nine small craft Robert J. Cressman, *The Official Chronology of the U.S. Navy in World War II* (Washington, DC: Contemporary History Branch, Naval Historical Center, 1999), p. 465.

19 United States Strategic Bombing Survey (Pacific), Naval Analysis Division, *The Campaigns of the Pacific War* (Washington, DC: United Government Printing Office, 1946), p. 207.

20 Commander in Chief, U.S. Pacific Fleet and Pacific Ocean Area to Commander in Chief, U.S. Fleet, *Operations in Pacific Area–October 1944*, 31 May 1945, M233, Reel 12, U.S. *Navy Strategic Planning: Its Evolution and Execution, 1891–1945, Admin. and Operational History* (Wilmington, DE: Scholarly Resources, Inc., 1977), pp. 83–86.

21 Ministry of Defence (Navy), *War with Japan*, Vol. VI: *Advance to Japan* (London: Her Majesty's Stationary Office, 1995) p. 55.

22 David C. Evans, editor and translator, *The Japanese Navy In World War II: In the Words of Former Japanese Naval Officers* (Annapolis, MD: Naval Institute Press,), p. 314; *Philippine Area Naval Operations*, Part II, Oct–Dec 1944, Background of Leyte Battle, Folder G-27, Box 9, RG 23: BEG, NHC, p. 3; Shigeru Fukudome, "The Air Battle off Taiwan," in David C. Evans, editor, *The Japanese Navy in World War II. In the Words of Former Japanese Naval Officers*, pp. 345–46; Richard W. Bates, *The Battle For Leyte Gulf, October 1944: Strategical and Tactical Analysis*, Vol. I: *Preliminary Operations Until 0719 October 17th Including Battle off Formosa* (Newport,

RI: U.S. Naval War College, 1953), p. 93; Commander in Chief, U.S. Pacific Fleet and Pacific Ocean Areas, *Operations in the Pacific Ocean Areas During the Month of October 1944* (Annapolis, MD: Nimitz Library Special Collection, U.S. Naval Academy, 31 May 1945), pp. 7, 9. TF 38's pilots claimed to have sunk or damaged ten naval vessels and four cargo ships. These included one submarine depot vessel, minesweeper, destroyer escort, and small escort vessel each; two 120-foot mine craft; four midget submarines; and four medium cargo ships. The Japanese acknowledged the loss of one submarine depot ship, 12 torpedo boats, two midget submarines, four commercial vessels totaling 11,000 tons, and numerous smaller craft. They also admitted losing 31 aircraft on the ground and in the air, plus five naval search aircraft. TF 38 lost 14 aircraft but only five pilots and four crew members Richard W. Bates, *The Battle for Leyte Gulf, October 1944: Strategical and Tactical Analysis*, Vol. I: *Preliminary Operations Until 0719 October 17th Including Battle off Formosa* (Newport, RI: U.S. Naval War College, 1953), pp. 94–95.

23 Charles R. Anderson, *Leyte* (Washington, DC: U.S. Government Printing Office, CMH 72–27, 1994), p. 8; Samuel Eliot Morison, *History of United States Naval Operations in World War II*, Vol. 12: *Leyte: June 1944–January 1945* (Boston: Little, Brown, reprint 1984), pp. 92–94.

24 Samuel Eliot Morison, *History of United States Naval Operations in World War II*, Vol. 12: *Leyte: June 1944–January 1945* (Boston: Little, Brown, reprint 1984), p. 94; Richard W. Bates, *The Battle for Leyte Gulf, October 1944: Strategical and Tactical Analysis*, Vol. I: *Preliminary Operations Until 0719 October 17th Including Battle off Formosa* (Newport, RI: U.S. Naval War College, 1953), pp. 100–03.

25 Samuel Eliot Morison, *History of United States Naval Operations in World War II*, Vol. 12: *Leyte: June 1944–January 1945* (Boston: Little, Brown, reprinted 1984), p. 107.

26 Wesley F. Craven and James L. Cate, *The Army Air Forces in World War II*, Vol. 5: *The Pacific: Matterhorn to Nagasaki, June 1944 to August 1945* (Washington, DC: Office of Air Force History, 1983), p. 350.

27 Ministry of Defence (Navy), *War with Japan*, Vol. 6: *The Advance to Japan* (London: Her Majesty's Stationery Office, 1995), pp. 60–62.

28 Jeremiah S. Heathman, *The Bombing of Brittany: Solving the Wrong Problem* (Fort Leavenworth, KS: School of Advanced Military Studies, U.S. Army Command and General Staff College, 12 May 2010), p. 9.

29 Jeremiah S. Heathman, *The Bombing of Brittany: Solving the Wrong Problem* (Fort Leavenworth, KS: School of Advanced Military Studies, U.S. Army Command and General Staff College, 12 May 2010), p. 10.

30 Stephen W. Roskill, *History of the Second World War. The War at Sea*, Vol. III: *The Offensive*, Part II: *1st June–14th August 1945* (London: Her Majesty's Stationery Office, 1961), pp. 170–71.

31 Stephen W. Roskill, *History of the Second World War. The War at Sea*, Vol. III: *The Offensive*, Part II: *1st June–14th August 1945* (London: Her Majesty's Stationery Office, 1961), p. 170.

32 Stephen W. Roskill, *History of the Second World War. The War at Sea*, Vol. III: *The Offensive*, Part II: *1st June–14th August 1945* (London: Her Majesty's Stationery Office, 1961), p. 162.

33 Stephen W. Roskill, *History of the Second World War. The War at Sea*, Vol. III: *The Offensive*, Part II: *1st June–14th August 1945* (London: Her Majesty's Stationery Office, 1961), p. 168.

34 Ministry of Defence (Navy), *War with Japan*, Vol. II: *Defensive Phase* (London: Her Majesty's Stationery Office, 1995), p. 22.

35 Ministry of Defence (Navy), Naval Historical Branch, *War with Japan*, Vol. III: *The Campaigns in the Solomons and New Guinea* (London: Her Majesty's Stationery Office, 1995), p. 13.

36 Samuel E. Morison, *History of United States Naval Operations in World War II*, Vol. IV: *Coral Sea, Midway and Submarine Operations, May 1942–August 1942* (Boston: Little, Brown and Company, 1984), p. 66.

37 Ministry of Defence (Navy), Naval Historical Branch, *War with Japan*, Vol. III: *The Campaigns in the Solomons and New Guinea* (London: Her Majesty's Stationery Office, 1995), p. 13.

38 Carl Boyd and Akihiko Yoshida, *The Japanese Submarine Force and World War II* (Annapolis, MD: Naval Institute Press, 1995), p. 88.

39 Ministry of Defence (Navy), Naval Historical Branch, *War with Japan*, Vol. III: *The Campaigns in the Solomons and New Guinea* (London: Her Majesty's Stationery Office, 1995), pp. 14–15.

40 Samuel Eliot Morison, *History of United States Naval Operations in World War II*, Vol. IV: *Coral Sea, Midway and Submarine Operations, May 1942–August 1942* (Boston: Little, Brown and Company, 1984), p. 68.

41 Carl Boyd and Akihiko Yoshida, *The Japanese Submarine Force and World War II* (Annapolis, MD: Naval Institute Press, 1995), p. 88.

42 Carl Boyd and Akihiko Yoshida, *The Japanese Submarine Force and World War II* (Annapolis, MD: Naval Institute Press, 1995), p. 89.

43 Stephen W. Roskill, *History of the Second World War, The War at Sea*, Vol. III: *The Offensive*, Part I: *1st June 1943–31st May 1944* (London: Her Majesty's Stationery Office, 1960), p. 65.

44 Stephen W. Roskill, *History of the Second World War, The War at Sea*, Vol. III: *The Offensive*, Part I: *1st June 1943–31st May 1944* (London: Her Majesty's Stationery Office, 1960), pp. 65–66; Barry M. Gough, "The Crimean War in the Pacific: British Strategy and Naval Operations," *Military Affairs*, Vol. 37, No. 4 (December 1973), p. 84.

45 Stephen W. Roskill, *History of the Second World War, The War at Sea*, Vol. III: *The Offensive*, Part I: *1st June 1943–31st May 1944* (London: Her Majesty's Stationery Office, 1960), pp. 66–67.

46 Stephen W. Roskill, *History of the Second World War, The War at Sea*, Vol. III: *The Offensive*, Part I: *1st June 1943–31st May 1944* (London: Her Majesty's Stationery Office, 1960), p. 68.

47 Stephen W. Roskill, *History of the Second World War, The War at Sea*, Vol. III: *The Offensive*, Part I: *1st June 1943–31st May* 1944 (London: Her Majesty's Stationery Office, 1960), pp. 68–69.

48 Ze'ev Almog, "Israel's Navy Beat the Odds," *United States Naval Institute Proceedings*, Vol. 123, No. 3 (March 1997), p. 107.

49 K.G. Weiss, *The Enemy Below – The Global Diffusion of Submarines and Related Technology* (Monterey, CA: Center for Global Security Research in Cooperation with the U.S. Naval Postgraduate School, 30–31 May 2002), p. 5.

50 Brian McCue, *U-Boats in the Bay of Biscay: An Essay in Operations Research* (Washington, DC: National Defense University, 1990), p. 22.

51 A. Timothy Warnock, *The U.S. Army Air Forces in World War II. Air Power Versus U-Boats: Confronting Hitler's Submarine Menace in the European Theater* (Washington, DC: Air Force History and Museums Program, Air Force Historical Studies Office, 1999), p. 15.

52 Arthur J. Marder, *From the Dreadnought to Scapa Flow: The Royal Navy in the Fisher Era, 1904–1919*, Vol. 5: *Victory and Aftermath (January 1918–June 1919)* (London: Oxford University Press, 1970). p. 50.

53 Arthur J. Marder, *From the Dreadnought to Scapa Flow: The Royal Navy in the Fisher Era, 1904–1919*, Vol. 5: *Victory and Aftermath (January 1918–June 1919)* (London: Oxford University Press, 1970), pp. 55–56.

54 Arthur J. Marder, *From the Dreadnought to Scapa Flow: The Royal Navy in the Fisher Era, 1904–1919*, Vol. 5: *Victory and Aftermath (January 1918–June 1919)* (London: Oxford University Press, 1970), p. 56; out of some 1,700 men, the British losses

totaled 214 men killed in action, 385 wounded, and about 20 captured. The German losses were ten killed and 16 wounded *Der Krieg zur See 1914–1918. Der Krieg in der Nordsee*, Vol. 7: *Vom Sommer 1917 bis zum Kriegsende 1918*. Reprint prepared by Gerhard P. Gross with assistance of Werner Rahn (Hamburg/Berlin/Bonn: Verlag E. S. Mittler & Sohn, 2006), p. 318.

55 Arthur J. Marder, *From the Dreadnought to Scapa Flow: The Royal Navy in the Fisher Era, 1904–1919*, Vol. 5: *Victory and Aftermath (January 1918–June 1919)* (London: Oxford University Press, 1970), p. 60.

56 Arthur J. Marder, *From the Dreadnought to Scapa Flow: The Royal Navy in the Fisher Era, 1904–1919*, Vol. 5: *Victory and Aftermath (January 1918–June 1919)* (London: Oxford University Press, 1970), p. 34.

57 *Der Krieg zur See 1914–1918. Der Krieg in der Nordsee*, Vol. 7: *Vom Sommer 1917 bis zum Kriegsende 1918*. Reprint prepared by Gerhard P. Gross with assistance of Werner Rahn (Hamburg/Berlin/Bonn: Verlag E. S. Mittler & Sohn, 2006), p. 324.

58 Eric J. Grove, editor, *The Defeat of the Enemy Attack on Shipping 1939–1945* a revised edition of the Naval Staff History, Vols. 1A (Text and Appendices) and 1B (Plans and Tables); Aldershot, UK: Ashgate, The Navy Records Society, 1997, p. 165.

59 Craig Baker, *The Strategic Importance of Defeating Underground Facilities* (Carlisle, PA: U.S. Army War College, 2012), pp. 7–8.

60 Ministry of Defence (Navy), *The U-Boat War in the Atlantic 1939–1945*, Vol. 1: *1939–1941, German Naval History* (London: Her Majesty's Stationery Office, 1989), p. 48.

61 Craig Baker, *The Strategic Importance of Defeating Underground Facilities* (Carlisle, PA: U.S. Army War College, 2012), p. 9; Eric J. Grove, editor, *The Defeat of the Enemy Attack on Shipping 1939–1945* a revised edition of the Naval Staff History, Vols. 1A (Text and Appendices) and 1B (Plans and Tables); Aldershot, UK: Ashgate, The Navy Records Society, 1997, p. 171.

62 Eric J. Grove, editor, *The Defeat of the Enemy Attack on Shipping 1939–1945*, a revised edition of the Naval Staff History, Vols. 1A (Text and Appendices) and 1B (Plans and Tables); Aldershot, UK: Ashgate, The Navy Records Society, 1997, p. 171.

63 Bernard Ireland, *Battle of the Atlantic* (Annapolis, MD: Naval Institute Press, 2003), p. 120.

64 Ministry of Defence (Navy), *The U-Boat War in the Atlantic 1939–1945*, Vol. 3: *June 1943–May 1945, German Naval History* (London: Her Majesty's Stationery Office, 1989), p. 77.

65 Bernard Ireland, *Battle of the Atlantic* (Annapolis, MD: Naval Institute Press, 2003), p. 120.

66 Eric J. Grove, editor, *The Defeat of the Enemy Attack on Shipping 1939–1945*, a revised edition of the Naval Staff History, Vols. 1A (Text and Appendices) and 1B (Plans and Tables); Aldershot, U.K.: Ashgate, The Navy Records Society, 1997, p. 171.

67 Eric J. Grove, editor, *The Defeat of the Enemy Attack on Shipping 1939–1945*, a revised edition of the Naval Staff History, Vols. 1A (Text and Appendices) and 1B (Plans and Tables); Aldershot, UK: Ashgate, The Navy Records Society, 1997, p. 333.

68 A. Timothy Warnock, *The U.S. Army Air Forces in World War II. Air Power Versus U-Boats: Confronting Hitler's Submarine Menace in the European Theater*, (Washington, DC: Air Force History and Museums Program, Air Force Historical Studies Office, 1999), p. 21.

69 Bernard Ireland, *Battle of the Atlantic* (Annapolis, MD: Naval Institute Press, 2003), p. 182.

70 Bernard Ireland, *Battle of the Atlantic* (Annapolis, MD: Naval Institute Press, 2003), p. 81.

71 Henry Guerlac and Marie Boas, "The Radar War Against the U-Boat," *Military Affairs*, Vol. 14, No. 2 (Summer 1950), p. 105.

72 John Terraine, *The U-Boat Wars 1916–1945* (New York: G.P. Putnam's Sons, 1989), pp. 119, 141–42.

73 "Appendix 2: German U-Boats Destroyed," in Eric J. Grove, editor, *The Defeat of the Enemy Attack on Shipping 1939–1945* (Aldershot: Ashgate, Publications of the Navy Records Society, Vol. 137, 1997), p. 245.

74 "Appendix 2: Italian U-Boats Destroyed," Eric J. Grove, editor, *The Defeat of the Enemy Attack on Shipping 1939–1945* (Aldershot: Ashgate, Publications of the Navy Records Society, Vol. 137, 1997), p. 246.

75 "Appendix 2: Japanese U-Boats Destroyed," in Eric J. Grove, editor, *The Defeat of the Enemy Attack on Shipping 1939–1945* (Aldershot: Ashgate, Publications of the Navy Records Society, Vol. 137, 1997), p. 247.

76 Marine Corps Concept Paper (MCCP), *A Concept for Future Naval Mine Counter-measures in Littoral Power Projection* (Quantico, VA: Marine Corps Combat Development Command, 1998), p. 4.

77 T. Michael Cashman, *Sweeping Changes for Mine Warfare: Controlling the Mine Threat* (Monterey, CA: Naval Postgraduate School, December 1994), p. 35.

78 Jürg Meister, *Der Seekrieg in den osteuropäischen Gewaessern 1941/45* (Munich: J. F. Lehmans Verlag, 1958), pp. 148–49.

79 Robert C. Duncan, *America's Use of Mines* (White Oak, MD: U.S. Naval Ordnance Laboratory, 1962), pp. 68–69.

80 Roy F. Hoffmann, "Offensive Mine Warfare: A Forgotten Strategy," *Naval Review* (1977), p. 145; Andrew Patterson, Jr., "Mining: A Naval Strategy," *Naval War College Review* (May 1971), p. 55.

81 Gerhard Freiherr von Ledebur, *Die Seemine* (Munich: J. F. Lehmanns Verlag, 1977), p. 62.

82 V.V. Nikolayev and V.N. Romanovsky, *A History of Mine Warfare in the Russian and Soviet Navies*. Translated from the Russian *Morskiye Sapery* Washington, DC: Naval Intelligence Support Center, 1 March 1984 (Moscow: Voyenizdat, 1967), p. 12.

83 Gerhard von Ledebur, *Die Seemine* (Munich: J. F. Lehmanns Verlag, 1977), p. 185.

84 Gregory K. Hartmann, with Scott C. Truver, *Weapons That Wait*, updated version (Annapolis, MD: Naval Institute Press, 1991), p. 242; V.V. Nikolayev and V.N. Romanovskiy, *A History of Mine Warfare in the Russian and Soviet Navies*. Translated from the Russian *Morskiye Sapery* Washington, DC: Naval Intelligence Support Center, 1 March 1984 (Moscow: Voyenizdat, 1967), p. 12.

85 Gerhard von Ledebur, *Die Seemine* (Munich: J. F. Lehmanns Verlag, 1977), p. 192.

86 Milija Jovanovi, "Uticaj minskog oružja na taktiku i operatiku ratne mornarice," *Mornari ki Glasnik* (Belgrade), 6 (November–December 1982), p. 1004.

87 Chief of Naval Operations, *German, Japanese, and Italian Submarine Losses in World War II* (Washington, DC: Navy Department, OPNAV-P33–100 NEW 5–46, 1946), pp. 1–18.

88 Ellis A. Johnson and David A. Katcher, *Mines Against Japan* (White Oak, Silver Spring, MD: Naval Ordnance Laboratory, 1947; Washington, DC: U.S. Government Printing Office, 1973), p. 30; Chief of Naval Operations, *German, Japanese, and Italian Submarine Losses in World War II* (Washington, DC: Navy Department, OPNAV-P33–100 NEW 5–46, 1946), pp. 22–25.

7   Containing the enemy's forces

The destruction of the enemy's naval forces is usually combined with their containment or neutralization. Containment might be applied in the event either that the enemy fleet is too strong to be destroyed by a decisive action or that it is weak but could escape to a certain area where the stronger fleet does not have sufficient presence.[1] This method is directed not only against the enemy naval forces but also against the ground forces deployed in the coastal area. It is generally difficult to contain enemy land-based aircraft because they can be redeployed, on very short notice, hundreds and thousands of miles from their home bases. Containment could be conducted either after the enemy forces are substantially weakened or simultaneously with a decisive action.

The main methods of containing enemy naval forces are (1) naval blockade, (2) posing a threat to critical positions/areas, and (3) strategic diversions.[2] In each case, the predominant methods of the combat employment of naval forces are major or minor tactical actions. The enemy forces would be destroyed or neutralized over time. The only exception is a naval blockade, which could be planned as a major naval/joint operation. However, in contrast to a major fleet-vs.-fleet operation, a naval blockade would accomplish its ultimate operational and in many cases partial strategic objective only over time. The great majority of actions in conducting a naval blockade would be tactical in size.

Naval blockade

The most prevalent method of containment of the enemy fleet is by conducting a blockade of its bases/ports. In general, a naval blockade is aimed to prevent the enemy's use of its naval power.[3] The initial objective is to fix the enemy fleet in a place where it cannot do particular harm to one's forces. The ultimate objective is to create conditions that the enemy fleet would have only two options: remain in its bases/ports or sail out and accept the risk of its destruction.[4] Admiral Richmond observed that "in no case in all the many wars at sea in which an enemy has been forced to keep under the shelter of the defenses of his ports has a blockade forced him to fight.

Neither Spain, Holland, France nor Germany in their wars with England sent their fleets out to fight the stronger British Navy."[5] However, Richmond was not entirely correct in the case of the Dutch Navy. For example, during the first three Anglo-Dutch Wars, the Dutch fleet came out on several occasions to lift the British blockade of their coast, which then led to a major naval battle (e.g., the Battle of Katwijk on 8 August 1653 and Battle of Lowestoft on 13 June 1665). Also, the Battle of Heligoland on 9 May 1864 during the Second War of Schleswig was the result of the Austro-Prussian effort to lift the Danish blockade of the Prussian coast in the North Sea.

Castex wrote that a naval and commercial blockade is established almost simultaneously. No artificial boundaries could be drawn between a naval and a commercial blockade.[6] Both the naval and the commercial blockades are conducted parallel with each other. The reason is that the decision to establish one contributes to the establishment and maintenance of the other. Castex also noted that, more commonly, the main purpose of each of them is very different. A naval blockade is one of main methods to obtain and maintain sea control, whereas a commercial blockade is largely a part of exercising sea control. Also, a commercial blockade aims to weaken the enemy's economic potential at sea by interrupting or cutting off the movement of his commercial shipping within a given theater and overseas. It is an integral part of maritime trade warfare. The key prerequisite for the success of a commercial blockade is an effective naval blockade.[7] Also, by weakening the enemy's war-making potential, a commercial blockade indirectly contributes to the success of a naval blockade.

In general, a naval blockade requires the availability of geographically favorably located bases for the blockading forces. Bases flanking the enemy transit routes are especially valuable in conducting a naval blockade. For example, during the French Revolutionary Wars (1792–1802), the string of naval bases along England's Channel coast, combined with control of the Strait of Gibraltar, Mallorca (Balearic Islands), and La Maddalena (Sardinia), allowed the Royal Navy to blockade the French and Spanish fleets from Texel (fronting the entrance to Amsterdam) to Toulon. In contrast, the French did not have on their side of the Channel's coast a harbor large enough to provide shelter for the major part of their fleet. In addition, the prevailing winds blew up the Channel and toward the southern coast of England. The French were unable to obtain permanent control of Antwerp, the only large port within striking distance of the British major naval bases. The British policy was always to have close and friendly relations with the Low Countries and thereby deny the use of Antwerp to the French fleet.

During the American Civil War (1861–1865), the Federal Navy captured many islands and ports, primarily to reinforce the Union blockade of the Southern states. [8] In the Franco-Prussian War of 1870–1871, the French attempt to blockade the Prussian coast did not last long because of the lack of bases close to the Prussian coast in the North Sea.[9] In the Spanish-American War of 1898, the U.S. Navy used temporary bases in

Cuba, especially at Guantanamo. In the Russo-Japanese War of 1904–1905, the Japanese used the Elliot island group as an advanced base in their blockade of Port Arthur.[10] Because of the need to monitor the movements of the enemy ships within a blockaded area, the stronger side must have a sufficient number of ships/aircraft for blockading duties. For example, it was believed that, for an effective close blockade, the blockading force had to be between 25 and 33 percent larger than a blockaded fleet.[11]

In general, the effectiveness of a blockading force is much higher if it is composed of both deep- and shallow-draft vessels. In the era of sail, the blockaded fleet was often able to escape from the port if composed of shallow draft vessels and the blockading force lacked the same. For example, in July 1790, the Russians blockaded the Swedish fleet in the Vyborg Bay, in eastern part of the Gulf of Finland. However, they did not have shallow-draft ships capable of operating close to the Swedish coast. Consequently, the Swedes slipped out of the ports with their small galleys and transports through shallow waters under cover of diversionary raids and gun fire from larger warships.[12]

The lack of suitable platforms was one of the reasons for the rather ineffectual British blockade of the Russian fleet in the Baltic in 1854–1855. British Vice Admiral Sir Charles Napier (1786–1860) entered the Baltic in March 1854 with a largely steam-powered force. Napier's orders called for establishing a naval blockade and to reconnoiter the Russian defenses. Among other things, he had a shortage of local pilots and a lack of shallow-draft vessels. Hence, he had great difficulties in monitoring the enemy-held coast.[13] Very often, blockade breakers moved within sight of the fleet, but the British were unable to stop the traffic.[14]

Types

Depending on the distance of a blockading force from the blockaded forces, a naval blockade could be close, distant, or semi-distant. In general, a naval blockade can be conducted against a single or several naval bases/ ports or against the entire enemy coast. A specific type of blockade prevents enemy naval/commercial movements through a strait/narrows or artificial canal. A close or semi-distant blockade is usually established against a single or several major naval base/port, whereas distant blockade usually requires the physical control of one or several straits/narrows.

Close blockade

Until the end of the nineteenth century, a naval blockade meant *close blockade*. By conducting a close blockade, a stronger fleet was able to exploit the benefits of the command of the sea without fighting and hence without large losses.[15] Normally, a close blockade required relatively large forces to be effective. It was also extremely exhausting and demanding on one's ships' crews. Yet sometimes a close blockade played into the hands of a weaker fleet by tying the stronger fleet to a given sea area, thereby reducing or even preventing it from operating elsewhere.[16]

Naval classical thinkers recognized the great importance of a close naval blockade. For example, in Mahan's view, a close blockade might succeed in keeping both merchant and naval vessels bottled up in their own harbors. However, if the enemy warships inevitably escape to sea, they must be sought and destroyed.[17] Corbett wrote that close blockade is an "arrested offensive." It is essentially an offensive operation, although its objective is usually negative. It is aimed at preventing the enemy from carrying out some offensive operation and making the enemy's coast your frontier.[18] He explained that by establishing a naval blockade, the stronger fleet would try to "either prevent an enemy armed force leaving port, or to make certain that he shall be brought to action before it can carry out the ulterior [ultimate] purpose for which it puts to sea."[19] Corbett noted that in establishing a close blockade, the objective "is inseparable from the ulterior object of naval war."[20] For him, a close blockade was a method for securing local and temporary command.[21] Corbett also believed that in his era close blockade was no longer practicable.[22]

One of the major advantages of a close naval blockade is that it considerably reduced or even eliminated entirely the weaker fleet's ability to operate outside its bases/ports. In the era of sail, the enemy controlled with his coastal guns only a few hundred meters of the sea surface, or an area no larger than his ports. A close naval blockade was the most economical method of watching the enemy fleet's movements instead of trying to find its scattered parts in the vast expanses of an ocean.[23] Brodie wrote that in conducting a close blockade, the size of the sea area left to the enemy control was practically nil.[24] At the same time, the seamanship and morale of the blockading forces were increased while the blockaded forces were forced to be idle.[25]

Rudiments of a close naval blockade could be found in Greek and Roman naval warfare. In the ancient era, naval vessels had poor seaworthiness and a small radius of action. Classical war galleys were unable to be at sea in front of a blockaded port for too long. Hence, a naval blockade never extended to a large part of the enemy-controlled coast and was seldom conducted during the night (the ships were beached, and the crews slept ashore). A secure permanent station close to the blockaded harbor was necessary for a blockade to be effective. In general, naval blockades in the ancient era were unsuccessful or of dubious value.[26]

The effectiveness of a naval blockade was greatly increased with the advent of large and seaworthy sailing ships in the late sixteenth century. A naval blockade was established against several enemy detachments and encompassed a large part of the enemy coast. A stronger fleet was then usually deployed off the enemy bases/ports to watch enemy ship movements from a distance. Hence, it exerted only a general control of local waters.

The objective was to prevent the enemy from concentrating his forces. The individual elements of the blockading fleet had to be deployed within a mutually supporting distance. Yet bad weather often forced the blockading squadrons to leave their patrolling areas off the enemy ports, thereby giving an alert enemy an opportunity to escape.

By the end of the eighteenth century, the ability of large navies to maintain a blockade for a long time became possible. As practiced by the British Navy, a naval blockade became a strategic extension of its sea power to the enemy coast. The coppering of ship bottoms dramatically extended the time between ship refits. The British adopted lightweight carronade (smoothbore cast iron cannon) in 1779, which reduced ship's tonnage, crewing needs, and costs. This, in turn, also allowed smaller ships to be employed for blockading duties. By the late 1700s, naval medicine conquered scurvy (vitamin C deficiency). Dramatic improvements in shipboard hygiene and medicine allowed crews to spend months and sometimes years at sea.[27]

The steady and uninterrupted resupply of the blockading ships was critical for the success of a close blockade, as shown in the Dutch efforts to maintain a blockade of the Spanish fleet at anchor in the Downs in 1639. Also, Admiral Edward Hawke's (1705–1781) ships were able to remain on station in 1750s due to constant resupply from Portsmouth.[28] In the eighteenth century, Gibraltar and Minorca provided the Royal Navy resupply and refit for ships assigned to a long period of blockade duty in the Mediterranean. In 1794, the British lost Minorca but obtained a new base on Corsica used for resupply of the British ships blockading the French Mediterranean ports. (The ports of Naples and Sicily were closed to British ships.) In 1803, Admiral Horatio Nelson lacked favorably situated bases to conduct a close blockade of Toulon. Although his nine ships of the line were badly in the need of repairs, he kept them constantly at sea. Nelson did not have a regular base nearer than Gibraltar and Malta. Gibraltar was inadequate as a fleet base, plus it is about 900 miles from Toulon. Likewise, Malta is located about 700 miles away from Toulon – six to seven weeks of sailing time.[29]

In the era of steam, a blockading force was more limited in range and endurance than were sailing ships. The ships greatly depended on the supply of coal. Hence, it was critical to have coaling stations available and not too far away from the blockaded coast.[30] For example, in the Spanish-American War of 1898, Key West was the main U.S. base for operations. Most U.S. ships had a range of about 4,000 nm, or about two weeks of continuous sailing. They heavily depended on supplies of coal for maintaining the blockade of Cuba. However, at the beginning of war, the U.S. Navy had only six colliers. In August 1898, an additional 11 colliers were purchased.[31] The U.S. commanders were greatly concerned about having adequate supplies of coal. The shortages of coal, in turn, almost allowed Admiral Cervera to escape.[32]

The first example of a close blockade in the era of sail was in September–October 1639 when the Dutch fleet of 100 ships under Admiral Maarten (Harpertszoon) Tromp blockaded the Spanish fleet of 70 ships in the Downs along the English coast. In the first three Anglo-Dutch Wars, several major battles took place when a weaker side tried to either prevent a blockage or lift an existing one by a stronger side. For example, in the First Anglo-Dutch War, the Dutch fleet blockaded the English fleet on the island of Elba and Leghorn for six months between September 1652 and March 1653. Both of these blockades were effective, and in the latter case, the Dutch destroyed the English fleet as it tried to escape.[33] In the aftermath of the British victory at Outer Gabbard on 2–3 June 1653, the British established blockade of the Dutch coast from Nieuwpoort to Texel.[34] In the Third Anglo-Dutch War, the Battle of Lowestoft on 13 June 1665 was fought because the Dutch tried to prevent a second blockade of their coast by the British.[35] A close blockade of the British ports by the Dutch fleet in 1667 forced the British to discuss peace terms with the Dutch in matter of weeks.[36]

During the Seven Year's War, William Pitt the Elder (1708–1778) made a naval blockade during his tenure as Secretary of State (1757–1761) an integral part of the national strategy. The Royal Navy combined a blockade of the enemy fleet with occasional raids against the enemy bases. For the protection of its naval and commercial ports, France depended upon strong coastal fortresses, which within a few days might be reinforced by the mobilization of scattered detachments of militia.[37] The objective was to keep the French fleet divided between the Atlantic and the Mediterranean ports.

The first continuous and close naval blockade was conducted under Admiral George Anson's (1697–1762) tenure as First Lord of the Admiralty in the Seven Years' War (1756–1763). In 1759, Admiral Edward Hawke was the first to apply such a blockade as the commander of the Channel Fleet.[38] He was directed to blockade Brest with his 25 men-of-war. Hawke's fleet was deployed at Saint-Mathieu near Pierres Noiers. With westerly winds, he cruised some forty miles southwest of Quessant.[39] He kept his blockading squadron off Brest instead of returning to Torbay, Devon, some 130 nm away. The reason was that he wanted to prevent the French from sending a squadron from Brest to the West Indies. That task could not have been successfully carried out from the western ports in southern England.[40]

The French fleet that escaped Brest was decisively beaten in the Battle of Quiberon Bay on 20 November 1759.[41] Afterward, the British maintained the unopposed blockade of French ports that eliminated French ships from the high seas. The Royal Navy kept its main forces back at Torbay or even Spithead and relied on smaller ships off the French coast to keep an eye on the French ships if they tried to come out. The French merchant marine was devastated and the finances of the country exhausted. The British further restricted French trade by seeking out contraband in neutral shipping. By the end of the Seven Years' War, the British were firmly in command of the sea.[42]

Britain applied naval blockades extensively during the French Revolutionary Wars (1792–1802) and the Napoleonic Wars (1803–1815). For example, in 1795, the British blockaded Lorient for five months. The naval base at Brest was constantly watched. A major part of the Royal Navy was on station in England. The escape of the French Admiral Justin Bonaventure Morard de Galles (1741–1809), with a fleet of 45 ships, pointed out the need for a more strict blockade. Hence, after 1797, the British extended the blockade to Rochefort and Lorient in the Bay of Biscay and to Toulon in the Mediterranean. Eventually, the British blockaded Texel, the Netherlands, and the Spanish ports of Ferrol an Cádiz. [43] The French were able to choose among many points for attack, while the British had to keep close watch over many ports.[44]

The key position for the British blockading force off the main French naval base at Brest was the island of Ushant.[45] The British ships were constantly at sea and far from their bases. Very often, stormy weather swept the blockading ships away. In westerly winds, the French squadron in Brest could not sail out, but the British fleet could regain their station with the first easterly winds in time to prevent the enemy to escape. This, in turn, depended on the speed of the British movements and thereby the distance of the port of refuge. Spithead was unfavorably situated as a port of refuge. Yet Admirals Richard Howe and Samuel Hood chose it for their squadrons. They also added the practice of keeping the main body of the fleet in port during the winter months.[46] Although Brest was the most important port, the British did not monitor it with the necessary diligence. For the British, the problem was complicated because the French fleet was divided among several ports.[47] Hence, it was difficult to have a sufficient force monitoring all the ports. For example, Vice Admiral Étienne Eustache Bruix (1759–1805), after escaping Brest with 25 ships in May 1799, appeared suddenly in front of Cádiz. The British Western Squadron with 50 ships signally failed to prevent that escape.[48] Admiral George Keith Elphinstone (1st Viscount Keith) (1746–1823), with 18 ships, was blockading the Spanish fleet in Cádiz. Although superior in strength, Bruix decided to avoid the British ships. Hence, his escape from Brest did not have serious consequences for the British.[49] Nevertheless, Bruix's escape caused a three-month-long crisis for the British.[50]

In April 1800, Admiral John Jervis (Lord St. Vincent) (1735–1823) became commander of the Channel Fleet (40 ships and five admirals).[51] He introduced a much stricter blockade than his predecessors. Among other things, Jervis made new arrangements to expedite refitting of his ships and thereby extend their time on station.[52] He directed his ships to be refitted at either Torbay or Cawsand Bay (southeast of Plymouth). They never stayed more than six days in these two ports. They were not allowed to go to Spithead unless special orders were issued by the Admiralty or Jervis personally.[53] In 1801, the number of ships of the line was increased from 24 to 30 for the blockade of the principal French naval base at Brest.[54] The central station for the blockading force was changed from eight leagues (24 nm) west of Ushant in the presence of easterly winds to six leagues (18 nm) in westerly winds.[55] Jervis changed the blockade of Brest and Rochefort to a tight blockade in winter and summer. This made any French breakout virtually impossible.[56]

After England declared war against France in May 1803, the Royal Navy blockaded the entire French coast. In effect, England thus moved its frontiers to France. With one stroke, French shipping, trade, and colonies were cut off. Never before or afterward was a naval blockade as successful as in 1803–1805. During the Napoleonic Wars (1803–1815), the British did not try to hermetically seal all the French or Spanish ports but rather to effectively prevent any large French-led force to sail out to sea. They then blockaded enemy ships at Brest, Toulon, and Rochefort, as well as Spanish ships at Cádiz and Franco-Spanish ships in Ferrol.[57] However, for some reason, the French public, including Napoleon I himself, believed that the blockade was not serious. The French were maintaining their fleet in good order, and the British were wearing themselves out. Certainly such constant cruising entailed excessive fatigue. However, blockading duties also created incomparably skilled crews and officers.[58]

The most successful British close blockade was conducted by Admiral William Cornwallis (1744–1819) between the winter of 1804/1805 and after the Battle of Trafalgar in October 1805. For Napoleon I, it was essential that parts of his fleet could escape out to the open sea but to do so at the time of his own choosing and by using routes that would ensure a rapid concentration at a particular point.[59] To prevent this from happening, the British declared a close blockade of the French bases in the English Channel. In the event of the enemy detachments escaping out of the ports, orders were given for the outlying British squadrons to fall back on their central position off Brest and thereby be able to pursue the French if they sailed either to Ireland or up to the Channel. If the French moved up the Channel, they would be met by the British squadron based at Downs and in the North Sea.[60]

The British blockade of France lasted 20 years. Bad weather allowed the French fleet to escape, but many ships were dispersed, and it was difficult to assemble them. The ships blockaded in Ferrol and Brest remained blockaded for years. Also, coastwise traffic was almost completely stopped. This made it very difficult to supply and provision French ports. A great advantage was that it raised the morale of the British crews and demoralized the French crews.[61]

In the War of 1812 between Britain and the United States, the Royal Navy blockaded the U.S. East Coast. The blockade was primarily intended to cut off commercial traffic. However, The Royal Navy also tried to prevent U.S. privateers from attacking British commercial vessels. In 1812, the Royal Navy had 686 ships in active service, including 120 ships of the line and 145 frigates. It had some 75 ships on the American station, whereas the American Navy had only 16 ships (the best were three 44-gun frigates).[62] American privateers enjoyed great freedom of action because the Royal Navy was preoccupied with the war against Napoleon I, and England was unable to send substantial naval reinforcements to Canada. This situation drastically changed in 1813 when England started to exercise greater general control at sea After the first downfall of Napoleon I in the spring 1814, the war entered a third phase. The Royal Navy completely dominated the U.S. East Coast and many inland waters. It practically stopped U.S. naval operations and commerce at sea. The British army was reinforced and began an invasion of the United States. This effort failed because of the U.S. victory on Lake Champlain on 1 June 1814. The final phase was characterized by attacks of strong British expeditions against U.S. cities on the coast.[63]

During the Crimean War (1854–1856), the Anglo-French fleet established a blockade of the Russian ports in both the Baltic and the Black Sea. In the Baltic, British Admiral Charles Napier (1786–1860), by mid-April 1854, blockaded Libau (Liepāja today), the Gulf of Livonia (Gulf of Riga today), and the approaches to the Gulf of Finland. He also dispatched a squadron of four steamers into the Gulf of Bothnia.[64]After the arrival of the French squadron, Napier imposed, on 20 June 1854, a full blockade of the Russian-controlled coast and across the Gulf of Finland. However, he had too few ships for imposing a total blockade.[65] By the end of June, the combined Anglo-French fleet consisted of 51 ships (28 ships of the line, five first-class frigates, and 18 steamers), with 50,000 seamen and marines.[66] The blockade of the Gulf of Bothnia was extended north as additional ships became available, and the southern coast was blockaded by 22 June 1854. By mid-July 1854, the entire Gulf of Bothnia was blockaded.[67]

In 1854, the British Admiralty directed Vice Admiral Sir James Dundas (1785–1862) to impose a blockade of the Russian coast in the Black Sea. However, Dundas found out that his French counterpart Admiral Francois-Adolphe Hamelin (1796–1864) did not have orders from his government to do the same.[68] Hence, the Anglo-French fleet blockaded only the Danube Estuary on 1 June 1854. The Anglo-French ships patrolled area around the port of Sulina and sporadically shelled the Russian positions on the coast.[69] However, by December 1854, the Admiralty, realizing that the French were not going to help, directed Dundas to blockade ports. However, the blockade was ineffective because of the shortage of ships.[70]

In the war between Austria and Franco-Piedmontese coalition (Second Italian War of Independence) on 3 May 1859 – or only four days after the Austrian Army invaded Piedmont – the first French and Sardinian warships arrived in the Adriatic. The French deployed to the Adriatic only six ships of the line plus several frigates and smaller vessels. This force proved to be more than sufficient to keep the Austrian fleet in check.[71] Because of the inferiority of his fleet, the Austrian Navy's Commander Archduke Ferdinand Max (1832–1867) (brother of Emperor Francis Joseph) took a defensive posture. He assembled his screw-driven ships to Pola with the best of his sailing vessels and paddle steamers. On 2 June, the French declared a blockade of Venice and other harbors. The allied fleet did not reach the full strength until weeks later. In early July, the allied fleet occupied Lussin Piccolo (Mali Lošinj today) as a base for an amphibious assault on Venice. However, by then the war had already been decided by the Austrian defeats at Magenta on 4 June and Solferino on 24 June.[72] The war ended with the Armistice of Villafranca on 11 July 1859.

In the American Civil War (1861–1865), the Union blockade of the Confederacy (Plan ANACONDA) was the Navy's greatest contribution to victory. Some 3,500-mile sea border from Chesapeake Bay to the Mexican border was blockaded. To wage the war, the Confederate armies needed guns, ammunition, medical supplies, and clothing. European manufacturers desperately needed cotton from the Southern states. With the increased strength of the Union Navy, the blockade became progressively more and more effective.[73]

In 1861, the Federal Navy consisted of only 40 steamers (including five steam-powered frigates) and 50 sailing vessels in commission. This number included steamers available immediately for blockading duties; the remainder were too old to be of much use.[74] The Union Navy had only 7,000 men in active service. Navy Secretary Gideon Wells (1802–1878) increased ship construction program dramatically. By the end of war in 1865, some 670 ships were built. The Union Navy's personnel strength stood at 225,000 men. The Confederate States had a small navy. Yet in the course of the war 150 ships were built despite all the economic difficulties.[75]

The Union blockading force was divided into four groups: (1) the North Atlantic Squadron covering the coast from the Chesapeake Bay and its tributaries and the coast south to the South Carolina boundary near Wilmington; (2) the South Atlantic Squadron responsible for blockading the coast from Wilmington in the north to Cape Canaveral in the south, with its main operating base in Port Royal, South Carolina. After January 1862, the Gulf Coast was divided in two blockading sectors: (3) the East Gulf blockading squadron responsible for the coast from Cape Canaveral to St. Andrew's Bay and (4) the West Coast blockading squadron, patrolling from the latter point to the Rio Grande at the Mexican border with Texas.[76]

In the Spanish-American War of 1898, President William McKinley directed the U.S. Navy to start a blockade of Cuba on 21 April. Spain followed with a declaration of war on 23 April, and two days later, the U.S. Congress declared war against Spain. The Spanish Navy had only four armored cruisers while one older battleship and an armored cruiser were not ready for combat at the beginning of the war. It also had in service five smaller cruisers and 13 torpedo gunboats plus six double-turreted and essentially useless monitors. Despite the courage and devotion of its officers and crews, the Spanish Navy suffered from numerous problems ranging from lack of engineering competence, bad equipment, passivity, lack of training, and corruption in supply service.[77]

At the beginning of 1898, the U.S. Navy had in service four new battle-ships, one old battleship, two fast armored cruisers, 13 protected cruisers, six steel monitors, eight old iron monitors, 33 unprotected cruisers and gunboats, six torpedo boats, and 12 tugs. Its biggest weakness was the lack of colliers, supply ships, transports, hospital ships, and repair ships – all necessary to maintain an effective naval blockade.[78]

The Spaniards attempted to loosen the blockade by building new batteries and engaging smaller vessels with gunboats. They also tried to lure larger us ships within the range of shore batteries. On several occasions, the Spaniards were successful. The U.S. blockading ships cut off telegraphic communications from Cienfuegos, Santiago, and Guantanamo to Madrid.[79] In conducting the blockade of the port of Santiago, Rear Admiral William T. Sampson (1840–1902), contrary to all precedents, distributed his ships on an extended line that doubled the cordon of light vessels and enclosed the narrow entrance of the harbor. He established a military blockade on the principles of commercial blockade. Yet doing so had no serious consequences because the Spaniards decided not to fight.[80]

Semi-distant blockade

In the era of sail, the lack of a sufficient number of ships forced the stronger fleet to apply the method of a so-called open, or semi-distant, blockade. For example, Nelson used a different method in blockading the French naval base at Toulon in 1803–1805 than Jervis and Cornwallis used in blockading the French ports in the English Channel. Because of the lack of a sufficient number of ships for the blockading duties, he kept only scouting frigates off Toulon to timely inform him about the movements of the French ships. Nelson appeared off Toulon from time to time but not staying for too long.[81] He stayed at sea with his entire squadron. He withdraw sporadically to Agincourt Sound anchorage at La Maddalena, Sardinia (which was then neutral) in order to give his crews a rest, leaving only some frigates on guard.[82] He took his ships to La Maddalena only six times during the two-year long blockade of Toulon.[83] Nelson said that "his system is the very contrary of blockading. Every opportunity has been offered the enemy to put to sea."[84] Corbett called Nelson's method an "open" blockade. For him, an open blockade was aimed at the destruction of the enemy naval force. Hence, it was a definite step toward securing permanent command.[85]

Nelson's method of blockading the enemy port failed on two occasions because his ships were too far away. For example, on 14 January 1805, Admiral Pierre-Charles-Jean-Baptiste-Silvestre de Villeneuve (1763–1806) escaped from Toulon with the intent to pass the Strait of Gibraltar and then head to the Caribbean. Yet he returned to Toulon after only two days. Nelson was misled by false information to search for the French squadron in the eastern Mediterranean. He returned to Malta on 19 February and then learned that Villeneuve was back in Toulon. In the second attempt, on 30 March 1805, Villeneuve sailed out with 11 ships of the line, avoided Nelson's ships, transited the Strait of Gibraltar, and then headed for the Caribbean.[86] La Maddalena, some 250 miles away from Toulon, was obviously too far away to allow for an effective blockade.[87] In contrast, the method applied by Admirals Jervis and Cornwallis was more effective in blockading the enemy fleet. By conducting a close blockade of the French ports, British morale was enhanced, and the need for constant sailing increased the skills of the British sailors. The blockaded French fleet was demoralized. The French crews lacked sailing practice, and over time they lost the ability to fight both the enemy and the elements.[88]

With the advent of mines and torpedoes, a close blockade became more difficult to apply in the late nineteenth century. This, in turn, led some commanders to keep the blockading ships farther away from the enemy's bases and ports. In the Russo-Japanese War of 1904–1905, Admiral Heihachirō Tōgō, commander of the Japanese Navy, conducted a semi-distant blockade of the Russian naval base at Port Arthur for about ten months.[89] He took as an advanced base Elliot island group, where he permanently detached his torpedo boats and light vessels to maintain a watch of Port Arthur.[90] For example, on 19 August 1904, Tōgō deployed in the vicinity of Port Arthur three destroyer flotillas with ten destroyers and eight torpedo boats. About ten miles off Port Arthur's entrance, he had five cruisers, three armored cruisers, and seven torpedo boats. About 20–40 miles from Port Arthur was deployed the Japanese main force of four battleships and three cruisers. In short, the Japanese deployed 15 out of 20 large ships in a semicircle some 40 miles away from Port Arthur.[91]

The Japanese fleet in front of Port Arthur suffered disproportionately high losses from the Russian mines. Not only did Admiral Tōgō lose two battleships, or one-third of his battle force, but he was also forced to loosen his pressure on Port Arthur. Tōgō's problems were increased greatly by the Imperial General Staff's delay in landing an army at Yentoa Bay on the Liaoutung Peninsula, only 53 miles from Port Arthur. This action was very risky because the Russian squadron at Port Arthur could have possibly intervened and attacked the Japanese Army's flank during one of absences of the Japanese battleships for coaling or maintenance. Tōgō asked for a dozen merchant ships to be used for the blockade of Port Arthur, but that request was denied because of the general shortage of shipping needed for the transport of troops and supplies.[92]

Distant blockade

The disadvantages of a close blockade increased in the age of steam. The blockading ships' large consumption of fuel greatly expanded the logistical needs of the fleet. Shifts in wind no longer granted respite to the blockading squadrons. Also, the coal-burning ships did not have the sailing ships' almost unlimited range and endurance. By the late nineteenth century, a close blockade had become progressively more costly for a stronger fleet because of the defender's use of mines and torpedoes. The advent of submarines, and eventually aircraft meant that the blockading squadrons were increasingly exposed to a dangerous level of attrition.[93]

Mahan realized, perhaps earlier than many of his contemporaries, that the advent of the torpedo and submarine would impose much greater stress on the blockading force. This, in turn, would force the attacker to keep the ships at a much greater distance from enemy bases and ports. Expressed differently, a close blockade would be converted into a distant blockade.[94] Thus, a distant (or broad) blockade emerged as the solution for a stronger fleet to neutralize an inferior opponent.

Corbett was the first theoretician who differentiated between close and observation (or distant) blockade. Close blockade was designed to prevent an enemy from sailing out from its bases/ports, whereas an observation blockade was aimed at enticing the enemy forces to sail out in order to do combat with them in a decisive encounter.[95]

Castex observed that a close blockade secures, with great efforts, direct and temporary control of the sea. This was important but sometimes could be brought into the question if the weaker side escaped. In contrast, an open blockade could lead, if the enemy fleet was destroyed, to a permanent and full command of the seas.[96]

In contrast to a close blockade, the fleet conducting a distant blockade occupies operationally several exterior positions and hence operates along converging lines of operation. Generally, a distant blockade is less effective than a close blockade. A stronger fleet has to be deployed at a distance and therefore concedes to the inferior fleet a certain freedom of movement. One can perhaps argue that a weaker fleet is not blockaded at all. The stronger fleet does not keep the enemy within his bases; it only threatens with interception and punishment, and possible destruction, if the enemy ships go too far away from their bases.[97] The stronger side cannot choose the time for decisive encounter but does have control over the enemy's communications.[98]

A distant blockade leads usually to a disputed control of the sea. It is generally more effective against surface ships than against submarines. In a war against a strong opponent, the distant blockade requires the employment of a considerable number of surface ships and aircraft. For example, in World War I, the Royal Navy had to concentrate large forces on the line Scapa Flow-Cromarty-Rosyth in the North Sea.[99] The weaker opponent can strike at any of several widely separated areas, thereby forcing the stronger fleet to keep strong forces in more than one place. The enemy often controls the larger part of the sea.[100] For example, in World War I, the British had to keep capital ships not only at Scapa Flow also in the south of England. In World War II, the British had to keep capital ships at Scapa Flow, Gibraltar, and Alexandria.[101]

In a distant blockade, the weaker fleet undergoes much less of the humiliation and deterioration than if it is locked in a port. It also could largely control the shipping within the sea area left to it.[102] No complete and permanent control of surface, subsurface, and the air can be obtained, as long the enemy fleet is not destroyed. A small or even a large part of the enemy fleet has the opportunity to break through the blockade. The weaker side is not doomed to inactivity. For example, in World War I, the German Navy was able to control the Baltic Sea and eastern part of the North Sea.

Changes in the legal regime

The law of blockade did not emerge until the late seventeenth century. In the early years, warring states issued proclamations or similar instruments to inform neutrals of the nature of their blockade and which conduct violated the conditions of blockade. However, because a blockade was one-sided, it often led to friction between the blockading states and neutrals.[103] After the blockade became more common in the seventeenth century, neutral states began to respond to it. The early legal scholars were initially more concerned with justifying a blockade. They also tried to reconcile conflict between the interests of a blockading state and neutrals. The neutral states either tacitly agreed or protested its application by a stronger sea power. Very often, neutrals went to a war to protect their interests at sea. Over time emerged a common recognition that the general principles of a lawful blockade should rest on adequate notice, effective enforcement, impartial implementation, and respect for neutrals' rights.[104]

In the modern era, the conduct of a naval blockade became one of the main issues of international law. At the conference in Paris in 1856 that ended the Crimean War, one of the major issues discussed was naval blockade. In the Paris Declaration Respecting Maritime Law issued on 16 April 1856, it was stipulated, among other things, that "blockades, in order to be binding must be effective, that is to say, maintained by a force sufficient really to prevent access to the coast of the enemy." It also stated that "the present Declaration is not and shall not be binding, except between those Powers who have acceded or shall accede, to it."[105] This declaration was repeated in the Declaration Concerning the Laws of Naval War, issued in London on 26 February 1909. It also stipulated in article 1 that a blockade "must not extend beyond the ports and coasts belonging to or occupied by the enemy." Article 5 stated that "a blockade must be applied impartially to the ships of all nations."[106] However, Declaration of London was never ratified by Britain and did not enter into force as a binding instrument for any state that negotiated it.[107]

Naval blockades in world wars

The introduction of submarine, mines, and aircraft radically changed blockade practice. The weaker side using such weapons forced the stronger power to move its warships hundreds of miles away from the blockaded shore. Instead of deployed blockading squadrons as in the past, the new weapons led to establishing a blockade zone that is off-limits to all vessels. Notices were issued to all states to stay away from these areas. Neutral ships found within such a zone were liable to indiscriminate attack.[108] Blockade zones allow for the indiscriminate destruction of merchant ships, eliminating the traditional neutral's rights of capture when found in violation of blockade.[109]

In World War I, a naval blockade had little resemblance to those envisioned under traditional law. Various war zones were declared encompassing large areas of the ocean/sea and were rendered dangerous to shipping. Within a war zone, also known as "operational zone," and "exclusion zone," a "barred area" or a "military" area was declared. All rules of naval warfare were suspended through the use of mines and submarines, thereby rendering the areas dangerous not only for the enemy merchant shipping but also to neutrals.[110]

In World War I, the objective of a blockade was primarily to bring the enemy down by inflicting starvation and denying the transport of war materials. This was opposite to what the Japanese did in 1904.[111] At that time, the Japanese government authorized the Navy Minister or the commander in chief to designate certain area adjacent to the islands of the Japanese Empire as a "sea defense area" on and after the outbreak of war. About one dozen of such areas were declared. In some cases, their boundaries ran as far as 10 miles from land.[112] The concept of the so-called long-distance blockade (or distant blockade) led to radical changes in the way a blockade was conducted.[113] The Entente powers justified, in November 1914, their long-distance blockade not as legally permissible strategy but only on the basis of their claim that belligerent reprisals, namely the retaliation for the German use of contact mines on the open sea around the British Isles, were a violation of the 1907 Hague Convention VIII Relative to the Laying of Automatic Submarine Contact Mines.[114] The offensive use of mines and submarines required the establishment of a blockade zone within which all ships were sunk indiscriminately. This in fact rendered traditional law obsolete.[115]

From 1905 to 1911, the Royal Navy focused on the so-called observation blockade of the German coast in the North Sea in case of war with Germany. The mainstay of the blockade would be light forces. Close blockade with heavy ships was not possible due to the high risk. A decisive role in these considerations was to enable light forces to remain in the area.[116] By 1911, the Admiralty decided to institute a distant blockade of the German High Seas Fleet in the North Sea in case of a European war. This was formally adopted in war orders in mid-December 1912.[117] Specifically, the Grand Fleet would deploy its battle fleet at Scapa Flow; the Second Fleet, or the Channel Fleet, would be deployed at the Strait of Dover and on the southern coast of England, while the Third Fleet would serve as reserve and for local defense.[118] Parallel with the naval blockade, the British also decided to institute a commercial blockade by closing the Strait of Dover and the northern exit from the North Sea by employing the 10th Cruiser Squadron.[119]

A distant blockade was instituted by the Grand Fleet in the North Sea shortly after the outbreak of war in August 1914. The British moved their blockade line far away from the German bases. In case the High Seas Fleet tried to break through either the northern or the southern exit from the North Sea, the Grand Fleet was nearby and ready to attack. The ultimate objective was to isolate Germany from all links with overseas.[120] The Germans deployed their ships in a triangle-like base of operations formed by naval bases on the rivers Weser, Ems, and Jade. Because the initial ratio of forces was three to two, the Germans tried to balance naval strength by conducting attrition warfare before seeking a general fleet action. However, these actions were not a part of an overall military strategic objective, nor were they an integral part of an operational plan. Despite pressure to go on the offensive, the High Seas Fleet remained on the strategic defensive but acted offensively on the tactical level.[121]

The British were successful in protecting the country's maritime interests behind the blockading line. Offensively, the control of German shipping that the Grand Fleet exercised from Scapa Flow to the Channel ports was no less complete than if the German North Sea ports had been blockaded at close range. It was probably even more effective in the final result because the blockade included neutral countries adjoining Germany as well. Defensively, the British distant blockade was sufficient in accomplishing its main purpose. As long as the northern and southern exits from the North Sea were firmly controlled, the German surface ships were unable to attack British shipping on the Atlantic routes.

In World War I, a distant blockade of a semi-enclosed sea normally did not prevent the weaker force from exercising control of the adjacent enclosed sea theater. For example, the Germans had general control of the Baltic throughout the entire war, despite the British distant blockade of the German fleet in the North Sea. Yet a distant blockade provided the stronger fleet with the best means of containing a weaker but potentially dangerous enemy – and so improved its chances of being able to use the sea in relative security. But at the same time, technology and strategic circumstances gave the blockaded navies (Germany and Austria-Hungary) much more freedom of action. The Allies blockaded the sea's only exit in the Adriatic, but that did not prevent the Austro-Hungarian Navy to have de facto control of major parts of the Adriatic.

In World War II, the western Allies used the blockade as a method to cut off the Axis powers from their links overseas. On 27 November 1939, the British Order-in-Council established a long-distance blockade of Germany. The neutral states, including Italy, strongly protested. After Italy entered the war on 11 June 1940, the Allies blockaded Italy too. As in World War I, the western Allies justified their naval blockade as retaliation.[122] Britain felt justified because Germany had violated the London (Submarine) Protocol of 1936 and the 1907 Hague Mining Convention (Article VIII) and because of Germany's indiscriminate attacks on commerce between the Allies and neutrals.[123]

After the attack on Pearl Harbor in December 1941, the United States declared a huge blockading zone encompassing the entire Pacific Ocean from the Arctic Circle to the Antarctica, or some 69-million-square-mile-large area. It ordered U.S. submarines to attack, without warning, all Japanese warships and merchant ships found in the declared zone.[124]

Blockades since 1945

After the end of World War II, naval blockades were declared in several regional wars. The first naval blockade after the end of World War II was declared by the U.S. President Harry S. Truman (1884–1972) shortly after the North Korean invasion of South Korea. On 30 June 1950, Truman declared a naval blockade of North Korea by naval and air forces.[125] The primary purpose of the U.N. blockade was not to contain North Korean naval forces but to exert economic pressure by using naval and air attacks against the enemy logistics.[126] No part of North Korea is more than 120 miles away from the sea. Hence, it was believed that the communists were vulnerable to pressure from naval power. The United States had to take many ships from its mothballed fleet and many aircraft from distant theaters. By the summer of 1951, typically two or three U.S. aircraft carriers, one battleship, several cruisers, and accompanying destroyers were deployed off the eastern coast of North Korea. The British Commonwealth force revolved around one or two carriers, with accompanying cruisers and destroyers. Also, the French, Australian, and Colombian navies took part in the blockade. The United States organized Task Force (TF) 77, deployed in the Sea of Japan, to prevent seaborne traffic from the Soviet port of Vladivostok. In addition, the blockade encompassed the western coast of North Korea, where the main objective was to cut off coastal traffic from China. (The North Koreans used mostly small unarmed junks or sampans in carrying cargo.)[127]

One of the major reasons for the Six-Day War of June 1967 was Egypt's blockade of the Strait of Tiran, declared on 22 May 1967. Egypt announced that the strait would be closed to all ships flying the Israeli flag or carrying strategic material, effective 23 May.[128] On the first day of the war, 6 October. Egypt's zone encompassed the sea area southward of 33° N and east of 29° 30'. Syria's war zone encompassed an area north of 33° N and east of 34° E.[129] Any ship within the blockaded zone sailed at its own risk.[130] Egypt also declared a war zone in the Red Sea and mined the southern exit of the Gulf of Suez to prevent Israeli tanker traffic between the southwestern oil fields and Eilath.[131]

In the past three decades, the term "blockade" has been replaced in the practice of many states with a more benign term, "exclusion zone," and its variants. The United States used the term "quarantine "during the Cuban Missile Crisis of October 1962. Despite the use of these terms, the blockading country still has to follow the rules stipulated in international law governing blockades. For example, during the Falklands/Malvinas War of 1982, several exclusion zones were declared by both belligerents. Initially, both the British and Argentine declarations were aimed at limiting the conflict to combat forces. On 12 April, the British government declared a maritime exclusion zone (MEZ) some 200 nm around the Falklands from the point approximately at the center of the Falkland islands. Only Argentine warships and naval auxiliaries found in that zone were liable to be attacked.[132] The zone was intended to constrain Argentine aircraft, warships, and auxiliaries from entering the area.[133] On 28 April, the British government announced a total exclusion zone (TEZ) to take effect on 30 April. It had the same extent as the MEZ but stipulated that "any . . . aircraft, whether military or civil found within this zone without the authority from the Ministry of Defence in London will be regarded as operating in support of the illegal occupation and will therefore be regarded hostile. . . ."[134] Declaration of TEZ was accompanied by a statement that establishment of the zone was "without prejudice to the right of United kingdom to take additional measures which may be needed in exercise of its rights of self-defense under Article 51 of the UN Charter." [135] The British TEZ was challenged only by Argentine and the former USSR.[136] On 7 May, the British government announced that because hostile forces can cover the distance involved in resupplying Argentine forces on the Falklands or in taking other hostile action undetected, particularly at night and in bad weather, any Argentine warships or military aircraft that are found more than 12 miles from the Argentine coast will be regarded as hostile.[137] This announcement came in response to the Argentine aircraft sinking of HMS *Sheffield* four days earlier.[138] On 13 April, the Argentine government established the 200-nm exclusion zone off Argentina's coast and around the Malvinas.[139] On 29 April, the Argentines strengthened their exclusion zone and on 11 May formally declared the South Atlantic War Zone.[140]

The "San Remo Manual on International Law Applicable to Armed Conflicts at Sea," adopted in June 1994, provides a legal basis for establishing a naval blockade. It states that the purpose of a blockade is to deny the enemy the use of his own and neutral vessels or aircraft to transport personnel and goods to or from enemy territory. It is also the only method of naval warfare by which belligerents may interfere with enemy exports.[141] The "San Remo Manual" stipulates that "the declaration of blockade shall specify the commencement, duration, location, extent of the blockade and the period

within which vessels of neutral states may leave the blockaded coastline."
The blockade must be effective.[142] It "must be enforced and maintained by
a combination of legitimate methods and means of warfare" and be consistent with the rules set out in the "San Remo Manual." Blockade also cannot
prevent access to the ports and coasts of neutral states. It must be applied
impartially to the vessels of all states.[143] It also stated that a blockade may be
enhanced and maintained by military aircraft, which in most cases would
operate from a warship.[144]

Threat to the enemy's critical positions/areas

Posing a threat to the enemy critical positions/areas is another method of
containment. It is often used simultaneously with a naval blockade but could
also be used separately. The objective is to use one's naval forces in such a
way as to pose a considerable threat to something that the enemy holds
valuable and that would compel him to deploy his naval and/or ground
forces nearby in order to protect it. Only a stronger side could establish a
naval blockade, but the threat to enemy critical positions or areas can be
applied by both the stronger and the weaker side.[145]

   In posing a threat to the enemy's positions or areas, two main methods are
used: (1) tying up disproportionately large enemy forces in the main theater
of operations and/or (2) diverting a large part of the enemy strength to a
theater of operations that is of secondary importance to the stronger side.
A stronger side can threaten or actually conduct amphibious raids along a
large stretch of the coastline. Although such raids are rarely decisive, they
might force the enemy to deploy a larger part of its ground troops in the
coastal area. The constant threat of raids or invasions can adversely affect
the morale of the enemy populace. A key requirement for carrying out
raids against the enemy's critical positions is credible amphibious capability.
Experience shows that some raids were successful and some were not. For
example, during the Seven Years' War (1756–1763), the British threatened
raids up and down the French Atlantic coast, forcing the French to deploy
large numbers of troops to vulnerable areas. For the defense of the naval
bases and commercial ports, the French relied on strong coastal fortresses
that could be reinforced within days by the scattered detachments of militia.
Some 300,000 men from the national guard defended French shores against
possible landings by the British force of about 30,000 men embarked in transports at the Downs.[146] In 1758, the major part of the French Army operated
against Hannover and Prussia. The British threat prevented the French from
sending additional troops to their forces operating in Westphalia against the
Prussians. Moreover, the French were unable to send reinforcements to their
hard-pressed garrisons in Louisburg and Quebec in Canada.[147]

   The British not only threatened with raids but also carried them out. For
example, in June 1758, Admiral Howe, with a small escort and supporting

detachment, landed about 13,000 troops at St. Malo. He then blockaded the port. Anson placed his Channel Fleet in a position to intercept the Brest squadron if it tried to interfere with the expedition from England. However, he kept the fleet sufficiently away from Brest to allow the French fleet to sortie if it desired. The purposes of the expedition were to destroy the French ships that were shortly to sail for Canada, to force France to weaken its army in Germany by withdrawing troops for the strengthening of its coastal defense, and to induce the French fleet to leave Brest to protect St. Malo and thereby permit Admiral Anson to engage it decisively.[148]

Although the British Army was unable to capture the fortress, within the port the troops destroyed four frigates, eight privateers, 62 merchant-man, and various small craft.[149] British troops were reembarked before the French troops could assemble.

During the Crimean War (1854–1856), the presence of the Franco-British fleet in the Baltic implicitly threatened attacks on Russian ports, such as Helsingfors, Kronshtadt, and many others. This, in turn, tied up significant Russian forces that might otherwise have been dispatched to the Crimea.[150] In the Franco-Prussian war of 1870–1871, the French Navy was a much larger and more potent force than the North German Federal Navy (created in October 1867).[151] The French plan envisaged weakening the Prussian/German Army on the main front by tying up its forces in the Baltic. The French planned to send a squadron of 14 armored frigates and a number of scouting ships (avisos) to the Baltic. This force would be followed by a transport squadron carrying some 30,000 troops and accompanied by floating batteries and gunboats.[152]

On 24 July 1870, or nine days after the beginning of the war, the French assembled a squadron of some seven armored ships (or half of the original strength) plus only a single scouting ship.[153] The squadron, under the command of Admiral Édouard Bouët-Willaumez (1808–1871), reached Sound (Öresund), a 2.5-mile-wide strait separating the Danish island of Zealand from the Swedish province of Scania on 28 July. On 2 August, he received the order from the French government to enter the Baltic. In the meantime, the French organized a second squadron from the Mediterranean fleet composed of eight armored ships and four craft. This squadron would be ready to sail for the Baltic on 9 August.[154]

The French hoped to entice the Danes to declare war on Prussia by promising that landing troops would be deployed to the Baltic too.[155] They believed that it would be possible to successfully land their troops on north Germany's beaches. Yet that it would be extremely difficult to sustain them unless Denmark entered the war on the side of France. However, the Danes were unimpressed with the French arguments. The early Prussian successes on the land front convinced them to remain neutral.[156] Interestingly, General Helmut von Moltke, Sr. (1800–1891), chief of the Prussian general staff, considered, in a memo written in the winter of 1868/1869, the possibility of the French landing in the Baltic. Hence, he foresaw the need to have some 40,000 field troops to guard against such a landing.[157]

The French clearly lacked a clear plan of action for their squadrons in the Baltic. Their activity was limited to patrolling and seizing German merchant ships. Neither admiral tried to blockade the German north coast. The defeat and capture of Napoleon III at Sedan on 2 September led to a quick withdrawal of the French squadrons from the Baltic to Cherbourg.[158] Despite this apparent lack of success in accomplishing the main objective, Castex claimed that in fact Moltke Sr. was forced to keep significant forces in the northern part of Prussia because of the fear of the French invasion.[159]

In the modern era, the great advantage of possessing a credible amphibious capability has been shown repeatedly. The constant threat of raids or invasions can tie up a large part of the enemy's ground and naval forces for the defense of the coast and offshore islands. In this way, the success of a large-scale amphibious landing in the main theater of effort could be greatly enhanced. For example, the perceived threat of Allied amphibious landings forced the Germans to deploy, along the 8,000-mile-long European coastline, 53 divisions, or 27 percent of their total strength, on the eve of their invasion of Russia in June 1941. At the same time, the Germans used 120 divisions, or 60 percent of their total strength, in that invasion.[160] Hitler and the Supreme Command of the Wehrmacht (Oberkommando der Wehrmacht, OKW) were especially concerned with the possibility of the Allied invasion of Norway in 1941–1942. On 14 December 1941, Hitler directed the buildup of defense installations in Norway and the improvement of the roads in the coastal area. In his view, if the enemy was successful in seizing Norway, then the Allies would be able to regularly supply the Soviet Union and thereby pose a serious threat to the German northern front. The enemy would also be able to operate in the Baltic. In that case, the Germans would be cut off from the critical Swedish iron ore and the Finnish nickel deposits from Petsamo. These views were also given new urgency based on the information by German agents and statements in Western media and by Western leaders. The German fears were increased in the aftermath of the British commando raids on Vågsøy-Lofoten and Måløy, south of Trondheim, on 27 December.[161] In his meetings with the CINC of the German Navy, Admiral Erich Raeder (1876–1960), on 29 December 1941 and 12 January 1942, Hitler stated that the enemy threat to Norway requires the redeployment of heavy German ships as a deterrent against such a landing. Based on some Swedish sources, Hitler also believed that the British and Americans might land between Trondheim and Kirkenes. He directed Raeder to deploy all available naval forces to Norway.[162] By the end of January 1942, Hitler became convinced that a major enemy landing, with possible support of Sweden and Finland, was in preparation. In his view, every ship that was not in Norway was in the wrong place. Raeder agreed with that assessment.[163]

In 1943, the Germans also committed some 18 divisions to Italy against the possible landing of 15 Allied divisions. They deployed another 15 divisions, or twice the previous strength level, to the Balkans because of the widely held view that the Allies would land there.[164]

The inestimable value of a potent and credible amphibious capability was also well understood by the U.N. high command in Korea. The Korean Peninsula was an almost ideal place to threaten with landings at multiple places. The U.N. commanders, Generals Matthew Ridgway (1895–1993) and Mark W. Clark (1896–1984), took every opportunity to highlight the threat of amphibious landings to their North Korean and Chinese opponents. They ordered amphibious exercises to be held both in Japan and in South Korea. The Marine 1st Division held an amphibious landing exercise at Hwachon Reservoir so that the North Korean communists could observe it.[165] In response to the threat of landing plus the U.N. air superiority, the North Koreans exerted enormous efforts in time and material to strengthen their anti-amphibious and anti-air defenses. They were found unpleasantly surprised with the highly successful U.S. amphibious landing at Inchon on 15 September 1950 (Operation CHROMITE) and did not want any such landing in the future. The North Korean defenses on the land front consisted of a honeycomb of underground tunnels stretching from the east to west coast of the peninsula. Many of these tunnels were burrowed so deep that they were impervious to bombs and artillery fire. They also greatly strengthened coastal defenses.[166] Several hundreds of thousands of the North Koreans were engaged in building and manning coastal defenses. Like defenses on the front line, the North Korean coastal defenses included a large number of underground installations. In addition, they established multiple trench lines of defense in the coastal area, plus minefields. Large areas of rice paddy acreage were flooded. They also made preparations to flood other areas in case of an invasion from across the sea.[167]

The value of possessing a credible amphibious threat capability was shown relatively recently in the Gulf War of 1990–1991. General Norman Schwarzkopf (1934–2012) kept the 13th Marine Expeditionary Unit (MEU) to deceive the Iraqis and pin down their forces in Kuwait. Reportedly, the Iraqis were forced to deploy at least three infantry divisions to defend the Kuwaiti coast from Kuwait City in the south to the Saudi-Kuwaiti border.[168] The U.S. Marines conspicuously prepared for an amphibious landing along the Kuwaiti coast, conducting highly publicized exercises with ominous names like IMMINENT THUNDER. Meanwhile, the U.S./Coalition tried to convince the late Iraqi dictator Saddam Hussein that a major land assault would be launched against Iraq's most heavily defended areas along the Saudi border.[169]

Strategic diversion

Another method of containing enemy forces is by using a *strategic diversion*. Although this method is normally used by a weaker side, sometimes a stronger side can use it too. Strategic diversion aims to obtain a more favorable ratio of forces (or even superiority) in the principal theater of war, inducing or deceiving the weaker opponent to concentrate a major part of his forces in a secondary theater of war. Strategic concentration and diversion have one characteristic in common: both are conducted only once. In addition, like surprise, the effect of both is temporary. A successful strategic diversion has an effect similar to strategic concentration because a large part of the enemy forces is removed or made unavailable in the principal theater of war. For example, during the Seven Years' War (1756–1763), both the British and the French used strategic diversion in trying to force the other side to misdistribute its forces and efforts. However, the British were more successful. The British principal strategic objective of the war was the expulsion of the French from Canada. Hence, North America was their principal theater of war. To tie the French forces, they decided to help, with money but only a few troops, their Prussian ally, King Frederick the Great (1712–1786), in his operations against the common Austrian and French foes. The objective was to tie up as many French troops as possible in Europe so that they could not be used to reinforce the French garrisons in Canada. Another objective was to force France to make such a great effort on the continent that it could devote but few resources to building up its Navy. After the outbreak of hostilities, the British created favorable conditions for the success of British operations against the French possessions in Canada by forcing the French to focus on war in Europe, that is, a theater of war which was by no means vital to England.[170]

Containment of enemy forces is an important method used by a stronger side to obtain sea control. A stronger side should combine decisive actions against enemy forces with containment. Even though, in the initial phase of a war, the focus should be always on destroying enemy forces by a decisive action, naval blockade is perhaps one of the most effective methods for neutralizing inferior naval forces within a larger ocean/sea area. Generally, a naval blockade should be declared shortly after the beginning of the hostilities. In contrast to a major fleet-vs.-fleet operation, a blockade requires much more time to be effective. It also requires a large number of smaller, less capable, but also less costly ships. All naval combat arms, plus the combat arms/branches of other services, should be employed in enforcing a blockade. Today, aircraft are probably one of the most effective platforms for blockading duties. In a blockade, an operational and ultimately partial strategic objective cannot be accomplished quickly but only over time. The principal methods of the combat forces' employment are major and minor tactical actions. Major naval/joint operations would be rarely conducted in enforcing a naval blockade.

Posing a threat to important enemy positions/areas is one of the well-proven containment methods. The most effective is posing a credible threat of possible large-scale amphibious landings and raids against the enemy's controlled mainland coast and offshore islands/archipelagoes. Experience shows that such a method is especially effective in the event that a weaker side occupies an insular or peninsular position. To be credible, a stronger side must possess highly capable and well trained amphibious forces. This would normally force a weaker side to build strong and extensive beach defenses and to deploy large numbers of troops. In addition, the weaker side would also assign relatively large number of ships in support of the troops on the coast. Hence, such forces would not be available for disputing sea control. In case of a war in two or more theaters and against the same opponent, a stronger side might attempt to deceive the enemy about its true theater of main effort. If successful, a weaker side would assign much larger forces than necessary to the stronger side's theater of secondary effort.

Notes

1   Elwin F. Cutts, *Operations for Securing Command of the Sea Areas*, Part 1 (Newport, RI: Naval War College, 8–9 July 1938), p. 46.
2   Staff Presentation, *Operations in Sea Areas Under Command*, Part 1 (Newport, RI: Naval War College, July 17, 1941), p. 1.
3   Alexander Meurer, *Seekriegsgeschichte in Umrissen. Seemacht und Seekriege vornehmlich vom 16. Jahrhundert ab* (Leipzig: Verlag v. Hase & Koehler, 1925), p. 49.
4   Elwin F. Cutts, *Operations for Securing Command of the Sea Areas*, Part 1 (Newport, RI: Naval War College, 8–9 July 1938), p. 49.
5   Geoffrey Till, editor, *Maritime Strategy and the Nuclear Age*, 2nd ed. (New York: St. Martin's Press, 1984), p. 123.
6   Raoul Castex, *More Protiv Kopna*, Vol. 1. Translated by Hijacint Mundorfer (*Théórie stratégiques*, Vol 1: *La Mer Contre La Terre*) (Belgrade: Geca Kon AD, 1939), p. 26.
7   Raoul Castex, *More Protiv Kopna*, Vol. 1. Translated by Hijacint Mundorfer (*Théórie stratégiques*, Vol. 1: *La Mer Contre La Terre*) (Belgrade: Geca Kon AD, 1939), p. 25.
8   Raoul Castex, *More Protiv Kopna*, Vol. 1. Translated by Hijacint Mundorfer (*Théórie Stratégiques*, Vol. 1: *La Mer Contre La Terre*) (Belgrade: Geca Kon AD, 1939), p. 35.
9   Raoul Castex, *More Protiv Kopna*, Vol. 1. Translated by Hijacint Mundorfer (*Théórie Stratégiques*, Vol. 1: *La Mer Contre La Terre*) (Belgrade: Geca Kon AD, 1939), p. 34.
10 Raoul Castex, *More Protiv Kopna*, Vol. 1. Translated by Hijacint Mundorfer (*Théórie stratégiques*, Vol. 1: *La Mer Contre La Terre*) (Belgrade: Geca Kon AD, 1939), p. 35.
11 Geoffrey Till, editor, *Maritime Strategy and the Nuclear Age*, 2nd ed. (New York: St. Martin's Press, 1984), p. 125.
12 David T. Cunningham, *The Naval Blockade: A Study of Factors Necessary for Effective Utilization* (Fort Leavenworth, KS: School of Advanced Military Studies, U.S. Army Command and General Staff College, June 1987), p. 38.
13 Cited in Andrew D. Lambert, "The Crimean War Blockade: 1854–56," in Bruce A. Elleman and S.C.M. Paine, editors, *Naval Blockades and Seapower. Strategies and Counterstrategies, 1805–2005* (London: Routledge, 2006), p. 49.
14 Wilhelm True, *Der Krim Krieg und seine Bedeutung für die Entstehung der modern Flatten* (Herford/Bonn: E. S. Mittler & Sohn GmbH, 1980), pp. 98–99.
15 Gabriel Darrieus, *War on the Sea. Strategy and Tactics* (Annapolis, MD: United States Naval Institute, 1908), p. 212.

16 David T. Cunningham, *The Naval Blockade: A Study of Factors Necessary for Effective Utilization* (Fort Leavenworth, KS: School of Advanced Military Studies, U.S. Army Command and General Staff College, June 1987), pp. 16–17.

17 Philip A. Crowl, "Alfred Thayer Mahan: The Naval Historian," in Peter Paret, editor, *Makers of Modern Strategy. From Machiavelli to the Nuclear Age* (Princeton, NJ: Princeton University Press, 1986), p. 459.

18 Julian S. Corbett, *Some Principles of Maritime Strategy* (London: Longmans, Green and Co., 1918), p. 182.

19 Julian S. Corbett, *Some Principles of Maritime Strategy* (London: Longmans, Green and Co., 1918), p. 164.

20 Julian S. Corbett, *Some Principles of Maritime Strategy* (London: Longmans, Green and Co., 1918), p. 182.

21 Julian S. Corbett, *Some Principles of Maritime Strategy* (London: Longmans, Green and Co., 1918), p. 167.

22 Julian S. Corbett, *Some Principles of Maritime Strategy* (London: Longmans, Green and Co., 1918), p. 165.

23 David T. Cunningham, *The Naval Blockade: A Study of Factors Necessary for Effective Utilization* (Fort Leavenworth, KS: School of Advanced Military Studies, U.S. Army Command and General Staff College, June 1987), pp. 16–17.

24 Bernard Brodie, *A Layman's Guide to Naval Strategy* (Princeton, NJ: Princeton University Press, 1942), p. 89.

25 Nikola Krajnović, *Prevlast Na Moru* (Belgrade: Viša Vojno-Pomorska Akademija, 1 November 1983), pp. 4–5.

26 Arthur MacCartney Shepard, *Sea Power in Ancient History. The Story of the Navies of Classic Greece and Rome* (London: William Heinemann Ltd., 1925), pp. 35–36.

27 Wade G. Dudley, "The Flawed British Blockade, 1812–15," in Bruce A. Elleman and S.C.M. Paine, editors, *Naval Blockades and Seapower. Strategies and Counter-strategies, 1805–2005* (London: Routledge, 2006), pp. 36–37.

28 David T. Cunningham, *The Naval Blockade: A Study of Factors Necessary for Effective Utilization* (Fort Leavenworth, KS: School of Advanced Military Studies, U.S. Army Command and General Staff College, June 1987), pp. 33, 31.

29 G.J. Marcus, *A Naval History of England*, Vol. 2: *The Age of Nelson. The Royal Navy 1793–1815* (New York: Viking Press, 1971), pp. 239, 241.

30 Raoul Castex, *More Protiv Kopna*, Vol. 1. Translated by Hijacint Mundorfer (*Théórie stratégiques*, Vol 1: *La Mer Contre La Terre*) (Belgrade: Geca Kon AD, 1939), p. 35.

31 Mark L. Hayes, "The Naval Blockade of Cuba During the Spanish-American War," in Bruce A. Elleman and S.C.M. Paine, editors, *Naval Blockades and Seapower. Strategies and Counterstrategies, 1805–2005* (London: Routledge, 2006), p. 84.

32 Mark L. Hayes, "The Naval Blockade of Cuba During the Spanish-American War," in Bruce A. Elleman and S.C.M. Paine, editors, *Naval Blockades and Seapower. Strategies and Counterstrategies, 1805–2005* (London: Routledge, 2006), p. 83.

33 David T. Cunningham, *The Naval Blockade: A Study of Factors Necessary for Effective Utilization* (Fort Leavenworth, KS: U.S. Army Command and General Staff College,, June 1987), pp. 26, 19–20.

34 Alexander Meurer, *Seekriegsgeschichte in Umrissen. Seemacht und Seekriege vornehmlich vom 16. Jahrhundert ab* (Leipzig: Verlag v. Hase & Koehler, 1925), p. 188.

35 Alfred Stenzel, *Seekriegsgeschichte in ihren wichtigsten Abschnitten mit Berücksichtigung der Seetaktik*, Part 3: *Von 1600 bis 1720* (Hannover/Leipzig: Hahnsche Buchhandlung, 1909), p. 156.

36 David T. Cunningham, *The Naval Blockade: A Study of Factors Necessary for Effective Utilization* (Fort Leavenworth, KS: U.S. Army Command and General Staff College, June 1987), pp. 26, 19–20.

37 Elwin F. Cutts, *Operations for Securing Command of Sea Areas* (Newport, RI: Naval War College, 8–9 July 1938), p. 42.

38 Julian S. Corbett, *Some Principles of Maritime Strategy* (London: Longmans, Green and Co., 1918), p. 171.

39 Raoul Castex, *More Protiv Kopna*, Vol. 1. Translated by Hijacint Mundorfer (*Théorie stratégiques*, Vol. 1: *La Mer Contre La Terre*) (Belgrade: Geca Kon AD, 1939), p. 28.

40 Julian S. Corbett, *Some Principles of Maritime Strategy* (London: Longmans, Green and Co., 1918), p. 171.

41 Raoul Castex, *More Protiv Kopna*, Vol. 1. Translated by Hijacint Mundorfer (*Théorie stratégiques*, Vol. 1: *La Mer Contre La Terre*) (Belgrade: Geca Kon AD, 1939), p. 28.

42 David T. Cunningham, *The Naval Blockade: A Study of Factors Necessary for Effective Utilization* (Fort Leavenworth, KS: U.S. Army Command and General Staff College, June 1987), pp. 20–23; Geoffrey Till, *Maritime Strategy and the Nuclear Age*, 2nd ed. (New York: St. Martin's Press, 1984), p. 122.

43 Rene Daveluy, *The Genius of Naval Warfare*, Vol. I: *Strategy* (Annapolis, MD: United States Naval Institute 1910), p. 220.

44 Alfred T. Mahan, *Influence of Sea Power upon the French Revolution and Empire, 1793–1812*, Vol. I, 8th ed. (Boston: Little, Brown, and Company, 1897), p. 241.

45 Alfred T. Mahan, *Influence of Sea Power upon the French Revolution and Empire, 1793–1812*, Vol. I, 8th ed. (Boston: Little, Brown, and Company, 1897), p. 344.

46 Alfred T. Mahan, *Influence of Sea Power upon the French Revolution and Empire, 1793–1812*, Vol. I, 8th ed. (Boston: Little, Brown, and Company, 1897), p. 345.

47 Alfred T. Mahan, *Influence of Sea Power upon the French Revolution and Empire, 1793–1812*, Vol. I, 8th ed. (Boston: Little, Brown, and Company, 1897), p. 339.

48 C.J. Marcus, *The Age of Nelson. The Royal Navy in the Age of Its Greatest Power and Glory 1793–1815* (New York: Viking Press, 1971), p. 157.

49 Rene Daveluy, *The Genius of Naval Warfare*, Vol I: *Strategy* (Annapolis, MD: United States Naval Institute, 1910), p. 223.

50 Raoul Castex, *More Protiv Kopna*, Vol. 1. Translated by Hijacint Mundorfer (*Théorie Stratégiques*, Vol. 1: *La Mer Contre La Terre*) (Belgrade: Geca Kon AD, 1939), p. 30.

51 Alfred T. Mahan, *Influence of Sea Power upon the French Revolution and Empire, 1793–1812*, Vol. I, 8th ed. (Boston: Little, Brown, and Company, 1897), p. 339.

52 Alfred T. Mahan, *Influence of Sea Power upon the French Revolution and Empire, 1793–1812*, Vol. I, 8th ed. (Boston: Little, Brown, and Company, 1897), p. 345.

53 C.J. Marcus, *The Age of Nelson. The Royal Navy in the Age of Its Greatest Power and Glory 1793–1815* (New York: Viking Press, 1971), p. 157.

54 C.J. Marcus, *The Age of Nelson. The Royal Navy in the Age of Its Greatest Power and Glory 1793–1815* (New York: Viking Press, 1971), p. 159; Alfred T. Mahan, *Influence of Sea Power upon the French Revolution and Empire, 1793–1812*, Vol. I, 8th ed. (Boston: Little, Brown, and Company, 1897), pp. 368–69.

55 Alfred T. Mahan, *Influence of Sea Power upon the French Revolution and Empire, 1793–1812*, Vol. I, 8th ed. (Boston: Little, Brown, and Company, 1897), p. 369.

56 Alexander Meurer, *Seekriegsgeschichte in Umrissen. Seemacht und Seekriege vornehmlich vom 16. Jahrhundert ab* (Leipzig: Verlag v. Hase & Koehler, 1925), p. 334.

57 Department of Operations, *Naval Strategy* (Newport, RI: U.S. Naval War College, August 1936), p. 43.

58 Rene Daveluy, *The Genius of Naval Warfare*, Vol I: *Strategy* (Annapolis, MD: United States Naval Institute, 1910), p. 223.

59 Geoffrey Till, *Maritime Strategy and the Nuclear Age*, 2nd ed. (New York: St. Martin's Press, 1984), pp. 122, 124–25.

60 G.J. Marcus, *A Naval History of England*, Vol. 2: *The Age of Nelson. The Royal Navy 1793–1815* (New York: the Viking Press, 1971), pp. 242–43.

61 Rene Daveluy, *The Genius of Naval Warfare*, Vol I: *Strategy* (Annapolis, MD: United States Naval Institute, 1910), pp. 221–22.

62 William Oliver Stevens and Allan Westcott, *A History of Sea Power* (New York: Doubleday, Doran & Company, Inc., 1942), p. 240.

63 Dudley W. Knox, *A History of the United States Navy* (New York: G. P. Putnam Sons, 1948), p. 82.

64 Cited in Andrew D. Lambert, "The Crimean War Blockade: 1854–56," in Bruce A. Elleman and S.C.M. Paine, editors, *Naval Blockades and Seapower. Strategies and Counterstrategies, 1805–2005* (London: Routledge, 2006), p. 49.

65 Andrew D. Lambert, "The Crimean War Blockade: 1854–56," in Bruce A. Elleman and S.C.M. Paine, editors, *Naval Blockades and Seapower. Strategies and Counterstrategies, 1805–2005* (London: Routledge, 2006), p. 51.

66 Peter Duckers, *The Crimean War at Sea. The Naval Campaigns Against Russia 1854–56* (Barnsley, South Yorkshire: Pen & Sword Maritime, 2011), pp. 21–22.

67 Andrew D. Lambert, "The Crimean War Blockade: 1854–56," in Bruce A. Elleman and S.C.M. Paine, editors, *Naval Blockades and Seapower. Strategies and Counterstrategies, 1805–2005* (London: Routledge, 2006), p. 52.

68 Cited in Andrew D. Lambert, "The Crimean War Blockade: 1854–56," in Bruce A. Elleman and S.C.M. Paine, editors, *Naval Blockades and Seapower. Strategies and Counterstrategies, 1805–2005* (London: Routledge, 2006), p. 52.

69 Peter Duckers, *The Crimean War At Sea. The Naval Campaigns Against Russia 1854–56* (Barnsley, South Yorkshire: Pen & Sword Maritime, 2011), p. 52.

70 Andrew D. Lambert, "The Crimean War Blockade: 1854–56," in Bruce A. Elleman and S.C.M. Paine, editors, *Naval Blockades and Seapower. Strategies and Counterstrategies, 1805–2005* (London: Routledge, 2006), p. 54.

71 Lawrence Sondhaus, *The Habsburg Empire and the Sea. Austrian Naval Policy, 1797–1866* (West Lafayette, IN: Purdue University Press, 1989), pp. 191–92.

72 Lawrence Sondhaus, *The Habsburg Empire and the Sea. Austrian Naval Policy, 1797–1866* (West Lafayette, IN: Purdue University Press, 1989), pp. 191–92.

73 Harold and Margaret Sprout, *The Rise of American Naval Power, 1776–1918* (Princeton, NJ: Princeton University Press, 1939), p. 154.

74 Stuart Anderson, "1861: Blockade vs. Closing the Confederate Ports," *Military Affairs*, Vol. 41, No. 4 (December 1977), p. 190.

75 Alexander Meurer, *Seekriegsgeschichte in Umrissen. Seemacht und Seekriege vornehmlich vom 16. Jahrhundert ab* (Leipzig: Verlag v. Hase & Koehler, 1925), p. 373.

76 Dudley W. Knox, *A History of the United States Navy* (New York: G. P. Putnam Sons, 1948), p. 275.

77 Allan Westcott, editor, et al, *American Sea Power Since 1775* (Chicago/Philadelphia/New York: J.B. Lippincott, 1947), p. 221.

78 Mark L. Hayes, "The Naval Blockade of Cuba During the Spanish-American War," in Bruce A. Elleman and S.C.M. Paine, editors, *Naval Blockades and Seapower. Strategies and Counterstrategies, 1805–2005* (London: Routledge, 2006), p. 83; Allan Westcott, editor, *American Sea Power Since 1775* (Chicago, IL/Philadelphia, PA/New York, NY: J.B. Lippincott, 1947), p. 221.

79 Mark L. Hayes, "The Naval Blockade of Cuba During the Spanish-American War," in Bruce A. Elleman and S.C.M. Paine, editors, *Naval Blockades and Seapower. Strategies and Counterstrategies, 1805–2005* (London: Routledge, 2006), p. 85.

80 Rene Daveluy, *The Genius of Naval Warfare*, Vol I: *Strategy* (Annapolis, MD: United States Naval Institute 1910), p. 227.

81 Raoul Castex, *More Protiv Kopna*, Vol. 1. Translated by Hijacint Mundorfer (*Théorie stratégiques*, Vol 1: *La Mer Contre La Terre*) (Belgrade: Geca Kon AD, 1939), p. 33.

82 Rene Daveluy, *The Genius of Naval Warfare*, Vol. I: *Strategy* (Annapolis, MD: United States Naval Institute 1910), p. 224.

83 Colin White, *Nelson Encyclopedia* (Mechanisburg, PA: Stackpole Books, 2002), p. 54.

84 Julian S. Corbett, *Some Principles of Maritime Strategy* (London: Longmans, Green and Co., 1918), p. 165.

85 Julian S. Corbett, *Some Principles of Maritime Strategy* (London: Longmans, Green and Co., 1918), p. 167.

86 N.A.M. Rodger, *The Command of the Ocean. A Naval History of Britain, 1649–1815* (New York/London: W. W. Norton & Company, 2004), pp. 533–34.

87 Rene Daveluy, *The Genius of Naval Warfare*, Vol. I: *Strategy* (Annapolis, MD: United States Naval Institute 1910), p. 224.

88 Raoul Castex, *More Protiv Kopna*, Vol. 1. Translated by Hijacint Mundorfer (*Theórie stratégiques*, Vol 1: *La Mer Contre La Terre*) (Belgrade: Geca Kon AD, 1939), p. 34.

89 Raoul Castex, *More Protiv Kopna*, Vol. 1. Translated by Hijacint Mundorfer (*Theórie stratégiques*, Vol 1: *La Mer Contre La Terre*) (Belgrade: Geca Kon AD, 1939), p. 36.

90 Donald G.F. Macintyre, *Sea Power in the Pacific: A History from the Sixteenth Century to the Present Day* (New York: Crane, Russak, 1972) p. 142.

91 Raoul Castex, *More Protiv Kopna*, Vol. 1. Translated by Hijacint Mundorfer (*Theórie stratégiques*, Vol 1: *La Mer Contre La Terre*) (Belgrade: Geca Kon AD, 1939), p. 36.

92 Herbert Rosinski, *The Development of Naval Thought* (Newport, RI: Naval War College Press, 1977), pp. 10–11; M. Rene Daveluy, *The Genius of Naval Warfare*, Vol I: *Strategy* (Annapolis, MD: United States Naval Institute 1910), p. 227–28.

93 Geoffrey Till, *Maritime Strategy and the Nuclear Age*, 2nd ed. (New York: St. Martin's Press, 1984), p. 126.

94 Alfred T. Mahan, *Naval Strategy: Compared and Contrasted with the Principles and Practice of Military Operations on Land* (Boston: Little, Brown, and Company, 1911), p. 3.

95 Barry M. Gough, "Maritime Strategy: The Legacies of Mahan and Corbett as Philosophers of Sea Power," *RUSI Journal* (Winter 1988), p. 59.

96 Raoul Castex, *More Protiv Kopna*, Vol. 1. Translated by Hijacint Mundorfer (*Theórie Stratégiques*, Vol. 1: *La Mer Contre La Terre*) (Belgrade: Geca Kon AD, 1939), pp. 26–27.

97 Bernard Brodie, *A Layman's Guide to Naval Strategy* (Princeton, NJ: Princeton University Press, 1942), p. 91.

98 Raoul Castex, *More Protiv Kopna*, Vol. 1. Translated by Hijacint Mundorfer (*Theórie stratégiques*, Vol. 1: *La Mer Contre La Terre*) (Belgrade: Geca Kon AD, 1939), p. 52.

99 Nikola Krajnović, *Prevlast Na Moru* (Belgrade: Viša Vojno-Pomorska Akademija, 1 November 1983), p. 7.

100 Nikola Krajnović, *Prevlast Na Moru* (Belgrade: Viša Vojno-Pomorska Akademija, 1 November 1983), p. 6.

101 Bernard Brodie, *A Layman's Guide to Naval Strategy* (Princeton, NJ: Princeton University Press, 1942), p. 91.

102 Bernard Brodie, *A Layman's Guide to Naval Strategy* (Princeton, NJ: Princeton University Press, 1942), p. 90.

103 Cited in Michael G. Fraunces, "The International Law of Blockade: New Guiding Principles in Contemporary State Practice," *The Yale Law Journal*, Vol. 101, No. 4 (January 1992), p. 895.

104 Michael G. Fraunces, "The International Law of Blockade: New Guiding Principles in Contemporary State Practice," *The Yale Law Journal*, Vol. 101, No. 4 (January 1992), p. 895.

105 International Relations and Security Network, Primary Resources in International Affairs (PRIA), "Paris Declaration Respecting Maritime Law," p. 1; accessed at www.isn.etyhz.ch
106 Declaration concerning the Laws of Naval War, London, 26 February 1909; pp. 1–2; accessed at http://www.lawfareblog.com/wp-content/uploads/2013/01/Declaration-concerning-the-Laws-of-Naval-War.pdf
107 L.F.E. Goldie, "Maritime War Zones & Exclusion Zones," in Horace B. Robertson, editor, *International Law Studies*, Vol. 64: *The Law of Naval Operations* (Newport, RI: Naval War College Press, 1991), p. 163.
108 Michael G. Fraunces, "The International Law of Blockade: New Guiding Principles in Contemporary State Practice," *The Yale Law Journal*, Vol. 101, No. 4 (January 1992), p. 906.
109 Michael G. Fraunces, "The International Law of Blockade: New Guiding Principles in Contemporary State Practice," *The Yale Law Journal*, Vol. 101, No. 4 (January 1992), p. 908.
110 Cited in Ross Leckow, "The Iran-Iraq Conflict in the Gulf: The Law of War Zones," *British Institute of International and Comparative Law*, Vol. 37, No. 3 (July 1988), p. 632.
111 L.F.E. Goldie, "Maritime War Zones & Exclusion Zones," in Horace B. Robertson, editor, *International Law Studies*, Vol. 64: *The Law of Naval Operations* (Newport, RI: Naval War College Press, 1991), p. 160.
112 L.F.E. Goldie, "Maritime War Zones & Exclusion Zones," in Horace B. Robertson, editor, *International Law Studies*, Vol. 64: *The Law of Naval Operations* (Newport, RI: Naval War College Press, 1991), pp. 158–59.
113 Michael G. Fraunces, "The International Law of Blockade: New Guiding Principles in Contemporary State Practice," *The Yale Law Journal*, Vol. 101, No. 4 (January 1992), p. 894.
114 L.F.E. Goldie, "Maritime War Zones & Exclusion Zones," in Horace B. Robertson, editor, *International Law Studies*, Vol. 64: *The Law of Naval Operations* (Newport, RI: Naval War College Press, 1991), p. 164.
115 Michael G. Fraunces, "The International Law of Blockade: New Guiding Principles in Contemporary State Practice," *The Yale Law Journal*, Vol. 101, No. 4 (January 1992), p. 894.
116 Cited in Uwe Dirks, *Waren Grundzüge britischer Seekriegführung bereits vor dem Ersten Weltkrieg den Schriften Corbetts zu entnehmen?* (Hamburg: Führungsakademie der Bundeswehr, 30 October 1979), p. 23.
117 Raoul Castex, *More Protiv Kopna*, Vol. 1. Translated by Hijacint Mundorfer (*Théórie stratégiques*, Vol 1: *La Mer Contre La Terre*) (Belgrade: Geca Kon AD, 1939), p. 41.
118 "Chapter VI: The German Operations in the North Sea (1914–1916)," Vol. II, Extracts from Raoul Castex, *Theories Strategiques*. Translated from French by R.C. Smith and assisted by E.J. Tiernan (Newport, RI: Naval War College, April 1939), p. 6.
119 Raoul Castex, *More Protiv Kopna*, Vol. 1. Translated by Hijacint Mundorfer (*Théórie stratégiques*, Vol. 1: *La Mer Contre La Terre*) (Belgrade: Geca Kon AD, 1939), p. 43.
120 Günther Poeschel, *Die Rolle und Bedeutung der Seeherrschaft in Vergangenheit und Gegenwart. Analyse der theoretischen Aussagen zum Begriff der Seeherrschaft* (Dresden: Militaerakademie "Friedrich Engels," Schriften der Militaerakademie, Heft 165, 1978), p. 43.
121 Hans Fuchs, "Die Diversion als strategisches Mittel zur Erzielung eines Kräfteausgleiches, dargelegt an geschichtlichen Beispielen," *Marine Rundschau*, No. 4 (April 1938), p. 240.

122 L.F.E. Goldie, "Maritime War Zones & Exclusion Zones," in Horace B. Robertson, editor, *International Law Studies*, Vol. 64: *The Law of Naval Operations* (Newport, RI: Naval War College Press, 1991), p. 168.

123 L.F.E. Goldie, "Maritime War Zones & Exclusion Zones," in Horace B. Robertson, editor, *International Law Studies*, Vol. 64: *The Law of Naval Operations* (Newport, RI: Naval War College Press, 1991), p. 168.

124 L.F.E. Goldie, "Maritime War Zones & Exclusion Zones," in Horace B. Robertson, editor, *International Law Studies*, Vol. 64: *The Law of Naval Operations* (Newport, RI: Naval War College Press, 1991), pp. 170, 186.

125 Malcolm Muir, Jr, "A Failed Blockade. Air and Sea Power in Korea, 1950–53," in Bruce A. Elleman and S.C.M. Paine, editors, *Naval Blockades and Seapower. Strategies and Counterstrategies, 1805–2005* (London: Routledge, 2006), p. 145.

126 Malcolm Muir, Jr, "A Failed Blockade. Air and Sea Power in Korea, 1950–53," in Bruce A. Elleman and S.C.M. Paine, editors, *Naval Blockades and Seapower. Strategies and Counterstrategies, 1805–2005* (London: Routledge, 2006), p. 146.

127 Malcolm Muir, Jr, "A Failed Blockade. Air and Sea Power in Korea, 1950–53," in Bruce A. Elleman and S.C.M. Paine, editors, *Naval Blockades and Seapower. Strategies and Counterstrategies, 1805–2005* (London: Routledge, 2006), p. 147.

128 "Egypt Closes Gulf of Aqaba to Israeli Ships: Defiant Move by Nasser Raises Middle East Tension," *The Times*, May 23, 1967, p. 1.

129 Walter Jablonsky, "Die Seekriegfüehrung im Vierten Nahostkrieg aus ägyptischer Sicht," *Marine Rundschau*, July 1978, p. 442.

130 Benyamin Telem, "Die israelischen FK-Schnellboote im yom-Kippur-Krieg," *Marine Rundschau*, October 1978, p. 638.

131 Walter Jablonsky, "Die Seekriegführung im Vierten Nahostkrieg aus ägyptischer Sicht," *Marine Rundschau* (July 1978), p. 445.

132 Cited in L.F.E. Goldie, "Maritime War Zones & Exclusion Zones," in Horace B. Robertson, editor, *International Law Studies*, Vol. 64: *The Law of Naval Operations* (Newport, RI: Naval War College Press, 1991), p. 172.

133 Niklas Bergdahl Jonsson, *Legal Issues on Self-Defense and Maritime Zones in Naval Operations* (Lund: Faculty of Law, University of Lund, unpublished MA thesis, spring 2008), p. 30.

134 Cited in L.F.E. Goldie, "Maritime War Zones & Exclusion Zones," in Horace B. Robertson, editor, *International Law Studies*, Vol. 64: *The Law of Naval Operations* (Newport, RI: Naval War College Press, 1991), p. 173.

135 Cited in Niklas Bergdahl Jonsson, *Legal Issues on Self-Defense and Maritime Zones in Naval Operations* (Lund: Faculty of Law, University of Lund, unpublished MA thesis, spring 2008), p. 30.

136 Niklas Bergdahl Jonsson, *Legal Issues on Self-Defense and Maritime Zones in Naval Operations* (Lund: Faculty of Law, University of Lund, unpublished MA thesis, spring 2008), p. 30.

137 L.F.E. Goldie, "Maritime War Zones & Exclusion Zones," in Horace B. Robertson, editor, *International Law Studies*, Vol. 64: *The Law of Naval Operations* (Newport, RI: Naval War College Press, 1991),p. 173.

138 Niklas Bergdahl Jonsson, *Legal Issues on Self-Defense and Maritime Zones in Naval Operations* (Lund: Faculty of Law, University of Lund, unpublished MA thesis, spring 2008), p. 30.

139 L.F.E. Goldie, "Maritime War Zones & Exclusion Zones," in Horace B. Robertson, editor, *International Law Studies*, Vol. 64: *The Law of Naval Operations* (Newport, RI: Naval War College Press, 1991), p. 172.

140 L.F.E. Goldie, "Maritime War Zones & Exclusion Zones," in Horace B. Robertson, editor, *International Law Studies*, Vol. 64: *The Law of Naval Operations* (Newport, RI: Naval War College Press, 1991), p. 174.

141 Wolff Heintschel von Heinegg, "The Current State of the Law of Naval War-
     fare: A Fresh Look at the San Remo Manual," in Anthony M. Helm, editor,
     International Law Studies, Vol. 82: *The Law of War in the 21st Century: Weaponry
     and the Use of Force*, published in Yoram Dinstein and Fania Domb, editors, *Israel
     Yearbook on Human Rights*, Vol. 36, 2006 (Tel Aviv: Faculty of Law, Tel Aviv Uni-
     versity, August 2006), p. 276.
142 Louise Doswald-Beck, editor, "San Remo on International Law Applicable to
     Armed Conflicts at Sea" (Cambridge: Cambridge University Press, first pub-
     lished 1996, reissued 2005), p. 26.
143 Louise Doswald-Beck, editor, "San Remo on International Law Applicable to
     Armed Conflicts at Sea" (Cambridge: Cambridge University Press, first pub-
     lished 1996, reissued 2005), p. 27.
144 Wolff Heintschel von Heinegg, "The Current State of the Law of Naval War-
     fare: A Fresh Look at the San Remo Manual," in Anthony M. Helm, editor,
     International Law Studies, Vol. 82: *The Law of War in the 21st Century: Weaponry
     and the Use of Force*, published in Yoram Dinstein and Fania Domb, editors,
     Israel Yearbook on Human Rights Vol. 36, 2006 (Tel Aviv: Faculty of Law, Tel Aviv
     University, August 2006), p. 277.
145 Elwin F. Cutts, *Operations for Securing Command of the Sea Areas*, Part 1 (Newport,
     RI: Naval War College, 8–9 July 1938), p. 48.
146 Julian S. Corbett, *Some Principles of Maritime Strategy* (London: Longmans,
     Green and Co., 1918), p. 59.
147 Elwin F. Cutts, *Operations for Securing Command of Sea Areas* (Newport, RI: Naval
     War College, 8–9 July 1938), p. 21.
148 Elwin F. Cutts, *Operations for Securing Command of the Sea Areas*, Part 1 (Newport,
     RI: Naval War College, 8–9 July 1938), p. 43.
149 Elwin F. Cutts, *Operations for Securing Command of the Sea Areas*, Part 1 (Newport,
     RI: Naval War College, 8–9 July 1938), p. 42.
150 Cited in Peter Duckers, *The Crimean War at Sea. The Naval Campaigns Against
     Russia 1854–56* (Barnsley, South Yorkshire: Pen & Sword Maritime, 2011),
     p. 17; WilhelmTreue, *Der Krim Krieg und seine Bedeutung für die Entstehung der
     modernene Flotten* (Herford: E. S. Mittler & Sohn GmbH, 1980), p. 109.
151 The French fleet consisted of 34 armored ships 25 armored craft; 24 ships of
     the line; 130 frigates, corvettes, and scouting vessels (avisos); 68 gunboats; and
     60 transport ships; in the summer of 1870, the North German Federal Navy
     consisted of three armored frigates, two armored vessels, one ship of the line,
     nine corvettes, three scouting ships, 22 steam-powered gunboats, and three
     sail frigates and brigs Hermann Kirchhoff, *Seemacht in der Ostsee: Ihre Einwirkung
     auf die Geschichte der Ostseeländer Im 19. Jahrhundert*, Vol. II (Kiel: Verlag von Rob-
     ert Cordes, 1908), pp. 254–55.
152 Hermann Kirchhoff, *Seemacht in der Ostsee: Ihre Einwirkung auf die Geschichte der
     Ostseeländer Im 19. Jahrhundert*, Vol. II (Kiel: Verlag von Robert Cordes, 1908),
     p. 256.
153 Hermann Kirchhoff, *Seemacht in der Ostsee: Ihre Einwirkung auf die Geschichte der
     Ostseeländer Im 19. Jahrhundert*, Vol. II (Kiel: Verlag von Robert Cordes, 1908),
     p. 256.
154 Hermann Kirchhoff, *Seemacht in der Ostsee: Ihre Einwirkung auf die Geschichte der
     Ostseelaender Im 19. Jahrhundert*, Vol. II (Kiel: Verlag von Robert Cordes, 1908),
     p. 259.
155 Hermann Kirchhoff, *Seemacht in der Ostsee: Ihre Einwirkung auf die Geschichte der
     Ostseelaender Im 19. Jahrhundert*, Vol. II (Kiel: Verlag von Robert Cordes, 1908),
     p. 258.
156 Lawrence Sondhaus, *Navies of Europe, 1815–2002* (London: Taylor & Francis,
     2002), pp. 383–85.

157 Hermann Kirchhoff, *Seemacht in der Ostsee: Ihre Einwirkung Auf Die Geschichte Der Ostseelaender Im 19. Jahrhundert*, Vol. II (Kiel: Verlag von Robert Cordes, 1908), pp. 264–65.

158 Lawrence Sondhaus, *Navies of Europe, 1815–2002* (London: Taylor & Francis, 2002), p. 389.

159 Raoul Castex, *Théories Stratégiques*, Vol. I: *Généralites sur la stratégie-La mission des forces maritimes. La Conduite des operations* (Paris: Société d'Editions Géographiques Maritimes et Coloniales, 1929), translated by Ekrem Đurić and Boško Ranitović, *Strategijske Teorije*, Vol. I (Belgrade: Vojno-Izdavački Zavod, 1960), pp. 108–09.

160 B.H. Liddell Hart, "The Value of Amphibious Flexibility And Forces," *R.U.S.I. Journal*, Vol. 105, No. 620 (1960), pp. 483–85.

161 F.W. Müller-Meinhard, "Der Einfluss der Feindlagebeurteilung auf Operationsplanung, Entschlussfassung und Operationsführung (I)," *Marine Rundschau*, No. 9 (September 1970), p. 516.

162 F.W. Müller-Meinhard, "Der Einfluss der Feindlagebeurteilung auf Operationsplanung, Entschlussfassung und Operationsführung (I)," *Marine Rundschau*, No. 9 (September 1970), p. 517.

163 Naval Staff History, Second World War, Battle Summary No. 22: *Arctic Convoys 1941–1945* (London: Historical Section Admiralty, November 1954), p. 2.

164 B.H. Liddell Hart, "The Value of Amphibious Flexibility And Forces," *R.U.S.I. Journal*, Vol. 105, No. 620 (1960), pp. 483–85.

165 Malcolm W. Cagle and Frank A. Mason, *The Sea War in Korea* (Annapolis, MD: Naval Institute Press, 1957), p. 388.

166 Malcolm W. Cagle and Frank A. Mason, *The Sea War in Korea* (Annapolis, MD: Naval Institute Press, 1957), p. 389.

167 Malcolm W. Cagle and Frank A. Mason, *The Sea War in Korea* (Annapolis, MD: Naval Institute Press, 1957), p. 390.

168 Department of Defense, *Conduct of the Persian Gulf War. Final Report to Congress* (Washington, DC: Government Printing Office, April 1992), p. 294.

169 *The New York Times*, February 28, 1991, pp. A8–9.

170 Elwin F. Cutts, *Operations for Securing Command of Sea Area*, Part 1 (Newport, RI: Naval War College, 8–9 July 1938), p. 58.

8 Choke point control

Do you know that there are five keys to the world? The Strait of Dover, the Straits of Gibraltar, the Suez Canal, the Straits of Malacca, the Cape of Good Hope. And everyone of these keys we hold. Aren't we the lost tribes?

Admiral John Fisher (1841–1920)[1]

Straits, or "choke points,"[2] have had a very great importance in the struggle for sea control throughout the ages. Choke point control is only the first, although the most important step, for obtaining control of a given enclosed or semi-enclosed sea theater. Hence, a stronger side should be operationally and tactically on the offensive; otherwise, having control of a choke point is of little value or even essentially useless.

A stronger side at sea could exercise operational or even strategic control of a given enclosed or semi-enclosed sea by virtue of its possession of one or both shores of an important strait/narrows, either already in peacetime or obtained in the course of hostilities. A more difficult situation for a stronger side is when control must be obtained by blockading the approaches to a choke point controlled by a weaker opponent.

Straits are both the hubs and the most vulnerable segments of sea communications. A stronger side, by possessing physical control of either a strait or its approaches, is able to control naval/commercial movements of all powers to/from a given enclosed or semi-enclosed sea. Control of one shore or, preferably, both shores of a strait/narrows in peacetime greatly enhances one's ability to obtain control of the adjacent sea or ocean areas soon after the outbreak of hostilities. The control of a strait/narrow includes control not only of the water but also of the adjacent land area and associated airspace.

Importance

There are several hundred straits worldwide, and most of them are important only to a certain littoral state. However, some straits have "international"

importance because their significance transcends the interests of the littoral states. The number of international straits varies from 95 to 121.[3] International straits are free for navigation by ships of all nations, regardless
whether they overlap with the territorial waters of littoral states. Normally,
various international agreements regulate the transit of naval vessels and
commercial shipping through these straits in peacetime.[4]

Several international straits have had extraordinarily large geopolitical
importance in the policies of major powers. For example, the Danish Straits
(the collective name for the Skagerrak and Kattegat) and the Turkish Straits
have had in the past and still have an inordinately large role and importance in the policies of the European great powers. In the medieval age,
Denmark obtained control and jurisdiction of both shores of the Sound, as
well as of the Little and Great Belt. It lost control of northern shore to Sweden in the seventeenth century. Yet it continued to have control over the
Sound dues until 1857 when the European nations paid Denmark a sum of
money for the imposition of this prescriptive imposition upon Baltic commerce.[5] During the Napoleonic Wars (1803–1815), Britain had a big stake
in the neutrality of Denmark. Among other things, England was very much
concerned that the Danish fleet might come under French control. During
the era of sail, it was essential that British warships and merchantman could
freely transit the Danish Straits.

The Danish Straits had great economic significance not only for the riparian states in the Baltic but also for other great powers, Britain and France
in particular. From the plains and forests of the north came the timber and
naval stores with which England and France equipped their navies. Danish
Straits were also critical for the trade in grain and other products that made
waging a war possible. Denmark was in a position to interrupt this trade.[6]

Several international straits have a potentially strategic importance, in
case of open hostilities, because they would have a major impact on the
course or even outcome of a war in a certain maritime theater. Usually, the
sole exit from an enclosed sea, such as the Danish Straits and the Turkish
Straits, or a strait connecting a narrow sea with an ocean, such as the Strait
of Gibraltar or an artificial waterway linking two oceans, such as the Panama
Canal, have strategic importance. For example, Germany's de facto control
of the approaches to the Danish Straits in 1914–1918 effectively prevented
Great Britain from sending reinforcements to its embattled Russian ally.
The occupation of Denmark in April 1940 gave the Germans full control of
the Baltic approaches. Thereby, the Royal Navy was cut off from the Baltic,
and the Germans were free to use the economic resources of the Scandinavian countries, especially Sweden's ores, to set up bases in Finland, and
generally to improve conditions for the employment of their naval forces
in the Atlantic.

The Strait of Gibraltar is the only passageway between the Atlantic and
the Mediterranean. On the Atlantic side, access to the Strait of Gibraltar
is formed by a triangle running from the Cape of Saint Vincent to Rota to

Tarifa and Ceuta. Historically, its strategic value to the British would have been much greater if they also controlled the island of Madeira some 620 miles to the west and the Azores another 520 miles to the west. In World War II, the British control of Gibraltar was critical for the Allied position in the eastern part of the Atlantic. Without it, the value of the Allied position in the Azores and Cape Verde would have been greatly diminished.[7] The Indian Ocean and the Pacific are connected with several straits, of which the Strait of Malacca and the Sunda Strait are the most important. The powers that controlled one or both shores of the Strait of Malacca dominated the principal shipping route to and from the Indian Ocean. By their control of the Strait of Malacca, they also had easy access to the Java Sea and the Moluccas Archipelago.

The strategic value of a sea's exit is greater if the same power also controls a number of operationally important positions in its relative proximity and within a given narrow sea. Control of the sea's exits is insufficient in itself to prevent the weaker side from having freedom of action in some areas of a given enclosed or semi-enclosed sea. For example, in World War I, Britain had a partial strategic control of the Mediterranean because it controlled two most important exits, the Strait of Gibraltar and the Suez Canal, while the Turkish Strait was under control of the Centrals Powers. However, Britain and its allies, France and Italy, controlled all other operationally important choke points in the Mediterranean such as the Sicilian Narrows and the straits of Otranto, Messina, and San Bonifacio. In World War II, the Allies were in full control of the two Mediterranean exits – the Strait of Gibraltar and the Suez Canal. They lacked control of the Turkish Straits because Turkey was formally neutral. Nevertheless, the Allies had for all practical purposes strategic control of the Mediterranean. Yet the Allies did not control either the western or the eastern part of the Mediterranean because all the operationally important straits (Strait of Bonifacio, Messina Strait, and the Strait of Otranto) were in Axis hands until the summer of 1943. To complicate the matter, the Axis hotly disputed control of the Sicilian Narrows (also called the Strait of Sicily) with aircraft, submarines, and mines in 1940–1943. The island of Malta barely functioned as a naval and air base because of the almost constant attacks by the German and Italian aircraft based on Sicily and Sardinia.

In World War II, the Germans had a strategic control of the Baltic because they controlled one side of the Danish Straits (Sweden was neutral). However, they needed to obtain control of several positions within the Baltic to secure full control Baltic. The most critical was control of the Gulf of Finland. The German plans for the invasion of Soviet Russia envisaged the capture by the Finns of the Åland Islands and Hanko, key positions dominating the western end of the Gulf of Finland.[8] After the German troops captured Estonia and besieged Leningrad, their operational control of the western and central parts of the Gulf of Finland was secured. Except for submarines, no Soviet surface ships were able to operate outside the Gulf of Finland until the Soviet counteroffensive in the summer of 1944. However, the Germans and the Finns never obtained control of the Bay of Kronshtadt because the Soviets retained an air base on the island of Lavansaari. The German and Finns controlled the exit from the Gulf of Finland until the Soviet counteroffensive in the summer of 1944.

The Iranians, in their war with Iraq (1980–1988), controlled one shore of the Strait of Hormuz. That waterway was within effective range of the Iranian coastal antiship missile batteries and was controlled by Iranian surface warships. The Iranians also captured the Fāw Peninsula (in the northern Gulf) in 1986. To reinforce their control of the Strait of Hormuz and its approaches, the Iranians deployed small detachments of the Revolutionary Guards (Pasdaran) to Lārak, Hengion, and Sirrī Islands. Field gun and AA gun positions were built up on the Qeshm and Greater Tunb Islands. In addition, the Iranians reinforced their forces on Fārsī Island.[9] However, Iran lacked control of operationally significant positions elsewhere within the confines of the Persian (Arabian) Gulf.

Operating environment

The straits represent a unique but also a very challenging operating environment for one's naval forces. Almost all the advantages are on the side of a defender. They are both the hubs and the most vulnerable segments of sea communications linking a sea with other sea/open ocean areas. Obviously, one's surface ships and submarines are far more vulnerable to enemy attack while transiting a strait/narrows than they are on the open ocean. Hence, a strait can also be used to effectively block the exit or entry of hostile naval forces or the transit of the enemy's merchant shipping. In addition, control of a sea's only exit can be used to move one's naval forces from one sea/ocean area to another.

The physical features of a strait, such as its length, width, depth, tides, and currents, considerably affect both the offensive and the defensive employment of naval forces. There are great differences in the lengths of international straits.. For example, the Mozambique Channel, the Strait of Malacca, and the Strait of Hormuz are 1,000, 550, and 170 miles long, respectively. In contrast, the Strait of Gibraltar is about 40 miles long. The Strait of Tiran (Gulf of Aqaba) is only about 3.5 miles long.

The width of international straits can also vary greatly. For example, the Strait of Malacca's width ranges from 30 to 200 miles. The Strait of Gibraltar is 8 to 24 miles wide. The Sicilian Narrows are some 70 miles wide. In the Danish Straits, the Skagerrak is 75 to 90 miles wide, while Kattegat is 37 to 100 miles in width. The Strait of Malacca is only about 1.7 miles wide at its narrowest point, as is the Phillips Channel in the Singapore Strait. The Strait of Hormuz is 24 to 30 miles wide. The Red Sea's only exit, Bab el-Mandeb (Gate of Tears), is about 20 miles wide. The Bungo-suidō (between Kyūshū and Shikoku islands in Japan) varies in width from about 27 miles at its southern part to about five miles at its northern end. Some international straits are very narrow and thereby greatly affect a ship's speed and maneuverability. For example, the width of the Bosporus is only 1,000 yards. The entrance of the Dardanelles is about two miles wide. Inside, the channel opens up to four and a half miles, then gradually comes together again at the Narrows some 14 miles upstream.

The depths of international straits also greatly. For example, the Strait of Malacca is only about 70–120 feet deep. The Bosporus and Dardanelles are 110 and 160 feet deep, respectively.[10] The depth of the straits of Malacca and Singapore is only 70 feet, while the Strait of Hormuz is 160 feet deep. The average depth of the continental shelf in the Sicilian Narrows is about 490 feet. The main channel of the Strait of Gibraltar is about 1,100 feet deep.[11] Depths in San Bernardino Strait (between Luzon and Samar) are between 180 and 390 feet.

Some important straits pose significant challenges for navigation because of their strong currents. For example, in the San Bernardino Strait, the tidal currents can attain speeds of four to eight knots. The current in the Shimonoseki Strait (between Honshu and Kyushu) is up to 8 knots. The Dardanelles are essentially tideless, but the water flowing from the Black Sea rivers and from the melting snow of the Caucasus Mountains creates a permanent current of two to four knots.[12]

Because of the much reduced physical space, all straits are favorable places for the employment of small surface combatants, mines, and coastal missile/gun batteries. Straits with deep water allow the employment of conventionally-powered attack submarines (SSKs) and midget submarines. The highly indented coast of some straits, such as the Strait of Hormuz, can provide sanctuaries for fast-attack craft (FAC), which can launch missile strikes against large surface combatants with little or no warning. Another advantage of the weaker force is that sometimes it can obtain and maintain sea control of a strait and its approaches by employing non-naval forces alone, such as aircraft and/or strong coastal defenses.

A great advantage for a defender of a choke point is that its forces operate along multiple and much shorter lines of operation. In contrast, the attacking force transiting the strait can use only a single line of operation and a single line of retreat. For example, in the Leyte Operation, the Japanese First Diversionary Attack Force moved along a planned single line of operation from Brunei Bay to Balabac Strait (630 miles), across the Sibuyan Sea to the San Bernardino Strait (230 miles), and then to Tacloban anchorage (230 miles).[13] Likewise, the 3rd Section (Force C) of the First Diversionary Attack Force and the Second Diversionary Attack Force operated along a single line of operation once they entered the Bohol Sea between the islands of Negros and Mindanao toward the Surigao Strait on their way to their assigned objective in the Leyte Gulf.

Objectives and methods

The principal objectives in establishing choke point control are to pre-vent the enemy surface combatants/submarines and military/commer-cial shipping from operating outside the confines of a given enclosed or semi-enclosed sea, to destroy the enemy fleet within a strait, and to capture one or both shores of a strait/narrows. The main method of preventing enemy naval/commercial movements is containment. The latter, in turn, is accomplished by either blockading the outer and/or inner approaches of a strait controlled by a weaker side. The enemy fleet could be attacked and destroyed by forcing a strait or if it tries to exit and operate freely. The main method in obtaining physical control of one or both shores of a strait is by an attack on the land side and/or an amphibious landing.

Preventing the enemy's naval movements

In the event that a stronger side already controls the sea exit(s), prevent-ing the enemy naval/commercial movements would require deployment of relatively large and diverse forces and strong defenses ashore. Then naval forces should be deployed near or within a striking distance of the sea exit(s); otherwise, it would be difficult if not impossible to maintain control of the strait. For example, in World War I, the British Grand Fleet estab-lished a distant blockade of Germany in the North Sea by stationing strong forces in the vicinity of the Strait of Dover and the Shetland–southern Norway line.

Alternatively, a stronger side has to establish a semi-distant blockade of one or both approaches to a sea exit controlled by a weaker side, as the Entente Powers did in the Aegean in 1915. In the past, a stronger side some-times tried to obtain control of a strait by destroying defenses on the coast by using its surface ships. However, such attempts, if conducted solely by naval forces, usually failed, as the British experience in the Dardanelles in 1807 and 1915 illustrates.

At the beginning of World War I in August 1914 and until the entry of Italy into the war on 23 May 1915, the French navy provided most forces for blockading the sole exit from the Adriatic Sea, the 45-mile-wide Strait of Otranto. In August 1914, the French fleet was able to exercise its supe-riority by blockading the Austro-Hungarian coast. However, it did not have any base in the Adriatic, nor was it possible to capture such a base. After an Austro-Hungarian U-boat torpedoed the French dreadnought *Jean Bart* on 21 December 1914, operating north of the Strait of Otranto became too dangerous for French large surface combatants. They were withdrawn farther away to the Ionian Islands. The Entente's naval blockade was greatly limited because of the absence of favorably located and well equipped bases. Fuel and food were obtained in Cephalonia and Zante from the merchant ships and on the open sea, later at anchor. The Entente's ships used two anchorages on the Epirian coast and one in Morea (Peloponnesus). Because of the threat of the Austro-Hungarian and the German U-boats, the French fleet was moved even farther away to the Gulf of Morea (near Cape Matapan) and even Crete.[14] The French wanted to keep the Strait of Otranto under observation by using cruisers. However, after the torpedoing of the armored cruiser *Léon Gambetta* by an Austro-Hungarian U-boat on 27 April 1915, that was abandoned too. The situation dramatically improved with the entrance of Italy into the war in May. Afterward, the French forces were able to use the bases of Taranto and Brindisi. The bases at Argostoli and Corfù were used for the first time in April 1916.[15]

The Entente navies made only occasional forays farther north into the southern Adriatic. This situation left the much weaker Austro-Hungarian fleet with almost undisputed control of the Adriatic throughout the war. If the Entente navies had made a strong effort to destroy a major part of the Austro-Hungarian fleet, they would have probably prevented the German and Austro-Hungarian U-boats from making their deadly attacks on Entente shipping in the Mediterranean.[16]

Sometimes a weaker but more offensively minded fleet could successfully blockade the stronger fleet guarding a strait and defeat the enemy attempts to lift a blockade. For example, in the First Balkan War (1912–1913), the Greek Navy blockaded the entrance of the Dardanelles and the coast of Asia Minor. The objective was to prevent the Turks from reinforcing their armies in Thrace and Macedonia by sending troops from Smyrna to the port of Dedeağaç (Alexandroupoli today).[17] The much stronger Turkish Navy remained bottled up in the Sea of Marmara, allowing the Greek fleet to operate freely in the Aegean Sea. The Greek fleet sailed toward the Dardanelles on 12 October. It captured the island of Lemnos (Limni) on 21 October.[18] This island is located only about 30 miles west of the Dardanelles' entrance. In quick succession, the Greeks captured poorly defended islands of Samothrace (Semendirek), Thassos (Tasoez), Imbros (Imroz, now Gokceada), and Agios Efstratios (Aystrati) (31 October); Psara (west of Chios) (4 November); Tenedos (Bozcaada) (7 November); and Ikaria (Icaria) (17 November). [19]

The Turks made two unsuccessful attempts to break up the Greek blockade. In the first, the Battle of Elli on 16 December, the Turkish detachment consisted of four battleships, nine destroyers, and six torpedo boats. The Greek squadron consisted of one armored cruiser, three coastal defense battleships, and four destroyers.[20] The Turkish coastal forts on both shores of the Dardanelles' entrance supported the fleet. In the ensuing clash, both sides suffered some damage. The Turkish ships withdrew to their base after one hour of fighting. The Turks had 58 killed and the Greeks one killed and seven wounded.[21] Two days later, the Turks made another attempt to break up the blockade but again withdrew without accomplishing anything.[22] The largest naval battle of the war took place some 12 miles southeast of the island of Lemnos on 18 January 1913. Both sides were roughly equal in strength; the Greek squadron consisted of three battleships, one armored cruiser, and seven destroyers. The Turkish squadron consisted of three battleships, one cruiser, and five destroyers. The battle ended with a clear Greek victory. After some three hours of gunnery dueling, the Turks had three ships heavily damaged and the Greeks none. The Turks also had considerable losses in personnel killed and wounded. The Greeks pursued the Turkish fleet to the entrance of the Dardanelles. This victory secured the Greek control of the Aegean. The Greeks also closed the Aegean to Ottoman shipping.[23] The Greeks continued their patrols for another four months, but the naval war in the Aegean was practically over. [24]

The Entente navies also established a semi-distant blockade of the Dardanelles after the evacuation of their last troops from Gallipoli in January 1916. The Aegean Sea became a backwater. The British and the French retained a sizeable force of older ships to support their army in Salonika, protecting the long lines of supplies against the German and Austro-Hungarian U-boats.[25] The British maintained watch over the Dardanelles to prevent the German battle cruiser *Goeben* (transferred to Turkey on 16 August 1914 and renamed Yavuz Sultan Selim) from breaking out. For patrols, they used two semi-dreadnoughts, occasionally supported by the older French battleships.[26]

As in World War I, the Royal Navy again conducted a distant blockade of Germany in World War II. The British established a blockade line between the Shetlands and southern Norway. They also tried to control the northern approaches to the Atlantic through the 180-mile-wide Denmark Strait and the 430-mile-wide passage between Iceland and Faroes (Føroyar) and the other 206-mile stretch of water to the Shetlands. The objective was to prevent German surface forces from operating on the open expanses of the Atlantic. Britain also controlled one shore of the sea's only southern exist, the Strait of Dover. In addition, the British deployed several of their submarines to monitor the German movements through the Danish Straits from the beginning of the hostilities in September 1939 until March 1940. Yet they were not allowed to attack German forces.[27] Only after the Germans started the invasion of Denmark and Norway on 10 April 1940 (Operation WESERÜBUNG) did British aircraft lay some 260 mines in the Great Belt, in Kattegat, in Kiel Canal, and in the approaches to Kiel. According to the British sources, 24 German ships ran into these mines at the cost of some ten British aircraft.[28]

In World War I, the stronger side already in control of the sea exit(s) tried to prevent the movement of the enemy submarines by using primarily mines and net defenses, combined with surface patrolling and aircraft. These efforts were only moderately successful. For example, in 1914–1918, the Royal Navy used mines extensively to block the transit of U-boats through the Strait of Dover, the southern exit from the North Sea. The Dover Barrage between Dover and Calais was initially established in February 1915. It consisted of both deep and shallow minefields with indicator nets and flare drifters.[29] Nine indicator nets were laid from Goodwin to the Outer Ruytingen in September 1916. The Dover Barrage experienced some serious difficulties because of the unfavorable oceanographic conditions and bad weather. Among other things, indicator nets could not stand up to the strong currents and stormy weather and were repeatedly ripped loose. There were plans to make nets from stronger material, but the material was diverted to the Dardanelles in 1915. Mines had weak moorings, and many broke loose even in moderately adverse weather. However, one of the most serious problems was that the British failed to properly organize patrolling by mobile forces. Until late 1917, patrols kept their watch only in daylight hours and during good weather.[30]

The mine-net barrage in the Strait of Dover never prevented the U-boats from reaching the open waters of the Atlantic. For example, from the beginning of 1917 until the end of November 1917, some 153 transits were made by the U-boats, or 23 transits per month on average.[31] However, this situation drastically changed in early 1918, when the British established new systems of patrol in the Strait of Dover. Existing buoys and nets were not replaced when they came loose and broke adrift in stormy weather. As a result, many small boats were released for patrolling duties. After the beginning of 1918, the British assigned a much larger number of ships to patrol the strait and also used brilliant illumination in the deep minefield between Folkestone and Cap Gris-Nez. Some 80–100 ships were patrolling the strait day and night at any given time. Drifters and trawlers were assigned areas north of the barrage, while destroyers were divided into two groups: East and West Barrage Patrols.[32]

Until 19 December 1917, the Germans lost only two U-boats trying to cross the Strait of Dover. This situation began to change in 1918. Three U-boats were sunk from mines between 19 January and 8 February; another U-boat was depth-charged and sunk by a British destroyer on 26 January. But more important was the psychological effect of the new patrolling system in the Strait of Dover. It had become too risky for crews in the German U-boats attempting to transit the strait. The combination of the intensive patrolling by air and sea and the illumination forced the U-boats to sail at night and dive into a deep minefield.[33] The increased effectiveness of the barrage was combined with the almost incessant air attacks on Flanders U-boat bases.[34]

After March 1918, Flanders Flotilla U-boats started to use the Strait of Dover less and less. During June 1918, only a single U-boat left Flanders for the Strait of Dover, and nine boats in July. During the war, about a dozen U-boats were destroyed while trying to cross the Dover Barrage. In addition, two heavily damaged U-boats were put out of commission.[35]

Because of the increased difficulties in transiting the Strait of Dover, the Flanders Flotilla U-boats began to use the northern route between the Faeroes and the coast of southern Norway. The 240-mile Northern Barrage, between the Orkneys and the Hardanger Fjord (Norway), was established primarily by U.S. initiative between March and early June 1918 in order to restrict the movements of German U-boats from the North Sea into the Atlantic. The initial requirements called for about 200,000 mines, though only about 71,100 mines (15,100 British and 56,000 American) were actually laid.[36] The American-designed antenna mines were set too deep and hence were ineffective against surfaced U-boats. This new type of mine was introduced into service without being properly tested. The antenna mines had a tendency to be set off prematurely. The deep minefield was of little value without a mobile patrolling force that would compel the U-boats to dive into the minefield. In addition, there was a need to have a naval base and air base on the adjacent Norwegian coast.[37] However, the Norwegians did not mine their territorial waters, although that was the only way to prevent the U-boats from sailing close to Norway's coast. After much diplomatic pressure, the Norwegian government announced on 29 September that, starting 7 October, the Norwegian waters would be mined. Yet that was not done because the war was by then almost over.[38] The effectiveness of the Northern Barrage is hard to evaluate because there is no common agreement on how many U-boats were destroyed. The number ranges from two to six. The British Admiralty's postwar list cited three U-boats destroyed plus three more "probables."[39]

In September 1915, the Entente navies made the first attempt to blockade the Strait of Otranto, the Adriatic Sea's only exit to the Mediterranean Sea. The Strait of Otranto is very deep – 300 to 500 fathoms (1,800 to 3,000 feet) – hence, it was very difficult to block the exit against the Austro-Hungarian and German U-boats based in the Bay of Cattaro and Pola, Istria. The only favorable feature was the absence of tides and currents. Initially, drifters and nets were used to block the passage of U-boats.[40] Starting in September 1915, the British maintained a force of drifters with nets and motor launches, plus destroyers, to protect the Otranto Mobile Barrage Force. This force was assisted by seaplanes based at Otranto and occasionally by submarine diving patrols.[41] Drifters were withdrawn in the summer of 1917. The French and Italians used a net composed of mines and supported by buoys some distance beneath the sea's surface. This work started in October, and on 20 November 1917, drifters laid the first section. It was suspended 33 feet below the surface, and it had a depth of 150 feet. The basic problem was that the Strait of Otranto was too deep for effective mining, and surface and air patrols by themselves were not sufficient for the task at hand. [42] Hence, the barrage was unable to prevent the transit of the German and Austro-Hungarian U-boats from their base in the Bay of Cattaro to the Mediterranean. The U-boats were able to withstand the pressure up to the depth of 180 and 250 feet. They simply sailed under the barrage.[43]

In 1918, lines of hydrophones were laid on both sides of the Strait of Otranto. They were patrolled by motor launches (MLs), while seaplanes and flying boats carried out a daylight patrol. The Allies committed huge resources to patrol the Otranto Barrage – some 300 large and small warships, squadrons of aircraft, submarine flotillas, minefields, and A/S nets. From April through August 1918, 121 U-boats passed the strait, or 24 passages per month. The barrage force carried out 58 attacks, mostly with depth charges (DCs) but achieved only two kills.[44] The Otranto Barrage was completed by 30 September 1918.[45] Lines of deeply laid mines were intended to catch the U-boats that dived under the nets. A shallow mine field barrage was laid between Otranto and Cape Linguetta.[46] Some sources claim that three U-boats were sunk and three others damaged, while others claim six confirmed sinkings.[47]

In World War II, the British tried again to keep German U-boats from their basing area in the North Sea and the open waters of the Atlantic. In September 1939, the Royal Navy instituted a blockade of the English Channel, the Strait of Dover, and the North Sea's northern exit between the Shetlands and southern Norway, through which passed the deployment routes of the German U-boats. In the first weeks of September 1939, the British laid some 6,600 mines in the Strait of Dover aimed to prevent the exit of German U-boats and to protect the flank of the British Expeditionary Force (B.E.F.).[48] Yet none of the attempts were successful. About 10,000 mines were laid in St. George's Channel (in the Irish Sea), but not a single U-boat was lost to any mine laid. The East Coast Barrage, laid in 1939–1940 and consisting of about 35,000 mines, also did not have any appreciable influence on the activities of the German U-boats.[49] In July 1940, the British tried but failed to block the passage of German U-boats from the North Sea to the northern Atlantic by mining the area between the Faroe Islands and Iceland. However, the barrage was ineffective because the water was too deep (some 200 fathoms). The new barrage absorbed 90,000 mines and tied up a large number of destroyers as escorts for minelayers.[50] The entire effort was a huge waste of time and resources.

In World War II, the Allies tried to block the passage of the German U-boats and Italian submarines to/from the Mediterranean through the Strait of Gibraltar. These efforts were only partially successful. In April 1941, the German Navy High Command (Oberkommando der Marine, OKM) considered sending some U-boats then in the Atlantic to the Mediterranean. The only way of doing that was by sending the U-boats through the well defended Strait of Gibraltar. On 7 September 1941, a decision was made to send U-boats to be based in Salamis, Greece. The first six U-boats left the Bay of Biscay bases and transited the Strait of Gibraltar between 22 September and 3 October 1941.[51] Because of the worsening military situation for the Axis in the Mediterranean, a second wave of U-boats was ordered to enter the Mediterranean on 4 November. Four U-boats transited the strait at night between 12 and 15 November.[52] A third wave, composed of four U-boats, passed the strait without any incident between 16 and 20 November.[53]

The British advance into Cyrenaica led to the German decision to shift more U-boats from the Atlantic to the Mediterranean. On 29 November, the OKM decided to deploy 15 U-boats in the western Mediterranean, plus ten U-boats in the eastern Mediterranean. The same day, four U-boats left their bases in the Bay of Biscay. Yet none of these U-boats, for variety of reason, were able to transit the Strait of Gibraltar.[54] The British strengthened air patrols in the vicinity of Gibraltar that forced U-boats approaching the strait from the west to remain submerged for extended periods of time.[55]

From late September to mid-December 1941, the U-boats usually made transit during the dark new moon periods, sailing on the surface at their top speed and taking advantage of the easterly surface current. This method proved to be very effective because no U-boat was detected. However, this situation changed after an Area Combined Headquarters was established. It combined R.A.F. day patrols and F.A.A. night air patrols.[56]

The British steadily strengthened defenses against the U-boats in the Strait of Gibraltar. The most effective were extended daylight air patrols. From 27 November 1941 to 26 January 1942, the British used radar-fitted aircraft to patrol during both the day and the night. These aircraft were capable of detecting U-boats on surface. They forced the U-boats to submerge during the day and to transit the strait at night. After being detected, the U-boats were illuminated and attacked with depth charges.[57] These patrols made it increasingly difficult for the U-boats to transit the strait on the surface. Before the night air patrols were established, some 14 U-boats and 43 Italian submarines passed the strait in either direction. However, once the air patrols were put in place, seven of 14 U-boats that attempted transit were sunk, damaged, or forced to abandon their attempt.[58] The transit of the U-boats through the Strait of Gibraltar became so dangerous that the Germans were forced to abandon their plans of basing U-boats operating in the Mediterranean in their Bay of Biscay bases.[59]

From February to September 1942, due to several reasons, not a single U-boat entered the Mediterranean. On 19 September, the German naval high command ordered the deployment of six U-boats to the Mediterranean; two of them returned, but four other transited the strait.[60] On 4 November, the OKM decided to send seven U-boats to reinforce the then existing 18 U-boats in the Mediterranean.[61]

Between October 1942 and January 1943, 15 U-boats and one Italian submarine successfully transited the Strait of Gibraltar. No more submarines were sent through the strait until April 1943. However, between April and June 1943, five U-boats transited the strait without, [although the Allied aircraft carried ASV (airborne surface vessel) radars, Leigh Lights (powerful searchlights), and depth charges]. The U-boats were fitted with search receivers, (FuMB-1 Metox) capable of detecting aircraft radar transmissions. In September 1943, four U-boats tried to enter the Mediterranean. However, by then the Allied aircraft had been fitted with centimetric radars whose transmissions the U-boats were unable to detect. Only a single U-boat got through the strait; another was damaged, and other two were ordered back.[62] By October 1943, the U-boats were fitted with a search receiver (FuMB-7 Naxos) capable of detecting centimetric radar transmissions. In that month, five U-boats were ordered to the Mediterranean, but the Allies knew about that order. Only two U-boats successfully transited the strait; one was intercepted and sunk at night off the west coast of Spain, and the remaining two were sunk by air and surface patrols in the strait while trying to transit submerged.[63]

Between December 1943 and mid-February 1944, seven U-boats passed the strait without difficulty and submerged. Afterward and until mid-May 1944, only four out of eight U-boats directed to enter the Mediterranean successfully transited the strait. Because of these high losses, Admiral Karl Doenitz (1891–1980), CINC of the German Navy, decided not to send any more U-boats to the Mediterranean.[64]

During the entire war, the number of the German U-boats in the Mediterranean was rarely higher than 20. Yet they inflicted rather large losses on Allied shipping and warships. Out of 95 U-boats directed by the OKM to enter the Mediterranean, 11 boats did not sail because of variety of reasons; one was damaged and two others sunk while on the way to transit the Strait of Gibraltar. Out of the remaining 82 U-boats that attempted transit, three were sunk on their way to the strait. Yet no fewer than 62 successfully transited the strait. Of the remaining 16 boats, six were sunk and six damaged from the Allied ASW defenses; two U-boats were deterred and ordered back because of the strong Allied defenses. All of 30 Italian submarines sent to the Atlantic between June 1940 and the end of 1943 successfully transited the strait, as did 13 Italian submarines that returned from the Atlantic to the Mediterranean.[65]

Perhaps the most successful effort in World War II to prevent enemy submarines from operating in open waters was the German–Finnish A/S defenses in the Gulf of Finland in 1941–1944. The major reasons for this success were the geography and the favorable military situation ashore. The 12,000-square-mile Gulf of Finland extends for some 250 miles from the Hanko (Hangö) Peninsula to Leningrad (Saint Petersburg today). Its width varies from about 43 miles at its western entrance to some 81 miles on the line connecting the cities of Kotka (Finland) and Meriküla (Estonia) at the longitude of the island of Moshchnyy. The gulf is only about 7.5 miles wide at Neva Bay. It is also relatively shallow. The deepest part of the Gulf is at its entrance: 260–330 feet. The depths in the Neva Bay are only about 20 feet. The average depth of the Gulf of Finland is 125 feet. The depths off the gulf's southern shore are about 330 feet, while the depths of the northern coast do not exceed 200 feet. The Gulf of Finland is usually partly frozen between November and late April and often completely frozen in late January.

In preparing for war with Soviet Russia, the Germans planned to completely close the Gulf of Finland by laying several mine barriers. These barriers would be patrolled by surface craft and defended by the coastal gun batteries. By late June 1941, the German naval staff believed that it was only a matter of time before the Soviet Baltic Fleet would be bottled up in its bases in the inner part of the Gulf of Finland and ultimately eliminated from the war.[66] The first mine barrier in the Gulf of Finland was laid on 12 June 1941 by German ships camouflaged as merchant vessels.[67]

The Germans laid two mine barriers in the Gulf of Finland on the night of 21/22 June 1941. The mines were code-named *Apolda* (Örö-Takhkona line) and *Corbetha* (Kallbadagrund- Pakerort line).[68] After the Finns entered the war on 26 June, their ships laid the *Kipinola* and *Kuolemanjarvi* minefields. The Finnish submarines laid a number of mine banks between Hochland and Great Tueters.[69] The Germans laid another large mine barrier, *Juminda* (Cape Juminda-Kallbada), in late August 1941.[70]

After the start of their invasion of Soviet Russia on 22 June 1941, German troops advanced rapidly along the Baltic coast, By early September 1941, the Germans reached the gates of Leningrad (St. Petersburg today). The Soviet Baltic Fleet, including more than 20 submarines, was bottled up in the Bay of Kronshtadt.[71] The Germans and Finns reinforced existing mine barriers and laid new ones throughout the course of 1942. About 12,875 mines and mine obstructors were laid in the Gulf of Finland and its western approaches.[72] The Germans and Finns controlled both the northern and southern shores of the Gulf of Finland.[73] They also used small patrol craft and aircraft in daylight to protect their mine barriers.

For the Germans and Finns, the blockade of the Gulf of Finland had been critical in preventing Soviet submarines from freely operating in the open waters of the Baltic. The German ships carried the great majority of supplies and troops to the front. The German war industry was also heavily dependent on the uninterrupted flow of iron ore and other materials from Sweden to German ports in the Baltic. This situation remained essentially unchanged until the start of the Soviet major offensive in June 1944, which led eventually to the lifting of the siege of Leningrad and the Soviet reconquest of the Baltic States.

Today, preventing the movements of the enemy submarines through a strait would be probably much more effective than in World War II. The combined employment of one's SSNs/air-independent propulsion (AIP)–fitted SSKs, "smart" mines, surface ships, and both maritime patrol aircraft and ASW helicopters, plus a shore-based detection/surveillance system would make such movements extremely hazardous for enemy submarines.

Forcing the straits

Experience shows that forcing a strait by using only naval forces and in the face of the enemy's strong defenses is fraught with great danger and rarely successful. Such actions could be successful only when combined with attack on the land side and by achieving surprise. For example, on 30 December 1806, the British government directed Vice Admiral Cuthbert Collingwood, Commander of the Mediterranean Fleet, to send the fleet detachment to the Dardanelles and force the Porte (central government) in Constantinople to stay out of the war between Russia and France (the Ottoman Empire had declared war on Russia, then nominally Britain's ally). Because of the Russian invasion of the Danubian principalities (Moldavia and Wallachia) in December 1806, the Porte closed the Dardanelles to Russian ships.

Collingwood, in turn, sent on 15 January 1807, Vice Admiral John T. Duckworth (1748–1817) with a squadron composed of eight ships of the line, two frigates, two bomb ships, and one transport.[74] However, the fleet was not accompanied by any land forces. Britain then had only 11,000–12,000 troops available for overseas expeditions.[75] The Ottoman forces consisted of some 14 ships of the line, nine frigates, and a dozen brigs and gunboats, plus several hundred siege cannons.[76] The objective was to show force at Constantinople and put heavy pressure on Turkey to reverse its decision to go to war with Russia. Failing that, the Ottoman fleet would be destroyed or captured.[77] This might have possibly worked if Duckworth's action had been accompanied by a credible threat of land attack. Otherwise, Duckworth could apply little pressure on the Porte and was at risk of being trapped.[78] Also, the mission to be successful needed a skillful negotiator, but Duckworth lacked the diplomatic skills, and the British ambassador at Constantinople, Charles Arbuthnot (1767–1850), was ill and depressed. On 18 February, Duckworth forced the Dardanelles, passed the coastal batteries, and entered into the Sea of Marmara.[79] He destroyed one Turkish ship of the line and some smaller ships but then hesitated and delayed his arrival at Constantinople until 3 March.[80] Duckworth issued an ultimatum that the Porte make peace with Russia and dismiss the French ambassador. However, Sultan Selim III decided to resist.[81] Duckworth achieved nothing at Constantinople. On the way back, his ships were damaged by huge Turkish bombards (medieval mortars throwing stone balls) at Dardanelles. This fruitless effort was followed by a British landing in Egypt in March 1807.[82]

After Duckworth left, the Russian Admiral Dmitry Senyavin (1763–1831) blockaded the Dardanelles and twice defeated the Ottoman fleet, second time on 1 July 1807 when he won a clear victory.[83] However at Til'sit (Sovetsk today), Eastern Prussia, Tsar Alexander I agreed to abandon the Mediterranean and transfer the Ionian Islands to France. Senyavin was left to make his own way back to the Baltic.[84]

The British apparently learned nothing from their sorry experience in forcing a strait with naval forces alone in 1807. Almost 100 years later, they tried to force the Dardanelles again in February 1915. Already in August 1914, the Admiralty and the War Office had discussed the possible capture of the Gallipoli peninsula. On 3 November 1914, the British fleet actually bombarded the outer forts for about ten minutes to test Turkish defenses.[85] In this action, two 15-inch-gun dreadnoughts and 16 French and British pre-dreadnoughts bombarded the outer forts at a range of 13,000 yards. Only one fort was slightly damaged. The attack proved to be costly in the long run because it alerted the Turks, who from then on began to pay much greater attention to the defenses of the Straits. Moreover, there was no possibility to achieve a surprise in the future.[86]

Winston S. Churchill (1874–1965), First Lord of the Admiralty (1911–1915), proposed a combined naval and land attack on the Dardanelles in order to enhance the defense of Egypt. However, no ships or men were available for the operation until the seas could be cleared of German shipping and firm defensive position established on the Western Front. This was accomplished by the end of December 1914.[87] The British Secretary of State for War, Field Marshal Lord Kitchener (1850–1916) agreed with the idea but was unable to spare any troops. Another major concern was that an attack on the Dardanelles might have negative repercussions because Russia might be suspicious of the British real motives. This was resolved on 21 January 1915, when Grand Duke Nicholas Nikolayevich (1859–1919) (grandson of Tsar Nicholas I), Commander-in-Chief of the Russian Army, sent a telegram asking whether England could divert the Ottoman armies by "bringing pressure to bear on Turkey in her most vulnerable and sensitive spot."[88] After receiving the request from Grand Duke Nikolayevich that western allies reduce Turkish pressure on the Caucasian front, Churchill went ahead with a naval attack only. He believed, apparently erroneously, that the Dardanelles were defended only by old guns that could be outranged by the Anglo-French heavy guns. Also, the attacking ships did not need to come close in. The ships alone could overcome the Turkish guns ashore. The British believed that the Turkish minefields could be rapidly cleared and that the Anglo-French ships would be free to sail into the Sea of Marmara.[89] They also believed that Turkey was a weak state and would certainly surrender as the Anglo-French battleships approached the capital. In the case that Turkey refused to surrender, then the same battleships would bombard Constantinople into submission. Such an attack would be very destructive because Constantinople was built of wood. Turks' only munitions and primary gun and rifle factories were located within the range of naval gunfire from the Sea of Marmara. After Turkey was pacified, the sea route to Russia would be reopened, allowing the transport of war material and supplies to Russia. Also, Russian wheat would flow to the Western Front. In addition, neutral Balkan states, specifically Greece, Romania, and Bulgaria, would be ready to join the allies.[90]

Churchill asked for an opinion from Admiral Sackville Carden (1857–1930), commander of the blockading squadron at the Dardanelles, about the chances of success in forcing the Dardanelles. On 5 January, Carden replied, "I consider it impossible to rush the Dardanelles. If extended operation were undertaken with a considerable number of ships, a passage might be forced." Carden prepared a plan, which Churchill presented to the Cabinet.[91] In the weeks preceding Turkey's entry into the war (29 October 1914), the Turks had added 21 batteries, followed by nine batteries between October 1914 and 19 February 1915. However, the Turks made little effort to strengthen the defenses of Sidd-el-Bashar and Kum-Kale. They believed that this position could not withstand a determined attack. Both shores of the Dardanelles were dotted with dummy positions. By 2 November 1914, five mine lines had been in place, mostly in the Narrows.[92]

The first Anglo-French naval attack was carried out on 19 February, with 16 battleships, plus numerous craft. By then, the Turks had deployed more than 100 medium- and heavy-caliber guns in the Straits.. [93] In the first attack on 19 February 1915 the Anglo-French battleships quickly reduced the defenses of the outer forts at Kum-Kale and Sidd-el-Bashar. In the second attack, on 25 February British battleships inflicted severe damage on the forts and gun emplacements. However, many guns remained operational, and many minefields were unswept. The morale of the Turkish defenders remained high.[94] After a preliminary minesweeping, Anglo-French ships bombarded the batteries in the Turkish Narrows on 18 March and succeeded in silencing them. But Anglo-French losses due to the Turkish mines were heavy; three old battleships were sunk, and three others were damaged. This prompted the British and French to call off the attack and hastily leave the Straits. Unknown to them, the Turks were at the end of their resources; all gunfire control had broken down, and the Turks had almost run out of ammunition. In the meantime, Carden was replaced by Admiral Sir John Michael de Robeck (1862–1928), who decided on 23 March to discontinue with the attack.[95] The naval effort then ceased to await the arrival of Anglo-French troops. The first units did not arrive until 25 April 1915.[96]

A major lesson of the Dardanelles action was that fleet bombardment of coastal forts should have never been undertaken until the troops are ready shortly thereafter to land and seize the objective area. The only way to take the offensive against a land power is to carry out a combined operation. The Anglo-French error was in thinking that a fleet alone could deal with the situation and force the Straits without troops.

In January 1940, British Prime Minister Winston S. Churchill concocted an utterly implausible plan (codenamed CATHERINE). It envisaged the penetration of the Danish Straits with a force composed of two battleships, five cruisers, two destroyer flotillas, and some submarines and subsequent operations in the Baltic The objective was to prevent a German attack on Denmark, to exert pressure on the Scandinavian countries, and to tie up the German Navy in the Baltic.[97] Not surprisingly, this plan was never carried out.

An example of the lack of success by a stronger side at sea to prevent the movements of the enemy surface combatants through a narrows and an international strait is the escape of two German battle cruisers (*Scharnhorst, Gneisenau*) and one heavy cruiser (*Prinz Eugen*) from Brest, Brittany, in February 1942 (Operation CERBERUS). Originally, the Germans planned to use the battleship *Tirpitz* and the heavy cruiser *Admiral Hipper* to operate jointly with the Brest Group against Allied maritime traffic in the Atlantic. In July 1941, the *Scharnhorst* completed repairs and was sailing to La Pallice for a shakedown when it was attacked by British aircraft. It was hit by three bombs and suffered extensive damage. It had to return to Brest and go to the dockyard. The British attacks against the Brest Squadron became more intense despite improved AA defenses and camouflage. It was only a matter of time before the vessels would be damaged again.[98] This was one of the main reasons for Hitler's decision to move the Brest Group to by forcing the English Channel and the Strait of Dover. The alternative was to move the Brest Group though the Denmark Strait, but that course of action was equally dangerous. The British kept close watch on Brest and knew exactly when the Brest Group would be ready for sea. However, the British believed – as it turned out, wrongly – that the Germans would not dare to move the Brest Squadron through the Dover Strait.[99]

At 2300 on 11 February 1942, the Brest Group (two battle cruisers, one heavy cruiser, six destroyers, and three torpedo boats) left Brest. The entire operation was under the command of Vice Admiral Otto Ciliax (1891–1964). The Brest Group's departure was delayed for two hours because of an enemy air attack. The Germans were fortunate that the British aircraft assigned to monitor their movement had to leave their station because of aircraft trouble and a relief plane did not arrive in time.[100] The Germans kept an air alarm and smokescreen until the next morning to hide from the British the fact that the ships had left Brest. The Brest Group was not detected until it reached the area near Le Havre.[101] Its escorts were then reinforced with eight torpedo boats and ten S-boats. At the beginning of daylight, at least 16 Luftwaffe fighter aircraft provided continuous air cover. Some 175 heavy bombers and fighters of the 3rd Air Fleet were also assigned for air support of the Brest Group.[102]

By 1100 on 12 February, the German ships were in the vicinity of the Somme River estuary when they were sighted by British aircraft. The report by the aircraft reached the Admiralty shortly after 1200, and the German ships passed Dover Strait around 1300. Some 16 minutes later, the British coastal batteries opened the fire but failed to score any hits. Equally unsuccessful were attacks by five motor torpedo boats (MTBs) from Dover and three MTBs from Ramsgate.[103] Also, attacks by many bombers and torpedo bombers failed to inflict any damage on the German ships.[104] The Germans lost one patrol boat and 17 aircraft, and many British aircraft were shot down by the Luftwaffe.[105] The British also used some five destroyers based in Harwich in carrying out torpedo attacks against the German ships. However, their attacks failed due to the strong German defenses. One British destroyer was damaged in these attacks.[106] Mines proved to be the most effective British weapon. The British laid some 1,100 ground mines in 16 minefields in southern part of the North Sea. The *Scharnhorst* ran on two mines, and the *Gneisenau* on one. However, both were able to reach Wilhelmshaven and the Elbe Estuary, respectively, on their own power.[107] The Germans also lost from mines one destroyer and one minesweeper.[108]

Attack on the enemy fleet

In some rare cases, an opportunity might exist or be created to attack and destroy or to capture a major part of the enemy fleet within a strait and thereby indirectly undermine or break up the hostile coalition. For example, on 2 April 1801, the British fleet under Admiral Hyde Parker (1784–1854) attacked the Danish fleet at Copenhagen. The reason for this action was that Denmark joined Russia, Sweden, and Prussia in the League of Armed Neutrality, aimed to enforce free trade with France. Britain viewed the League as the tool of Napoleon I's policy and decided to break up the League. Denmark occupied key positions by reason of its control of the Skagerrak and Kattegat. The timing of the attack was chosen before the melting of the ice in the Baltic, thereby preventing the League from having a much more formidable force to oppose the British fleet. The First Lord of the Admiralty, Admiral St. Vincent, doubted that the fleet could do anything unless it carried 20,000 of the best troops under the most capable of commanders. He did not have the confidence that bombardment alone would have the desired effect on the Danish government. St. Vincent reportedly said, "shells thrown from ships are impotent weapons and will be laughed at when the first consternation is over."[109]

The British fleet sailed from Yarmouth on 12 March 1801.[110] Admiral Parker was informed by a British diplomat that the Danish government had rejected the British ultimatum and that they had taken advantage of all the delays to strengthen the defense of Copenhagen.[111] Parker's fleet did not reach Skaw until 21 March. He had under his command two three-deck and 18 two-deck ships of the line, five frigates, 28 craft with 2,000 guns, and 15,000 men.[112] The Danish fleet, anchored off Copenhagen, consisted of seven ships of the line and some 30 smaller vessels.

Admiral Horatio Nelson (1758–1805), who was second in command of the expedition, sent a letter to Parker on 12 March (the day the Danish government rejected British demands), in which he argued that no moment should be lost in attacking Copenhagen.[113] Nelson remarked that as long as the British fleet remained in the Sound, without entering the Baltic, the way was open for both the Swedes and the Russians, if released by the ice, to make a junction with the Danes. He suggested that a sufficiently strong force of the lighter ships of the line should pass the Middle Ground shoal (between the city of Copenhagen and the island of Saltholm) and, despite difficulties in navigation, which in Nelson's view were not insuperable, the British detachment would interpose itself between the Danish fleet and their Swedish and Russian allies. Hence, the British would be in a position to assail the weaker part of the enemy force. Nelson offered himself to lead that detachment.[114] The British estimated that the Russians then had some 20, the Swedes 11, and the Danes ten ships of the line, respectively. [115]

At a second council of war on 30 March, the plan of attack suggested by Nelson was finally adopted. Nelson proposed to take ten of the lighter ships of the line with frigates eastward of the Middle Ground by the Outer Channel or Hollaender Deep Channel and then approach the city through the narrow and intricate King's Deep Channel.[116] Nelson's detachment consisted of 12 ships of the line (seven 74-gun, three 64-gun, and two 52-gun), five frigates, and two corvettes, plus 17 smaller ships (two brigs, two fireships, seven bombardment craft, and six small brigs armed with cannons), for a total of 36 ships with 1,280 guns and 9,400 men. In reserve under Admiral Parker were two three-deckers (98-guns) and four two-deckers (two with 74-guns and two with 64-guns).[117]

In the British attack on 2 April, the general action lasted for nearly four hours. The Danes fought doggedly and well. The British were handicapped by the stranding of their three ships of the line. The Danes were also able to replace their losses by the boatloads of men from the shore.[118] Yet in the end Nelson's squadron prevailed.[119] Out of some 5,300 men, the Danish losses were 370 killed, 665 wounded, 205 missing, and 1,780 taken prisoner. The British losses were 255 killed and 688 wounded.[120] Nelson ordered the sinking of all the captured ships with the exception of one 74-gun ship of the line to be commissioned as a hospital ship. Nelson's squadron moved out to rejoin Parker's fleet. Afterward, the British positioned their bombardment ships in the King's Deep Channel, thereby threateninng to bombard the Danish Capital.[121] To save Copenhagen from bombardment, Nelson consented to a permanent armistice to give the Danes time to suspend their alliance with Russia but to refrain from fitting out their warships for another 14 weeks. They also had to agree to supply the British fleet with provisions.[122]

Nelson's attack was bold, but he nearly lost the battle. He later observed that the French fought bravely, but they could not have stood for one hour the fight that the Danes had endured for four.[123] Danes called the encounter the "Anchorage Battle" and considered it their success. The British were not entirely satisfied with the results of their attack on Copenhagen inasmuch as no gold medals were given to the participants.[124]

The 14-week armistice was signed on 12 April, and the British fleet entered the Baltic. Nelson relieved Parker as the fleet commander. He sailed for Reval (Tallinn today), Estonia. However, the Russian fleet escaped

Reval and moved to Kronshtadt some ten days before Nelson's arrival. On 17 June, the convention was signed between Britain and Russia and later accepted by the northern states. Under its terms, Britain conceded that neutrals might engage in trade from one enemy port to another, with the exception of the colonial ports. It was also agreed that naval stores should not be considered as contraband (goods that are imported or exported illegally, either in defiance of a ban or without payment of duty). On its part, Russia agreed that enemy goods under certain conditions might be seized in neutral ships and that ships under naval escort might be searched by ships of war.[125]

In another example, the British decided to send a fleet to Copenhagen in 1807 in order to destroy or capture the Danish fleet, thereby preventing its alliance with France. Napoleon I crushed Prussia in the dual battle at Jena-Auerstedt on 14 October 1806. Afterward, France obtained control of the rivers Weser, Elbe, Trave, and Oder, as well as the entire Baltic coast. Napoleon I entered Berlin on 21 November. He issued what was later known the "Berlin Decrees," which declared a blockade of England. Napoleon I's objective was to cut off England completely from its markets in Europe. The Berlin Decrees were Napoleon I's retaliation for the British blockade of France declared on 16 May 1806. Napoleon I believed that the British blockade was illegal.[126] He proceeded to defeat the Russians at Battle of Eylau on 7–8 February 1807 and the Battle of Friedland on 14 June 1807. After these defeats, the Tsar Alexander I (1777–1825) immediately asked for an armistice. In a secret article of the peace treaty between France and Russia signed at Til'sit on 7 July, the tsar promised to combine his navy with Napoleon I's against Britain. Sweden, Denmark, Portugal, and Austria were compelled to close their ports to Britain and to declare war if Britain did not accept the settlements. With these navies at his disposal, Napoleon I would have more than 100 ships of the line and would be able to resume the struggle for command of the sea. In the meantime, in June 1807, the British sent some 7,000 men to the Baltic to help the Swedes in defending Stralsund.[127]

London heard about the peace between Russia and France but did not know about the secret articles. Yet the situation was clear to the British. Denmark was consistently hostile to England. The Danish fleet had 18 ships of the line. If Denmark joined France, the Sound would be closed to British shipping. The British were adamant about not allowing this to happen.[128] By pure deduction, George Canning (1770–1827), the British Foreign Secretary, at once organized a powerful expedition to reinforce the 7,000–8,000 men already in the Baltic, to be escorted and supported by a fleet of 24 ships of the line and to take a position against the Danish fleet at Copenhagen.[129]

On 26 July, Admiral James Gambier (1756–1833) left Yarmouth with 17 ships of the line. At the same time, General Lord William Cathcart (1755–1843) was ordered to bring his troops from Ruegen to Copenhagen to join some 17,000 troops sent with Gambier.[130] The sending of the fleet to the Danish Straits was kept in utmost secrecy except for the First Sea Lord. The Admiralty did not know about the true purpose of the expedition. Gambier received orders to attack Copenhagen not from the Admiralty but directly from Canning. Gambier was instructed to cooperate with the king of Sweden, to protect any reinforcement to Pomerania, and to secure British trade and the supply of naval stores in the Baltic.[131]

The British fleet arrived off Gothenburg (Göteborg today) on 1 August. Four ships of the line, three frigates, and ten brigs were sent at once under Commodore Richard G. Keats (1757–1834) to seize the Great Belts to prevent any of the Danish troops in Holstein from reaching Zealand (Sjælland). On 3 August, Admiral Gambier entered the Sound and anchored off Helsingør, Sweden. During the next few days, eight ships of the line and one frigate joined his fleet. The troops from Ruegen also arrived. Everything was ready for the attack.[132]

The Danes did not have a clue about the British intentions. However, they put Copenhagen in an increased state of readiness for defense. The English representative Mr. Francis Jackson met the Danish-Norwegian Crown Prince (who commanded the majority of the army then deployed in Schleswig-Holstein) at Kiel and presented his government's demands on 8 August. The English representative demanded that the Danish fleet be handed over to England until the conclusion of peace between England and France. He assured the Crown Prince that England would protect Denmark from French attacks. However, if the Danish government refused these demands, the Danish fleet would be taken by force and retained. Not surprisingly, the Crown Prince refused the British demands. Yet not until 18 August was the British representative able to transmit orders to Admiral Gambier to proceed with action against the Danish fleet. The Danish defenses were not as formidable as they were in 1801.[133]

On 1 September, the British batteries were ready for the bombardment of Copenhagen. Gambier and Cathcart sent demands to the Danes to surrender. After the Danes rejected the British demands, the bombardment started on 2 September. Three days later, the Danish General Ernst Peymann (1737–1823), commander of Copenhagen, asked for truce as a preliminary to surrendering to the British. The British commander insisted on the surrender of the Danish fleet. The agreement on surrender was signed on 7 September. The Danish fleet was ceded to England, and hostilities would cease.[134] The British were to take control of the citadel and dockyard but were to withdraw as soon as they had taken their prizes.[135]

The Danish fleet that surrendered numbered some 76 ships, including 14 ships of the line; three ships of the line were destroyed, along with 16 frigates, ten brigs, 14 gun sloops, two bombardment vessels, plus seven other vessels. On 20 October, the British troops were reembarked, and the following day the fleet sailed for England with its prizes. The Danish Navy almost ceased to exist.[136]

Capturing straits

Optimally, a stronger side should obtain physical control of either one or, even better, both shores of a strait/narrows. This would greatly increase its ability to obtain a greater degree of control of the sea both in the respective narrow sea and in a larger ocean/sea area. For example, the rise of England as a global sea power rested in large part on its control of four narrow seas adjacent to the British Isles (the Irish Sea, the North Sea, the English Channel, and the Bay of Biscay), plus physical control of some key choke points of maritime trade: the Strait of Gibraltar, Cape of Good Hope, Bab-el Mandeb, Strait of Hormuz, and the Singapore Strait.

The British captured Gibraltar during the War of the Spanish Succession (1701–1714) on 1–3 August 1704 and has retained control ever since. Before the British took control, Gibraltar was known as a third-rate port town with works designed to defend against the Barbary pirates.[137] British Admiral George Rooke (1650–1709) and his Anglo-Dutch squadron of 17 ships of the line, plus three mortar boats carrying some 1,800 marines, was directed to enter the Mediterranean.[138] He made the risky decision to go ahead with the capture of Gibraltar even though he did not know the whereabouts of the French fleet from Toulon.[139] The Spanish defenders consisted of some 100 regular soldiers, plus 400 militia and some 100 guns.[140] Under cover of the main body of his ships, a select squadron conducted a bombardment of Gibraltar. Then the marines landed at some distance from the town and marched against the fortress over the sandy isthmus. While the Spanish defenders were distracted by the marines, another English landing detachment of seamen seized the Rock.[141] Shortly afterward, the French sent their Toulon squadron to recapture Gibraltar. This led to a clash between the French and the allied fleets off Malaga on 13 August 1704. Its results were tactically inconclusive. However, the battle was an operational victory for the Anglo-Dutch fleet. The Toulon squadron was forced to withdraw, and the British retained control of Gibraltar.[142] With bases at Lisbon and Gibraltar, the British fleet was able for the first time to remain in the Mediterranean throughout the year and continuously monitor the French and Spanish movements in the western Mediterranean.[143]

The British presence in Singapore was established in 1819 when Sir Stamford Raffles (1781–1826) established a port. In 1867, Singapore, then called the "Straits Settlements," became a separate Crown colony, directly overseen by the Colonial Office in London. The British captured Aden, Yemen, in 1839 from the Abdali Sultan of Lahey.[144] Thereby they obtained control of the eastern shore of the critically important Strait of Bab-el-Mandeb. Aden had only some 600 inhabitants living in a 3-square-mile area.[145] The reason for obtaining control of Aden was the need to establish a coal depot for the steamers of the East India Company en route to India. Britain had expressed great interest in obtaining control of the Suez Canal, built by a French company. It took full control of the canal in August 1882, some 13 years after it was completed. The canal was administered and managed by the Suez Canal Authority. The British also established the first permanent military presence in Egypt in 1882.

Experience shows that capturing a strait would normally require close cooperation between the land forces and the navy; otherwise, the entire effort might be found wanting. For example, the Austro-Hungarian Army failed to capture the eastern shore of the Strait of Otranto because it lacked the support of naval forces. The Austro-Hungarians planned to seize control of the Albanian coast southward up to Valona, which guarded the eastern shore of the Strait of Otranto. Their army reached the port of Durazzo (Durrës today) in late February 1916. However, their advance stopped, and the front remained stationary until almost the end of war.[146] This failure had momentous consequences for the ability of the Austro-Hungarian and German U-boats based in the Bay of Cattaro to reach the open waters of the Mediterranean undisturbed.

Two of the Entente Powers, Great Britain and France, tried but failed to capture one shore of the Turkish Straits in 1915. The landing was conducted over the commanded sea, but the lack of adequate cooperation between the services doomed the entire enterprise. The main objectives of the Gallipoli landing were to take Turkey out of war, to open a direct link with their embattled Russian ally, to force the Germans to shift troops from the Russian front, and to influence Greece to side openly with the *Entente Powers*.[147]

After the failure of the naval attack in February 1915, the Western Allies decided to commit ground troops to capture the Turkish Straits. The initial forces for the ground assault consisted of about 75,000 British troops under General Sir Ian Hamilton (1853–1947). Specifically, this force comprised the British 29th Division and the Royal Naval Division, as well as the Australian and New Zealand Army Corps (ANZAC), composed of the 1st Australian Division and the New Zealand Division. In addition, on 10 March, the French made available some 18,000 colonial troops of the 1st Division.[148] In the meantime, the Turkish defenses of the straits were greatly improved after 24 March when the German General Liman von Sanders (1855–1929) took command of the Turkish Fifth Army at the Dardanelles. He had to defend a coastline stretching for 150 miles with just 84,000 men (of whom only 62,000 were combat ready), organized in six divisions. Only about 20,000 men were defending the Gallipoli Peninsula.

The main landing at Cape Helles was carried out on 25 April by about 35,000 men of the 29th Division and elements of the Royal Naval Division. Smaller, diversionary landings took place the same day, involving some 17,000 largely untrained ANZAC troops, farther north at Ari Burnu (later renamed Anzac Cove). The 6th Colonial Regiment of the French 1st Division conducted a temporary landing at Kum Kale at the neck of the peninsula.[149] The allied troops seized the initial lodgment ashore but were unable to enlarge it because of the steadily stiffening resistance by the Turks. The fighting evolved into trench warfare. Neither side was able to gain much ground, and both suffered heavy losses. By August 1915, the allied forces amounted to 12 divisions. A new landing was conducted in early August at Suvla Bay, aimed to link with the ANZAC's forces at Anzac Cove. After some gains, the entire operation ultimately failed, and the Turks recaptured Suvla Bay.

Despite all these efforts, the Allied troops were unable to make much progress on land. In the end, there was no other option but to abandon the entire operation. The evacuation was carried out in two stages on 18–19 December 1915 and 8–9 January 1916. The losses on both sides were heavy. The allies committed eventually a total of about 490,000 troops (including 79,000 French) to the operation and suffered 252,000 casualties (including about 44,100 killed). The Turks employed some 500,000 troops and suffered about 251,300 casualties (including some 86,700 killed).[150]

In the modern era, capturing a major strait/narrows would normally require the planning and execution of a major joint operation. Such an operation would be an integral part of a littoral or maritime campaign. For example, the Soviet-led Warsaw Pact envisaged, as part of its plan for war against NATO, the capture of Schleswig-Holstein and the Jutland Peninsula. The naval part of the plan envisaged a struggle to obtain sea control and to capture the Danish Strait, while supporting one army operating in the coastal direction over 800–kilometer-long supply lines.[151] The objective of a major operation on the coastal front was to go on the offensive in the area Mecklenburg and destroy the West German-Danish forces in the area of lower Saxony and Schleswig-Holstein and on the territory of Denmark. Another objective was to create conditions for the operation of the Joint Baltic Fleets in the Baltic and the North Sea. The operation on the coastal flank would be about 310 miles in depth and 62 miles in width. The entire operation would last eight to nine days.[152] The plan envisaged the destruction of the NATO naval forces within seven and eight days, thereby obtaining sea control in the area of Cape Kullen-Island Samso-Frederica. In addition, naval forces would support an amphibious landing aimed to capture islands in the western part of the Danish Straits and to support the advance by friendly troops along the coast in the Jutland operational direction.[153]

Straits or choke points offer both opportunities and challenges for a stronger side at sea. Sometimes their control would not only enhance the country's maritime position but also have a much broader and greater non-military importance. Control of the sea exit(s) in peacetime would greatly facilitate the struggle for obtaining sea control in a time of open hostilities. If a stronger side does not possess control of the sea's exit(s), then it should attempt to physically seize one or both shores of the sea's exit. This would, in turn, normally require the planning and execution of a major naval/ joint operation. In some cases, it is possible that land forces alone might be able to physically seize control of one shore of strait during their offensive on the land front. Physical control of the sea exit(s) in itself is insufficient for obtaining control of an enclosed or semi-enclosed sea theater. Hence, a stronger side must also obtain control of additional tactically and operationally important positions and choke points within a given narrow sea. It must then attack and destroy a major part of the enemy's naval forces and those non-naval forces deployed in the littorals that could prevent friendly naval/commercial movements.

Notes

1 John Fisher, "Appendix H: Instant Readiness for War, Strategy – Fleet Distribution and Fleet Orders," in Peter Kemp, editor, *The Papers of Admiral Sir John Fisher*, Vol. 1 (London: Naval Records Society, 1960), pp. 160–61.
2 The term "choke point" (or bottleneck) is defined as a narrow passage, such as a strait through which shipping must pass; an alternate meaning is a point of congestion or obstruction *American Heritage Dictionary of the English Language*, 5th ed. (New York: Houghton Mifflin Company, 2011); the same term is also used in referring to both geographical features on land (e.g., valleys, mountain passes, defiles) and at sea (e.g., straits, narrows, channels, artificial canals); the term "maritime choke point" pertains in general to narrow waterways canals connecting two large bodies of water and to straits/narrows in particular; in transport geography, a choke point refers to locations that limit the capacity of circulation and cannot be easily bypassed, if at all; this implies that any alternative to a chokepoint involves a level of detour or use of an alternative that translates into significant financial costs and delays; maritime choke points are the result of the constraints of physical geography, whereas others, such as the Suez and Panama canals, are artificial creations Jean-Paul Rodrigue, "Straits, Passages and Chokepoints. A Maritime Geostrategy of Petroleum Distribution," *Cahers de Géographie du Québec*, Vol. 48, No. 135 (December 2004), p. 359.
3 Specifically, there are 22 international straits in the North Atlantic and Mediterranean; 13 in the Caribbean Sea/Gulf of Mexico; three in the Indian Ocean; 40 in the northwestern Pacific; 16 in the eastern Pacific; and 28 in southwest Pacific B. Fabiani, *Die seestrategische Bedeutung von Inseln und Meerengen unter Berücksichtigung der gegenwärtigen militärstrategischen Bedingungen und der Entwicklung des Seevölkerrechte* (Hamburg: Führungsakademie der Bundeswehr, 31 October 1980), p. 22.
4 Carl J. Kulsrud, "The Seizure of the Danish Fleet, 1807: The Background," *The American Jopurnal of International Law*, Vol. 32, No. 2 (April 1938), p. 283.
5 Carl J. Kulsrud, "The Seizure of the Danish Fleet, 1807: The Background," *The American Journal of International Law*, Vol. 32, No. 2 (April 1938), p. 283.
6 Carl J. Kulsrud, "The Seizure of the Danish Fleet, 1807: The Background," *The American Journal of International Law*, Vol. 32, No. 2 (April 1938), p. 284.
7 "Betrachtung über die Bedeutung Gibraltar," *Deutsche Kriegführung im Mittelmeer Februar 1941–Dezember 1941*, 2.12.1941, SKL Teil C, XIV, RM 7–234, BA-MA, p. 310.
8 Michael Salewski, *Die deutsche Seekriegsleitung 1935–1945*, Vol. I: *1935–1941* (Bonn: Bernard & Graefe, 1970), p. 370.
9 Anthony Cordesman, *The Iran-Iraq War and Western Security 1984–67: Strategic Implications and Policy Options* (London: Jane's Publishing Company, Ltd., 1987), p. 174.

10 Mark H. Huber, *Chokepoint Control: Operational Challenges for Blue-Water Navies* (Newport, RI: Naval War College, May 2003), pp. 4–5.

11 Mark K. Huber, *Chokepoint Control: Operational Challenges for Blue-Water Navies* (Newport, RI: Naval War College, 2003), p. 5.

12 Jonathan Schroden, *A Strait Comparison: Lessons Learned from the 1915 Dardanelles Campaign in the Context of a Strait of Hormuz Closure Event* (Alexandria, VA: Center for Naval Analyses, September 2011), p. 7.

13 Milan Vego, *The Battle for Leyte, 1944. Allied and Japanese Plans, Preparations, and Execution* (Annapolis, MD: Naval Institute Press, 2006), pp. 215–17.

14 Raoul Castex, *More Protiv Kopna*, Vol. 1. Translated by Hijacint Mundorfer (*Théórie stratégiques*, Vol. 1: *La Mer Contre La Terre*) (Belgrade: Geca Kon AD, 1939), p. 49.

15 Raoul Castex, *More Protiv Kopna*, Vol. 1. Translated by Hijacint Mundorfer (*Théórie stratégiques*, Vol. 1: *La Mer Contre La Terre*) (Belgrade: Geca Kon AD, 1939), p. 49.

16 Anthony Sokol, "Naval Strategy in the Adriatic Sea During the World War," *Proceedings*, 8 (August 1937), p. 1083.

17 Richard C. Hall, *The Balkan Wars 1912–1913: Prelude to the First World War* (London: Routledge, Taylor & Francis Group, 2000), p. 64.

18 Zisis Fotakis, *Greek Naval Strategy and Policy, 1910–1919* (London/New York: Routledge, Taylor & Francis Group, 2005), p. 48.

19 Edward J. Erickson, *Defeat in Detail. The Ottoman Army in the Balkans, 1912–1915* (Westport, CT/London: Praeger Publishers, 2003), p. 157; Zisis Fotakis, *Greek Naval Strategy and Policy, 1910–1919* (London/New York: Routledge. Taylor & Francis Group, 2005), p. 48.

20 Richard C. Hall, *The Balkan Wars 1912–1913: Prelude to the First World War* (London: Routledge, Taylor & Francis Group, 2000), p. 64; Zisis Fotakis, *Greek Naval Strategy and Policy, 1910–1919* (London/New York: Routledge, Taylor & Francis Group, 2005), p. 50.

21 Zisis Fotakis, *Greek Naval Strategy and Policy, 1910–1919* (London/New York: Routledge. Taylor & Francis Group, 2005), p. 50.

22 Richard C. Hall, *The Balkan Wars 1912–1913: Prelude to the First World War* (London: Routledge, Taylor & Francis Group, 2000), p. 65.

23 Richard C. Hall, *The Balkan Wars 1912–1913: Prelude to the First World War* (London: Routledge, Taylor & Francis Group, 2000), p. 65.

24 Zisis Fotakis, *Greek Naval Strategy and Policy, 1910–1919* (London/New York: Routledge. Taylor & Francis Group, 2005), p. 50.

25 Paul G. Halpern, *The Naval War in the Mediterranean 1914–1918* (Annapolis, MD: Naval Institute Press, 1987), p. 289.

26 Paul G. Halpern, *The Naval War in the Mediterranean 1914–1918* (Annapolis, MD: Naval Institute Press, 1987), p. 289.

27 Herbert Henning, *Analyse des Kampfes der Seestreitkräfte um Meerengen in Verlaufe des Zweiten Weltkrieges* (Dresden: Militärakademie Friedrich Engels, 1967), p. 13; that prohibition was lifted only in April 1940 cited in Herbert Henning, *Analyse des Kampfes der Seestreitkräfte um Meerengen in Verlaufe des Zweiten Weltkrieges* (Dresden: Militärakademie Friedrich Engels, 1967), p. 14.

28 Cited in Herbert Henning, *Analyse des Kampfes der Seestreitkräfte um Meerengen in Verlaufe des Zweiten Weltkrieges* (Dresden: Militärakademie Friedrich Engels, 1967), p. 14.

29 James A. Meacham, "Four Mining Campaigns: An Historical Analysis of the Decisions of the Commanders," *Naval War College Review*, Vol. 19, No. 10 (June 1967), p. 88; Eric J. Grove, editor, *The Defeat of the Enemy Attack on Shipping 1939–1945* a revised edition of the Naval Staff History, Vols. 1A (Text and

Appendices) and 1B (Plans and Tables); Aldershot, UK: Ashgate, Navy Records Society, 1997), p. 150.

30 Jan S. Breemer, *Defeating the U-Boat: Inventing Antisubmarine Warfare*, Newport Paper 36 (Newport, RI: Naval War College Press, 2010), 26.

31 R.H. Gibson and Maurice Prendergast, *The German Submarine War 1914–1918* (Constable & Co. Ltd., 1931; reprinted Annapolis, MD: Naval Institute Press, 2002), p. 222.

32 Arthur J. Marder, *From the Dreadnought to Scapa Flow: The Royal Navy in the Fisher Era, 1904–1919*, Vol. 5: *Victory and Aftermath (January 1918–June 1919)* (London: Oxford University Press, 1970), p. 41.

33 Arthur J. Marder, *From the Dreadnought to Scapa Flow: The Royal Navy in the Fisher Era, 1904–1919*, Vol. 5: *Victory and Aftermath (January 1918–June 1919)* (London: Oxford University Press, 1970), 41.

34 Arthur J. Marder, *From the Dreadnought to Scapa Flow: The Royal Navy in the Fisher Era, 1904–1919*, Vol. 5: *Victory and Aftermath (January 1918–June 1919)* (London: Oxford University Press, 1970), p. 65.

35 Arthur J. Marder, *From the Dreadnought to Scapa Flow: The Royal Navy in the Fisher Era, 1904–1919*, Vol. 5: *Victory and Aftermath (January 1918–June 1919)* (London: Oxford University Press, 1970), pp. 65–66.

36 Henry Newbolt, *Naval Operations, History of the Great War Based on Official Documents*, Vol. 5: *From April to the End of the War*, Julian Stafford Corbett, editor (London: Longmans, Green and Co., 1931), 207; Arthur J. Marder, *From the Dreadnought to Scapa Flow: The Royal Navy in the Fisher Era, 1904–1919*, Vol. 5: *Victory and Aftermath (January 1918–June 1919)* (London: Oxford University Press, 1970), p. 66, the British estimated that, because of the great depth of water in the area, about 400,000 mines would be required to prevent the transit of U-boats; however, the invention of the Mk 6 antenna mines by the United States allowed for the reduction of the total number of mines for the barrage; these mines were laid in the deep sections of the barrage, while the British chemical-horn H mines were used at both ends of the barrage James A. Meacham, "Four Mining Campaigns: An Historical Analysis of the Decisions of the Commanders," *Naval War College Review*, Vol. 19, No. 10 (June 1967), p. 89.

37 Arthur J. Marder, *From the Dreadnought to Scapa Flow, The Royal Navy in the Fisher Era, 1904–1919*, Vol. 5: *Victory and Aftermath (January 1918–June 1919)* (London: Oxford University Press, 1970), pp. 68–69.

38 Arthur J. Marder, *From the Dreadnought to Scapa Flow, The Royal Navy in the Fisher Era, 1904–1919*, Vol. 5: *Victory and Aftermath (January 1918–June 1919)* (London: Oxford University Press, 1970), p. 72.

39 Arthur J. Marder, *From the Dreadnought to Scapa Flow, The Royal Navy in the Fisher Era, 1904–1919*, Vol. 5: *Victory and Aftermath (January 1918–June 1919)* (London: Oxford University Press, 1970), 73; Eric J. Grove, editor, *The Defeat of the Enemy Attack on Shipping 1939–1945* a revised edition of the Naval Staff History, Vols. 1A (Text and Appendices) and 1B (Plans and Tables); Aldershot, UK: Ashgate, Navy Records Society, 1997), p. 149; James A. Meacham, "Four Mining Campaigns: An Historical Analysis of the Decisions of the Commanders," *Naval War College Review*, Vol. 19, No. 10 (June 1967), pp. 90–91; Gregory K. Hartmann, *Weapons That Wait: Mine Warfare in the U.S. Navy* (Annapolis, MD: Naval Institute Press, 1979), p. 53.

40 R.H. Gibson and Maurice Prendergast, *The German Submarine War 1914–1918* (Constable & Co. Ltd., 1931; reprinted Annapolis, MD: Naval Institute Press, 2002), p. 264.

41 Arthur J. Marder, *From the Dreadnought to Scapa Flow, The Royal Navy in the Fisher Era, 1904–1919*, Vol. 5: *Victory and Aftermath (January 1918–June 1919)* (London: Oxford University Press, 1970), p. 32.

42 Arthur J. Marder, *From the Dreadnought to Scapa Flow, The Royal Navy in the Fisher Era, 1904–1919*, Vol. 5: *Victory and Aftermath (January 1918–June 1919)* (London: Oxford University Press, 1970), p. 35.

43 R.H. Gibson and Maurice Prendergast, *The German Submarine War 1914–1918* (Constable & Co. Ltd., 1931; reprinted Annapolis, MD: Naval Institute Press, 2002), pp. 264–65.

44 Arthur J. Marder, *From the Dreadnought to Scapa Flow, The Royal Navy in the Fisher Era, 1904–1919*, Vol. 5: *Victory and Aftermath (January 1918–June 1919* (London: Oxford University Press, 1970), pp. 34–35.

45 R.H. Gibson and Maurice Prendergast, *The German Submarine War 1914–1918* (Constable & Co. Ltd., 1931; reprinted Annapolis, MD: Naval Institute Press, 2002), p. 265.

46 Eric J. Grove, editor, *The Defeat of the Enemy Attack on Shipping 1939–1945* a revised edition of the Naval Staff History, Vols. 1A (Text and Appendices) and 1B (Plans and Tables) (Aldershot, UK: Ashgate, Navy Records Society, 1997), p. 149.

47 James A. Meacham, "Four Mining Campaigns: An Historical Analysis of the Decisions of the Commanders," *Naval War College Review*, Vol. 19, No. 10 (June 1967), pp. 90–91.

48 Hartmut Waltz, *Die Problem moderner Minelegeplanungen vor dem Hintergrund historischer Erfahrungen in der Nordsee 1939–1944* (Hamburg: Führungsakademie der Bundeswehr, October 1985), p. 9.

49 Eric J. Grove, editor, *The Defeat of the Enemy Attack on Shipping 1939–1945* a revised edition of the Naval Staff History, Vols. 1A (Text and Appendices) and 1B (Plans and Tables) (Aldershot, UK: Ashgate, Navy Records Society, 1997), pp. 151–52.

50 Arthur J. Marder, "The Influence of History on Sea Power: The Royal Navy and the Lessons of 1914–1918," *Pacific Historical Review*, Vol. 41, No. 4 (November 1972), p. 430.

51 Eric J. Grove, editor, *The Defeat of the Enemy Attack on Shipping 1939–1945* a revised edition of the Naval Staff History, Vols. 1A (Text and Appendices) and 1B (Plans and Tables) (Aldershot, UK: Ashgate, Navy Records Society, 1997), p. 134.

52 Eric J. Grove, editor, *The Defeat of the Enemy Attack on Shipping 1939–1945* a revised edition of the Naval Staff History, Vols. 1A (Text and Appendices) and 1B (Plans and Tables) (Aldershot, UK: Ashgate, Navy Records Society, 1997), p. 134.

53 Eric J. Grove, editor, *The Defeat of the Enemy Attack on Shipping 1939–1945* a revised edition of the Naval Staff History, Vols. 1A (Text and Appendices) and 1B (Plans and Tables) (Aldershot, UK: Ashgate, Navy Records Society, 1997), p. 135.

54 Eric J. Grove, editor, *The Defeat of the Enemy Attack on Shipping 1939–1945* a revised edition of the Naval Staff History, Vols. 1A (Text and Appendices) and 1B (Plans and Tables) (Aldershot, UK: Ashgate, Navy Records Society, 1997), p. 135.

55 Eric J. Grove, editor, *The Defeat of the Enemy Attack on Shipping 1939–1945* a revised edition of the Naval Staff History, Vols. 1A (Text and Appendices) and 1B (Plans and Tables) (Aldershot, UK: Ashgate, Navy Records Society, 1997), p. 135.

56 Eric J. Grove, editor, *The Defeat of the Enemy Attack on Shipping 1939–1945* a revised edition of the Naval Staff History, Vols. 1A (Text and Appendices) and 1B (Plans and Tables) (Aldershot, UK: Ashgate, Navy Records Society, 1997), p. 137.

57 Eric J. Grove, editor, *The Defeat of the Enemy Attack on Shipping 1939–1945* a revised edition of the Naval Staff History, Vols. 1A (Text and Appendices) and 1B (Plans and Tables) (Aldershot, UK: Ashgate, Navy Records Society, 1997), p. 144.

58 Eric J. Grove, editor, *The Defeat of the Enemy Attack on Shipping 1939–1945* a revised edition of the Naval Staff History, Vols. 1A (Text and Appendices) and 1B (Plans and Tables) (Aldershot, UK: Ashgate, Navy Records Society, 1997), p. 144.

59 Eric J. Grove, editor, *The Defeat of the Enemy Attack on Shipping 1939–1945* a revised edition of the Naval Staff History, Vols. 1A (Text and Appendices) and 1B (Plans and Tables) (Aldershot, UK: Ashgate, Navy Records Society, 1997), p. 144.

60 Eric J. Grove, editor, *The Defeat of the Enemy Attack on Shipping 1939–1945* a revised edition of the Naval Staff History, Vols. 1A (Text and Appendices) and 1B (Plans and Tables) (Aldershot, UK: Ashgate, Navy Records Society, 1997), p. 138.

61 Eric J. Grove, editor, *The Defeat of the Enemy Attack on Shipping 1939–1945* a revised edition of the Naval Staff History, Vols. 1A (Text and Appendices) and 1B (Plans and Tables) (Aldershot, UK: Ashgate, Navy Records Society, 1997), p. 139.

62 Eric J. Grove, editor, *The Defeat of the Enemy Attack on Shipping 1939–1945* a revised edition of the Naval Staff History, Vols. 1A (Text and Appendices) and 1B (Plans and Tables) (Aldershot, UK: Ashgate, Navy Records Society, 1997), p. 144.

63 Eric J. Grove, editor, *The Defeat of the Enemy Attack on Shipping 1939–1945* a revised edition of the Naval Staff History, Vols. 1A (Text and Appendices) and 1B (Plans and Tables) (Aldershot, UK: Ashgate, Navy Records Society, 1997), p. 144.

64 Eric J. Grove, editor, *The Defeat of the Enemy Attack on Shipping 1939–1945* a revised edition of the Naval Staff History, Vols. 1A (Text and Appendices) and 1B (Plans and Tables) (Aldershot, UK: Ashgate, Navy Records Society, 1997), pp. 144–45.

65 Eric J. Grove, editor, *The Defeat of the Enemy Attack on Shipping 1939–1945* a revised edition of the Naval Staff History, Vols. 1A (Text and Appendices) and 1B (Plans and Tables) (Aldershot, UK: Ashgate, Navy Records Society, 1997), p. 144.

66 Michael Salewski, *Die deutsche Seekriegsleitung 1935–1945*, Vol. 1, *1935–1941* (Frankfurt a.M.: Bernard & Graefe, 1970), p. 418.

67 Jürgen Rohwer, "Der Minenkrieg im Finnischen Meerbusen, Part I: June–August 1941," *Marine Rundschau*, 1 (January 1967), p. 21.

68 Jürg Meister, *Der Seekrieg in den osteuropäischen Gewässern 1941–45* (Munich: J.F. Lehmanns Verlag, 1958), pp. 13–14.

69 Jürgen Rohwer, "Der Minenkrieg im Finnischen Meerbusen, Part I: June–August 1941," *Marine Rundschau* 1 (January 1967), p. 21.

70 Jürgen Rohwer, "Der Minenkrieg im Finnischen Meerbusen, Part I: June–August 1941," *Marine Rundschau* 1 (January 1967), p. 16.

71 According to a German source, the Soviet Baltic Fleet had in service some 65 submarines of various classes on 22 June 1941 Friedrich Ruge, *The Soviets as Naval Opponents 1941–1945* (Annapolis, MD: Naval Institute Press, 1979),

12; between 22 June and 1 September 1941, the Soviets lost some 12 submarines in combat, five were scuttled, and two were damaged Jürgen Rohwer and Gerhard Hümmelchen, *Chronology of the War at Sea 1939–1945: The Naval History of World War Two*, 2nd revised and expanded edition (Annapolis, MD: Naval Institute Press, 1992), pp. 69–72, 77, 81; according to a Soviet source, by mid-September 1941, the Soviets had deployed 17 submarines in the Gulf of Finland for attacks against the enemy shipping, while four other submarines were deployed in the open waters of the Baltic V. I. Achkasov and N. B. Pavlovich, *Soviet Naval Operations in the Great Patriotic War 1941–1945* (Annapolis, MD: Naval Institute Press, 1981), p. 223.

72 Jürg Meister, *Der Seekrieg in den osteuropäischen Gewässern 1941–45* (Munich: J. F. Lehmanns Verlag, 1958), p. 50.

73 The Soviet Navy in World War II," pt. 4, "Soviet Submarines Operations, 1941–1945," *ONI Review*, No. 1 (1953). p. 13.

74 R. Ernest Dupuy and Trevor N. Dupuy, *The Encyclopedia of Military History from 3500 B.C. to the Present*, 2nd rev. ed. (New York: Harper & Row, Publishers, 1986), p. 766.

75 Herbert Richmond, *Statesmen and Sea Power* (Oxford: Clarendon Press, first published 1946, reprinted 1947), p. 231.

76 R. Ernest Dupuy and Trevor N. Dupuy, *The Encyclopedia of Military History from 3500 B.C. to the Present*, 2nd rev. ed. (New York: Harper & Row, Publishers, 1986), p. 766.

77 Roger C.B. Anderson, *Naval Wars in the Baltic During the Sailing-Ship Epoch, 1522–1850* (London: C. Gilbert-Wood, 1910, reprinted Charleston, SC: Nabu Press, 2014), p. 314.

78 N.A.M. Rodger, *The Command of the Ocean. A Naval History of Britain, 1649–1815* (New York/London: W.W. Norton & Company, 2005), p. 550.

79 N.A.M. Rodger, *The Command of the Ocean. A Naval History of Britain, 1649–1815* (New York/London: W.W. Norton & Company, 2005), p. 551.

80 Roger C.B. Anderson, *Naval Wars in the Baltic During the Sailing-Ship Epoch, 1522–1850* (London: C. Gilbert-Wood, 1910, reprinted Charleston, SC: Nabu Press, 2014), p. 314.

81 R. Ernest Dupuy and Trevor N. Dupuy, *The Encyclopedia of Military History from 3500 B.C. to the Present*, 2nd rev. ed., (New York: Harper & Row, Publishers, 1986), p. 766.

82 N.A.M. Rodger, *The Command of the Ocean. A Naval History of Britain, 1649–1815* (New York/London: W.W. Norton & Company, 2005), p. 551.

83 Roger C.B. Anderson, *Naval Wars in the Baltic During the Sailing-Ship Epoch, 1522–1850* (London: C. Gilbert-Wood, 1910, reprinted Charleston, SC: Nabu Press, 2014), p. 314.

84 N.A.M. Rodger, *The Command of the Ocean. A Naval History of Britain, 1649–1815* (New York/London: W.W. Norton & Company, 2005), p. 551.

85 A.L. MacFie, "The Straits Question in the First World War, 1914–1918, *Middle Eastern Studies*, Vol. 19, No. 1 (January 1983), p. 52.

86 Arthur J. Marder, *From the Dreadnought to Scapa Flow: The Royal Navy in the Fisher Era, 1904–1919*, Vol. 2: *The War Years to the Eve of Jutland (1914–1916)* (London: Oxford University Press, 1965); p. 201; S.W.C. Pack, *Sea Power in the Mediterranean. A History From the Seventeenth Century to the Present Day* (London: Arthur Barker Ltd., 1971), pp. 160–61.

87 A.L. MacFie, "The Straits Question in the First World War, 1914–1918, *Middle Eastern Studies*, Vol. 19, No. 1 (January 1983), p. 52.

88 Cited in A.L. MacFie, "The Straits Question in the First World War, 1914–1918, *Middle Eastern Studies*, Vol. 19, No. 1 (January 1983), p. 53.

89 Jonathan Schroden, *A Strait Comparison: Lessons Learned from the 1915 Dardanelles Campaign in the Context of a Strait of Hormuz Closure Event* (Alexandria, VA: Center for Naval Analyses, September 2011), p. 9.

90 Jonathan Schroden, *A Strait Comparison: Lessons Learned from the 1915 Darda-nelles Campaign in the Context of a Strait of Hormuz Closure Event* (Alexandria, VA: Center for Naval Analyses, September 2011), p. 9.

91 A.L. MacFie, "The Straits Question in the First World War, 1914–1918, *Middle Eastern Studies*, Vol. 19, No. 1 (January 1983), p. 53.

92 A.L. MacFie, "The Straits Question in the First World War, 1914–1918, *Middle Eastern Studies*, Vol. 19, No. 1 (January 1983), p. 54.

93 Arthur J. Marder, *From the Dreadnought to Scapa Flow: The Royal Navy in the Fisher Era, 1914–1919*, Vol. 2: *The War Years to the Eve of Jutland (1914–1916)* (London: Oxford University Press, 1965), p. 201; S.W.C. Pack, *Sea Power in the Mediter-ranean. A History From the Seventeenth Century to the Present* Day (London: Arthur Barker Ltd., 1971), pp. 160–61.

94 A.L. MacFie, "The Straits Question in the First World War, 1914–1918, *Middle Eastern Studies*, Vol. 19, No. 1 (January 1983), p. 54.

95 A.L. MacFie, "The Straits Question in the First World War, 1914–1918, *Middle Eastern Studies*, Vol. 19, No. 1 (January 1983), p. 54.

96 Arthur J. Marder, *From the Dreadnought to Scapa Flow: The Royal Navy in the Fisher Era, 1914–1919*, Vol. 2: *The War Years to the Eve of Jutland (1914–1916)* (London: Oxford University Press, 1965), p. 201; S.W.C. Pack, *Sea Power in the Mediter-ranean. A History From the Seventeenth Century to the Present* Day (London: Arthur Barker Ltd., 1971), pp. 160–61.

97 Herbert Henning, *Analyse des Kampfes der Seestreitkräfte um Meerengen in Ver-laufe des Zweiten Weltkrieges* (Dresden: Militärakademie Friedrich Engels, 1967), p. 11.

98 Friedrich Ruge, *Der Seekrieg. The German Navy's Story 1939–1945* (Annapolis, MD: United States Naval Institute, 1957), p. 263.

99 Friedrich Ruge, *Der Seekrieg. The German Navy's Story 1939–1945* (Annapolis, MD: United States Naval Institute, 1957), p. 264.

100 Friedrich Ruge, *Der Seekrieg. The German Navy's Story 1939–1945* (Annapolis, MD: United States Naval Institute, 1957), p. 264.

101 Friedrich Ruge, *Der Seekrieg. The German Navy's Story 1939–1945* (Annapolis, MD: United States Naval Institute, 1957), p. 264.

102 Friedrich Ruge, *Der Seekrieg. The German Navy's Story 1939–1945* (Annapolis, MD: United States Naval Institute, 1957), p. 265; Jürgen Rohwer and Ger-hard Hümmelchen, *Chronology of the War at Sea 1939–1945*, 2nd revised and expanded edition (Annapolis, MD: Naval Institute Press, 1992), p. 122.

103 Jürgen Rohwer and G. Hummelchen, *Chronology of the War at Sea 1939–1945. The Naval History of World War Two*, 2nd revised and expanded edition (Annap-olis, MD: Naval Institute Press, 1992), p. 122.

104 Friedrich Ruge, *Der Seekrieg. The German Navy's Story 1939–1945* (Annapolis, MD: United States Naval Institute, 1957), p. 266.

105 Friedrich Ruge, *Der Seekrieg. The German Navy's Story 1939–1945* (Annapolis, MD: United States Naval Institute, 1957), p. 265.

106 Jürgen Rohwer and G. Hummelchen, *Chronology of the War at Sea 1939–1945. The Naval History of World War Two*, 2nd revised and expanded edition (Annap-olis, MD: Naval Institute Press, 1992), p. 122.

107 Jürgen Rohwer and G. Hümmelchen, *Chronology of the War at Sea 1939–1945. The Naval History of World War Two*, 2nd revised and expanded edition (Annap-olis, MD: Naval Institute Press, 1992), p. 122; Friedrich Ruge, *Der Seekrieg. The German Navy's Story 1939–1945* (Annapolis, MD: United States Naval Institute, 1957), p. 266.

108 Friedrich Ruge, *Der Seekrieg. The German Navy's Story 1939–1945* (Annapolis, MD: United States Naval Institute, 1957), p. 266.

109 Herbert Richmond, *Statesmen and Sea Power* (Oxford: Clarendon Press, first published 1946, reprinted 1947), p. 210.

110   Alfred T. Mahan, *Influence of Sea Power upon the French Revolution and Empire, 1793–1812*, Vol. II, 8th edition (Boston: Little, Brown, and Company, 1897), p. 43.

111   C.J. Marcus, *The Age of Nelson. The Royal Navy in the Age of Its Greatest Power and Glory 1793–1815* (New York: Viking Press, 1971), p. 178.

112   Alfred Stenzel, *Seekriegsgeschichte in ihren wichtigsten Abschnitten mit Berücksichtigung der Seetaktik*, Part 4: *Von 1720 bis 1850* (Hannover/Leipzig: Hahnsche Buchhandlung, 1911), p. 281.

113   Alfred T. Mahan, *Influence of Sea Power upon the French Revolution and Empire, 1793–1812*, Vol. II, 8th edition (Boston: Little, Brown, and Company, 1897), p. 43.

114   Alfred T. Mahan, *Influence of Sea Power upon the French Revolution and Empire, 1793–1812*, Vol. II, 8th edition (Boston: Little, Brown, and Company, 1897), p. 44.

115   Alfred Stenzel, *Seekriegsgeschichte in ihren wichtigsten Abschnitten mit Berücksichtigung der Seetaktik*, Part 4: *Von 1720 bis 1850* (Hannover/Leipzig: Hahnsche Buchhandlung, 1911), p. 281.

116   C.J. Marcus, *The Age of Nelson. The Royal Navy in the Age of Its Greatest Power and Glory 1793–1815* (New York: Viking Press, 1971), pp. 178–79.

117   Hermann Kirchhoff, *Seemacht in der Ostsee: Ihre Einwirkung Auf Die Geschichte Der Ostseeländer Im 19. Jahrhundert*, Vol. II (Kiel: Verlag von Robert Cordes, 1908), pp. 48–49.

118   C.J. Marcus, *The Age of Nelson. The Royal Navy in the Age of Its Greatest Power and Glory 1793–1815* (New York: Viking Press, 1971), p. 183.

119   C.J. Marcus, *The Age of Nelson. The Royal Navy in the Age of Its Greatest Power and Glory 1793–1815* (New York: Viking Press, 1971), p. 187.

120   Roger C.B. Anderson, *Naval Wars in the Baltic During the Sailing-Ship Epoch, 1522–1850* (London: C. Gilbert-Wood, 1910, reprinted Charleston, SC: Nabu Press, 2014), p. 308.

121   C.J. Marcus, *The Age of Nelson. The Royal Navy in the Age of Its Greatest Power and Glory 1793–1815* (New York: Viking Press, 1971), p. 187.

122   C.J. Marcus, *The Age of Nelson. The Royal Navy in the Age of Its Greatest Power and Glory 1793–1815* (New York: Viking Press, 1971), p. 188.

123   C.J. Marcus, *The Age of Nelson. The Royal Navy in the Age of Its Greatest Power and Glory 1793–1815* (New York: Viking Press, 1971), p. 187.

124   Alfred Stenzel, *Seekriegsgeschichte in ihren wichtigsten Abschnitten mit Berücksichtigung der Seetaktik*, Part 4: *Von 1720 bis 1850* (Hannover/Leipzig: Hahnsche Buchhandlung, 1911), p. 302.

125   William Oliver Stevens and Allan Westcott, *A History of Sea Power* (New York: Doubleday, Doran & Company, Inc., 1942), p. 217.

126   Herbert Richmond, *Statesmen and Sea Power* (Oxford: Clarendon Press, first published 1946, reprinted 1947), pp. 228–29.

127   Herbert Richmond, *Statesmen and Sea Power* (Oxford: Clarendon Press, first published 1946, reprinted 1947), p. 232.

128   Roger C.B. Anderson, *Naval Wars in the Baltic During the Sailing-Ship Epoch, 1522–1850* (London: C. Gilbert-Wood, 1910, reprinted Charleston, SC: Nabu Press, 2014), p. 315.

129   Herbert Richmond, *Statesmen and Sea Power* (Oxford: Clarendon Press, first published 1946, reprinted 1947), p. 232.

130   Roger C.B. Anderson, *Naval Wars in the Baltic During the Sailing-Ship Epoch, 1522–1850* (London: C. Gilbert-Wood, 1910, reprinted Charleston, SC: Nabu Press, 2014), p. 315.

131   Herbert Richmond, *Statesmen and Sea Power* (Oxford: Clarendon Press, first published 1946, reprinted 1947), pp. 232–33.

132 Roger C.B. Anderson, *Naval Wars in the Baltic During the Sailing-Ship Epoch, 1522–1850* (London: C. Gilbert-Wood, 1910, reprinted Charleston, SC: Nabu Press, 2014), p. 315.
133 Roger C.B. Anderson, *Naval Wars in the Baltic During the Sailing-Ship Epoch, 1522–1850* (London: C. Gilbert-Wood, 1910, reprinted Charleston, SC: Nabu Press, 2014), p. 316.
134 Roger C.B. Anderson, *Naval Wars in the Baltic During the Sailing-Ship Epoch, 1522–1850* (London: C. Gilbert-Wood, 1910, reprinted Charleston, SC: Nabu Press, 2014), p. 318.
135 Roger C.B. Anderson, *Naval Wars in the Baltic During the Sailing-Ship Epoch, 1522–1850* (London: C. Gilbert-Wood, 1910, reprinted Charleston, SC: Nabu Press, 2014), p. 319.
136 Roger C.B. Anderson, *Naval Wars in the Baltic During the Sailing-Ship Epoch, 1522–1850* (London: C. Gilbert-Wood, 1910, reprinted Charleston, SC: Nabu Press, 2014), p. 319; Geoffrey Callender, *The Naval Side of British History* (Boston: Little, Brown, and company, 1924), p. 138.
137 Julian S. Corbett, *England in the Mediterranean. A Study of the Rise and Influence of British Power Within the Straits, 1603–1713*, Vol. II (London: Longmans, Green and Co., 1904), p. 257.
138 Alfred Stenzel, *Seekriegsgeschichte in ihren wichtigsten Abschnitten mit Berücksichtigung der Seetaktik*, Part 3: *Von 1600 bis 1720* (Hannover/Leipzig: Hahnsche Buchhandlung, 1909), p. 410.
139 Geoffrey Callender, *The Naval Side of British History* (Boston: Little, Brown, and Company, 1924), p. 137.
140 Alfred Stenzel, *Seekriegsgeschichte in ihren wichtigsten Abschnitten mit Berücksichtigung der Seetaktik*, Part 3: *Von 1600 bis 1720* (Hannover/Leipzig: Hahnsche Buchhandlung, 1909), p. 210.
141 Geoffrey Callender, *The Naval Side of British History* (Boston: Little, Brown, and company, 1924), p. 138.
142 Herbert Richmond, *Statesmen and Sea Power* (Oxford: Clarendon Press, first published 1946, reprinted 1947), p. 88.
143 Herbert Richmond, *Statesmen and Sea Power* (Oxford: Clarendon Press, first published 1946, reprinted 1947), p. 89.
144 Shihan de Leila Ingram and Richard Pankhurst, "Somali Migration to Aden," in Silva Jayasuriya and Jean-Pierre Angenot, editors, *Uncovering the History of Africans in Asia* (Leiden: Brill Academic Publications, 2008), p. 108.
145 Caesar E. Farah, The *Sultan's Yemen: 19th Century Challenges to Ottoman Rule* (London: I. B. Tauris Publishers, 2002) p. 120.
146 Anthony Sokol, "Naval Strategy in the Adriatic Sea During the World War," *Proceedings*, 8 (August 1937), p. 1087.
147 James B. Agnew, "From Where Did Our Amphibious Doctrine Come?" *Marine Corps Gazette*, Vol. 63, No. 8 (August 1979), p. 53.
148 Tim Travers, *Gallipoli 1915* (Gloucestershire: Tempus Publishing, Stroud, 2001), p. 270.
149 Jenny Macleod, *Reconsidering Gallipoli* (Manchester/New York: Manchester University Press, 2004), p. 3.
150 Alan Moorehead, *Gallipoli* (London: Hamish Hamilton, 1956), p. 361; Tim Travers, *Gallipoli 1915* (Gloucestershire: Tempus Publishing, Stroud, 2001), p. 229.
151 Torstem Diedrich, "Zur rolle der Nationalen Volksarmee der DDR in der operativen Plannung des Warschauer Paktes unter besonderer Berücksichtigung der 1960s Jahre," in Rüdiger Wentzke, editior, *Die Streitkräfte der DDR und Polens in der Operationsplanung des Warschauer Paktes* (Potsdam: Militärgeschichtliches Forschungsamt, 2010), p. 26.

152 Zbigniew Moszumanski, "Die Polnische Küstenfront auf dem Westlichen Kriegschauplatz," in Rüdiger Wentzke, editor, *Die Streitkräfte der DDR und Polens in der Operationsplanung des Warschauer Paktes* (Potsdam: Militärgeschichtliches Forschungsamt, 2010), p. 80.

153 Czeslaw Szafran, "Die Seekriegsflotte der Volksrepublik Polen in den Vereinten Ostseeflotte des Warschauer Vertrages. Ein Buendnis in Krieg und Frieden," in Rüdiger Wentzke, editor, *Die Streitkräfte der DDR und Polens in der Operationsplanung des Warschauer Paktes* (Potsdam: Militärgeschichtliches Forschungsamt, 2010), p. 92.

9 Capturing the enemy's important positions and basing areas

Another rarely discussed method for obtaining sea control is to capture, at the beginning of hostilities, key positions that afterward could be developed as major or advanced naval bases. In peacetime, such positions are acquired by diplomacy, political concessions or pressure, and economic enticements. In the time of hostilities, the stronger side must use military force to capture such positions for the employment of one's naval forces and aircraft. The control of such points would create prerequisites for the successful employment of one's naval and air forces in the struggle for sea control. Another method is to capture enemy naval/air basing areas from the land side by the quick advance of ground forces supported by the air force.

Capturing important positions/areas

History gives numerous examples of a stronger sea power acquiring some key positions in a given maritime theater, which then were used to employ its naval forces and, in modern era, aircraft in the struggle for sea control. Such positions could be acquired by diplomacy, political/economic pressure, or enticements or by the use of force. Perhaps the best examples of using nonmilitary means to obtain a commanding position in a given sea area are the naval policies and strategies of the Italian maritime republics, specifically Venice and Genoa, in the Mediterranean in the early medieval era. Venice was one of the strongest sea powers in the Mediterranean and Europe in the thirteenth century. Venice needed to have ports for its galleys on their voyages to the Black Sea and Eastern Mediterranean.[1] Its naval power rested largely on the control of several strategically located large islands in the eastern Mediterranean. In addition, Venice also had control of a number of ports in the Morea (classic Peloponnesus), the Aegean Sea, Albania, and Dalmatia. In contrast to other sea powers, it not only allowed but also encouraged various aristocratic Venetian families to govern various smaller islands and places on Greece's mainland coast.[2]

Venice had become a beneficiary of its support for the Fourth Crusade in 1203–1204. After the fall of Constantinople and the end of the Fourth Crusades in 1204, Venice concentrated on obtaining control of those parts of the Byzantine Empire that were of the greatest importance as bases for its fleet. It acquired new territories by using cash, inheritances, diplomacy, and military conquest.[3] Constantinople was Venice's most important naval base, even though it was formally the capital of the Byzantine Empire. Venice owned about three-eighths of the city, including the dockyards and arsenal.[4]

In 1204, Venice obtained control of the Aegean islands and a swath of land from Adrianople to Gallipoli.[5] Crete (formally the Kingdom of Candia) was acquired by Venice in 1205. This island occupied a critically important strategic position because it dominated all Venetian sea routes from the Ionian Sea to Egypt and Syria. A year later, Venice acquired the coastal fortresses of Methoni (Modon) and Koroni (Coron) in Messenia (southwestern part of Peloponnesus).[6] In 1206, Corfu and Durazzo, Albania, were first occupied by Venice. Venice also gained control of Nauplia (Nafplion today) and Argos in 1388. In about 1390, the Triarchy of Negroponte (a crusader state) on the island of Euboea became a Venetian colony. Afterward, it became the main Venetian base in the Aegean between Crete and Constantinople.

Between 1380 and 1420, Venice doubled its territory. Among other territorial acquisitions, Venice extended its control to Corfù (in 1386), Durazzo (1392), Scutari (1396), Lepanto (Naupaktos), and Patras (1406). [7] Venice also considerably extended its foothold in Dalmatia by acquiring control of Cattaro (Kotor today) (1419), Zara (Zadar today), Curzola (Korčula today) (1420), and Lesina (Hvar today) (1424). Venice failed, despite its repeated attempts, to acquire control of Ragusa (Dubrovnik today, which remained independent as a maritime republic). The Kingdom of Cyprus, a tributary state of the Egyptian Mamluks after 1426, became increasingly dominated by Venetian merchants. It came formally under Venice's control in 1489 when Queen Catherina Cornaro (1454–1510) was forced to abdicate.

In the sixteenth and the seventeenth centuries, Venice and the Ottoman Turks engaged in frequent wars for control of the Ionian and Aegean seas and the Levant. Unlike Venice, the Ottoman Turks obtained a commanding position in the Mediterranean exclusively by military conquest. In their war with Venice in 1499–1502, the Ottomans seized the important bases of Koron Modon, Navarino, and Lepanto and thereby firmly established their foothold in the Ionian Sea.[8] In 1517, the Turks conquered Egypt and Syria, as well as the island of Rhodes in 1522. The island of Rhodes was a stronghold of the Knight Hospitalers of St. John. It had a secure and fortified harbor and is separated by about a 12-mile-wide passage from Turkey's coast. Rhodes is located halfway between Istanbul and easternmost Mediterranean. Algiers came under the Ottoman's control in 1529. By the early sixteenth century, Ottoman Turkey was transformed from a continental power to a seaborne empire, both naval and commercial.[9]

In 1574, the Ottoman Turks extended their power into the central and western Mediterranean by conquering Tunis. Thereby, they obtained partial control of the Sicilian Narrows, a gateway between the eastern and western Mediterranean. The Turks captured the islands of Cyprus in 1571 and Crete in 1669.[10] Control of these islands was important for the Turks to eliminate any potential threat to the security of their shipping traffic to/from the Dardanelles and mainland Greece. Venice put up a staunch resistance to the Turks after they landed on Crete in 1645. Its navy defeated the Turks in a battle south of Naxos on 8–10 July 1651 and in the Dardanelles on 21 June 1655 and on 26–27 June 1656. Yet despite all these successes at sea, the main fort of Candia fell to the Turks after a 21-year-long siege.[11]

In the era of sail and early steam, one of the often used methods to establish or reinforce a permanent naval presence in a certain strategically important ocean/sea area was to capture at the very beginning of a war one or several favorably located ports/anchorages. The newly acquired positions would then serve as bases for the fleet operating in a given area. Capturing new positions required very close cooperation between a navy and army. The army would provide troop contingents, and the navy would ensure their safety during the sea transit.

The struggle for obtaining control of strategically important islands and ports characterized naval wars in the Caribbean and the Mediterranean from the late seventeenth and eighteenth centuries in the Caribbean and the Mediterranean. For example, almost any war in Europe between Britain and France and/or Spain quickly spread to the West Indies or the Caribbean. Until the rise of Britain and Dutch sea power, Spain was the paramount power in the Caribbean. Spain controlled most of the mainland coast in the Caribbean and the Gulf of Mexico, plus the islands of Cuba, Puerto Rico, and Hispaniola, or what was then known as the "Spanish Main." This area was the source of enormous wealth (gold, silver, gems, and spices), which made Spain the richest European power. In the late seventieth century, Britain, the Dutch Republic, and France gradually acquired control of many small islands and archipelagoes in the Caribbean. Mahan pointed out that these islands were too small to be held except by a naval power.[12] In the seventeenth century, the Dutch acquired a relatively large number of island groups known as the "Dutch Antilles."[13] Britain's main competitors for power and influence were France and Spain. By the early eighteenth century, Britain controlled Jamaica, Barbados, and some smaller islands, while France acquired Guadalupe, Martinique, and western part of Hispaniola.[14] Britain eventually acquired extensive colonial possessions in the West Indies and in the process greatly reduced the power of Spain.[15] In contrast, France was far less successful than Britain in extending its power to the West Indies.[16]

Dominant positions in the British West Indies were occupied by Jamaica, Barbados, and St. Lucia.[17] Kingston Harbor on Jamaica served for a long time as the principal naval base. The only good anchorage on Trinidad was the Gulf of Paria. Tobago had a number of good sheltered anchorages. One of the key positions in the British West Indies was the 40-mile-wide Anegada Passage between the Virgin Islands (west) and the Leeward group (southeast), which links the Atlantic Ocean and the Caribbean Sea. Other important passages are the 85-mile-wide Grenada Passage (between Grenada and Tobago) and the 19-mile-wide passage between Tobago and Trinidad. More difficult to guard was the 65-mile-wide stretch of Grenadine between St. Vincent and Grenada.[18]

During several major wars in Europe, France, often allied with Spain, tried to wrest control of some key island groups in the British West Indies. Similarly, Britain attempted to reduce the colonial possessions of Spain and France in the West Indies. The British conducted numerous combined (army-navy) operations in the West Indies in the eighteenth century. For example, during the Seven Years' War (1756–1763), the British achieved some easy victories by capturing Barbados (in 1759) and Saint Domingue (1763). However, in their invasion of Martinique (1762), although ultimately successful, they encountered serious French resistance.[19] By the end of the war, France lost all its strongholds in French Canada (including Louisburg) and Martinique in the West Indies and in Pondicherry, India.[20]

Spanish colonial rule in the Americas ended in the aftermath of the American-Spanish War of 1898. By the Treaty of Paris signed on 10 December 1898, Spain ceded Guam, the Philippines, and Puerto Rico to the United States. The United States acquired the use of the excellently located base at Guantanamo in Cuba. Guantanamo has a commanding position in the Windward Passage. Culebra, an island off the east coast of Puerto Rico, guards one shore of the 61-mile-wide Mona Passage (between Puerto Rico and the eastern part of Haiti). In Cuba, the United States also acquired the use of Bahia Honda, nearly opposite Key West. Both of these bases guarded the entrance to the Gulf of Mexico.[21]

During its frequent wars with France and Spain in the seventeenth and eighteenth centuries, Britain captured a number of ports/anchorages in the Mediterranean to subsequently serve as the bases for the Royal Navy's detached squadrons. For example, during the early days of the rise of Britain as a major sea power, one of major problems for its presence in the Mediterranean was the lack of suitable and secure bases for its fleet. Until the beginning of the War of the Spanish Succession in 1701, the British did not have a single base for their fleet in the Mediterranean. In 1704, they captured their first base in the Mediterranean, Gibraltar. Afterward, they intensified their efforts to obtain bases in the western Mediterranean. For example, in August 1707, the Anglo-Dutch fleet, led by Admiral John Leake (1656–1720) arrived in the Mediterranean. Its main mission was to supply the Anglo-Dutch armies in Catalonia from Italy. In August 1707, Leake secured the surrender of Sardinia, then a part of the Spanish Mediterranean Empire. Sardinia served as a principal granary for Catalonia. It also possessed a good harbor at Cagliari. However, the British coveted to possess a much better located base at Port Mahón on the island of Minorca. This base is only some 300 miles away from Toulon. On 25 August 1708, Leake arrived at Port Mahón and landed marines. On 14 September, the

Anglo-Dutch troops under General James Stanhope (1673–1721) arrived from Barcelona and landed at Port Mahón. The defenders withdraw to the fortress at St. Philip. The entire island was conquered within a month. The capture of Mahón secured for the allies a foothold in the western Mediterranean. Yet it was too late to change the course of the war. The naval contribution to the war was to control the export of grain from North Africa, which supplied the Anglo-Dutch army in Catalonia and deny it to the French.[22]

By the Treaty of Utrecht signed in April 1713, Britain gained control of Gibraltar, Minorca, Acadia (renamed as Nova Scotia), all of Newfoundland and St. Kitts (hitherto divided), and undisputed possession of Hudson's Bay, Canada. The Spanish Netherlands was transferred to Austria.[23] Possession of Port Mahón increased rather than decreased British strategic difficulties in the Mediterranean. Although Port Mahón was very favorably located for operations against Toulon, it was also a liability. Even with a substantial garrison, it was too large to be defended because a determined enemy was able to land at many unexpected places on the island. The population remained stubbornly indifferent to British rule. Minorca could feed itself only in good years. The British troops had to be supplied from overseas, usually from Algiers. British operations were hampered by the necessity of defending their base and its communications. In peacetime, the Royal Navy left only a few ships in the Mediterranean; so in the spring of 1756 when the Seven Years' War started, there was nothing to protect Minorca but an understrength garrison.[24] The French captured the island in 1756 but were forced to return it to the British under the terms of the Treaty of Paris, which ended the Seven Years' War. In 1782, the British lost control of Minorca to the combined French-Spanish force. The British formally ceded the island to Spain in 1783 under the Treaty of Versailles, which ended the American Revolutionary War. Minorca was again invaded and occupied by the British in 1798 during the French Revolutionary Wars. It was permanently returned to France under the terms of the Treaty of Amiens in March 1803.

Britain acquired the island of Malta in 1800 when the island voluntarily came under its rule. Under the terms of Treaty of Amiens, Britain was obliged to relinquish its control of Malta but refused to do so. Malta occupies a commanding position in the central Mediterranean. This 122-square-mile island is located some 50 miles south of Sicily, 175 miles east of Tunisia, and about 210 miles from Libya. It was one of the most important British naval and later air bases until 1964 when Malta became independent.

In the modern era, the capabilities of naval forces to support the transport and landing of friendly troops over long distances were substantially increased, compared with what they were in the era of sail and early steam. This allowed a stronger side to obtain a large degree of control of the sea surface by focusing initially not on the destruction of enemy naval forces but on capturing selected "decisive points" on enemy-held islands/archipelagoes or mainland coast. These decisive points are usually major ports/

naval bases and/or airfields. Very often, the larger objective was to obtain control of some economically or politically important area. The initial landings were often conducted over the uncommanded sea. After capturing the initial landing point, the follow-on ground forces were employed to consolidate and expand control over the larger land area. By seizing control of the key airfields, it is possible to establish control of the air and partial control of the sea surface within the effective range of one's fighter aircraft. This, in turn, allows the attacker to bypass enemy strongpoints and land in the enemy's rear. Initially, naval forces would be employed primarily for providing protection to the transport of friendly troops. Afterward, they would play a critical role in obtaining control of the subsurface and, jointly with land-based aircraft, a larger degree of control of the surface.

An excellent example of obtaining control relatively quickly over a larger part of the ocean/sea area was the Japanese conquest of Malaya, Philippines, the Netherlands East Indies (NEI), the Andamans, and Burma in December 1941–April 1942. The Japanese were highly successful although they did not initially possess either general or local sea control.

The primary reason for the Japanese decision to invade and occupy British Malaya and the NEI was to obtain control over their natural resources. The 130,000-square-mile-large British Malaya (the Malay Peninsula, British Borneo) was the world's leading producer of rubber and tin.[25] The NEI occupied a land area of about 733,000 square miles and had population of some 70 million.[26] The NEI extended for some 3,000 miles along the Equator.[27] In 1939, the NEI produced 35 percent of the world's oil and 17 percent of tin.[28] Most oilfields in the NEI were located in Dutch Borneo, eastern Java, and eastern Sumatra.[29] However, only oil extracted on the island of Tarakan could be used for diesel engine without refining it. The rest of the NEI's oil had to be sent mostly to three refineries in Balikpapan in Borneo, at Brandan (near Marda), and at Pladjoi (near Palembang) on Sumatra. Tin was extracted on the islands of Banka, Billiton, and Singkep off Sumatra.[30] Coal was extracted at Ombilin and Boekitasem. In the Philippines, gold was found on Luzon and Mindanao. The Philippines also had quantities of iron ore and chrome and limited deposits of coal.[31] Nevertheless, for the Japanese, the Philippines were strategically not economically important.[32]

The Japanese prepared detailed studies on the sequence of operations aimed at eliminating Allied power in the Far East in case a decision for going to war was made. They considered two basic courses of action: capturing: either (1) Philippine Islands (PI), the NEI, and Malaya or (2) Malaya, the NEI, and the Philippines. The question of whether to invade the Philippines and Malaya simultaneously or consecutively depended on the potential effectiveness of preliminary air strikes. The only advanced Japanese air bases were on Formosa and southern French Indochina. The distances of these bases from the initial landing points were just within the effective range of Zero fighters (300–400 miles).[33] The initial plan to use fast carriers in support of these operations was dropped in November 1941 because the Combined Fleet needed every available carrier for the attack on Pearl Harbor. In addition, the night performance of Zero fighters had been improved so that morning strikes could be more effective without carriers.[34] The Japanese' final decision was to invade simultaneously with an attack on the U.S. Pacific Fleet in Pearl Harbor, the Philippines, and Malaya, followed by the capture of Borneo, Celebes (Sulawesi today), Sumatra, and Java.[35]

The Japanese divided their First Operational Stage of War into three phases: (1) invasion of the Philippines, British Malaya, Borneo, Celebes, Timor, northern Sumatra, and the Bismarck Archipelago; (2) invasion of Java and the occupation, at opportune times, of airfields in southern Burma; and (3) the pacification of the occupied territories and, depending on the situation, the completion of operations in Burma.[36] They believed that the capture of the Philippines could be accomplished within 50 days, Malaya within 100 days, and the NEI within 150 days.[37]

For the Japanese, a major consideration in selecting their initial objectives was the need for a quick capture of the selected ports/naval bases and airfields, which then would be used to obtain air superiority over a larger land/sea area. The Japanese also wanted to capture major oilfields/refineries quickly so that they could be put to use for their war effort. Another consideration was the need to protect their flanks from possible enemy attacks.[38] For example, the Philippines had to be captured because they flanked the NEI. If left in U.S. hands, they would pose a significant threat to Japanese communications between the home islands and the Southern Resources Area. The U.S.-controlled Wake and Guam and the British-controlled Gilberts had to be seized in order to eliminate potential attacks from the flanks on the Japanese strongpoints in the Mandated Islands.[39]

Because of the heavy commitment of Army forces in China, the Japanese had assigned only 11 (out of a total of 51) divisions for the pending conquests in Southeast Asia. They also assigned two Army air groups with 700 aircraft. The IJN committed a major part of its forces and 1,700 naval aircraft to its attack on Pearl Harbor and in support of the army operations in Southeast Asia and the central Pacific. The Japanese planners were convinced of success despite an apparent large disconnect between the factors of space and force.[40]

The Japanese made extensive preparations to seize British Malaya and Singapore. The objective was to destroy British power in Malaya and thereby establish a protective right flank for a major thrust into the South Seas.[41] The initial landing was made at Kota Bharu, British Malaya, shortly after midnight on 7/8 December. On the same day, the Japanese landed at two places on Thailand's east coast: Singora (Songkhla today) and Pattani (some 65 miles south of Singora).[42] Both landings were unopposed.[43] After Singora, Patani, and Kota Bharu were captured, Japanese army aircraft obtained air superiority over Malaya, and provided direct air support to forces advancing on Singapore.[44] On 8 January, the Japanese landed at several places on Singapore Island. By dawn, some 23,000 Japanese troops were already ashore.[45] Japanese troops entered the naval base on 11 February. Singapore fell to the Japanese four days later. In fewer than eight days, the Japanese captured an island defended by more than 60,000 troops. The Japanese force that conquered British Malaya was half as large as the Allied forces.[46]

Singapore occupies an extremely favorable strategic position. It is some 1,500 nautical miles away from both Colombo and Hongkong. It is about 3,000 nm away from Tokyo and Yokohama. In 1941, the radius of action of naval forces based at Singapore was estimated at 2,000 nm and encompassed three-fourths of the territories under British control in Asia. The entire trade to/from Europe to the Far East passed through the Strait of Malacca. From Singapore, it was possible to control access routes in the Indian Ocean and the Pacific and in Siam (Thailand).[47]

In the invasion of the Philippines, the Japanese objective was to eliminate U.S. air and naval strength in the Philippines. It mattered little to the Japanese how long and desperate the defense of the U.S. Army troops would be in the Philippines.[48] To achieve a quick victory, the Japanese assigned overwhelming strength to cover amphibious landings. They also carried out multiple-pronged attacks. The initial landings were aimed at capturing airfields so that Army aircraft could provide support to the troops on the ground. The key element for the successful invasion of the Philippines was to achieve surprise. Hence, the Japanese eliminated surface preliminary bombardments of the landing objectives and tactical air fires. The principal Japanese objective was to quickly capture Luzon, the largest island and also where the bulk of the American forces were deployed. The main landing at Lingayen Gulf was aimed at capturing the capital of Manila.[49]

The Japanese invasion of the Philippines started with massive air attacks on Clark and Nichols airfields, near Manila, on 8 December 1941. By then, the U.S. commanders in the Philippines were well aware of the Japanese attack on Pearl Harbor. The Japanese were greatly surprised that the U.S. heavy bombers and almost all the fighters were still on the ground. The Japanese destroyed half of the heavy bombers and one-third of the U.S. Far East Air Force (FEAF). Many U.S. aircraft were damaged. On 10 December, all the remaining U.S. heavy bombers were withdrawn to the south. The reconnaissance aircraft followed four days later, after losing half of their strength.[50]

The Japanese preliminary landings in the Philippines started on 8 December, when a small number of troops landed on the island of Batan in the Bashi Channel to develop an airfield for the use by Army aircraft. However, the success of the air attacks on Manila airfields made this airfield redundant. Hence, two days later, part of the same force was withdrawn and landed on Kamigin Island in the Babuyan Islands.[51] The invasion of Luzon started on 10 December, when the Japanese troops landed at Aparri to capture an advanced air base.[52] To protect the rear of the main forces at Lingayen Gulf and to secure the northern part of

Luzon, the Japanese planned a landing at Pandan, some 3 miles southeast of Vigan.[53] The landing at Legaspi on 11 December was aimed at controlling the San Bernardino Strait.[54] After the initial landing, the Japanese rapidly repaired airfields and sent troop reinforcements to the landing points.[55] On 22 December, the Japanese main forces landed at Lingayen Gulf, and two days later one element landed at Lamon Bay. The Japanese entered Manila on 2 January 1942. The last strongholds of the American and Filipino troops on the Bataan Peninsula and Corregidor fell to the victorious Japanese on 9 April 1942.[56]

In the meantime, the Japanese landed at Davao, Mindanao, on 20 December. The same day, they established a seaplane base at Talomo Bay, south of Davao. A part of the same force, reinforced by one aircraft carrier, landed on Jolo Island, Sulu Archipelago. Mindonao was occupied by 25 December. The first fighters of the Eleventh Air Fleet arrived at Mindanao on 23 December.[57]

Borneo had great military importance to the Japanese because the enemy could threaten the sea routes to Japanese-held Malaya and form a barrier to an east-west Japanese advance. Most of Borneo was in Dutch possession, except for northern part, which was under British control.[58] In British Borneo, most oilfields were located at Miri, northern Sarawak.[59] On 16 December, the Japanese troops landed at Miri and captured the nearby airfield.[60] A hastily built British airfield at Kuching fell on 24 December.[61] On 19 January, British forces in Borneo surrendered. By 22 December, the 22nd Air Flotilla was already operating from the airfield at Miri.[62]

The Japanese plan for the conquest of the NEI focused on seizing oil-rich resources as quickly as possible. The Japanese began to concentrate their Army, Navy, and Air forces over an area 2,000 miles from east to west and some 1,000 miles from north to south. Operations had to be carried out nearly simultaneously to prevent the enemy from destroying resources, especially oilfields. The Japanese operational idea (scheme) for capturing Java envisaged landings at selected points in Dutch Borneo, Celebes, Ambon, Timor, and Sumatra, followed by an all-out attack on Java. They carefully synchronized their advances toward the NEI. The Central Invasion Force would initially capture the island of Tarakan, the port of Balikpapan, and the city of Banjarmasin in Dutch Borneo. The Eastern Invasion Force would capture Menado (Manado today), Kendari, and Makassar in Celebes, the island of Ambon in the Moluccas (Maluku islands today), and the islands of Timor and Bali. The Western Invasion Force would capture the oilfields at Palembang and on Banka Island in southern Sumatra. Two naval air flotillas based in Formosa would be moved to the newly acquired bases and provide air support to the Army forces.[63]

The Japanese landed on Tarakan on 11 January 1942, and the island was secured after brief but fierce resistance the next day. Only five days later, the Japanese started to use the airfield there. On 24 January, the Japanese landed at Balikpapan.[64] Bandjarmasin was captured on 16 February.

By 28 January, Japanese naval land-based aircraft began to the airfield at Balikpapan and after 23 February at Bandjarmasin. With these landings, the Japanese obtained control of the northern approaches to the Makassar Strait.[65] In only ten days, the Japanese were able consolidate their positions in both British and Dutch Borneo and then use them as staging points for successive landings.[66]

The 67,400-square-mile island of Celebes occupies a central position between Borneo and the Moluccas. It extends for some 520 miles in an east-west direction and 420 miles along north-south axis. Celebes guards one shore of the Makassar Strait. The Japanese captured Menado on 23/24 January and Kendari one day later. The air base at Kendari, the best in the NEI, was immediately put into operation by the 21st Air Flotilla. These bases put Japanese bombers within range of Surabaya with its naval base and allowed the Japanese to disrupt the arrival of ABDA (American-British-Dutch-Australian) air reinforcements. A primary naval base was established at 45-square-mile Staring Bay, just to the south of Kendari. [67]

The capture of Kendari also opened the sea route to Ambon Island, east of Makassar. The 300-square-mile island of Ambon in the Banda Sea occupied the most important defensive position between Surabaya, east Java, and Darwin, Australia.[68] The Japanese attacked Ambon town on 30 January. It fell only three days later.[69] On Ambon, the Japanese also acquired the use of the 35-square-mile Amboina Bay, flanking the route between the Philippines and Australia via the Torres Strait.[70]

The 11,880-square-mile island of Timor is the easternmost of the Lesser Sunda Islands. The island was partly under Portuguese rule, with its capital in Kupang, and partly under the Dutch, with its capital in Dili. Timor had negligible natural resources. However, it was militarily very important for the Japanese. The airfields at Kupang and Dili served as staging areas for aircraft reinforcements to Java.[71] Australia was within the range of fighter aircraft from Timor.[72] It also flanked the sea route from Australia to the Indian Ocean via the Torres Strait.[73] On 20 February, a Japanese troop contingent landed at Kupang and Dili.[74] Only four days later, all of Timor was under Japanese control.[75]

The Japanese planned to seize the 186,000-square-mile island of Sumatra as a buffer against an attack on Malaya from the west.[76] Sumatra also guarded the western shore of the Strait of Malacca. The Japanese had to both capture the oilfields and drive out enemy forces from the southeastern part of Sumatra and thereby acquire positions from which to attack western Java. The Japanese made their initial assaults on Palembang and Bangka on 14 February. By 28 March 1942, all of Sumatra was in their hands.

By capturing Celebes, Ambon, Timor, and Sumatra, the Japanese isolated Java from the rest of the NEI territory. The most important part of their plan for the invasion of Java was cutting off communications with Australia, Port Darwin in particular.[77] This was the reason for the Japanese carrier raid on Port Darwin on 19 February. It resulted in eight enemy ships sunk, nine damaged, and 18 aircraft destroyed, plus the destruction of valuable stores ashore and heavy damage to the airport. Darwin was temporarily abandoned for fear of another Japanese raid.[78]

The 53,600-square-mile island of Java occupied the most important position in the entire NEI. With its 30 million inhabitants (in 1941), Java was the most densely populated island in the archipelago. It was the principal administrative and industrial center in the entire NEI.[79] On 19 February, as a preliminary to the invasion of Java, a Japanese troop contingent, staged at Makassar, landed on the island of Bali, just off the eastern tip of Java.[80] The Japanese main initial objectives on Java were to capture the airfields at Surabaya, Semarang, Bandung, and Batavia (Jakarta today). The naval base at Surabaya, some 360 miles eastward of Batavia, had good anchorages for seaplanes. Three airfields were located within a short distance of the port.[81] The Japanese forces assigned to the invasion of Java moved from Cam Ranh Bay, French Indochina, Jolo, Sulu archipelago, and Makassar Strait. These forces aimed to land troops at the eastern, central, and western parts of Java.[82]

For the invasion of Java, the Japanese assigned some 100,000 men of the 16th Army, supported by the Eastern and Western Naval Forces. On 25 February, a preliminary landing took place on Bawean Island some 85 miles north of Surabaya.[83] The main landings took place in the Surabaya and Batavia areas on 28 February/01 March.[84] By 9 March 1942, the entire NEI was in Japanese hands. In the process, they had decimated the ABDA Command's forces that opposed them. Australia became directly threatened by the Japanese control of the NEI.

The Japanese advance toward Java resembled a giant octopus with multiple tentacles. The initial landings were aimed at capturing not a large land area but only few selected key ports/cities and nearby airfields. From each newly acquired position, the Japanese obtained local sea and air superiority before making another landing. They concentrated overwhelming naval and air power at each point of attack. The Japanese land and naval forces never operated beyond the effective range of land-based aircraft unless they had carrier support. Each time the ABDA command tried to consolidate its defensive positions, they were faced by Japanese airbases in their front and flanks and sometimes even in their rear.[85] Although the Japanese fought several major and many minor engagements with the ABDA forces, most of them took place after their troops had already captured airfields and ports. The most important were the night action off Balikpapan on 23/24 January, the Battle of Makassar Strait (also known as the Action of Madura Strait) on 4 February, the encounter in the Bandung Strait (off Bali) on 18–20 February, the Battle of the Java Sea on 27 February (main action), and the night battle in the Sunda Strait on 28 February/1 March. Except for the encounter off Balikpapan, where ABDA forces sunk several transports, the Japanese won victories in all the naval actions with the ABDA forces.

The Japanese planned to capture resource-rich Burma. Afterward, Burma would be used for staging attacks on British shipping off eastern India and on the British Eastern Fleet.[86] On 22 January 1942, the Japanese main forces moved into Burma. By 7 March, British troops evacuated Rangoon. By mid-May 1942, the Japanese occupied Burma. With that, they cut off supplies to China from overseas by land and sea and threatened northeastern India.[87]

The occupation of British Malaya greatly increased for the Japanese importance of obtaining control of the Andaman/Nicobar archipelago in the Bay of Bengal. The Andamans/Nicobars are located some 250 miles southwest of Rangoon. They guard the northern approaches to the Strait of Malacca and the Singapore Strait. Control of the Andamans/Nicobars was also important for protecting sea routes for the Japanese 15th Army in Burma. The only military objective on the Andamans/Nicobars was Port Blair, which Japanese force captured on 23 March without encountering any resistance.

The Japanese also moved to strengthen their position in the Mandated Islands. On 8 December, the Japanese began air attacks on the U.S.-controlled islands of Guam, Wake, and Howland. Two days later, the Japanese troops invaded Wake and Guam. They suffered a temporary setback in the initial assault on Wake but succeeded in their second attempt on 22–23 December.[88]

The original Japanese plan for war envisaged the occupation of positions in the Gilberts and Ellice Islands, plus Nauru and Ocean islands. The Gilberts and Ellices were British-mandated territories. They could provide airstrips for American attacks in the Marshalls or for Japanese attacks on American supply lines to Australia. The Japanese captured Makin on 9 December 1941, and one day they landed on Tarawa in the Gilberts. These islands would be used as air bases to strengthen the defense of the strategic outer defense line.[89] The IJN planned to occupy Ocean and Nauru islands so that it could disrupt U.S. lines of communication from Australia. However, these plans were delayed.[90]

The Japanese incorporated the invasion of the Bismarck Archipelago into their plan for the First Operational Stage of War in the Pacific, developed in November 1941. In their view, a major base at Truk, Central Carolines, would not be secure as long as Rabaul was left in the enemy's hands.[91] On 23 January 1942, the Japanese occupied Rabaul, New Britain, and Kavieng, New Ireland. Rabaul has an excellent landlocked harbor. It was the key position for controlling the Bismarck Sea and New Guinea.[92] The fall of Rabaul greatly alarmed the Australian government and populace. Australia's Northeast Area became virtually unprotected.[93] The Japanese spread out of Rabaul and captured several decisive points in eastern New Guinea and the northern Solomons. On 8 March, they captured Lae and Salamaua, the key positions for control of the northern Huon Peninsula and entrance to the Bismarck Sea.[94] On 30 March, they captured the Buka Island and Shortlands guarding the northern and southern approaches to

Bougainville, which was occupied the next day.[95] They then started the construction of airfields on each of these three islands.[96] The Admiralty Islands in the Bismarck Sea were captured on 8 April 1942.[97] They occupy a central position in regard to New Britain and northern coast of New Guinea.

By end of March 1942, the Japanese had gained control of Southeast Asia and the southwest Pacific, rich in natural resources, and incorporated it into their Greater Asia Co-Prosperity Sphere. Their success was due to excellent planning and execution, as well as superiority in tactics and training.[98] The obtained control of a rather large land/sea area in remarkably short time and with minimum losses.

Seizing enemy basing areas

Ground forces can make a significant contribution in the struggle for sea control in the littorals. For a side on the strategic offensive on land, ground forces, by their advance along the coast, would capture naval/air bases and ports and thereby steadily reduce the ability of the enemy's naval forces in the struggle for sea control. In the extreme case, the loss of the entire naval basing area would preclude the employment of the enemy's naval forces, and it might even lead to their internment in the ports of a neutral country. In some cases, the side on the strategic offensive on land was able to obtain sea control by relying almost exclusively on its ground forces and with little or no support by its naval forces. For example, Alexander the Great (356–323 BC), in his conquest of Asia Minor and Egypt as a prelude to attacking the heart of the Persian Empire, decided first to secure his rear base by eliminating the Persian naval presence in the eastern Mediterranean. In 334 BC, he advanced to Miletus (Milet today) a few miles southeast of the island of Samos and the most important Persian naval base on the Aegean. The Persian emperor Darius III (Artashata) (c. 380–330 BC) suffered a heavy defeat at Granicus River (Biga Çayı today) but still had enormous military resources at his disposal. Alexander the Great did not fear Darius III's army, but the Persians with their 400 ships were greatly superior in naval strength to Alexander's fleet of 160 ships. He avoided fighting a battle off Miletus and instead decided to capture Persian controlled harbors and ports by using his army. Alexander the Great believed (falsely) that his fleet would be of little use, so he lay up his ships, paid his seamen, and turned them into soldiers. He then advanced to the port of Halicarnassus (Bodrum today), Anatolia, which he stormed and destroyed. With that, the Persians lost their last base in the Aegean. Afterward, Alexander the Great advanced toward Lycia (Likya today) and Pamphylia (the stretch of southern coast of Asia Minor between Lycia and Cilicia) to wrest control of the coast and thereby render the Persian fleet useless. He steadily deprived the Persians of their bases and ports as he advanced southward along the Eastern Mediterranean coast. By the fall of 333 BC, the entire coastline from Cilicia (Cukurova today) (the southern coast of Asia Minor) to the Hellespont (Dardanelles; Çanakkale Boğazi in Turkish) was in his hands.[99]

Darius was decisively beaten in the Battle of Issus (near Iskenderun) on 5 November 333 BC, Anatolia. By then, Alexander the Great controlled the coastline as far as Alexandretta (Iskenderun today). He decided to continue his advance down the Syrian coast to Gaza and thence to Egypt. His principal military objective was to capture Babylon. He was aware that to do that, he must have his home base secure from any Persian attack. To obtain that security, Alexander needed to utterly destroy Persian naval supremacy. He decided to build a large fleet to capture the entire coastline all the way to the Nile River. Alexander believed that the Phoenicians and Cypriots would be compelled to join him. By adding their fleets to his own, he would obtain full naval control and complete mercantile supremacy. A second line of communications with Alexander's home base would be established, thereby obviating, if necessary, the difficulties of using routes overland should any of the former Persian states revolt against him.[100]

In the era of mobile warfare as was the case in World War II, armies supported by air forces greatly contributed to the successful outcome of the struggle for sea control by capturing the enemy's naval/air basing areas. Then enemy surface forces and submarines were unable to either dispute sea control or freely support ground troops in their defensive operations on the coast. For example, in the German invasion of Soviet Russia, Army Group North advanced quickly along the Baltic coast in the first few weeks after the beginning of the hostilities on 22 June 1941. By 1 July, German troops seized Windau (Ventspils today), and Riga fell into their hands three days later. The southern shore of the Gulf of Riga, including the port of Dünamünde (Daugavgr va today), was captured, and by 8 July, the Germans entered the port of Pernau (Pärnu today), Estonia. By mid-July, however, the German advance slowed down because of stiffening Soviet resistance, and the front stabilized northeast of Riga. The Soviets held off the German troops along the coast and thereby retained control of Reval (Tallinn today). The German 18th Army advanced farther east and by 7 August reached the coast of the Gulf of Finland at Kunda and Juminda Cape, about 30 miles east of Reval. By doing this, the Germans cut off the land connection between Reval and Narva. On 27 August, the German 42nd Army Corps reached the suburbs of Reval. The Soviet troops continued to hold off German attacks on the Baltic islands of Moon, Oesel, and Dago (Hiiumaa). They also stubbornly defended the fortress Hanko at the western entrance of the Gulf of Finland.

By September 1941, Army Group North seized the entire Soviet-controlled coast with the exception of the eastern part of the Gulf of Finland. The German army, supported by the Luftwaffe, played the principal role in reducing the Soviet naval position to only a small stretch of coast in the inner part of the Gulf of Finland. Besides Kronshtadt and Leningrad, the Soviets also retained control of two islands in the inner part of the Gulf, Lavansaari and Seiskari.[101] On 3 December 1941, the Soviets evacuated their base at Hangö.[102] Yet the Germans and the Finns could not operate in the Bay of Kronshtadt and therefore could not destroy the remainder of Soviet surface ships.[103]

In late October, the Supreme Command of the Wehrmacht (Oberkommando der Wehrmacht, OKW) believed that the Soviets might send their heavy ships to be interned in Sweden. To prevent this, a so-called Baltic Fleet was formed (it included, among other ships, the 52,600-ton (full load) battleship *Tirpitz*). This "fleet" was in existence for only a few days before it was dissolved because it became clear that the Soviets intended to keep their remaining battleships and cruisers in the Kronshtadt-Leningrad area.[104]

The situation in the Black Sea was more complicated than in the Baltic because initially the Germans did not have any naval forces deployed in that area. The German Army Group South and the Romanian Army, supported by the Luftwaffe, made a major contribution in denying the Soviet Black Sea Fleet control of the surface. The German Army Group South advanced through the southern part of Ukraine with a twofold objective: (1) to capture the Crimean Peninsula, with its large naval base Sevastopol and other Ukrainian ports; and (2) to capture the oil fields in the Caucasus. The German and Romanian troops advanced quickly along the coast and seized the Soviet naval bases and ports on their way. However, they encountered, not unexpectedly, heavy Soviet resistance in their attack on the port of Odessa. In mid-October, the Soviets were forced to evacuate Odessa, but they were successful in delaying the German advance. Because of unexpectedly strong Soviet resistance, German troops did not reach the shore of the Sea of Azov until the end of September 1941. One month later, the Germans occupied most of the Crimea, including the Kerch Peninsula. The Sevastopol fortress did not fall into German hands until early July 1942.

The German summer 1942 offensive in Southern Russia was initially highly successful. By mid-July, the German troops crossed the Kerch Strait, and their advance units entered Krasnodar on the Kuban River in early August. The major port Novorossiysk was captured in September. The Soviets were left with only the small naval bases of Tuapse, Poti, and Batum on the Caucasus coast.[105] They were never captured by the Germans. The activity of Soviet naval forces remained a constant nuisance to German supply traffic in the Black Sea.[106]

Soviet ground forces were the principal factor in the reoccupation of the Baltic coast in 1944–1945. The Soviet offensive against Army Group North started in January 1944, when the German 18th Army was thrown back from its positions around Leningrad. By late June, after some very heavy fighting, the Soviets broke through the fortifications of the Finnish Mannerheim Line and captured the city of Vyborg. In July, they resumed their offensive against Narva and forced the Germans to fall back. Reval was cut off, and soon Estonia was lost to the Germans. By September 1944, the situation became even more precarious for the Germans after the Finns signed the armistice with the Soviets. Soon afterward, the Soviets began to recapture the Baltic Islands. The Germans offered a stubborn defense but were forced to evacuate their last remaining troops from the Sörve Peninsula on 23 November.

Soviet fortunes in the Black Sea Theater took a turn for the better after the end of the Battle for Stalingrad in January 1943. The Soviet offensive forced the Germans and their allies to fall back, and the front stabilized temporarily along the Mius River. The Germans established the Kuban bridgehead on the Taman Peninsula in January 1963 to supply by sea the troops on the southernmost part of their front. The Germans abandoned the Kuban bridgehead during the Soviet Novorossiysk-Taman operation (10 September-9 October 1943) and withdrew to Crimea. The Soviet advance continued along the coast, and by late October 1943, Soviet troops stood on the Dniester River. This forced the Germans to evacuate the port of Kherson, and the front stabilized until the end of February 1944.

After the Soviets resumed their offensive in southern Ukraine in February 1944, their troops recaptured several smaller ports. By late March, the Soviets captured a large port of Nikolayev, thereby cutting off a large number of German troops in the Crimea. The Germans conducted a large-scale evacuation of Odessa in April 1944, followed by the evacuation of their troops from the Crimea in May. The Soviet successes on land had other consequences. In the summer of 1944, the Turks closed the Straits to Axis ships, and in August, Romania and Bulgaria capitulated. With this, German naval forces lost their base of operations in the Black Sea.[107]

History also provides examples what negative consequences might ensue if ground forces fail to capture a critically important part of the enemy coast. For example, in World War I, one of the major reasons for the German Navy's inability to operate freely on the open spaces of the ocean was the Entente's control of both exits of the North Sea. The situation would have been very complicated for Britain and France if the Germans had occupied the French coast of the English Channel. The Schlieffen Plan was focused exclusively on defeating the major part of the French Army by advancing south of Paris and then northward toward the French fortifications in Alsace and Lorraine. Consequently, the German Great General Staff did not envisage capturing the Channel ports in the first months of the war. Clearly, the German General Staff did not consider the Navy's need to use the French Channels and Atlantic ports and thereby obtain better strategic position to fight a general fleet action. Yet this was not done. In contrast, the main mission of the Royal Navy in the initial phase of war was to provide unconditional security of the B.E.F.; everything else had secondary importance.[108]

Although the British did not know the German plan, they were alarmed with the German advance in France in August 1914, which potentially threatened the loss of the Channel ports of Ostend, Boulogne, and Le Havre. In addition, the possible British defeat in the Battle of Mons on 23 August led

Admiral Sir John Jellicoe (1859–1935) to warn that the Grand Fleet would shift its bases in case the Germans seized Calais and thereby obtained control of one shore of the Strait of Dover. Also, as a direct result of a possible major defeat on land, the British were faced with the prospect of a drastic redistribution of their fleet. The British Admiralty began to prepare plans to withdraw from the fleet all stores not immediately required by the army. Cherbourg was favored by the War Office as a new base because of the ease with which the Cotentin Peninsula could be made impregnable, so long as the British had command of the Channel. For that, however, it was critical that the Flemish ports did not fall into German hands. Therefore, the Admiralty, while pushing all preparations for transferring the base, did not want to abandon the more easterly Channel harbors, specifically Dunkirk, Calais, and Boulogne.[109]

Since the antiquity navies have required a sufficient number of favorably located and developed naval bases in home waters. This problem is more complicated for a major sea power because it must secure a number of major or advanced bases in the operating areas far away from home waters. It was one of the major responsibilities of grand and naval strategy to obtain access to naval bases overseas by using diplomacy, political influence, and economic incentives. In time of war, new bases in a maritime theater would be obtained primarily by means of military force. Yet in some cases, diplomatic pressure might be sufficient to force a weaker power to give access to its naval bases and airfields.

In the modern era, the greatly increased mobility and reach of naval forces and aircraft allowed a stronger side to occupy a rather large area relatively quickly. The newly obtained positions were then used to establish air superiority over a larger land/sea area within the effective range of the land-based aircraft. This method of bypassing enemy strongpoints, or "leapfrogging," is more likely to be successful against peninsular or archipelago positions because they offer a selection of multiple objectives. The defender would then have generally great difficulties in deducing where the next blow would come. It requires that a stronger side achieve surprise both in the selection of the decisive points and in the timing of the attacks. This method also requires bringing an overwhelming powet to bear at a decisive point and time.

Another method of obtaining a large degree of sea control is the capture of enemy naval bases/airfields by friendly ground troops on the coast. This was not always fully appreciated by both naval theoreticians and practitioners. Success in offensive operations on the coast would require strong and effective support from the air. Yet ground troops alone cannot obtain control of the sea in the littorals. They can only facilitate the employment of one's naval forces in the struggle for sea control. Likewise, land-based aircraft can obtain control of the air and a large degree of control of the surface. However, they have only limited capabilities to obtain control of the subsurface. They also lack the staying power and presence needed to maintain sea control.

Notes

1 Siriol Davies and Jack L. Davis, "Greeks, Venice, and the Ottoman Empire," *Hesperia Supplements*, Vol. 40, *Between Venice and Istanbul: Colonial Landscape in Early Modern Greece*, (2007), p. 26.
2 Kenneth M. Setton, *The Papacy and the Levant, 1204–1571*. Vol. 1: *The Thirteenth and Fourteenth Centuries* (Philadelphia, PA: American Philosophical Society, 1976), p. 19.
3 Monique O'Connell, *Men of Empire: Power and Negotiation in Venice's Maritime State* (Baltimore, MD: Johns Hopkins University Press, 2009), p. 23
4 Frederic C. Lane, *Venice. A Maritime Republic* (Baltimore, MD: John Hopkins University Press, 1973), p. 43.
5 Monique O'Connell, *Men of Empire: Power and Negotiation in Venice's Maritime State* (Baltimore, MD: Johns Hopkins University Press, 2009), p. 18
6 Monique O'Connell, *Men of Empire: Power and Negotiation in Venice's Maritime State* (Baltimore, MD: Johns Hopkins University Press, 2009), p.19; Siriol Davies and Jack L. Davis, "Greeks, Venice, and the Ottoman Empire," *Hesperia Supplements*, Vol. 40, *Between Venice and Istanbul: Colonial Landscape in Early Modern Greece*, (2007), p. 25.
7 Monique O'Connell, *Men of Empire: Power and Negotiation in Venice's Maritime State* (Baltimore, MD: Johns Hopkins University Press, 2009), p. 22.
8 Svatopluk Soucek, "Naval Aspects of the Ottoman Conquests of Rhodes, Cyprus and Crete," *Studia Islamica*, No. 98/99 (2004), p. 240.
9 Svatopluk Soucek, "Naval Aspects of the Ottoman Conquests of Rhodes, Cyprus and Crete," *Studia Islamica*, No. 98/99 (2004), pp. 219–20.
10 Svatopluk Soucek, "Naval Aspects of the Ottoman Conquests of Rhodes, Cyprus and Crete," *Studia Islamica*, No. 98/99 (2004), p. 219.
11 Frederic C. Lane, *Venice. A Maritime Republic* (Baltimore, MD: Johns Hopkins University Press, 1973), p. 409.
12 Alfred T. Mahan, *The Influence of Sea Power upon History, 1660–1783* (Boston: Little, Brown, and Company, 1939), p. 256.
13 They consisted of the "windward" islands (Aruba, Bonaire, and Curacao) and the "leeward" islands (Sint Maarten, Saba, and Sint Eustatius).
14 Alfred T. Mahan, *The Influence of Sea Power upon History, 1660–1783* (Boston: Little, Brown, and Company, 1939), p. 256.
15 They included the Bahamas, Bermuda, the British Leeward Islands (Anguilla, Antigua/Barbuda. British Virgin Islands, Dominica, Montserrat, and St. Kitts/ Nevis), and the British Windward Islands (Barbados, Grenada, St. Lucia, St. Vincent/Grenadines), Jamaica, Cayman Islands, Trinidad and Tobago, Turks and Caicos Islands, and Guyana.
16 The French West Indies encompassed French Guiana, plus four major island groups in the Antilles (Guadeloupe, Martinique, Saint Martin, and Saint Barthélemy).
17 Stephen B. Luce, "Our Future Navy," *The North American Review*, Vol. 149, No. 392 (July 1889), p. 56.
18 C.M.C., "The British West Indies – II," *Bulletin of International News*, Vol. 20, No. 9 (May 1, 1943), pp. 383–84.
19 Kristian M. Marks, *"Like Thunder and Lightning." British Force Protection in the West Indies, 1739–1800* (Columbus: Ohio State University, MA thesis, 1999), p. 18.
20 Alfred T. Mahan, *The Influence of Sea Power upon History, 1660–1783* (Boston: Little, Brown, and Company, 1939), p. 329.
21 W.P. Livingston, "The Future of the British West Indies," *The North American Review*, Vol. 182, No. 592 (March 1906), p. 426.
22 N.A.M. Rodger, *The Command of the Ocean. A Naval History of Britain, 1649–1815* (New York/London: W.W. Norton & Company, 2005), pp. 172–73.

23 N.A.M. Rodger, *The Command of the Ocean. A Naval History of Britain, 1649–1815* (New York/London: W.W. Norton & Company, 2005), p. 179.

24 Cited in N.A.M. Rodger, *The Command of the Ocean. A Naval History of Britain, 1649–1815* (New York/London: W.W. Norton & Company, 2005), p. 264.

25 Rupert Emerson, "The Dutch East Indies Adrift," *Foreign Affairs*, Vol. 18, No. 4 (July 1940), p. 737.

26 Amry Vandenbosch, "The Netherlands Indies," *Annals of the American Academy of Political and Social Science*, Vol. 226: Southeastern Asia and the Philippines (March 1943), p. 86.

27 Frances M. Earle, "Geography of the Southeast Tropics," *Annals of the American Academy of Political and Social Science*, Vol. 226: Southeastern Asia and the Philippines (March 1943), p. 4.

28 Rupert Emerson, "The Dutch East Indies Adrift," *Foreign Affairs*, Vol. 18, No. 4 (July 1940), p. 737; Amry Vandenbosch, "The Netherlands Indies," *Annals of the American Academy of Political and Social Science*, Vol. 226: Southeastern Asia and the Philippines (March 1943), p. 88.

29 Frances M. Earle, "Geography of the Southeast Tropics," *Annals of the American Academy of Political and Social Science*, Vol. 226: Southeastern Asia and the Philippines (March 1943), p. 5.

30 K.G. and H.G.L., "Scorched Earth Policy in the Netherlands East Indies," *Bulletin of International News*, Vol. 19, No. 5 (March 7, 1942), p. 178.

31 Frances M. Earle, "Geography of the Southeast Tropics," *Annals of the American Academy of Political and Social Science*, Vol. 226: Southeastern Asia and the Philippines (March 1943), p. 7.

32 Ministry of Defence (Navy), *War with Japan*, and Vol. II: *Defensive Phase* (London: Her Majesty's Stationery Office, 1995), p. 28.

33 Japanese Demobilization Bureaux Records, compiler, *Reports of General MacArthur, Japanese Operations in the Southwest Pacific Area*, Vol. II, Part I (Washington, DC: U.S. Army Military History, facsimile reprint 1994), p. 60.

34 Headquarters, Army Forces Far East, Military History Section, Japanese Research Division, Japanese Monograph No. 105: *General Summary of Naval Operations, Southern Force (November 1941–April 1942)* (Washington, DC: Office of the Chief of Military History, Department of the Army, 1952), p. 2.

35 Japanese Demobilization Bureaux Records, compiler, *Reports of General MacArthur, Japanese Operations in the Southwest Pacific Area*, Vol. II, Part 1 (Washington, DC: U.S. Government Printing Office, 1966), p. 39.

36 Japanese Demobilization Bureaux Records, compiler, *Reports of General MacArthur, Japanese Operations in the Southwest Pacific Area*, Vol. II, Part 1 (Washington, DC: U.S. Government Printing Office, 1966), p. 40.

37 Headquarters, Army Forces Far East, Military History Section, Japanese Research Division, Japanese Monograph No. 105: *General Summary of Naval Operations, Southern Force (November 1941–April 1942)* (Washington, DC: Office of the Chief of Military History, Department of the Army, 1952), pp. 1–2.

38 Der Eintritt Japans in den europäischen Krieg. Möglichkeiten und Auswirkungen, 3 February 1941, RM 7/253/a 1 Skl Teil XV Zusammenarbeit mit Japan Januar 1941–Dezember 1942, BA-MA, p. 4.

39 Betrachtung der Seekriegsleitung zur Frage (Dr. h.c, Gross), "Japan im Dreimächtepakt," 14.1, 1941— RM 7/253/a 1 Skl Teil XV Zusammenarbeit mit Japan Januar 1941–Dezember 1942, BA-MA, p. 2.

40 Japanese Demobilization Bureaux Records, compiler, *Reports of General MacArthur, Japanese Operations in the Southwest Pacific Area*, Vol. II, Part I (Washington, DC: U.S. Army Military History, facsimile reprint 1994), p. 61.

41 Paul S. Dull, *A Battle History of the Imperial Japanese Navy (1941–1945)*, 5th printing (Annapolis, MD: Naval Institute Press, 1978), p. 41.

42 Paul S. Dull, *A Battle History of the Imperial Japanese Navy (1941–1945)*, 5th print-ing (Annapolis, MD: Naval Institute Press, 1978), p. 38.

43 Louis Morton, *United States Army in World War II. The War in the Pacific. Strategy and Command: The First Two Years* (Washington, DC: Center of Military History, United States Army, 1989), p. 138.

44 Japanese Demobilization Bureaux Records, compiler, *Reports of General MacAr-thur. Japanese Operations in the Southwest Pacific Area*, Vol. II, Part 1 (Washington, DC: U.S. Government Printing Office, 1966), p. 75.

45 Ministry of Defence (Navy), *War with Japan*, Vol. II: *Defensive Phase* (London: Her Majesty's Stationery Office, 1995), p. 20.

46 Paul S. Dull, *A Battle History of the Imperial Japanese Navy (1941–1945)*, 5th print-ing (Annapolis, MD: Naval Institute Press, 1978), p. 64.

47 Otto Groos, "Stand und Bedeutung der maritimen Stützpunkte im Bereich das Stillen Ozean," *Nauticus 1939*, pp. 104–05.

48 Samuel Eliot Morison, *History of United States Naval Operations in World War II*, Vol. III: *The Rising Sun in the Pacific, 1931–April 1942* (Boston: Little, Brown and Company, 1959), p. 165.

49 Samuel Eliot Morison, *History of United States Naval Operations in World War II*, Vol. III: *The Rising Sun in the Pacific, 1931–April 1942* (Boston: Little, Brown and Company, 1959), pp. 166–67.

50 Ministry of Defence (Navy), *War with Japan*, Vol. II: *Defensive Phase* (London: Her Majesty's Stationery Office, 1995), p. 29.

51 Ministry of Defence (Navy), *War with Japan*, Vol. II: *Defensive Phase* (London: Her Majesty's Stationery Office, 1995), p. 33.

52 Samuel Eliot Morison, *History of United States Naval Operations in World War II*, Vol. III: *The Rising Sun in the Pacific, 1931–April 1942* (Boston: Little, Brown and Company, 1959), p. 174.

53 Samuel Eliot Morison, *History of United States Naval Operations in World War II*, Vol. III: *The Rising Sun in the Pacific, 1931–April 1942* (Boston: Little, Brown and Company, 1959), p. 176–77.

54 Ministry of Defence (Navy), *War with Japan*, Vol. II: *Defensive Phase* (London: Her Majesty's Stationery Office, 1995), p. 33.

55 Headquarters, Army Forces Far East, Military History Section, Japanese Research Division, Japanese Monograph No. 105: *General Summary of Naval Operations, Southern Force (November 1941–April 1942)* (Washington, DC: Office of the Chief of Military History, Department of the Army, 1952), p. 10.

56 Ministry of Defence (Navy), *War with Japan*, Vol. II: *Defensive Phase* (London: Her Majesty's Stationery Office, 1995), pp. 36–37.

57 Samuel Eliot Morison, *History of United States Naval Operations in World War II*, Vol. III: *The Rising Sun in the Pacific, 1931–April 1942* (Boston: Little, Brown and Company, 1959), p. 182.

58 Paul S. Dull, *A Battle History of the Imperial Japanese Navy (1941–1945)*, 5th print-ing (Annapolis, MD: Naval Institute Press, 1978), p. 42.

59 Ministry of Defence (Navy), *War with Japan*, Vol. II: *Defensive Phase* (London: Her Majesty's Stationery Office, 1995), p. 67.

60 Louis Morton, *United States Army in World War II. The War in the Pacific. Strategy and Command: The First Two Years* (Washington, DC: Center of Military His-tory, United States Army, 1989), p. 138; Samuel E. Morison, *History of United States Naval Operations in World War II*, Vol. III: *The Rising Sun in the Pacific, 1931–April 1942* (Boston: Little, Brown and Company, 1959), p. 191.

61 Paul S. Dull, *A Battle History of the Imperial Japanese Navy (1941–1945)*, 5th print-ing (Annapolis, MD: Naval Institute Press, 1978), p. 42.

62 Ministry of Defence (Navy), *War with Japan*, Vol. II: *Defensive Phase* (London: Her Majesty's Stationery Office, 1995), pp. 67–68.

63 Ministry of Defence (Navy), *War with Japan*, Vol. II: *Defensive Phase* (London: Her Majesty's Stationery Office, 1995), p. 73.

64 Paul S. Dull, *A Battle History of the Imperial Japanese Navy (1941–1945)*, 5th printing (Annapolis, MD: Naval Institute Press, 1978), pp. 61–62.

65 Samuel Eliot Morison, *History of United States Naval Operations in World War II*, Vol. III: *The Rising Sun in the Pacific, 1931–April 1942* (Boston: Little, Brown and Company, 1959), p. 281.

66 Samuel Eliot Morison, *History of United States Naval Operations in World War II*, Vol. III: *The Rising Sun in the Pacific, 1931–April 1942* (Boston: Little, Brown and Company, 1959), p. 283.

67 Paul S. Dull, *A Battle History of the Imperial Japanese Navy (1941–1945)*, 5th printing (Annapolis, MD: Naval Institute Press, 1978), p. 52; Staff Presentation, *The Strategic Area of the Philippines and the East Indian Islands* (Newport, RI: Naval War College, 19 October 1944), Folder 2461-F, Box 117, Publications, RG-4, Naval Historical Collection, Naval War College, Newport, RI., pp. 29–30.

68 Karl J. Pelzer, "Japan's Drive Against the Netherlands East Indies," *Far Eastern Survey*, Vol. 11, No. 3 (February 9, 1942), p. 38.

69 Paul S. Dull, *A Battle History of the Imperial Japanese Navy (1941–1945)*, 5th printing (Annapolis, MD: Naval Institute Press, 1978), pp. 52–53; Samuel E. Morison, *History of United States Naval Operations in World War II*, Vol. III: *The Rising Sun in the Pacific, 1931–April 1942* (Boston: Little, Brown and Company, 1959), p. 297.

70 Staff Presentation, *The Strategic Area of the Philippines and the East Indian Islands* (Newport, RI: Naval War College, 19 October 1944), Folder 2461-F, Box 117, Publications, Record Group 4, Naval Historical Collection, Naval War College, Newport, RI., p. 30.

71 Samuel Eliot Morison, *History of United States Naval Operations in World War II*, Vol. III: *The Rising Sun in the Pacific, 1931–April 1942* (Boston: Little, Brown and Company, 1959), p. 315.

72 Paul S. Dull, *A Battle History of the Imperial Japanese Navy (1941–1945)*, 5th printing (Annapolis, MD: Naval Institute Press, 1978), p. 61.

73 Staff Presentation, *The Strategic Area of the Philippines and the East Indian Islands* (Newport, RI: Naval War College, 19 October 1944), Folder 2461-F, Box 117, Publications, Record Group 4, Naval Historical Collection, Naval War College, Newport, RI., p. 27.

74 Samuel Eliot Morison, *History of United States Naval Operations in World War II*, Vol. III: *The Rising Sun in the Pacific, 1931–April 1942* (Boston: Little, Brown and Company, 1959), p. 315.

75 Paul S. Dull, *A Battle History of the Imperial Japanese Navy (1941–1945)*, 5th printing (Annapolis, MD: Naval Institute Press, 1978), p. 61.

76 Paul S. Dull, *A Battle History of the Imperial Japanese Navy (1941–1945)*, 5th printing (Annapolis, MD: Naval Institute Press, 1978), p. 98.

77 Samuel Eliot Morison, *History of United States Naval Operations in World War II*, Vol. III: *The Rising Sun in the Pacific, 1931–April 1942* (Boston: Little, Brown and Company, 1959), p. 16.

78 Samuel Eliot Morison, *History of United States Naval Operations in World War II*, Vol. III: *The Rising Sun in the Pacific, 1931–April 1942* (Boston: Little, Brown and Company, 1959), p. 320.

79 Paul S. Dull, *A Battle History of the Imperial Japanese Navy (1941–1945)*, 5th printing (Annapolis, MD: Naval Institute Press, 1978), p. 72.

80 Samuel Eliot Morison, *History of United States Naval Operations in World War II*, Vol. III: *The Rising Sun in the Pacific, 1931–April 1942* (Boston: Little, Brown and Company, 1959), pp. 320–21.

81 Staff Presentation, *The Strategic Area of the Philippines and the East Indian Islands* (Newport, RI: Naval War College, 19 October 1944), Folder 2461-F, Box 117,

Publications, Record Group 4, Naval Historical Collection, Naval War College, Newport, RI., pp. 24–25.

82 Samuel Eliot Morison, *History of United States Naval Operations in World War II*, Vol. III: *The Rising Sun in the Pacific, 1931–April 1942* (Boston: Little, Brown and Company, 1959), p. 335.

83 Ministry of Defence (Navy), *War with Japan*, Vol. II: *Defensive Phase* (London: Her Majesty's Stationery Office, 1995), pp. 89–90.

84 Ministry of Defence (Navy), *War with Japan*, Vol. II: *Defensive Phase* (London: Her Majesty's Stationery Office, 1995), p. 98.

85 Samuel Eliot Morison, *History of United States Naval Operations in World War II*, Vol. III: *The Rising Sun in the Pacific, 1931–April 1942* (Boston: Little, Brown and Company, 1959), pp. 292–93.

86 Paul S. Dull, *A Battle History of the Imperial Japanese Navy (1941–1945)*, 5th printing (Annapolis, MD: Naval Institute Press, 1978), p. 98.

87 Samuel Eliot Morison, *History of United States Naval Operations in World War II*, Vol. III: *The Rising Sun in the Pacific, 1931–April 1942* (Boston: Little, Brown and Company, 1959), p. 381.

88 Japanese Demobilization Bureaux Records, compiler, *Reports of General MacArthur. Japanese Operations in the Southwest Pacific Area*, Vol. II, Part 1 (Washington, DC: U.S. Government Printing Office, 1966), p. 74.

89 Japanese Demobilization Bureaux Records, compiler, *Reports of General MacArthur. Japanese Operations in the Southwest Pacific Area*, Vol. II, Part 1 (Washington, DC: U.S. Government Printing Office, 1966), p. 75; Paul S. Dull, *A Battle History of the Imperial Japanese Navy (1941–1945)*, 5th printing (Annapolis, MD: Naval Institute Press, 1978), pp. 95, 99.

90 Paul S. Dull, *A Battle History of the Imperial Japanese Navy (1941–1945)*, 5th printing (Annapolis, MD: Naval Institute Press, 1978), p. 100.

91 *Japanese Army Operations in the South Pacific Area*, translated by Steven Bullard (Canberra: the Australian War Memorial, 2007), p. 1.

92 Paul S. Dull, *A Battle History of the Imperial Japanese Navy (1941–1945)*, 5th printing (Annapolis, MD: Naval Institute Press, 1978), p. 100.

93 Louis Morton, *U.S. Army in World War II. The War in the Pacific. Strategy and Command: The First Two Years* (Washington, DC: U.S. Army Center for Military History, 1962, updated 1989), p. 201.

94 Paul S. Dull, *A Battle History of the Imperial Japanese Navy (1941–1945)*, 5th printing (Annapolis, MD: Naval Institute Press, 1978), p. 102.

95 Louis Morton, *United States Army in World War II. The War in the Pacific. Strategy and Command: The First Two Years* (Washington, DC: Center of Military History, United States Army, 1989), p. 291.

96 Paul S. Dull, *A Battle History of the Imperial Japanese Navy (1941–1945)*, 5th printing (Annapolis, MD: Naval Institute Press, 1978), p. 102.

97 Louis Morton, *United States Army in World War II. The War in the Pacific. Strategy and Command: The First Two Years* (Washington, DC: Center of Military History, United States Army, 1989), p. 291.

98 Louis Morton, *United States Army in World War II. The War in the Pacific. Strategy and Command: The First Two Years* (Washington, DC: Center of Military History, United States Army, 1989), p. 139.

99 J.F.C. Fuller, "The Grand Strategy of Alexander the Great," *The Royal Air Force Quarterly* 1 (January 1932), pp. 11–12.

100 J.F.C. Fuller, "The Grand Strategy of Alexander the Great," *The Royal Air Force Quarterly* 1 (January 1932), p. 12.

101 Friedrich Ruge, *The Soviets as Naval Opponents 1941–1945* (Annapolis, MD: Naval Institute Press, 1979), pp. 20–22; Jürg Meister, *Der Seekrieg in den osteuropäischen Gewässern 1941/45* (Munich: J. F. Lehmans Verlag, 1958), p. 23.

102 Friedrich Ruge, *The Soviets as Naval Opponents 1941–1945* (Annapolis, MD: Naval Institute Press, 1979), pp. 20–22; Jürg Meister, *Der Seekrieg in den osteuropäischen Gewässern 1941/45* (Munich: J. F. Lehmans Verlag, 1958), p. 22.

103 Jürg Meister, *Der Seekrieg in den osteuropäischen Gewässern 1941/45* (Munich: J. F. Lehmans Verlag, 1958), p. 340.

104 Friedrich Ruge, *The Soviets as Naval Opponents 1939–1945* (Annapolis, MD: Naval Institute Press, 1979), pp. 20–22; Jürg Meister, *Der Seekrieg in den osteuropäischen Gewässern 1941/45* (Annapolis, MD: Naval Institute Press, 1979), p. 22.

105 Friedrich Ruge, *The Soviets as Naval Opponents 1941–1945* (Annapolis, MD: Naval Institute Press, 1979), p. 77.

106 Michael Salewski, *Die deutsche Seekriegsleitung 1935–1945*, Vol. II: *1942–1945*, (Frankfurt a. M: Bernard & Graefe Verlag für Wehrwesen, 1975), p. 384.

107 Jürg Meister, *Der Seekrieg in den osteuropäischen Gewässern 1941/45* (Munich: J. F. Lehmans Verlag, 1958), p. 303.

108 Otto Groos, *Seekriegslehren im Lichte des Weltkrieges. Ein Buch für den Seemann, Soldaten und Staatsmann* (Berlin: Verlag von E. S. Mittler & Sohn, 1929), pp. 30–31.

109 Julian S. Corbett, *Official History of the Great War*, Vol. 1: *Naval Operations: To the Battle of the Falklands, December 1914* (London: Longmans, Green, 1920), p. 96.

Select bibliography

Articles

Bahnemann, Jörg. "Der Begriff der Strategie bei Clausewitz, Moltke und Liddell Hart: Eine Untersuchung de Beziehungen zwischen politischer und militärischer Führung," *Wehrwissenschaftliche Rundschau*, 1 (January 1968).

Carravagio, Angelo N. "The Attack at Taranto. Tactical Success, Operational Failure," *Naval War College Review*, Vol. 53, No. 3 (Summer 2006).

Charles, John F. "The Anatomy of Athenian Sea Power," *The Classical Journal*, Vol. 42, No. 2 (November 1946).

Davidonis, A.C. "Harbor Forcing Operations," *Military Affairs*, Vol. 8, No. 2 (Summer 1944).

Davies, Siriol, and Jack L. Davis, "Greeks, Venice, and the Ottoman Empire," *Hesperia Supplements*, Vol. 40, *Between Venice and Istanbul: Colonial Landscape in Early Modern Greece* (2007).

Engelmann, H. "Die Sicherstellung von Seeoperationen," *Militärwesen* (East Berlin), 3 (March 1980).

Fraunces, Michael G. "The International Law of Blockade: New Guiding Principles in Contemporary State Practice," *The Yale Law Journal*, Vol. 101, No. 4 (January 1992).

Fuchs, Hans. "Die Diversion als strategisches Mittel zur Erzielung eines Kräfteausgleiches, dargelegt an geschichtlichen Beispielen," *Marine Rundschau*, No. 4 (April 1938).

Fuller, J.F.C. "The Grand Strategy of Alexander the Great," *The Royal Air Force Quarterly*, 1 (January 1932),

Gadow, Walter. "Flottenstützpunkte," *Militärwissenschaftliche Rundschau*, No. 4 (April 1936).

Goldschmidt, Klaus. "Grundlagen der Strategie," *Wehrwissenschaftliche Rundschau*, 1 (January 1969)

Gough, Barry M. "Maritime Strategy: The Legacies of Mahan and Corbett as Philosophers of Sea Power," *RUSI Journal*, Vol. 133, No. 4 (Winter 1988).

Groos, Otto. "Stand und Bedeutung der maritimen Stützpunkte im Bereich das Stillen Ozean," *Nauticus 1939*.

Handel-Mazzetti, Peter. "Einfluss der Seemacht auf den Grossen Krieg," *Militärwissenschaftliche Mitteilungen*, No. 7 (July 1934).

Hayes, John D. "The Writings of Stephen B. Luce," *Military Affairs*, Vol. 19, No. 4 (Winter 1955).

Hess, Andrew C. "The Battle of Lepanto and Its Place in Mediterranean History," *Past & Present*, No. 57 (November 1972).

Hitz, Hans. "Taktik und Strategie. Zur Entwicklung kriegswissenschaftlicher Begriffe," *Wehrwissenschaftliche Rundschau*, No. 11 (November 1956).

Hümmelchen, Gerhard. "Unternehmen 'Eisstoss'—Der Angriff der Luftflotte 1 gegen die russischen Ostseeflotte im April 1942," *Marine Rundschau*, No. 4 (April 1959).

Jablonsky, Walter. "Die Seekriegführung im vierten Nahostkrieg," *Marine Rundschau*, No. 11 (November 1974).

Kulsrud, Carl J. "The Seizure of the Danish Fleet, 1807. The Background," *The American Journal of International Law*, Vol. 32, No. 2 (April 1938).

Kupfer, Max. "Die strategische Verteilung der Hauptflotten im Hinblick auf ihre Friedens – und Kriegsaufgaben," *Marine Rundschau*, No. 6 (June 1936).

Liddell Hart, B.H. "The Objective in War: National Object and Military Aim," lecture delivered at the Naval War College on 24 September 1952, *Naval War College Review* (December 1952).

Luce, Stephen B. "Naval Warfare Under Modern Conditions," *The North American Review*, Vol. 162, No. 470 (January 1896).

Luce, Stephen B. "Our Future Navy," *The North American Review*, Vol. 149, No. 392 (July 1889).

Luce, Stephen B. "The Navy and Its Needs," *The North American Review*, Vol. 193, No. 665 (April 1911).

MacFie, A.L. "The Straits Question in the First World War, 1914–1918," *Middle Eastern Studies*, Vol. 19, No. 1 (January 1983).

Mitchell, Donald W. "Admiral Makarov: Attack! Attack! Attack!" *United States Naval Proceedings* (July 1965).

Marraro, Howard. "Unpublished Documents on the Naval Battle of Lissa (1866)," *The Journal of Modern History*, Vol. 14, No. 3 (September 1942).

Pöschel, Günther. "Über die Seeherrschaft (I)" *Militärwesen* (East Berlin), No. 5 (May 1982).

Pöschel, Günther. "Über die Seeherrschaft (II)," *Militärwesen* (East Berlin), No. 6 (June 1982).

Pöschel, Günther. "Über die Seeherrschaft (III)," *Militärwesen*, No. 8 (August 1982).

Rohwer, Jürgen. "Der Minenkrieg im Finnischen Meerbusen, Part II: September–November 1941," *Marine Rundschau*, No. 2 (February 1967).

Salmon, E.T. "The Strategy of the Second Punic War," *Greece & Rome*, Vol. 7, No. 2 (October 1960).

Sokol, Anthony. "Naval Strategy in the Adriatic Sea During the World War," *Proceedings*, No. 8 (August 1937).

Soucek, Svatopluk. "Naval Aspects of the Ottoman Conquests of Rhodes, Cyprus and Crete," *Studia Islamica*, No. 98/99 (2004).

Stewart, James. "The Evolution of Naval Bases in the British Isles," *U.S. Naval Institute Proceedings*, No. 7 (July 1957).

Telem, Benyamin. "Die israelischen FK – Schnellboote im Yom-Kippur-Krieg," *Marine Rundschau*, No. 10 (October 1978).

Turner, Stansfield. "Mission of the U.S. Navy," *Naval War College Review* (March–April 1974).

Ze'ev, Almog. "Israel's Navy Beat the Odds," *U.S. Naval Institute Proceedings*, No. 3 (March 1997).

Monographs

Cunningham, David T. *The Naval Blockade: A Study of Factors Necessary for Effective Utilization* (Fort Leavenworth, KS: School of Advanced Military Studies, U.S. Army Command and General Staff College, June 1987).

Cutts, Elwin F. *Operations for Securing Command of the Sea* (Newport, RI: Naval War College, 8–9 July 1938).

Department of Operations, *Naval Strategy* (Newport, RI: U.S. Naval War College, August 1936).

Dirks, Uwe. *Waren Grundzuege britischer Seekriegführung bereits vor dem Ersten Weltkrieg den Schriften Corbetts zu entnehmen?* (Hamburg: Führungsakademie der Bundeswehr, 30 October 1979).

Henning, Herbert. *Analyse des Kampfes der Seestreitkräfte um Meerengen in Verlaufe des Zweiten Weltkrieges* (Dresden: Militärakademie Friedrich Engels, 1967).

Krajnović, Nikola. *Prevlast Na Moru* (Belgrade: Viša Vojno-Pomorska Akademija, 1 November 1983).

Pöschel, Günther. *Die Rolle und Bedeutung der Seeherrschaft in Vergangenheit und Gegenwart. Analyse der theoretischen Aussagen zum Begriff der Seeherrschaft* (Dresden: Militärakademie Friedrich Engels, 1978).

Rosinski, Herbert. *The Development of Naval Thought* (Newport, RI: Naval War College Press, 1977).

Schroden, Jonathan. *A Strait Comparison: Lessons Learned from the 1915 Dardanelles Campaign in the Context of a Strait of Hormuz Closure Event* (Alexandria, VA: Center for Naval Analyses, September 2011).

Seebens, Dieter Grundlagen. *Auffassungen und Pläne für eine Kriegführung in der Ostsee 1935–1939* (Hamburg: Führungsakademie der Bundeswehr, August 1971).

Seemann, Konrad. *Grundsätze der Seestrategie. Eine Analyse von konstanten und variable Elementen in den Konzeptionen von Seemächte* (Hamburg: Führungsakademie der Bundeswehr, 15 January 1990).

Settle, T.G.W. *The Strategic Employment of the Fleet* (Newport, RI: Staff Presentation, Naval War College, September 18, 1940).

Tritten, James J., and Luigi Donolo, *A Doctrine Reader* (Newport, RI: Naval War College, Newport Paper # 9, December 1995).

Turner, R.K. "Background of Naval Strategy," Lecture delivered before the Marine Corps Schools, Quantico, Virginia, 16 February 1938.

Uticaj Mora i Posebno Uskog Mora na Vodjenje Rata (Divulje: Viša Vojnopomorska Akademija, 1964).

Waltz, Hartmut. *Die Problem moderner Minelegeplanungen vor dem Hintergrund historischer Erfahrungen in der Nordsee 1939–1944* (Hamburg: Führungsakademie der Bundeswehr, October 1985).

Weyher, Hein-Peter. *Der Begriff "Seestrategie" und Seine Deutung in den Westlichen Kriegstheorien Des 20. Jahrhunderts* (Hamburg: Führungsakademie der Bundeswehr, July 1967).

Books

Anderson, Charles R. *Leyte.* (Washington, DC: U.S. Government Printing Office, CMH Pub 72–27, 1994.).

Anderson, Roger C.B. *Naval Wars in the Baltic During the Sailing-Ship Epoch, 1522–1850* (London: C. Gilbert-Wood, 1910, reprinted Charleston, SC: Nabu Press, 2014).

Arps, Th., Gadow, R., Hesse, H., and Niedermayer, D. Ritter von. *Kleine Wehrgeographie des Weltmeeres* (Berlin: E. S. Mittler & Sohn, 1938).

Bacon, Reginald, and McMurtries, Francis E. *Modern Naval Strategy* (London: Frederick Muller Ltd., 1940).

Bennett, Geoffrey. *Naval Battles of the First World War* (New York: Scribner's, 1968).

Boyd, Carl, and Yoshida, Akihiko. *The Japanese Submarine Force and World War II* (Annapolis, MD: Naval Institute Press, 1995).

Bridge, Cyprian. *Sea-Power and Other Studies* (London: Smith, Elder & Co., 1910).

Brodie, Bernard. *A Layman's Guide to Naval Strategy* (Princeton, NJ: Princeton University Press, 1942).

Cagle, Malcolm W., and Mason, Frank A. *The Sea War in Korea* (Annapolis, MD: Naval Institute Press, 1957).

Callender, Geoffrey. *The Naval Side of British History* (Boston: Little, Brown, and Company, 1924).

Castex, Raoul. *More Protiv Kopna*, Vol. 1. Translated by Hijacint Mundorfer (*Theórie stratégiques*, Vol 1: *La Mer Contre La Terre*) (Belgrade: Geca Kon AD, 1939).

Castex, Raoul. *Strategic Theories*. Selections translated and edited with an introduction by Eugenia C. Kiesling (Annapolis, MD: Naval Institute Press, 1993).

Clausewitz, Carl von. *On War*. Edited and translated by Michael Howard and Peter Paret (New York: Alfred A. Knopf, 1993).

Collins, John M. *Grand Strategy: Principles and Practices* (Annapolis, MD: Naval Institute Press, 1973).

Connaughton, Richard. *Rising Sun and Tumbling Bear. Russia's War with Japan* (London: Cassell, 2003).

Corbett, Julian S., editor, *Fighting Instructions, 1530–1816* (London: Publications of the Navy Records Society, Vol. XXIX, 1905 produced by Bibliothèque Nationale de France, Paris, reprinted September 15, 2005),

Corbett, Julian S. *Some Principles of Maritime Strategy* (London: Longmans, Green and Co., 1918).

Cordesman, Anthony H. *The Iran-Iraq War and Western Security 1984–87: Strategic Implications and Policy Options* (London: Jane's Publishing, 1987).

Crowl, Philip A. *United States Army in World War II. The War in the Pacific. Campaign in the Marianas* (Washington, DC: Office of the Chief of Military History, Department of the Army, 1960).

Custance, Reginald. *War at Sea. Modern Theory and Ancient Practice* (Edinburgh/London: William Blackwood and Sons, 1919).

Darrieus, Gabriel. *War on the Sea. Strategy and Tactics* (Annapolis, MD: The United States Naval Institute, 1908).

Daveluy, Rene. *The Genius of Naval Warfare*, Vol. I: *Strategy* (Annapolis, MD: United States Naval Institute 1910).

Doswald-Beck, Louise, editor. *San Remo on International Law Applicable to Armed Conflicts at Sea* (Cambridge: Cambridge University Press, first published 1996, reissued 2005).

Duckers, Peter. *The Crimean War at Sea. The Naval Campaigns Against Russia 1854–56* (Barnsley, South Yorkshire: Pen & Sword Maritime, 2011).

Ducrey, Pierre. *Warfare in Ancient Greece*. Translated by Janet Lloyd (New York: Schocken Books, 1986).

Dull, Paul S. *A Battle History of the Imperial Japanese Navy (1941–1945)*, 5th printing (Annapolis, MD: Naval Institute Press, 1978).

Duncan, Robert C. *America's Use of Mines* (White Oak, MD: U.S. Naval Ordnance Laboratory, 1962).

Dupuy, Ernest, and Dupuy, Trevor N. *The Encyclopedia of Military History from 3500 B.C. to the Present*, 2nd rev. ed. (New York: Harper & Row, Publishers, 1986).

Elleman, Bruce A., and Paine, S.C.M., editors. *Naval Blockades and Seapower. Strategies and Counterstrategies, 1805–2005* (London: Routledge, 2006).

Erickson, Edward J. *Defeat in Detail. The Ottoman Army in the Balkans, 1912–1915* (Westport, CT/London: Praeger Publishers, 2003).

Evans, David C., editor, *The Japanese Navy in World War II. In the Words of Former Japanese Naval Officers*, 2nd ed. (Annapolis, MD: Naval Institute Press, 1986).

Fiebeger, G.J. *Elements of Strategy* (West Point: United States Military Academy Press, 1910).

Fioravanzo, Giuseppe. *A History of Naval Thought*, translated by Arthur W. Holst (Annapolis, MD: Naval Institute Press, 1979).

Fotakis, Zisis. *Greek Naval Strategy and Policy, 1910–1919* (London/New York: Routledge. Taylor & Francis Group, 2005).

Gibson, R.H., and Prendergast, Maurice. *The German Submarine War 1914–1918* (Constable & Co. Ltd., 1931, reprinted Annapolis, MD: Naval Institute Press, 2002).

Goldsworthy, Adrian. *The Punic Wars* (London: Cassell & Co, 2001).

Goltz, Colmar von der. *Kriegführung. Kurze Lehre ihrer wichtigsten Grundsätze und Formen* (Berlin: R.v. Decker's Verlag, 1895).

Goltz, Colmar von der. *The Conduct of War: A Short Treatise on Its Most Important Branches and Guiding Rules*. Translated by G.F. Leverson (London: Kegan, Paul, Trench, Truebner, 1908).

Grainger, John D. *Hellenistic & Roman Naval Wars 336–31 BC* (Barnsley, South Yorkshire: Pen & Sword Maritime, 2011).

Gray, Colin S. *The Leverage of Sea Power* (New York: The Free Press, Maxwell MacMillan International, 1992).

Grenfell, Russell. *The Art of the Admiral* (London: Faber & Faber Ltd., 1937).

Grewe, Wilhelm G. *The Epochs of International Law*. Translated by Michael Byers (Berlin/New York: De Gruyter, 2000).

Groos, Otto. *Seekriegslehren im Lichte des Weltkrieges. Ein Buch für den Seemann, Soldaten und Staatsmann* (Berlin: Verlag von E. S. Mittler & Sohn, 1929).

Grove, Eric J., editor, *The Defeat of the Enemy Attack on Shipping 1939–1945* a revised edition of the Naval Staff History, vols. 1A (Text and Appendices) and 1B (Plans and Tables) (Aldershot: Ashgate, Navy Records Society, 1997).

Hall, Richard C. *The Balkan Wars 1912–1913: Prelude to the First World War* (London: Routledge, Taylor & Francis Group, 2000).

Halpern, Paul G. *The Naval War in the Mediterranean 1914–1918* (Annapolis, MD: Naval Institute Press, 1987).

Hartmann, Gregory K., with Truver, Scott C. *Weapons That Wait*, updated version (Annapolis, MD: Naval Institute Press, 1991).

Hodges, H.W., and Hughes, E.A., editors, *Select Naval Documents* (Cambridge: Cambridge University Press, 1922, reprinted by the Cornell University Library Digital Collections, 2015).

Ireland, Bernard. *Battle of the Atlantic* (Annapolis, MD: Naval Institute Press, 2003).

Johnson, Ellis A., and Katcher, David A. *Mines Against Japan* (White Oak, Silver Spring, MD: Naval Ordnance Laboratory, 1947; Washington, DC: U.S. Government Printing Office, 1973).

Jomini, Antoine-Henri de. *The Art of War.* Translated by G.H. Mendel and W.P. Craighill (Westport, CT: Greenwood Press Publishers, 1971, originally published Philadelphia: J. P. Lippincott & Co., 1862).

Kirchhoff, Hermann. *Seemacht in der Ostsee: Ihre Einwirkung auf die Geschichte der Ostseeländer Im 19. Jahrhundert,* Vol. II (Kiel: Verlag von Robert Cordes, 1908).

Knox, Dudley W. *A History of the United States Navy* (New York: G. P. Putnam Sons, 1948).

Lambert, Andrew, and Williamson, Arthur C. *The Dynamics of Air Power,* 1st ed. (London: Her Majesty's Stationery Office for Royal Air Force Staff College, Bracknell, 1996).

Lambi, Ivo N. *The Navy and German Power Politics, 1862–1914* (Boston: Allen & Unwin, 1984).

Lane, Frederic C. *Venice. A Maritime Republic* (Baltimore, MD: John Hopkins University Press, 1973).

Ledebur, Gerhard Freiherr von. *Die Seemine* (Munich: J. F. Lehmanns Verlag, 1977).

Lewis, Michael. *The Spanish Armada* (New York: T. Y. Crowell Co., 1968).

MacCartney Shepard, Arthur. *Sea Power in Ancient History. The Story of the Navies of Classic Greece and Rome* (London: William Heineman Ltd., 1925).

Macleod, Jenny. *Reconsidering Gallipoli* (Manchester/New York: Manchester University Press, 2004).

Mahan, Alfred T. *Naval Strategy: Compared and Contrasted with the Principles and Practice of Military Operations on Land* (Boston: Little, Brown, and Company, 1911).

Mahan, Alfred T. *Influence of Sea Power upon the French Revolution and Empire, 1793–1812,* Vol. I, 8th ed. (Boston: Little, Brown, and Company, 1897).

Mahan, Alfred T. *The Influence of Sea Power upon History 1660–1783* (Boston: Little, Brown, and Company, 1939).

Mahncke, Dieter, and Schwarz, Hans-Peter, editors, *Seemacht und Aussenpolitik* (Frankfurt a.M: Alfred Metzner Verlag, 1974).

Marcus, G.J. *A Naval History of England,* Vol. 2: *The Age of Nelson. The Royal Navy 1793–1815* (New York: Viking Press, 1971).

Marder, Arthur J. *From the Dreadnought to Scapa Flow. The Royal Navy in the Fisher Era, 1904–1919,* Vol. I: *The Road to War 1904–1914* (London: Oxford University Press, 1961).

Marder, Arthur J. *From the Dreadnought to Scapa Flow: The Royal Navy in the Fisher Era, 1914–1919,* Vol. 2: *The War Years: To the Eve of Jutland* (London: Oxford University Press, 1965).

Marder, Arthur J. *From the Dreadnought to Scapa Flow. The Royal Navy in the Fisher Era,* Vol. 3: *Jutland and After (May 1916–December 1916)* (London: Oxford University Press, 1966).

Marder, Arthur J. *From the Dreadnought to Scapa Flow: The Royal Navy in the Fisher Era, 1904–1919,* Vol. 5: *Victory and Aftermath (January 1918–June 1919)* (London: Oxford University Press, 1970).

Marolda, Edward J., and Schneller, Robert J. *Shield and Sword: The United States Navy and the Persian Gulf War* (Washington, DC: Naval Historical Center, 1998).

Meister, Jürg. *Der Seekrieg in den osteuropäischen Gewässern 1941/45* (Munich: J. F. Lehmans Verlag, 1958).

Meurer, Alexander. *Seekriegsgeschichte in Umrissen. Seemacht und Seekriege vornehmlich vom 16. Jahrhundert ab* (Leipzig: Verlag v. Hase & Koehler, 1925).

Ministry of Defence (Navy). *War with Japan,* Vol. II: *Defensive Phase* (London: Her Majesty's Stationery Office, 1995).

Ministry of Defence (Navy). *War with Japan*, Vol. III: *The Campaigns in the Solomons and New Guinea* (London: Her Majesty's Stationery Office, 1995).

Mordal, Jacques. *25 Centuries of Sea Warfare* (London: Abbey Library, 1959).

Morison, Samuel E. *History of United States Naval Operations in World War II*, Vol. III: *The Rising Sun in the Pacific, 1931–April 1942* (Boston: Little, Brown and Company, 1959).

Morison, Samuel E. *History of United States Naval Operations in World War II*, Vol. IV: *Coral Sea, Midway and Submarine Operations, May 1942–August 1942* (Boston: Little, Brown and Company, 1984).

Morison, Samuel E. *History of United States Naval Operations in World War II*, Vol VI: *Breaking the Bismarcks Barrier: 22 July 1942–1 May 1944* (Boston: Little, Brown and Company, 1975).

Morison, Samuel E. *History of United States Naval Operations in World War II*, Vol. XIII: *New Guinea and the Marianas, March 1944–August 1944* (Boston: Little, Brown and Company, 1953).

Morison, Samuel E. *The Two-Ocean War. A Short History of the United States Navy in the Second World War* (Boston: Little, Brown and Company, 1963).

Morton, Louis. *United States Army in World War II. The War in the Pacific. Strategy and Command: The First Two Years* (Washington, DC: Center of Military History, United States Army, 1989).

O'Connell, Monique. *Men of Empire: Power and Negotiation in Venice's Maritime State* (Baltimore, MD: Johns Hopkins University Press, 2009).

Pack, S.W.C. *Sea Power in the Mediterranean. A History from the Seventeenth Century to the Present Day* (London: Arthur Barker Ltd., 1971).

Paret, Peter, editor. *Makers of Modern Strategy. From Machiavelli to the Nuclear Age* (Princeton, NJ: Princeton University Press, 1986).

Potter, Elmer B., and Nimitz, Chester W., editors. *Seemacht. Eine Seekriegsgeschichte von der Antike bis zur Gegenwart*, rev. ed. (Hersching: Manfred Pawlak, 1986).

Richmond, Herbert. *Statesmen and Sea Power* (Oxford: Clarendon Press, first published 1946, reprinted 1947).

Rittmeyer, Rudolph. *Seekrieg und Seekriegswesen in ihrer weltgeschichtlichen Entwicklung mit besonderen Berücksichtigung der grossen Seekrieg XVII und XVIII Jahrhunderts*, Vol I: *Von den Anfängen bis 1740* (Berlin: Ernst Siegfried Mittler und Sohn, 1907).

Rittmeyer, Rudolph. *Seekrieg und Seekriegswesen in ihrer weltgeschichtlichen Entwicklung mit besonderen Berücksichtigung der grossen Seekrieg XVII und XVIII Jahrhunderts*, Vol II: *Von 1739–1793* (Berlin: Ernst Siegfried Mittler und Sohn, 1911).

Robertson, Horace B., editor, *International Law Studies*, Vol. 64: *The Law of Naval Operations* (Newport, RI: Naval War College Press, 1991).

Rodger, N.A.M. *The Command of the Ocean. A Naval History of Britain, 1649–1815* (New York/London: W. W. Norton & Company, 2004).

Rodgers, William Ledyard. *Greek and Roman Naval Warfare. A Study of Strategy, Tactics and Ship Design from Salamis (480 B.C.) to Actium (31 B.C.)* (Annapolis, MD: Naval Institute Press, 1937, 1964).

Rodgers, William Ledyard. *Naval Warfare Under Oars. A Study of Strategy, Tactics and Ship Design* (Annapolis, MD: Naval Institute Press, 1940, 1967).

Roeckel, Hermann. *Seeräume und Flottenstützpunkte* (Heidelberg/Berlin/Leipzig: Verlagsanstalt Huethig & Co., 1942).

Rohwer, Jürgen, and Hümmelchen, Gerhard. *Chronology of the War at Sea 1939–1945. The Naval History of World War II*, 2nd rev. ed. (Annapolis, MD: Naval Institute Press, 1992).

Roskill, Stephen W. *The War at Sea 1939–1945*, Vol. I: *The Defensive* (London: Her Majesty's Stationery Office, 1954).

Roskill, Stephen W. *The War at Sea 1939–1945*, Vol. II: *The Period of Balance* (London: Her Majesty's Stationery Office, 1956).

Roskill, Stephen W. *The War at Sea 1939–1945*, Vol. III: *The Offensive*, Part I: *1st June 1943–31st May 1944* (London: Her Majesty's Stationery Office, 1960).

Roskill, Stephen W. *History of the Second World War, The War at Sea*, Vol. III: *The Offensive* Part II: *1st June 1944–14th August 1945* (London: Her Majesty's Stationery Office, 1961).

Ruge, Friedrich. *The Soviets as Naval Opponents 1941–1945* (Annapolis, MD: Naval Institute Press, 1979).

Salewski, Michael. *Die deutsche Seekriegsleitung 1935–1945*, Vol. 1: *1935–1941* (Frankfurt am Main: Bernard & Graefe Verlag für Wehrwesen, 1970).

Salewski, Michael. *Die deutsche Seekriegsleitung 1935–1945*, Vol. 2: *1942–1945* (Frankfurt am Main: Bernard & Graefe Verlag für Wehrwesen, 1975)

Schottelius, Herbert, and Deist, Wilhelm, editors, *Marine und Marinepolitik im kaiserlichen Deutschland 1871–1914* (Düsseldorf: Droste Verlag, 1972).

Setton, Kenneth M. *The Papacy and the Levant, 1204–1571*. Vol. 1: *The Thirteenth and Fourteenth Centuries* (Philadelphia, PA: Amer Philosophical Society, 1976).

Sokol, Hans Hugo. *Des Kaisers Seemacht 1848–1914. Die k.k. oesterreichische Kriegsmarine* (Vienna: Amalthea, 2002).

Sondhaus, Lawrence. *The Habsburg Empire and the Sea. Austrian Naval Policy, 1797–1866* (West Lafayette, IN: Purdue University Press, 1989).

Sondhaus, Lawrence. *Navies of Europe, 1815–2002* (London: Taylor & Francis, 2002).

Sprout, Harold, and Sprout, Margaret. *The Rise of American Naval Power, 1776–1918* (Princeton, NJ: Princeton University Press, 1939).

Stenzel, Alfred. *Kriegführung zur See. Lehre vom Seekriege* (Hannover/Leipzig: Mahnsche Buchhandlung, 1913).

Stenzel, Alfred. *Seekriegsgeschichte in ihren wichtigsten Abschnitten mit Berücksichtigung der Seetaktik*, Part 2: *Von 400 vor Christen bis 1600 nach Christen* (Hannover/Leipzig: Hahnsche Buchhandlung, 1909).

Stenzel, Alfred. *Seekriegsgeschichte in ihren wichtigsten Abschnitten mit Berücksichtigung der Seetaktik*, Part 3: *Von 1600 bis 1720* (Hannover/Leipzig: Hahnsche Buchhandlung, 1910).

Stenzel, Alfred. *Seekriegsgeschichte in ihren wichtigsten Abschnitten mit Berücksichtigung der Seetaktik*, Part 4: *Von 1720 bis 1850* (Hannover/Leipzig: Hahnsche Buchhandlung, 1911),.

Stevens, William Oliver, and Westcott, Allan. *A History of Sea Power* (New York: Doubleday, Doran & Company, Inc., 1942).

Till, Geoffrey, *Maritime Strategy and the Nuclear Age*, 2nd ed. (New York: St. Martin's Press, 1984).

Travers, Tim. *Gallipoli 1915* (Gloucestershire: Tempus Publishing, Stroud, 2001).

Terraine, John, *The U-Boat Wars 1916-1945* (New York: G.P. Putnam's Sons, 1989),

True, Wilhelm. *Der Krim Krieg und seine Bedeutung für die Entstehung der modern Flotten* (Herford/Bonn: E. S. Mittler & Sohn GmbH, 1980).

Vego, Milan. *The Battle for Leyte, 1944: Allied and Japanese Plans, Preparations, and Execution* (Annapolis, MD: Naval Institute Press, 2006).

Warnock, A. Timothy. *Air Power Versus U-Boats: Confronting Hitler's Submarine Menace in the European Theater*, The U.S. Army Air Forces in World War II (Washington,

DC: Air Force History and Museums Program, Air Force Historical Studies Office, 1999).

Warry, John. *Warfare in the Classical World* (New York: Barnes & Noble, 1998).

Wegener, Wolfgang. *The Naval Strategy of the World War*, translated and with an Introduction and notes by Holger H. Herwig (Annapolis, MD: Naval Institute Press, 1989).

Wenzke, Rüdiger. editor. *Die Streitkräfte der DDR und Polens in der Operationsplanung des Warschauer Paktes* (Potsdam: Militärgeschichtliches Forschungsamt, 2010).

Westcott, Alan, editor. *American Sea Power Since 1775* (Chicago/Philadelphia/New York: J.B. Lippincott, 1947).

Woodward, David. *The Russians at Sea: History of the Russian Navy* (New York: Frederick A. Praeger, 1966).

Yates, Keith. *Flawed Victory: Jutland 1916* (Annapolis, MD: Naval Institute Press, 2000).

Zehrer, Hartmut, editor. *Der Golfkonflikt. Dokumentation, Analyse und Bewertung aus militärischer Sicht* (Herford/Bonn: Verlag E. S. Mittler & Sohn, 1992).

Index